Regression Analysis

With the rise of "big data," there is an increasing demand to learn the skills needed to undertake sound quantitative analysis without requiring students to spend too much time on high-level math and proofs. This book provides an efficient alternative approach, with more time devoted to the practical aspects of regression analysis and how to recognize the most common pitfalls.

By doing so, the book will better prepare readers for conducting, interpreting, and assessing regression analyses, while simultaneously making the material simpler and more enjoyable to learn. Logical and practical in approach, *Regression Analysis* teaches: (1) the tools for conducting regressions; (2) the concepts needed to design optimal regression models (based on avoiding the pitfalls); and (3) the proper interpretations of regressions. Furthermore, this book emphasizes honesty in research, with a prevalent lesson being that statistical significance is not the goal of research.

This book is an ideal introduction to regression analysis for anyone learning quantitative methods in the social sciences, business, medicine, and data analytics. It will also appeal to researchers and academics looking to better understand what regressions do, what their limitations are, and what they can tell us. This will be the most engaging book on regression analysis (or Econometrics) you will ever read!

Jeremy Arkes is Associate Professor at the Graduate School of Business and Public Policy, Naval Postgraduate School, U.S.A. He conducts research in a variety of fields, with a focus on military-manpower policy, substance-use policy, determinants of youth outcomes, sports economics, and using sports outcomes to make inferences on human behavior.

Regression Analysis
A Practical Introduction

Jeremy Arkes

Routledge
Taylor & Francis Group

LONDON AND NEW YORK

First published 2019
by Routledge
2 Park Square, Milton Park, Abingdon, Oxon OX14 4RN

and by Routledge
52 Vanderbilt Avenue, New York, NY 10017

Routledge is an imprint of the Taylor & Francis Group, an informa business

British Library Cataloguing-in-Publication Data
A catalogue record for this book is available from the British Library

Library of Congress Cataloging-in-Publication Data
A catalog record for this book has been requested

ISBN: 978-1-138-54140-5 (hbk)
ISBN: 978-1-138-54143-6 (pbk)
ISBN: 978-1-351-01109-9 (ebk)

Typeset in Bembo
by Apex CoVantage, LLC

Visit the eResources: www.routledge.com/9781138541405

To my mother, Judy Arkes (1941–2014). She was always a voice of love, support, and reason.

Contents

Figures

Tables

About the author

Jeremy Arkes grew up in Amherst, MA, in the midst of the fields of Amherst College. He left this bucolic setting to attend Georgetown University for his undergraduate studies and to later earn a Ph.D. in Economics from the University of Wisconsin. He spent his first ten years after graduate school working for think tanks: The Center for Naval Analyses (Alexandria, VA) and RAND Corporation (Santa Monica, CA). His main focus was on military–manpower research, but he sprouted out to other fields, such as the areas of substance use and divorce effects on children.

Since 2007, he has been teaching Economics and Applied (Regression) Analysis of Military Manpower in the Graduate School of Business and Public Policy at the Naval Postgraduate School in Monterey, California. At NPS, besides continuing to conduct research in military manpower, he has added a line of research that uses sports outcomes to make inferences on human behavior.

When not estimating regression models or writing about them, Dr. Arkes plays basketball and racquetball, and he hikes around the Big Sur and California Central Coast area with his wife, Jennifer. And, whenever they get a chance, he and Jennifer like to venture off to New England, the Rockies, the Cascades, British Columbia, Hawaii, or Alaska for hiking adventures.

Preface

I've played a lot of basketball in my life. I was mediocre in high school, being the 6th man (first guy off the bench) on my high-school team. At 5'9", I played all positions other than point guard (even center briefly, as I knew how to box out) . . . I could defend, jump, and rebound, but I couldn't dribble or shoot well.

Although I never developed a consistent outside shot until my 30s (and 3-point range in my mid-40s), it was at college (Georgetown University) where I learned to dribble, drive to the basket, and shoot mid-range jumpers – don't mind saying this helped me win a few 1-on-1 and 3-on-3 tournaments. And, it was in the Georgetown gym where I started to have experiences with the "hot hand," especially on those 95-degree-and-humid spring and summer days. The hot hand is a period of playing at a systematically higher level than what you normally play at, often called "being in the zone" or "*en fuego*." Those of you who play sports may have experienced it in whatever sport you play. My wife says she has experienced it in her dancing career. For me, some days, I just had a better feel for the ball, and I was more likely to make any type of shot I tried.

And, it is in one of those hot-hand events for myself that I briefly got the better of 7'2", future NBA-Hall-of-Famer, Dikembe Mutombo. (If you ever meet me and ask, I'll gladly tell you the story.)

So, you can imagine my surprise when I read that a bunch of famous economists, statisticians, and psychologists (including some Nobel Prize winners), were arguing, based on several studies that failed to find any evidence for the hot hand, that the hot hand is a figment of our imaginations. Many of them stated things along the lines of "The hot hand in basketball is a myth."

How could they conclude this? I had to investigate it on my own, applying some methods to try to increase the "power" of the test. Sure enough, in 2010, I found some evidence for the existence of the hot hand and published it. But, the real breakthroughs came in the next several years, with research by my friends Dan Stone (from Bowdoin College) and Josh Miller and Adam Sanjurjo (both from Universidad de Alicante). They found biases in the original studies (and mine) that would work against being able to detect the hot hand. Josh and Adam's most notable bias is from the Gambler's Fallacy (which I'll discuss briefly in Chapter 6). The bias Dan found (from measurement error) was more intuitive, as measurement error should be on any checklist for potential biases in a study. But, no one (including myself) had recognized it.

How could those famous researchers and Nobel Prize winners have made such huge errors? It wasn't just that they missed these sources of bias. But, they also used fallacious logic in their interpretations: the lack of evidence for the hot hand was not proof that it did not exist. (I'll discuss this more in Chapter 5).

This was a watershed moment for me that so many established researchers bought into this argument without critically assessing it. And, while I give myself a pass for missing the large biases that Josh and Adam found, I was guilty for not recognizing the measurement-error bias that Dan had found.

And so, this story arc on the hot hand confirmed a pattern I was seeing on other research topics, and it hit me. Yeah, most economists know the lingo and the formulas for why things could go wrong in regression analysis. But, many aren't trained well in recognizing these when they occur. And, many do not understand the proper way to interpret the results of regressions. I thought that there must be a better way to teach regression analysis.

It was at this point that I realized that I had a story to tell. I have come to understand many concepts on regression analysis that elude many researchers. These concepts came to me, not from my classes, but from my practical experience of estimating thousands of regressions . . . and from the many mistakes I have made in my research. And, the lessons I learned from poring over results helped me connect the dots between several of the essential concepts.

And so, from these experiences with various pitfalls of regression analysis, from mistakes I have made, from what helped me connect the dots between concepts, I have created a story on how to better understand, conduct, and scrutinize regression analysis.

Acknowledgments

I would first like to thank my wife, Jennifer. For much of my writing of this book, she was a doctoral student in Education, and we had numerous conversations about the methods I used and her perspectives on research from a curriculum focusing on qualitative research. I would also like to thank several of my colleagues/friends. Robert Eger was instrumental to me for his guidance on the process, and his encouragement to take a shot. For technical details, I benefited greatly from discussions with Thomas Ahn (Naval Postgraduate School), William A. Muir (U.S. Air Force and Naval Postgraduate School), John Pepper (University of Virginia), and my hot-hand-in-basketball colleagues, Joshua Miller (Universidad Alicante), Adam Sanjurjo (Universidad Alicante, and also my surf instructor), and Daniel Stone (Bowdoin College). And, for telling me when some of my attempts at humor worked and when they didn't, I am grateful to my friends at work: Ronda Spelbring, Houda Tarabishi, and Holly Shrewbridge.

The views expressed in this book are mine and do not reflect those of the Naval Postgraduate School, the U.S. Navy, the U.S. Department of Defense, or the U.S. government.

Abbreviations

2SLS	Two-stage Least Squares
ACF	Autocorrelation function
AFA	Air Force Academy
AFQT	Armed Forces Qualification Test
AIC	Akaike Information Criterion
AICc	Akaike Information Criterion (corrected)
AR	Autoregressive (model)
ARIMA	Autoregressive integrated moving average
ARMA	Autoregressive moving average
ATE	Average Treatment Effect
ATT	Average Treatment effect for the Treated
BIC	Bayesian Information Criterion
BPI	Behavioral Problems Index
CDF	Cumulative distribution function
CEO	Chief Executive Officer
CPS	Current Population Survey
CS	Class size
DD	Difference-in-difference (model)
d.f.	degrees of freedom
EITC	Earned Income Tax Credit
ExSS	Explained Sum of Squares
FD	First-difference (model)
FTE	Full-time-equivalent (worker)
GDP	Gross Domestic Product
GED	General Equivalency Diploma
GPA	Grade point average
HS	High School
IAT	Implicit Association Test
i.i.d.	Identically distributed
IQ	Intelligence Quotient

IV	Instrumental variable
LATE	Local Average Treatment Effect
LPM	Linear probability model
MAPE	Mean absolute percent error
MJ	Marijuana
MNL	Multinomial Logit (Model)
MSE	Mean Square Error
NBA	National Basketball Association
NCAA	National Collegiate Athletic Association
NFL	National Football League
NIH	National Institute of Health
NLSY	National Longitudinal Survey of Youth
NRA	National Rifle Association
NSDUH	National Survey on Drug Use and Health
OLS	Ordinary Least Squares
PACF	Partial autocorrelation function
PDF	Probability density function
PI/C	Personal income per capita
PTSD	Post-traumatic stress disorder
RCT	Randomized–control trial
RD	Regression discontinuity
RMSE	Root Mean Square Error
RMSFE	Root mean square forecast error
RP	Relative performance
RR	Restricted regression
RSS	Residual Sum of Squares
SAT	Scholastic Aptitude Test
SE	Standard Error
SETI	Search for Extraterrestrial Intelligence
SUR	Seemingly Unrelated Regression
TS	Test score
TSS	Total Sum of Squares
UR	Unrestricted regression
VAR	Vector Autoregression
var ( )	Variance

1 Introduction

If you don't read the newspaper you are uninformed, if you do read the newspaper you are mis-informed.

– Mark Twain

I'm on a mission, and I need your help.

My mission is to make this a better world.

I want society to make better choices and decisions. Sometimes, these decisions should be based on what is morally and ethically the right thing to do. I cannot help on that front. But, at other times, decisions need to be based on how they affect people and institutions. And, in that realm, sometimes statistical analysis can speak to best practices. Statistical analysis sometimes can tell us what health practices and interventions are most beneficial to people, what factors lead to better economic outcomes for people (individually or collectively), what factors contribute to the academic achievement of children, how to make government functions more cost-efficient (which could reduce the tax burden on society), and much more.

All that said, sometimes statistical analysis is unable to speak on many of these issues. This may be because the data are not adequate in terms of having sufficient observations and sufficient accuracy. Or, it could be because the statistical analysis was flawed, or that there are no solutions to certain biases. So, we need to be careful in how we interpret and use the results from statistical analyses so that we draw the correct and prudent conclusions, without overreaching or being affected by our pre-conceived notions and biases.

My goal with this book is not to answer the important questions on how to make the world better. In fact, I will address some research issues that some of you will care nothing about, such as whether discrimination is a self-fulfilling prophecy in France, whether a Medicaid expansion in Oregon improved health outcomes for participants, or whether the hot hand in basketball is real or just a figment of our imaginations. But, these research issues that I use will serve as useful applications to learn the concepts and tools of regression analysis.

So, my goal is to teach you the tools needed to address important issues. This book is designed to teach you how to better conduct, interpret, and scrutinize statistical analyses. From this, I hope you will help others make better decisions that will help towards making this world, eventually, a better place.

1.1 The problem

Jay Leno, in one of his *Tonight Show* monologues several years ago, mentioned a study that found that 50% of all academic research is wrong. His punchline: there's a 50% chance this study itself is wrong.

The study Leno referred to may actually *understate* the true percentage of studies that are inaccurate. The major causes of all these errors in research are likely faulty research designs and improper interpretations of the results. These accuracy issues bring into doubt the value of academic research.

Most quantitative academic research, particularly in the social sciences, business, and medicine, rely on regression analyses. The primary objective of regressions is to quantify cause–effect relationships. These cause–effect relationships are part of the knowledge that should guide society to develop good public policies and good strategies for conducting business, educating people, promoting health and general welfare, and more. Regressions are useful for estimating such relationships because they are able to "hold constant" other factors that may confound the cause–effect relationship in question. That is, regressions, if done well, can rule out reasons for two variables to be related, other than the causal-effect reason.

Here are some examples of how regressions can be used to estimate the causal effect of one factor (or a set of factors) on some outcome:

- How does some new cancer drug affect the probability of a patient surviving 10 years after diagnosis?
- How does a parental divorce affect children's test scores?
- What factors make teachers more effective?
- What encourages people to save more for retirement?
- What factors contribute to religious extremism and violence?
- How does parental cell phone use affect children's safety?
- How does oat-bran consumption affect bad cholesterol levels?
- Do vaccines affect the probability of a child becoming autistic?
- How much does one more year of schooling increase a person's earnings?
- Does smiling when dropping my shirt off at the cleaners affect the probability that my shirt will be ready by Thursday?

A regression is a remarkable tool in its ability to measure how certain variables move together, while holding certain factors constant. A natural human reaction is to be mesmerized by things people do not understand, such as how regressions can produce these numbers. And so, in the roughly 10 times that I have used regression results in briefings to somewhat-high-level officials at the Department of

Defense (mostly as a junior researcher, with a senior researcher tagging along to make sure I didn't say anything dumb), the people I was briefing never asked me whether there were any empirical issues with the regression analysis I had used or how confident I was with the findings. Most of the time, based on the leading official's response to the research, they would act as if I had just given them the absolute truth on an important problem based on these "magic boxes" called "regressions." Unfortunately, I was caught up in the excitement of the positive response from these officials, and I wasn't as forthright as I should have been about the potential pitfalls (and uncertainty) in my findings. And so, I usually let them believe the magic.

But, regressions are not magic boxes. The inaccuracy Leno joked about is real, as there are many pitfalls of regression analysis. And, from what I have seen in research, at conferences, from journal referees, etc., many researchers (most of whom have Ph.D.s) have a limited understanding of these issues. And so, published quantitative research is often rife with severely biased estimates and erroneous interpretations and conclusions.

How bad is it? In the medical-research field, where incorrect research has the potential to result in lost lives, John Ioannidis has called out the entire field on its poor research methods and records. The Greek doctor/medical-researcher was featured in a 2010 article in *The Atlantic* (Freedman 2010). Ioannidis and his team of researchers have demonstrated that a large portion of the existing medical research is wrong, misleading, or highly exaggerated. He attributes it to several parts of the research process: bias in the way that research questions were being posed, how studies and empirical models were set up (e.g., establishing the proper control group), what patients were recruited for the studies, how results were presented and portrayed, and how journals chose what to publish.

Along these lines, the magazine *The Economist* had a much-needed op-ed and accompanying article in 2013 on how inaccurate research has become.[1] Among the highlights they note are:

- Amgen, a biotech company, could replicate only 6 of 53 "landmark" cancer-research studies;
- Bayer, a pharmaceutical company was able to replicate just one-quarter of 67 important health studies;
- Studies with "negative results," meaning insignificant estimated effects of the treatment variables, constituted 30% of all studies in 1990 and just 14% today, suggesting that important results showing no evidence that a treatment has an effect are being suppressed – and/or extra efforts are being made to make results statistically significant.

All of this highlights an interesting irony. The potential for valuable research has perhaps never been greater, with more data available on many important outcomes (such as student test scores, human DNA, health, logistics, and consumer behavior, and ball and player movements in sports), yet the reputation of academic research has perhaps never been so low.

This is fixable!

This book is meant to effectively train the next generation of quantitative researchers.

1.2 The purpose of research

To understand where research goes wrong, we first have to understand the overall purpose of research. We conduct research to improve knowledge, which often involves trying to get us closer to understanding cause-effect and other empirical relationships. To demonstrate, let's start with the highly contentious issue of global warming. You may have some belief on the probability that the following statement is true:

Human activity is contributing to global warming.

And, hopefully that probability of yours lies somewhere between 0.3% and 99.7% – that is, you may have your beliefs, but you recognize that you probably are not an expert on the topic and so there is a possibility that you are wrong. I'm guessing that most people would be below 10% or above 90% (or, even 5% and 95%). But, for the sake of the argument, let's say that you have a subjective probability of the statement being true 45% of the time.

Suppose a study comes out that has new evidence that humans are causing global warming. This may shift your probability upwards. If the new research were reported on cable news channel MSNBC (which leans toward the liberal side of politics) and you tended to watch MSNBC, then let's say that it would shift your probability up by 7 percentage points (to 52%). If you tended to watch Fox News (a more conservative channel) instead, then the news from MSNBC may shift your probability up by some negligible amount, say 0.2 percentage points (up to 45.2%). But, ideally, the amount that your subjective probability of the statement above would shift upwards should depend on:

*   How the study contrasts with prior research on the issue;
*   The validity and extensiveness of the prior research;
*   The extent to which any viable alternative explanations to the current findings can be ruled out – i.e., how valid the methods of the study are.

With regression analysis, it should be the same thinking of shifting beliefs. People have some prior beliefs about some issue, say on whether class size is important for student achievement. Using regression analysis, a new study finds no evidence that class size has an effect on student achievement. This finding should not necessarily be taken as concrete evidence for that side of the issue. Rather, the evidence has to be judged based on the strength of the study relative to the strength of other studies, or the three criteria listed above. And, people would then shift their subjective probability appropriately. The more convincing the analysis, the more it should swing a person's belief in the direction of the study's conclusions.

This is where it is up to researchers, the media, and the public to properly scrutinize research to assess how convincing it is. As I will describe below, you cannot always rely on the peer-review process that determines what research gets published in journals.

1.3 What causes problems in the research process?

The only real fiction is non-fiction.

– Mark Totten

Where do I begin?

Well, let's discuss some structural issues first, which lead to misguided incentives for researchers.

One major problem in research is **publication bias** (discussed with more detail in Section 13.2), which results from the combination of the pressure among academics to publish and journals seeking articles with interesting results that will sell to readers, get publicity, and get more citations from subsequent research. All of this improves the standing of the journal. But, it leads to published research being biased towards results with significant (statistically and meaningfully) effects – so, studies finding statistically insignificant effects tend not to be disseminated. Given the greater likelihood of getting published with significant and interesting results, researchers at times will not spend time attempting to publish research that has insignificant results. In addition, research can be easily finagled, as adding or cutting a few semi-consequential variables can sometimes push the coefficient estimate on a key treatment variable over the threshold of "significance," which could make the difference between research being publishable or non-publishable or determine whether the research would be publishable in a high-quality journal.

Structural problems in research also result from the influence of sponsors of research. Who are the sponsors of research? One general set of sponsors comes from governments. In the U.S., several agencies sponsor research, with the National Institute of Health (NIH) and Department of Defense being two of the larger ones. NIH is generally an ideal sponsor of research in that a researcher obtains the funds and is often let alone to do the research and publish what they please from the research, regardless of the results. Still, similar to publication bias, there may be an incentive for the researcher to find something interesting, which would help towards receiving the next round of funding. But, for the most part, research conducted for the government, I believe, is less subject to sponsor-influence than that for other sponsors.

More concerning is research for corporations or foundations with an agenda. Economists are wrong on many things, but they are correct in their belief that corporations' primary goal is almost always to maximize profits. As a result, pressure for those profits may lead to immoral behavior on research. You probably do not want to trust research that is sponsored by an entity with a financial stake in the results.

This is largely the basis behind the concerns of Dr. Marcia Angell, a long-time Editor (and interim Editor-in-Chief) of the *New England Journal of Medicine*. She wrote an article that all law-makers and parents should be required to read (Angell 2009). In this article, Dr. Angell states:

> It is simply no longer possible to believe much of the clinical research that is published, or to rely on the judgment of trusted physicians or authoritative medical guidelines. I take no pleasure in this conclusion, which I reached slowly and reluctantly over my two decades as an editor of *The New England Journal of Medicine*.

The basis of Dr. Angell's realizations is the less than forthrightness involved with much medical research, particularly for pharmaceutical drugs. According to Dr. Angell, pharmaceutical companies pay influential academics large amounts of money and/or insert a representative into their sponsored research, usually at medical schools and hospitals. And, that representative (or the influenced academic) has power over the direction of the study and whether the final results can be published – meaning that negative results are often suppressed from the public domain.

This is fraud! And, it can kill people.

Beyond any fraud, pressure for interesting results, and publication bias, perhaps the primary underlying cause of poor research is a fundamental lack of understanding of statistical analysis, particularly regression analysis. Researchers often do not understand how to develop the best model to address a research question, the many things that could go wrong with a model, and the proper interpretation of results. Even research in top academic journals is sometimes based on misguided regression analyses and interpretation. There are certain topics for which almost every article on that topic has poorly executed regression analyses or interpretations. . . . I will get into a few of those later on.

Compounding these problems of poor research, the filtering process is quite weak. The scientific-review process to determine what gets published in academic journals turns out not to be as stringent and as good a quality-control as it sounds. The process involves:

- A researcher submits a paper to a journal.
- An editor or associate editor of the journal takes a quick look at the paper to determine if the paper might be of appropriate quality for the journal.
- If so, the editor seeks (typically) one to three referees who should be well-versed on the paper's topic and methods to evaluate the paper.
- The referees produce reports on what is good about the paper and what needs to be addressed. They also often make a recommendation to the editor for whether the paper should be rejected, accepted, or be allowed a "revise and resubmit" after addressing the comments.
- The editor (and perhaps higher-up editors) makes the final decision on whether the paper gets published in that journal.

I will speak more on the scientific (peer) review process in Chapter 13, with guidance on how to produce a responsible referee report. But, it seems clear that scientific reviews need improving, as evidenced by the somewhat laughable results of a few tests on the quality of peer reviews:

- The *British Medical Journal* sent an article to 200 of its reviewers, in which the journal created eight mistakes on the study design, the analysis, and the interpretation. On average, the reviewers found fewer than two of the eight mistakes.[2]
- Richard Smith (2006), the former editor of the *British Medical Journal* reported that there is evidence showing that referees on the same paper agree on whether a paper should be published just a little more than would be expected if they randomly decided.
- Similar evidence to Smith (2006) was found by Welch (2014) with regards to leading finance and economics journals.

If peer reviewers do not adequately screen research, then we cannot expect much better from the media (who report research results). For example, while the truth on regressions, that they can be rife with empirical problems, is often made loud and clear, it tends to be ignored by the media. An interesting article gets published, and the media report on the research as if it were a certainty, without much consideration of the soundness of the research or of any prior evidence to the contrary. In partial defense of the media, they rely on the (flawed) peer-review process to vet the article.

The fundamental problem comes down to all participants in the research process and its dissemination not knowing the right questions to ask to properly scrutinize research. This allows the low-quality research to get through the process.

The *Economist* article in the opening part of this chapter quoted an academic: "There is no cost [for researchers] to getting things wrong" (p. 26). In fact, there can be rewards for getting things wrong since it is unlikely anyone will ever notice. And, although any "fraud" may be isolated to a small percentage of researchers, the author of the article argues that there is a good chance that their results have a disproportionate share of research that gets publicly discussed.

Society needs to address issues of publication bias and the influence of sponsors with a vested interest. Beyond those problems, if the research process can be improved at all levels of the filtering process (by improving how we teach students the fundamentals, interpretations, and pitfalls of regression analysis), then there would be less room for faulty research methods, publication bias, and perhaps fraud. The research process could be more trusted.

1.4 About this book

I believe that regression analysis is often taught ineffectively and inefficiently. The ineffectiveness is suggested by mounting evidence that much academic research is inaccurate (often due to faulty methods). The inefficiency comes from the unnecessary reliance on high-level math, which squanders time on material that 99.3% of students will never use and makes the material inaccessible or unnecessarily difficult for those without strong math skills. I aim to improve how regression analysis is taught with a more logical and (relatively) low-math approach.

Compared to other books on regressions, this manuscript should better prepare readers for conducting, interpreting, and assessing regression analyses, while simultaneously making the learning of regression analysis simpler, more efficient, and (hopefully) more enjoyable.

The new low-math approach

I was great in math through high school, wasn't so great in college, and struggled mightily in undergraduate and graduate regression classes, given how highly mathematical they were. In college, I would spend way too much of my valuable basketball, socializing, and trying-to-find-a-girlfriend time attempting to decipher equations like this:

$$\hat{\beta}_2 = \frac{\sum\left(y_i x_{2i}\right)\left(\lambda^2 \sum x_{2i}^2 + \sum v_i^2\right) - \left(\lambda \sum y_i x_{2i} + \sum y_i v_i\right)\left(\lambda \sum x_{2i}^2\right)}{\sum x_{2i}^2 \left(\lambda^2 \sum x_{2i}^2 + \sum v_i^2\right) - \left(\lambda \sum x_{2i}^2\right)^2}$$

which comes from the popular *undergraduate* textbook that I had used in college.

Regression analysis is taught with high-level math, at least in economics curricula, as part of a rite of passage. Professors likely think that getting through these classes separates the real economists from the "partial" economists.

But now, after two decades of research using regression analysis, I know that the high-level math is not necessary for most practitioners. I have a pretty darn good intuitive feel for regression analysis. But, this came mostly from performing applications of regression analysis – applications in which I did not use any of the high-level math and proofs that I learned in the regression classes. Rather, I just used intuition and logic. And, these are largely based on a solid understanding of how regressions "hold other factors constant" and how different types of relationships between variables can cause problems – neither of which is taught with much detail and enough emphasis in regression classes/books. And, I would argue, a large portion of academics and practitioners lack this level of understanding.

You can develop this understanding and intuition, without the high-level math. The Linear Algebra and Calculus, used in most classes on regression analysis, are necessary only for regression theorists, not for practitioners. To teach regression analysis in the current complex way may prevent some sharp, creative researchers (who may not have such great math skills) from entering the world of research.

I wrote this book, in part, to shift the way that regression analysis is taught so that research can be opened up to creative people, almost regardless of their higher-math proficiency.

The primary focus is on what could go wrong with regression analysis

Surprisingly, most books on regression analysis give very little emphasis to the pitfalls of regression analysis regarding whether the estimated cause-effect relationships are biased. In fact, they tend to focus more on getting the standard errors correct. Standard errors (covered in Chapter 5) tell you how precise the estimates are, and they are used in the calculations for hypothesis tests. Certain types of regression models or the nature of some data require adjustments to standard errors to ensure that the correct standard errors are used for the hypothesis tests. Corrections are typically on the order of 0 to 25%.

But, in my view, it is more important for the hypothesis tests to have accurate coefficient estimates, which indicate the nature of the empirical relationships. And, the pitfalls of regression analysis cause coefficient estimates to be off by a much greater factor than for standard errors, often even reversing signs. It is most often errors in coefficient estimates rather than errors in standard errors that are the sources of wrong research. Compared to other regression books, this book pays much more attention and detail to avoiding, acknowledging, and addressing the things that could go wrong in regression analysis with coefficient estimates.

Scope of the book

This book is meant to be a guide for *conducting*, *interpreting*, and *assessing/scrutinizing* regression analysis. It brings a new approach to understanding regressions, replacing the high-level math with more figures demonstrating pathways and more intuition on what is occurring in the regressions. I direct the book both to students and researchers (as a guide on how to develop sound research) and to the consumers of research (to give the tools for properly scrutinizing research).

For students at the undergraduate or graduate level, I give almost all of the basic information needed to conduct valid regression analysis. By avoiding proofs and high-level math, a course using this book could cover more important information, such as giving more detail on how to interpret regressions, what methods to use for different types of outcome variables, what the pitfalls of regression analysis are (and, there are plenty of them), and how to address some of these pitfalls. For those who already have a regression/econometrics book, this book will serve as a nice supplement, as it relates many of the key concepts to "everyday" events, such as pouring a glass of beer, having a shooting contest with LeBron James, or searching for intelligent life elsewhere in the universe. Compared to other books on regressions, this book tends to use more stories and simple flow charts than complex mathematical equations to demonstrate the concepts.

Students will not learn every little detail for every specific situation. Rather, to make the book tractable I will present the details on issues that students are most likely to encounter in their research or others' research and the necessary details students need to develop strategies for their research. This is based on the thousands of regressions I have estimated, coming from several different fields of study. I have left out of this book minute details that are specific for certain topics. The details that are in most books are often complicated, bog people down, and distract readers from the important intuition and practical aspects of regression models.

There are some more advanced regressions that are not commonly used, for which I give an introduction without spending too much time on the details.[3] Thus, you will learn most of what you need to know about regression analysis much more efficiently than you would with the existing regression books.

The general game plan of the book is to:

- Describe the nuts and bolts of regression analysis, including the methods for hypothesis testing and its two main inputs (the coefficient estimate and the standard error);
- Indicate how coefficient estimates just tell us how variables move together, holding other factors constant. It is up to us to objectively assess whether it is causal;
- Stress how the coefficient estimate indicates causality only if alternative reasons for the variables moving together (or not) can be ruled out;
- Discuss those alternative reasons (to the causality argument) for variables moving together (or not) – these are the main pitfalls of regression analysis;
- Briefly discuss problems with standard errors and their corrections (for proper hypothesis testing);
- Present the pitfalls for regression analyses that have objectives other than estimating causal effects;
- Offer strategies for addressing some of the pitfalls for coefficient estimates;
- Provide alternative regression methods to use when the dependent variable (the outcome) has a non-standard form (such as being dichotomous);
- Provide examples of good research and research that could have been conducted better;
- Present how to conduct and write up a research project using regression analysis;
- Stress objectiveness and honesty for conducting and scrutinizing research.

1.5 The most important sections in this book

While I would argue that the whole book is extremely important for understanding regressions and improving the research process, I list here the most important sections.

2.12 Causal effects are "average effects"

This section highlights a simple and important (but often overlooked) concept, that coefficient estimates represent average effects or how two variables move together, on average. Coefficient estimates are not indicative of an absolute effect that applies to all subjects.

5.3 The drawbacks of p-values and statistical significance

This section highlights the fact that the conventional methods used for hypothesis tests (p-values and significance tests) do not tell you the probability that your conclusion is correct. The likelihood that there could be an effect, based on some subjective non-data assessment, would need to be considered.

5.5 What does an insignificant estimate tell you?

One of the most common flaws in research is misinterpreting insignificant effects. In addition, there may be hidden information in an insignificant effect.

5.6 Statistical significance is not the goal

It is exciting to find a result and conclude that you "found something." But, our goal in research is to advance knowledge, and so we should be guided by correct modeling strategies and not by what the results are.

Chapter 6

This is the chapter on the things that could go wrong with regression analysis and the BIG QUESTIONS that need to be considered to assess a regression. All researchers and consumers of research should know these issues.

8.1 to 8.3 Fixed-effects models

Fixed-effects models are one of the most common methods to address one of the most common problems in regression analysis, omitted-variables bias.

Chapter 12

This chapter discusses how to write and organize a research paper. It provides many tips for organization and the presentation of results, among other things.

13.1 Be aware of your cognitive biases

This section reminds researchers and consumers one of the most basic parts of research: keep an open mind for the possible findings rather than limiting your mind to just accepting what you believe to be the case.

1.6 Quantitative vs. qualitative research

From graduate school (at the University of Wisconsin), more than 20 years ago, I remember only one research seminar fairly clearly. An economist from Yale, Truman Bewley, talked to us about an investigation into what unemployment does to people, which ended up being part of a larger research project (Bewley 1999). His analysis was not based on formal surveys. But rather, Dr. Bewley had conversations with people who had been laid off by plant closings. From what I remember, he asked people about what they had experienced, how the lay-off made them feel physically and emotionally, what they were hoping for, and more.

I did not know it at the time, but what Dr. Bewley did was **qualitative research**, which is explorative research that is meant to describe (in-depth) opinions, attitudes, and behaviors. Qualitative research can be based on many types of data collection, with the more common ones being focus groups, individual interviews, and observations of behaviors. Focus groups and interviews tend to have minimal basic structure and are designed to allow the responses of the interviewee to direct the flow of the conversation to the thoughts and opinions that are more important to the interviewee.

The researcher would then compile the responses from the interviews and try to find commonalities and a story. I don't mean to simplify qualitative research, as there are five main methods of qualitative research.[4] This all stands in contrast to **quantitative research**, in which the information collected (e.g., survey or administrative data) would be the same for everyone.

There are advantages and disadvantages to each. I'll briefly describe some. Qualitative research can tell a much more detailed story, and it can speak to underlying motivations for certain behaviors or outcomes. Whereas quantitative research asks "what?", qualitative research asks "how?" and "why?". But, qualitative research is time-consuming, and so it is often difficult to generate enough data to make conclusions about a population.

With quantitative research, it is simple to deal with thousands or millions of observations, and so there could be plenty of power to draw conclusions on a population. Often, however, there are limits to what data can tell us. For example, with standard surveys, different types of questions are important to different people, and so the "general questions" may be too simplified for truly understanding behaviors and outcomes.

This book focuses on quantitative research. But, I want to give a shout-out to qualitative research, which can do many things that quantitative research cannot.

1.7 Stata and R code

I conducted the numerous regression analyses in this book using the statistical programs Stata and R. On the book's website (www.routledge.com/9781138541405), I have posted the data sets and the Stata and R code used for the analyses in the book. The Stata and R code are in two separate files, and I indicate what section in the book each set of code comes from. The data I posted can be used for other statistical programs besides these. The data are available as a Stata data set (*.dta) and in comma-delimited format (*.csv). If you do not know Stata or R, there are numerous online tutorials for learning them.

1.8 Chapter summary

Regression analysis can address important questions that can help people and organizations make better decisions. Unfortunately, the current state of academic research is marred by a slew of poorly conducted studies, which is giving the whole research community a bad name. This could be largely fixed if researchers were to gain a better understanding of research. Plus, bad research will not be disseminated as widely if the media could better distinguish between strong and questionable research. This book aims to build better researchers by promoting a stronger understanding of how to give the proper scrutiny to the research to assess its relevance and contribution to knowledge.

Notes

1 "Trouble at the Lab." *The Economist* 409 (8858), 26–30.
2 "Trouble at the Lab." *The Economist* 409 (8858), 26–30.
3 There are many sources on the internet or other textbooks for greater detail on any given regression topic.
4 See https://measuringu.com/qual-methods/, accessed July 10, 2018.

References

Angell, M. (2009). Drug companies & doctors: A story of corruption. *The New York Review of Books*, January 15, 2009 issue. (Available at www.nybooks.com/articles/2009/01/15/drug-companies-doctorsa-story-of-corruption/).

Bewley, T. F. (1999). *Why wages don't fall during a recession*. Cambridge, MA: Harvard University Press.

Freedman, D. H. (2010). Lies, damned lies, and medical science. *The Atlantic*. November 2010 issue. (Available at www.theatlantic.com/magazine/archive/2010/11/lies-damned-lies-and-medical-science/308269/).

Smith, R. (2006). Peer review: A flawed process at the heart of science and journals. *Journal of the Royal Society of Medicine*, 99(4), 178–182.

Welch, I. (2014). Referee recommendations. *Review of Financial Studies*, 27(9), 2773–2804.

2 Regression analysis basics

We regress, therefore we are.

– Me

2.1 What is a regression?

I'm pretty middle-of-the-road when it comes to politics – at least, that's what all the political tests I've taken show. But, my centrist views, along with my knowledge of regression analysis, once got me in trouble at a dinner party with my Aunt Jo's friends in San Francisco.

I merely said that I believe we over-educate people in the United States – except in educating people on statistical analysis. My aunt's friends took great exception to my statement. They cited stats that say how much more opportunity (i.e., income) people have from obtaining more schooling.

Besides the point that the costs of educating people need to be considered and that many people do not use the skills they learn in college, I applied what I knew about regression analysis to support my point. Yes, more-educated people make much more money than less-educated people, but it doesn't mean that education *caused* the entire income advantage. There are other differences between more- vs. less-educated people that could contribute to the income differences. So, the more-educated people would probably have made more money than the less-educated people even without the differences in education between them.

Regression analysis helps towards eliminating the influence of the other factors to get closer to the true, average causal effect of something – in this case, a year of schooling. (This is what would inform people on how much education to obtain, given the cost. And, it should have bearing on how much government should subsidize higher education.)

And so, I tried making this point about regressions to my aunt's friends. But, among the many limitations of regressions, one of the toughest is slicing through pre-conceived notions.

If I were able to play God for a moment (in geological terms), I would conduct an experiment in which I randomly assigned people to have different levels of schooling and compare their incomes at various points later in their lives. This would tell us, at least for this geological moment of the experiment, how much an extra year of schooling increased people's incomes, on average. From that information, I would have a sense of how much, as God, I should nudge people to obtain more schooling.

But, to the best of my knowledge, we do not live in an experimental world. And so, we need to devise other methods of examining how much an extra year of school, on average, increases a person's income. We might start with a scatterplot showing years-of-schooling completed and income from wages and salary, as in Figure 2.1. These data come from the National Longitudinal Survey of Youth (NLSY, Bureau of Labor Statistics, 2014), a survey tracking a cohort for over 30 years, starting in 1979.[1] I took a conveniently selected sample of 75 males (of ages 39 to 47) who were still in the survey in 2004, 25 years after the start of the survey. I purposefully made sure that the sample included observations at most levels of schooling, as a random sample would have a large concentration of observations at 12 years (a high-school diploma) and 16 years (a college degree).

A **regression** is an equation that represents how a set of factors explains an outcome and how the outcome moves with each factor. It is pretty clear, from Figure 2.1, that there is a positive correlation between education and income; when education is higher, income tends to be higher. And so, a regression model would probably show this positive relationship. But, the regression model does not indicate why the variables move with each other, and so we have not made the case for there being a causal effect or what the magnitude of any causal effect is because there are alternative explanations to why the variables move together. As mentioned above, before concluding that there is causality, we have to rule out other possible explanations first. This is why researchers use Multiple Regression

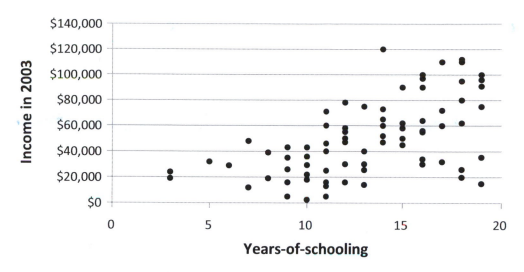

Figure 2.1 Scatterplot of years–of–schooling and income

Source: A random sample from the NLSY of 1979 (Bureau of Labor Statistics, 2014).

Models, which "hold constant" certain factors in an attempt to compare apples to apples when examining the effect of some treatment/factor on an outcome. But, after reviewing the main objectives of regression analysis, we need to start with the Simple Regression Model.

Before doing so, let me briefly address something you're probably asking yourself: Why is it called a "regression" model or analysis? That's a great question, and I do not know the answer. I searched the internet for a good explanation, but I couldn't find one. But, after much thought, I came up with a theory. But, you will need to wait until Box 2.1 in Section 2.4.2, as you will need some background information for my theory.

2.2 The four main objectives for regression analysis

> Little League baseball is a very good thing because it keeps the parents off the streets.
>
> — Yogi Berra

The most common use of regression analysis is to *quantify how one factor causally affects another*. For example, if a person obtains one additional year of schooling, how much would we expect that person's income to increase? Or, if a child's parents divorce, how much would that affect the child's academic outcomes, on average?

Second, regressions may be used to *forecast or predict an outcome*. The Army may want to have a good prediction of how many first–year soldiers would attrite (i.e., leave the service for some reason) so that the Army can set optimal recruiting targets for a given year. Or, Google may want to forecast how much space will be needed for Google Drive. The Army and Google would include in a regression model various factors that may help forecast attrition and Google Drive space needed.

A third use of regressions is to *determine the predictors of some factor.* For example, parents or school counselors may want to know what factors could predict whether a teenager is using drugs. In this case, certain factors, such as a parental divorce, may not itself have a causal effect on teenage drug use, but the divorce may be indicative of other factors (e.g., conflict at home) that could lead to the teenager's drug use. The causal effect of a parental divorce may in fact be zero, but the divorce may still be a strong predictor of teenage drug use.

And, the fourth main use of regression analysis is to *adjust an outcome for various factors.* For example, rather than just evaluating a teacher's effectiveness based on his/her students' test scores, we could adjust those scores based on the students' prior scores and perhaps the demographics and English-language status of the students. Or, a board of directors for a publicly traded firm, to properly evaluate the performance of a CEO, may want to evaluate quarterly profits after factoring out the industry's influences on the company's quarterly profits. This objective for regression analysis typically involves trying to gauge "relative performance" by factoring out certain variables that represent environmental and situational factors that are out of the control of the subject being evaluated.

Beyond these four main objectives, there is one other objective that is used in many studies: testing the "association" between variables. For example, some studies have examined the association between teenage drug use and early teenage sexual activity. I do not consider testing for "associations" as a main objective because these studies typically have the ultimate goal of knowing whether there is a causal effect of one variable on another, which would speak more to the effects of policies than would mere associations. The nature of their data or model makes it difficult to ascertain that any association they find is causal, and so they have to say they are testing for associations. This is not to criticize this type of research, as sometimes this research is meant to demonstrate an association which could suggest causation and which serves as a stepping stone for others to design a study or experiment to test for causality. But, it typically is not an ultimate objective of regression analysis.

Table 2.1 summarizes the four main objectives of regression analysis and the types of questions they address. The strategies for designing a regression would depend on which of these four purposes the researcher has.

As mentioned, this book concentrates on the first objective: quantifying cause-effect relationships. To this end, Chapter 6 goes into extensive detail about the main things that could wrong when estimating causal effects and what strategies should be used towards that goal. Chapter 7 describes the strategies to use when estimating regressions for the other objectives.

Table 2.1 The four main objectives of regression analysis and the questions addressed

Regression objective	Generic types of questions addressed
Estimating causal effects	How does a certain factor affect the outcome?
Determining how well certain factors predict the outcome	Does a certain factor predict the outcome? What factors predict the outcome?
Forecasting an outcome	What is the best prediction/forecast of the outcome?
Adjusting outcomes for various (non-performance) factors	How well did a subject perform relative to what we would expect given certain factors?

2.3 The Simple Regression Model

2.3.1 The components and equation of the Simple Regression Model

If you remember 8th grade Algebra, a straight line is represented by the equation:

$$y = a + bx$$

where:
- x is the horizontal-axis variable;
- y is the vertical-axis variable;
- a is the y-intercept;
- b is the slope of the line.

A Simple Regression is similar in that there is one X and one Y variable. But, it is different in that not all points fall on the straight line. Rather, the Simple Regression line indicates the line that best fits the data.

The **Simple Regression Model** (also known as the Bivariate Regression Model) is:

$$Y_i = \beta_0 + \beta_1 \times X_i + \varepsilon_i \qquad (2.1a)$$

$(i = 1, 2, 3, \ldots, N)$

This equation describes each of the N data points, not just the line. The five components of the model are:

- The **dependent variable** (Y), which is also called the *outcome, response variable, regressand,* or *Y variable.* (It is the Y-axis variable, or "income" in Figure 2.1.)
- The **explanatory variable** (X), which is also called the *independent variable, explanatory variable, treatment variable, regressor,* or simply *X variable.* Personally, I do not like the term "independent variable" because: (1) it is not descriptive of what the variable does; (2) sometimes, the X variable is "dependent" on the dependent (Y) variable or other factors that are related to the dependent variable; and (3) it often gets confused with "dependent variable." I prefer "explanatory variable" or simply "X variable." (It is the X-axis variable, or "years-of-schooling" in Figure 2.1.)
- The **coefficient on the explanatory variable** (β_1), which indicates the slope of the regression line, or how the outcome (Y) is estimated to move, on average, with a one-unit change in the explanatory variable (X).
- The **intercept term** (β_0), which indicates the Y-intercept from the regression line, or what the expected value of Y would be when $X = 0$. This is sometimes called the "constant" term.
- The **error term** (ε), which indicates how far off an individual data point is, vertically, from the true regression line. This occurs because regressions typically cannot perfectly predict the outcome. (Income depends on many things other than years-of-schooling.)

(Note that, following convention, I italicize variable names. But, when I speak generically about an X or Y variable, I do not italicize "X" or "Y.")

The i subscript in the regression line refers to individual i in the sample, so:

- Y_i = income for individual i;
- X_i = years-of-schooling for individual i;
- ε_i = the error for individual i.

Equation (2.1a) is actually N separate equations, one for each observation:

$$Y_1 = \beta_0 + \beta_1 \times X_1 + \varepsilon_1$$
$$Y_2 = \beta_0 + \beta_1 \times X_2 + \varepsilon_2$$
$$Y_3 = \beta_0 + \beta_1 \times X_3 + \varepsilon_3 \qquad (2.1b)$$
$$\ldots$$
$$Y_N = \beta_0 + \beta_1 \times X_N + \varepsilon_N$$

Note that the coefficients, β_0 and β_1, are the same for each observation.

Sometimes, shorthand is used and the subscripts (and the multiplication sign and subject-identifying subscripts) are left out, and the equation is just written as:

$$Y = \beta_0 + \beta_1 X + \varepsilon \qquad (2.2)$$

The X and Y variables

Y is the variable you are trying to explain or predict. Why is Y called the "dependent variable" and X the "independent variable"? Because, theoretically (and hopefully) Y depends on what X is and not *vice versa*. Hopefully, X is random with respect to Y, meaning that X changes for reasons that are unrelated to what is happening to Y. If X is affected by Y or if X and Y have common factors, then we have problems, which we will see in Chapter 6.

Sometimes a variable name other than X or Y is used if it is fairly self-explanatory. For example, if "marijuana use" is the X variable, then you could use *MJ* as the variable name. It gets confusing (and doesn't look good) if you use longer words for variable names. However, I will do so in a few places to keep it simple.

The coefficients

The two coefficients are:

- β_0 = the Y-intercept (known as the constant);
- β_1 = the slope of the line (the coefficient on X).

The interpretation would be that, if a person had 0 years-of-schooling ($X = 0$), they would be expected to have income of β_0, and each extra year of schooling *would be associated with* β_1 higher income, on average. Notice that I say "would be associated with" instead of "causes" or "leads to." I do so because, again, we have not established causality yet.

The error term

The **error term** is the difference between the actual Y value and the predicted Y value based on the true population regression equation (as opposed to what is estimated with the sample data). There are three main components of the error term, ε_i:

- The influence of variables not included in the regression. In the education–income regression, this could include, among other factors, gender, race, and motivation.
- The possibility that the X or Y variable is mis-coded. For example, if the person has a college degree (16 years-of-schooling) and is reported to have just 2 years of college (14), then the model may predict lower income than the person actually has, which would contribute positively to the error term.
- The effects of random processes affecting the outcome. This could come from a pay raise due to a promotion someone is given because the person who had been in the position randomly quit. Or, in examining students' test scores, a child may guess on some answers, and lucky or unlucky guesses will affect the outcome independently of any X variables.

The theoretical/true regression equation vs. the estimated regression equation

The equation from above:

$$Y_i = \beta_0 + \beta_1 X_i + \varepsilon_i \tag{2.1a}$$

is considered the theoretical or true regression equation. But, we can never know what the true regression equation is because of the randomness involved with sampling from the population and the random events that influence the outcome. And, without knowing the true coefficient estimates, we do not know the true error term. Thus, with data, we produce the estimated regression equation, as follows:

$$Y_i = \hat{\beta}_0 + \hat{\beta}_1 X_i + \hat{\varepsilon}_i \tag{2.3a}$$

$$\hat{Y}_i = \hat{\beta}_0 + \hat{\beta}_1 X_i \tag{2.3b}$$

The "hats" (^) over $Y, \beta_0, \beta_1,$ and ε indicate that they are predicted or estimated values. So, we would say that:

- $\hat{\beta}_0$ is the predicted intercept term.
- $\hat{\beta}_1$ is the predicted coefficient on the variable X.
- $\hat{\varepsilon}_i$ is the predicted error term (known as the **residual**) based on the actual X and Y values and the coefficient estimates.
- $\hat{Y}$ is the predicted value of Y based on the estimated coefficient estimates and value of the variable, X. Note that the predicted value of Y does not include the residual.

2.3.2 An example with education and income data

There are various methods for estimating the best-fitting regression line. By far, the most common one is the Ordinary Least Squares (OLS) method. The "Least Squares" part refers to minimizing the sum of the squared residuals across all observations. I will further discuss what this means and the mechanics behind OLS in Section 2.4.

Let's start with a sample on the full set of the 2772 males from the 2004 NLSY who had: (1) positive income from wages and salary reported in the 2004 survey (for 2003 income);[2] (2) a positive number of hours–worked–per–week in 2003; and (3) a non–missing score on the Armed Forces Qualification Test (AFQT), which is a test on aptitude that was taken by 94% of the NLSY respondents in the second year of the survey – we will use the AFQT score later in the chapter (Bureau of Labor Statistics, 2014).

I will just mention it here and not later, but you can follow along with the data set, called **income_data**, available on the book's website, and the Stata or R code. The two relevant variables for now are:

- $Y = income =$ income of the individual;
- $X = educ =$ years-of-schooling.

With the sample indicated above, we obtain the following regression equation (rounding):

$$\hat{Y} = -54,299 + 8121 \times X \tag{2.4a}$$

Or

$$\widehat{income} = -54,299 + 8121 \times (educ) \tag{2.4b}$$

This regression equation says that each year of schooling is associated with an estimated $8121 higher income in 2003. The $8121 figure is the coefficient estimate, $\hat{\beta}_1$. And, we can say that:

$$\hat{\beta}_1 = \frac{\Delta \hat{Y}}{\Delta X} = \$8121 \tag{2.5}$$

Note that equation (2.4a) is the regression equation (i.e., set of coefficient estimates) for the sample I have, which we hope would be representative of the population. If we had a different sample from the population, we would obtain a different set of coefficient estimates. Thus, the estimates will have sampling distributions and, hopefully, will have the desired properties (unbiased and consistent) mentioned in Section A.4 of the Appendix. The way that the uncertainty in the estimates is characterized is with the *standard error*, which will be discussed in Chapter 5 on hypothesis testing.

You might wonder how the intercept is negative and of such great magnitude, as it says that someone with 0 years-of-schooling is expected to earn negative $54,299. The reason for this is that the regression line is mostly derived from where most of the variation lies (see Section 2.6). And, most variation will lie in the 12 to 16 years-of-schooling range. So, the Least Squares regression line is fit in a way that is fairly steep in those years-of-schooling, which results in a negative predicted income for those with very low education. What this suggests is that there may be a better way to fit the data when a line that best fits the data is non–linear (not straight) . . . we'll get into non–linear models in Section 3.2.

2.3.3 Calculating individual predicted values and residuals

The **predicted value** indicates what we would expect income to be for a given level of schooling. In our example, there would be a different predicted value of *income* for each level of schooling.

The **residual**, how the actual Y value differs from the predicted value, would be how much more (or less) income is relative to the predicted income, given the level of schooling. With some regression methods, notably the most common one of OLS, the average residual equals 0. Thus, the amount of over-prediction and under-prediction are equal.

To calculate the predicted value and residual, recall from your classes on statistics or probability that: $E[a \mid b]$ = expected value of a, given b. The calculations are:

- Predicted value of $Y = \hat{Y} = E[Y \mid X] = \hat{\beta}_o + \hat{\beta}_1 \times X$

  (because $E[\hat{\varepsilon}] = 0$, or the average residual equals 0 in linear regression models);

- Residual $= \hat{\varepsilon} = Y - E[Y \mid X] = Y - \hat{Y}$.

As an example, one person in the sample has 10 years-of-schooling and $25,000 of income. His regression statistics would be:

- Predicted value of $Y = E[Y \mid X = 10] = -54,299 + 8121 \times 10 = \$26,911$.

- Residual $= Y - E[Y \mid X] = \$25,000 - \$26,911 = -\$1911$.

The interpretations are that:

- We predict that someone with 10 years-of-schooling would have an income of $26,911.
- This person with 10 years-of-schooling and an income of $25,000 has $1911 lower income than what would be predicted from the regression.

2.4 How are regression lines determined?

2.4.1 Calculating regression equations

Let's do an example with OLS with just four observations I made up to make an easy exercise. This simple exercise will help convey the intuition behind how regression equations are determined when using the most common method, OLS.

Table 2.2 Four-observation example of education and income

Person	Years-of-schooling (X)	Income ($1000s) (Y)	Deviation from mean X	Deviation from mean Y	Numerator for slope $(X_i - \bar{X}) \times (Y_i - \bar{Y})$	Denominator for slope $(X_i - \bar{X})^2$
1	10	40	−3	−5	15	9
2	12	45	−1	0	0	1
3	14	40	+1	−5	−5	1
4	16	55	+3	+10	30	9
	$\bar{X} = 13$	$\bar{Y} = 45$			40	20

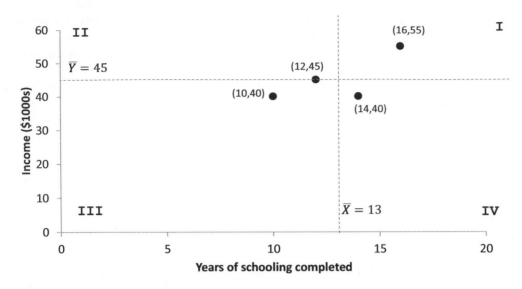

Figure 2.2 Data points for Table 2.2

The four observations from Table 2.2, based on the X and Y values in the second and third columns, are depicted in Figure 2.2, with the mean values (13 years-of-schooling for X and 45 or \$45,000 for Y), marked with dashed lines in the figure. The sign of the regression slope will be determined by whether the observations in quadrants I and III dominate those in quadrants II and IV or *vice versa*, based on the product of the deviations from the X and Y means. It looks as though the observations in quadrants I and III dominate, which means that we should have a positive regression slope. But, let's do the quick and easy math to check.

When using the OLS method, the following equation is the estimated slope of the regression line:

$$\hat{\beta}_1 = \frac{\sum_{i=1}^{n}(X_i - \bar{X})(Y_i - \bar{Y})}{\sum_{i=1}^{n}(X_i - \bar{X})^2} \tag{2.6a}$$

or more simply

$$\hat{\beta}_1 = \frac{\sum(X_i - \bar{X})(Y_i - \bar{Y})}{\sum(X_i - \bar{X})^2} \tag{2.6b}$$

Do not be intimidated by this. It is fairly straightforward. The equation represents how X and Y move together (the numerator) relative to how much variation there is in X (the denominator). So, when a given value of X is above its mean (the first quantity in the numerator is positive), does Y tend to be above or below its mean (the second quantity in the numerator)? Let's evaluate each observation.

- Person 1 has below-average years-of-schooling ($X = 10$) and income ($Y = 40$), so his value contributes $+15$ ($= -3 \times -5$) to the numerator, as seen in the second-to-last column of Table 2.2.

- Person 2 has the mean income. Even though the contribution to the numerator is 0, it does not mean that this observation is not contributing to the determination of the slope. The contribution is that Person 2 brings the coefficient more towards 0, as he has below-average years-of-schooling, but average income.
- Person 3 has above-average years-of-schooling and below-average income, so he contributes −5 (= 1 × −5) to the numerator.
- Person 4 has above-average years-of-schooling and income, so his value contributes +30 (= 3 × 10) to the numerator.

The sum for the numerator is, thus, 40, as shown in Table 2.2. The sign of the sum in the numerator indicates whether X and Y tend to move together in a positive or negative fashion, and the data indicate they move positively with each other. The denominator then scales the numerator based on how much variation there is in X. The denominator equals 20, based on the sum of values in the last column of Table 2.2.

Given these calculations, $\hat{\beta}_1 = 40 / 20 = 2$. This indicates how the two variables tend to move together. That is, when X changes by 1 unit, Y tends to be 2 units higher; or, when years-of-schooling is higher by one year, then income is higher by $2000, on average.

To then derive the coefficient estimate for β_0, we would use the centroid feature of Ordinary Least Squares:

$$\bar{Y} = \hat{\beta}_0 + \hat{\beta}_1 \bar{X} \tag{2.7}$$

That is, the regression line under OLS goes through the point that has the average X and Y values. This can then be rearranged as follows:

$$\hat{\beta}_0 = \bar{Y} - \hat{\beta}_1 \bar{X} = 45 - 2 \times 13 = 19 \tag{2.8}$$

The two estimates, $\hat{\beta}_0$ and $\hat{\beta}_1$, give the regression equation of:

$$\widehat{Y}_i = 19 + 2X_i \tag{2.9}$$

2.4.2 Total variation, variation explained, and remaining variation

To give more information on how the regression line is determined and what "Ordinary Least Squares" means, we need to understand the variation in the dependent variable. In Figure 2.3, we see the deviation from the mean $Y = 45$ for each of the four observations.

The **total variation** or **Total Sum of Squares** (*TSS*) of the outcome is the sum of the squared deviations from the mean, or:

$$TSS = \sum_{i-1}^{4} (Y_i - \bar{Y})^2 \tag{2.10}$$

In our example, using the deviations from the mean from the 5th column of Table 2.2:

$$TSS = \sum_{i=1}^{4} (Y_i - \bar{Y})^2 = (-5)^2 + (0)^2 + (-5)^2 + (10)^2 = 150 \tag{2.11}$$

Note that this is similar to the variance of a variable except that the "sum of squared deviations from the mean" is not divided by (the number of observations minus one). So, var(Y) = TSS / (n − 1).

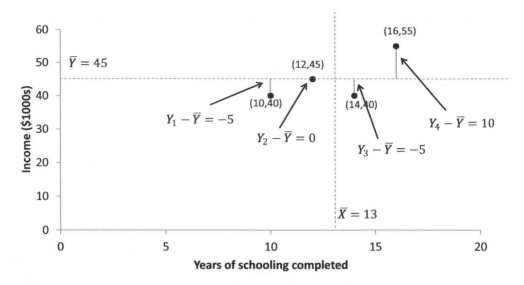

Figure 2.3 The data points relative to mean income for a four-observation regression

The total variation (*TSS*) can then be separated into two components:

- *ExSS* = Explained Sum of Squares = total variation explained by the regression model;
- *RSS* = Residual Sum of Squares = total variation remaining unexplained by the regression model (or the sum of the squared residuals).

The relationship between these different types of variation is:

TSS	=	ExSS	+	RSS	(2.12)
total variation	=	variation explained by the regression model	+	variation in the residuals	

or

RSS	=	TSS	−	ExSS	(2.13)
variation in the residuals	=	total variation	−	variation explained by the regression model	

Equation (2.13) helps highlight how linear regression models are calculated, when using **Ordinary Least Squares**. The model is estimated by finding the set of coefficients that maximizes *ExSS* (the amount of variation explained by the model). This, in turn, minimizes *RSS* (the amount of variation remaining unexplained) since *TSS* remains constant. Thus, "Least Squares" refers to the minimization of the sum of the squared residuals (*RSS*).

The regression line that explains most of the variation in *Y* is our regression equation from above:

$$\widehat{Y}_i = 19 + 2X_i \tag{2.9}$$

Table 2.3 Predicted values and residuals for the four-observation sample

Person	Years-of-schooling completed	Income ($1000s)	Predicted income = 19 + 2X ($1000s)	Residual
1	10	40	39	+1
2	12	45	43	+2
3	14	40	47	−7
4	16	55	51	+4

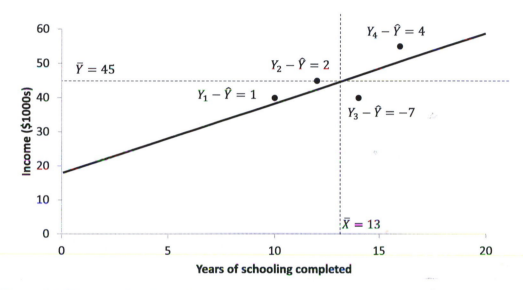

Figure 2.4 The regression line and residuals

With just the one variable, X, no other regression line would explain more variation (i.e., give a higher *ExSS* and a lower *RSS*) than this equation for the given four observations. Given this regression line, we can then calculate the predicted value and residual for each person, as shown in Table 2.3.

Person 1, who earns 40, has predicted income of 39. Thus, his residual is 1. This says that he has a one-unit (i.e., $1000) higher income than we would predict given his education of 10 years-of-schooling. Person 3, on the other hand, earns $7000 less than we would predict or expect, given his 14 years-of-schooling completed. Note that the average residual equals 0.

Figure 2.4 shows the graphical representation of the regression equation, as well as the residuals. In the figure, the predicted value would just be the height of the regression line for a given X value. Thus, the residual is the vertical distance (positive or negative, and not drawn) of the data point to the regression line.

In this model, *RSS* is calculated as:

$$RSS = \sum_{i-1}^{4} \left(Y_i - \hat{Y}\right)^2 = (1)^2 + (2)^2 + (-7)^2 + (4)^2 = 70$$

This means that:

$$ExSS = TSS - RSS = 150 - 70 = 80.$$

Again, no regression line different from equation (2.9), given these 4 data points, would produce a smaller RSS or a larger $ExSS$.

Box 2.1   Why is it called a "regression" model?

In Section 2.1, I raised this question and said that I did not know the answer, but I developed a theory (building off of a few I have seen). Another use of the word "regression" is in the term "regression to the mean," which means that outlying observations tend to revert towards the mean on the next go-around. For example, tall parents tend to have children who are shorter than them (for a given gender), and short parents tend to have children who are taller than them. This concept was represented well by Lester Bangs, the hip disc-jockey in the movie *Almost Famous*. When the 15-year-old William Miller said that he wasn't popular in his high school, Lester told him not to worry since he'd meet those popular kids again on the "long road to the middle."

So, how is there "regression to the mean" in regression analysis? Think about it this way. In the distribution of annual income across households, there is wide variation, with many people pretty far from the mean household income (on both the positive and negative side). But, after we account for some of the factors of income, residual household income will tend to be much closer to the mean (of 0). So, the variation in the residuals (RSS) will be much smaller than the total variation in the dependent variables (TSS). And so, for the most part, people have "regressed" to the mean. And, that may be why they call it a "regression" model.

But, I could be completely wrong on this!

2.5 The explanatory power of the regression

R-squared (R^2)

The discussion of TSS, $ExSS$, and RSS brings us to a relatively important statistic in regression analysis.

R-squared (or R^2) is the proportion of the variation in the outcome, Y, that is explained by the X variable(s). In other words:

$$R^2 = \frac{ExSS}{TSS} = \frac{TSS - RSS}{TSS} = 1 - \frac{RSS}{TSS} \tag{2.14}$$

In our example:

$$R^2 = \frac{TSS - RSS}{TSS} = \frac{150 - 70}{150} = 0.533$$

This says that variation in years-of-schooling explains 53.3% of the variation in income, for this sample of four people. For a Simple Regression Model, R^2 happens to be the square of the sample correlation, $r_{X,Y}$ (see equation A.8 in Section A.1 in the Appendix).

R^2 is one of many "goodness-of-fit" measures in regression analysis. It is the most straightforward of all of them, with a basic interpretation. Unfortunately, it cannot be calculated for certain non-linear models, as will be covered in Chapter 9.

What determines R^2 is how well the regression line explains variation in the dependent variable. The closer the data points are to the regression line, the lower RSS will be; the closer $ExSS$ will be to TSS, and the higher the R^2 will be.

The same formulas for TSS, $ExSS$, RSS, and R^2 are used for Multiple Regression Models, in which there is more than one explanatory variable. The interpretation for R^2 in such models is that it indicates how much of the total variation in the dependent variable (Y) can be explained by all of the explanatory (X) variables.

A high R^2 does not mean that the slope is high. Figure 2.5 shows four cases based on a low-vs.-high R^2 and a low-vs.-high slope. As you can see, there could be a relationship between the X and Y variables that has a steep slope but little explanatory power ("Low R^2, high slope") or *vice versa* ("High R^2, low slope"). Of course, characterizing an R^2 or slope as low vs. high is subjective, so these are just relative R^2's and slopes.

Researchers have different views on the value of the R^2 statistic. For the research objective of forecasting, a higher R^2 is usually the goal. However, for the objective of estimating causal effects, whereas some think it is important to be able to explain a large share of the variation in the outcome, others place less emphasis on R^2. The latter argue that what is important is how Y moves from changes in X,

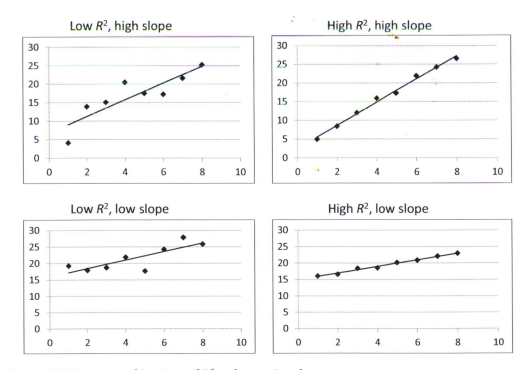

Figure 2.5 Various combinations of R^2 and regression slope

regardless of how much other factors play a role in determining Y. I would agree with this argument. What is most important for a model, when estimating a causal effect, is ruling out explanations for the relationship between X and Y that are alternative to X causing Y. The ability to explain a large portion of the dependent variable (Y) is irrelevant. And, as we will see later, adding more variables to a model, which increases R^2, can sometimes be detrimental to a model by causing a coefficient estimate to move away from the true causal effect.

Adjusted R-squared

When a new explanatory variable is added to a model (as in the Multiple Regression Model below), R^2 always increases, even if there is no systematic pattern between the new X variable and the dependent variable. This is because there is almost always at least some incidental correlation between two variables.

The **Adjusted R²** corrects for the incidental correlation. The formula is:

$$Adjusted\ R^2 = \bar{R}^2 = 1 - \frac{\sum \hat{\varepsilon}^2 / (n - K - 1)}{TSS / (n - 1)} \tag{2.15}$$

where R^2 in the numerator is the actual R^2, n is the sample size, and K is the number of explanatory variables (and $K + 1$ is the number of coefficients to be estimated).

When an X variable is added to the model, both the numerator and the denominator of the fraction in equation (2.15) would decrease. The Adjusted R^2 increases only if the new X variable explains more of the outcome, Y, than a randomized variable would be expected to explain variation in Y by chance.

What is typically reported for a regression model is R^2. Adjusted R^2 is mostly used when evaluating whether adding a variable helps the explanatory power of the model.

Mean Square Error and Standard Error of the Regression

An important statistic that will be used later is the estimated variance of the error, or the **Mean Square Error** (*MSE*), calculated as:

$$MSE = \hat{\sigma}^2 = \frac{\sum \hat{\varepsilon}^2}{(n - K - 1)} \tag{2.16}$$

The square root of *MSE*, or $\hat{\sigma}$, is referred to as:

*   The Standard Error of the Estimate,
*   The Standard Error of the Regression,
*   The Root Mean Square Error (RMSE).

This latter statistic will tell you the nature of the distribution of the residuals. In particular, the absolute value of 95% of the residuals should be less than roughly $1.96 \times$ RMSE.

These statistics will serve us later as the variance of the estimators of the $\hat{\beta}$'s are introduced and for determining how good a prediction is for the regression objective of forecasting and in time–series models (Chapters 7 and 10).

2.6 What contributes to slopes of regression lines?

The coefficient estimate on the explanatory variable (the slope, $\hat{\beta}_1$) depends on:

- Where most of the variation in X lies;
- How the Y variable changes with each increment of X, particularly where most of the variation in X lies;
- Outliers, as the regression line tries to minimize them.

Lets go back to the full-sample regression from Section 2.3.

$$\hat{Y}_i = -54,299 + 8121 \times X_i \qquad (2.4b)$$

Figure 2.6 shows the average income for each level of schooling, with the bubble size being representative of the number of observations at each level of schooling – note the small, almost-undetectable bubbles at 3 to 7 years-of-schooling. We see that most of the variation lies between 12 and 16 years-of-schooling – so completion of high school to completion of college. And, the relationship between years-of-schooling and income in that range appears to be more consistent with the regression line than the observations outside the 12–16 range. Thus, the average change in average income with each year of schooling over this range would, naturally, have greater weight towards determining the coefficient estimate than years-of-schooling outside this range. This is why the intercept, $\hat{\beta}_0$, is so largely negative.

Additionally, outliers can have disproportionate effects on a slope. This is the case because of the regression line minimizing the Residual Sum of Squared (RSS). Of all the possible regression lines,

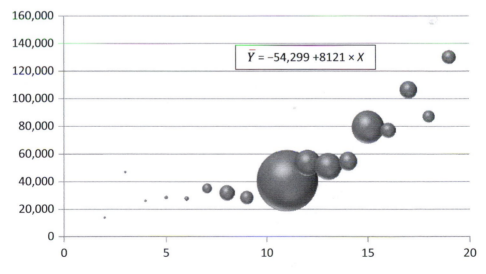

Figure 2.6 Average income by years-of-schooling

Note: Bubble size represents the number of observations at given years-of-schooling.
Source: Bureau of Labor Statistics, 2014 (n = 2772).

the regression that keeps the large residuals to a minimum would likely be the one that minimizes *RSS*. Thus, an added large outlier will cause the regression to change to something that minimizes the impact of that new high outlier, while not creating other large outliers.

The effect of an outlier on a coefficient estimate depends on where the outlier occurs:

- A large positive outlier at the average value of *X* would mostly just contribute to the regression line being higher (a higher constant or Y-intercept).
- A large positive outlier on the left side of the distribution of *X* would contribute to higher predicted values at that low *X* value, thus reducing the slope (making it less positive or more negative) and increasing the intercept. This would put an observation, in Figure 2.2, far from the origin in quadrant II, contributing negatively towards the coefficient estimate.
- A large positive outlier on the right side of the distribution of *X* would contribute to higher predicted values at the given *X* value (in quadrant I in Figure 2.2), thus increasing the slope (more positive or less negative) and decreasing the intercept.

2.7 Using residuals to gauge relative performance

One of my longest-standing debates has been with my friend, Rich, on who the best coach in NBA history is. (Technically, our other big debate, over whether *Shawshank Redemption* should have ended with Red getting on the bus, has lasted longer.) Anyway, Rich argues that Phil Jackson (of the Chicago Bulls and L.A. Lakers) is the best coach ever, even better than my pick of Gregg Popovich (of the San Antonio Spurs), citing Jackson's 11–5 edge in championships. But, is it correct to just compare the outcomes (championships) without considering what they had to work with? Put enough talent on a team, and Kim Kardashian could coach an NBA team to a championship.

A proper comparison would consider the quality of their players. Jackson had high-level talent on his teams, with several all-star players who were high-draft picks. Popovich mostly had just one perennial all-star who was a top pick (and another top pick towards the end of his career), but the rest of his players were low-draft-pick and undrafted players, many of whom were rejects from other teams in whom Popovich found value. Furthermore, whereas Jackson quit and signed on to coach teams with high championship potential, Popovich has stuck with the same team for 22 years and counting. Jackson, one could argue, should have won more championships than Popovich given the talent he had, if he could have just gotten them to like each other and want to win for each other. Popovich figured out how to reinvent his teams based on their skills. So, it is arguable that Popovich did more with less. Or, we might say, Popovich may have had the higher residual in that, compared to Jackson, he had more championships relative to what would be expected, given his talent – and this may be the better measure of the effectiveness of a coach.[3]

Along similar lines, I have the utmost respect for people who come from difficult backgrounds and end up finding their own way to get a strong education. I think specifically of a friend of mine who never knew her father and had no one in her family get more than an Associate's degree. She earned a Ph.D. and has become a highly successful academic. In a sense, she has a "high residual" in that she advanced in her education and had career success well beyond what would be predicted given her background.

Now, I don't exactly plug my friends' data onto a computer and run a regression, but you can do these basic comparisons. And, if I were to compare my friend above with myself, well I'm not looking so great. My father is a Ph.D. and has been a successful Political Science professor, and my mother earned a Masters in Teaching and served as the University Editor (and "safeguard of coherence") at a major university for 37 years until age 73. We were not rich as I grew up, but I certainly was given great models for hard work and academic and professional success. So, it certainly isn't as impressive for me to have earned my Ph.D., become an academic, and written this book. My residual isn't nearly as high as my friend's.

So, from this, you can probably gather that **the residual indicates how well the subject (observation) fared relative to what would be expected given the circumstances the subject had**.

Let's consider a more concrete example with data. One crucial debate in baseball is whether something should be done about the disparity in payrolls, as has been done in other major sports. Big-market teams (the Yankees, Red Sox, and Dodgers, for example) grab players from smaller-market teams during free agency because these big-market teams can pay significantly more. With these teams perennially paying far more than any other team, you would expect them to generally do better than other teams.

A residual analysis could indicate how well certain teams did, given how much they paid in salary. Using data from the 2013 season, regressing wins on payroll gives the following regression line:

$$\widehat{wins} = 71.24 \ + \ 0.09 \ \times \ \left(payroll \ in \ \$millions\right) \tag{2.17}$$

Figure 2.7 shows the graphical representation of the residual analysis. Each data point represents one of the 30 Major League teams. The regression line represents equation (2.17). And, the vertical distance between each point and the line represents the residual. The teams with the highest residual (most wins relative to what would be expected given their payroll) are:

- Oakland: 19.3 (96 wins),
- Pittsburgh: 15.6 (94 wins),
- Tampa Bay: 15.6 (92 wins).

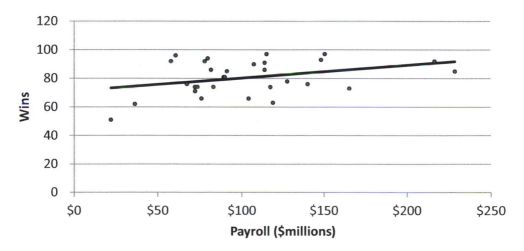

Figure 2.7 Wins and payroll, Major League Baseball, 2013

The teams with the lowest residual are:

- Houston: −22.2 (51 wins),
- Chicago White Sox: −19.0 (63 wins),
- Chicago Cubs: −14.6 (66 wins).

So, we would say that Houston had 22.2 fewer wins than would be expected, given their salary. The Yankees were not far behind, having 6.8 fewer wins than expected in 2013. The residual speaks to how well the team got value from its players or how well the team saw value in players that other teams did not. Of course, there is always a little (or a lot of) luck represented in the residual. Note that, in 2016 and 2017, two of those low-residual teams (the Chicago Cubs and Houston Astros) won the World Series.

The simple analyses in this section are based on one of the regression objectives from Section 2.2: to adjust outcomes for various factors. I introduce it here to give further insights into the workings of a regression and the meaning of the residual. More detail on how to use regressions for this objective will be given in Chapter 7.

2.8 Correlation vs. causation

A common mistake made by many is taking a correlation and concluding causation. Here is the difference.

A **correlation** is when two variables move together, positively or negatively. That is when one variable is higher, the other variable tends to be higher (a positive correlation) or lower (a negative correlation). In contrast, two variables having no correlation (or a correlation very close to zero) means that when one moves, there is no tendency for the other variable to be higher or lower, on average. Having a positive or negative correlation says nothing about the reason why the two variables move together – whether one of the variables affects the other variable, that there is a common factor that affects both at the same time, or that they move together just by coincidence.

A **causation** is when one variable has an effect on another variable. So, a causation is that if some randomness or some force were to cause variable X to change, then, on average, variable Y would change as a result.

The important point is this: **a correlation can exist without causation**. Although such a correlation could occur just by chance, a more common cause of a correlation without causation is that some other variable (a "third variable") affects both the X and Y variables. Here are some examples of relationships that may appear to be causal, but it is also possible that a third variable explains the correlation:

- In education, there is a negative correlation between a student being retained (held back a grade) and their eventual success in school. The potential third variable is the student's general academic aptitude that could affect both whether he is held back and his eventual academic success.
- Many researchers have found a positive correlation between a child experiencing a parental divorce and the child having behavioral problems. While a divorce may have an effect on behavioral problems, the correlation could largely be due to unhealthy family processes having

an effect on both the likelihood of a divorce and children's behavior. The divorce itself may have no effect.

Regression coefficient estimates indicate how two factors move together, which is indicative of the correlation. The regression itself has no say on whether the two factors are correlated due to one causing the other.

Now, let's return to an issue from earlier. From equation (2.4a) in Section 2.3.2, can we conclude that obtaining one more year of schooling would have increased income, on average, by $8121? We cannot because we need to be able to rule out other reasons for why those with more schooling had higher income. Let's consider a few other possible reasons. Those with higher levels of education probably *tend to*:

- Have greater motivation;
- Have higher innate ability/aptitude;
- Have more-educated parents, who could act as role models for aspiring to more highly skilled jobs and could be more likely to help foster the person's learning;
- Have grown up in an intact family;
- Be less likely to be a racial/ethnic minority;
- Have had a higher expected monetary return from schooling – i.e., they believed they had the skills to be handsomely rewarded for their schooling by becoming, say, a high-priced lawyer.

Given all these potential differences, we are comparing apples to oranges when comparing the incomes of more- vs. less-educated people. So, before we conclude that a year of schooling increases income by some amount close to $8121, we need to rule out these other reasons why those with more schooling earn more so that we can compare apples to apples. But, this would be a very difficult, if not an impossible, task. How would we possibly obtain data on all of these factors?

We will talk about more advanced strategies in Chapter 8, but in the next section we will turn to simple strategies that likely (but not certainly) help in getting closer to the causal effect – by adding more factors to the model.

2.9 The Multiple Regression Model

Continuing with the example from the prior section, for estimating the effects of schooling on income, we want to remove the influence of the other factors that could contribute to both the amount of schooling a person obtains and his income. That is, we want to hold these other factors constant so that we can compare incomes for people who are observationally similar except for the level of education they have.

One way to eliminate or reduce the influence of some of these other factors may be the **Multiple Regression Model**. There is one primary difference between the Simple and Multiple Regression Models: the simple model has one explanatory variable; the Multiple model has two or more explanatory variables. The model has the form:

$$Y_i = \beta_0 + \beta_1 X_{1i} + \beta_2 X_{2i} + \ldots + \beta_K X_{Ki} + \varepsilon_i \tag{2.18}$$

where K is the total number of explanatory variables.

Let's extend our model from above that attempts to estimate the causal effects of schooling on income by having two explanatory variables:

- X_1 = years-of-schooling;
- X_2 = aptitude score.

So, the model is:

$$Y_i = \beta_0 + \beta_1 X_{1i} + \beta_2 X_{2i} + \varepsilon_i \tag{2.19}$$

With two explanatory variables, equation (2.19) can be depicted as a plane in a 3-dimensional graph. With three explanatory variables, it becomes 4-dimensional.

The explanatory variables can be classified into two types, characterized here in terms of the objective of identifying causal effects:

- The **key explanatory (X) variable(s)** is the variable or set of variables for which you are trying to identify the causal effect. This is often called the "treatment." ("Years-of-schooling" is the key X variable in our example.)
- The **control variables** are the variables included in the model to help identify the causal effects of the key X variable(s). ("Aptitude score," X_2, is the control variable.)

Distinguishing between the key explanatory variables and the potential control variables is important for assessing a model and for determining the best set of other control variables to include in a model.

The determination of the coefficient estimates in the Multiple Regression Model is based on the same concept as in the Simple Regression Model in Section 2.4: the estimates are chosen so as to minimize the sum of the squared residuals across the observations. That is, with the actual residual (in contrast to the population error term, ε) being:

$$\hat{\varepsilon}_i = Y_i - E[Y_i \mid X_{1i}, X_{2i}] = \left(Y_i - \hat{Y}_i\right)$$
$$= Y_i - \left(\hat{\beta}_0 + \hat{\beta}_1 X_{1i} + \hat{\beta}_2 X_{2i}\right), \tag{2.20}$$

the estimates, $\hat{\beta}_0$, $\hat{\beta}_1$, and $\hat{\beta}_2$ are chosen to:

$$minimize \sum_{i=1}^{n} \left(\hat{\varepsilon}_i\right)^2 \ or \ minimize \sum_{i=1}^{n} \left(Y_i - \hat{Y}_i\right)^2.$$

With the NLSY data, I will now estimate equation (2.19), using as a measure of aptitude the percentile score from the Armed Forces Qualification Test (AFQT), which was administered to nearly all NLSY respondents at the time of the second round of interviews in 1980 (Bureau of Labor Statistics, 2014). The score represents a percentile, ranging from 0 to 99, from the distribution of AFQT scores in the U.S. population of 18–23-year-olds.

When we add AFQT percentile (hereafter, called "AFQT" or "AFQT score") to equation (2.4b), the regression equation (using descriptive variable names) is:

$$\left(\widehat{income}\right)_i = -34{,}027 + 5395 \times \left(educ\right)_i + 367 \times \left(afqt\right)_i \tag{2.21}$$

So, we would say that, *holding AFQT score constant*, an extra year-of-schooling is associated with $5395 higher income. To get an initial understanding of how the Multiple Regression Model holds other factors constant, let's first go back to the original simple model we had:

$$\widehat{\left(income\right)}_i = -54,299 + 8121 \times \left(educ\right)_i \qquad (2.4b)$$

One reason why those with more schooling may have had higher income was that they tend to have higher aptitude. Thus, part of the $8121 higher income for each year of schooling may be due to the higher aptitude a person with one more year of schooling tends to have – aptitude that (theoretically) would not depend on their education. But, as researchers, we are interested in how one extra year of schooling would affect a person's income, not the combined effects of an extra year of schooling plus some extra aptitude associated with that extra year of schooling.

Adding the AFQT score into the model helps towards this goal of controlling for aptitude and probably gets us closer to the causal effect of a year of schooling. The variation in income coming from the variation in years-of-schooling is now largely (but not entirely) independent of variation in aptitude. That is, the higher income for those with more schooling can no longer be attributable to higher aptitude, as measured *linearly* by the AFQT score. However, it remains unclear how well the AFQT score captures variation in people's aptitude that contributes to income or whether using a linear effect of the percentile, as opposed to categories of different levels of AFQT scores, is the best method of factoring out "aptitude." That is, perhaps the effect of the AFQT score on income from going from the 80th to 90th percentile is greater than the effect of going from the 10th to 20th percentile. But, the model is constraining these effects to be the same. Nevertheless, assuming that the model does a reasonable job in capturing the effects of aptitude, we have just partly addressed one of the reasons why those with more schooling have higher income. And, we are likely closer to the true causal effect, even though we may still be a good distance away from that true effect.

I will go into more detail on what "holding other factors constant" means in Chapter 4.

One common mistake in multiple regression analysis is that conclusions are made on the comparison of multiple coefficient estimates without consideration of the scale of the variable. For example, one might examine equation (2.21) and conclude that years-of-schooling is almost 15 times more important than the AFQT score to income. But, what would happen if we scaled the AFQT score by dividing it by 100 so it was on a 0 to 0.99 scale (instead of 0 to 99)? The coefficient estimate on *AFQT* would increase by 100 (to roughly, 36,700). It would then appear to be more important than years-of-schooling, but that assessment would be misguided as well. One thing that can be said is that one year of schooling is associated with a greater premium in predicted income than one percentile on the AFQT score.

2.10 Assumptions of regression models

Typical textbooks on regression analysis list several "assumptions" of regression models, often referred to as the "Gauss Markov assumptions" or a similar set called the "Classical Regression Model assumptions." Under these assumptions, OLS coefficient estimates and standard errors are unbiased estimators of the true population parameters – standard errors being the standard deviation in the estimated coefficient estimate.

Personally, I always questioned the use of the term "assumptions." The use of that word makes it seem like we can make the assumption and then we're okay. And, this is problematic because, as you will see, often many of these assumptions do not hold. I think of them more as *conditions* that are necessary to hold for the researcher to make firm conclusions. And so, the researcher needs to assess whether these conditions do in fact hold. But, "assumptions" is what they are normally called.

You can give theory as to why certain assumptions are valid. And, to be balanced and objective, you should mention plausible situations that would result in the assumptions being violated. In Chapter 6, on the things that may go wrong with regression models, we will discuss situations in which some of these assumptions may be violated. Giving an objective assessment of your model would then, ideally, spur you to design an approach that would address any problems and to make any corrections necessary. The last thing you want to do is assume that your model answers the research question because all these assumptions are true. Here are the assumptions, described in terms of the true regression equation.

A1. The average error term, ε, equals 0. That is, $E(\varepsilon) = 0$. This can be seen in Table 2.3 in Section 2.4.2. (This is indeed more a property of OLS than an assumption. The intercept automatically adjusts to make this so.)

A2. The error terms are independently and identically distributed (i.i.d.). This means that if one observation has, say, a positive error term, it should have no bearing on whether another observation has a positive or negative error term. That is, a given observation is not correlated with another observation. This could be violated if, for example, there were siblings in a sample. The siblings' incomes (beyond what would be explained by years-of-schooling and aptitude) would probably be correlated with each other, as they have common unobservable determinants. Thus, this would violate the i.i.d. assumption. Violations of this assumption could affect standard errors, and it could affect coefficient estimates in the case of estimating a time-series model (Chapter 10). This assumption will come into play in Chapter 6 when we discuss things that could go wrong with the standard errors. But, there are corrections for this situation to make the problem go away.

A3. The error terms are normally distributed. Supposedly, a common mistake is to believe that it is the dependent variable that needs a normal distribution, but it is the error terms that we hope are normally distributed. If error terms were not normal, then it would not mean that the coefficient estimates are biased. Rather, the main problem would be that the tests for significance (Chapter 5) may be off. With the Central Limit Theorem, however, almost any model that has an approximately continuous dependent variable and at least 200 observations should have an approximately normal distribution of error terms – that is, the errors would be asymptotically normal. Others say having 30–40 observations is adequate. And, Frost (2014) executes some simulations with various non-normal distributions and finds that 15 observations is adequate, as it results in just as many mistakes (false positives, or incorrectly concluding an empirical relationship when there is not any) as would be expected. Given all this, there should rarely be any concern with this assumption, and the hypothesis tests and confidence intervals for coefficient estimates can be estimated and calculated as they otherwise would be. However, in the case in which the dependent variable is a discrete variable that can only take on a few values (such as a dummy variable, as you will see in the next chapter), then there could be issues with non-normality. (I will discuss this in Sections 6.8 and 12.3.)

A4. The error terms are homoskedastic. This means that the variance of the error term, ε, is uncorrelated with the values of the explanatory variables, or $\text{var}(\varepsilon \mid X) = \text{var}(\varepsilon)$ for all values of X. When homoskedasticity does not hold, there is **heteroskedasticity**. The consequences of heteroskedasticity are that the estimated standard errors would be biased and wrong, which would in turn affect the hypothesis tests.

Because the assumption is often violated, it is good practice to always make a simple correction for heteroskedasticity. We will avoid it for now, until the deeper discussion on heteroskedasticity occurs in Section 6.6.2.

A5. The key explanatory variable(s) are uncorrelated with the error term, ε: If X_1 represents a key explanatory variable and X_2 the set of control variables, then $E[\varepsilon \mid X_1, X_2] = E[\varepsilon \mid X_2]$.

Note that the typical corresponding assumption used in most textbooks is that all of the explanatory variables, X, are uncorrelated with the error term. This is often called **conditional mean independence** and can be characterized as:

- $\text{cov}(X, \varepsilon) = 0$;
- $\text{corr}(X, \varepsilon) = 0$;
- $E[\varepsilon \mid X] = E[\varepsilon] = 0$.

But, this more stringent assumption is not necessary. Assumption **A5** says that it's okay if the control variables (X_2) are correlated with the error term, but the key explanatory variable (X_1) cannot be. That is, we want to select the right set of control variables so that the key explanatory variable is very close to being random and uncorrelated with the error term.

Recall that the error term captures the effects of factors that are not included as explanatory variables. If **A5** were violated, then if the error term were positive, X_1 would tend to be higher or lower than average. The variable, X_1, would no longer be randomly determined with respect to the outcome. Non-randomness of the key explanatory variable would cause bias if the objective were estimating causal effects.

Let us take the example of the issue of how years-of-schooling affects income. If years-of-schooling (the X_1 variable) were correlated with intelligence and intelligence were part of the error term since it cannot be properly controlled for, then the coefficient estimate on years-of-schooling would be biased because it would reflect the effects of intelligence on income. There are other stories that could cause an X variable to be correlated with the error term. These will be discussed in greater detail in Chapter 6.

Assumption **A5** is one of the key assumptions that dictate whether a model is validly capturing a causal effect. But, I've got some issues with **A5**:

- For two of the regression objectives (forecasting and determining predictors), it is not important that this condition hold. It is only important for estimating causal effects and adjusting outcomes. (I will discuss this more in Chapter 7.)
- This condition is often violated, so technically it might not be such a great idea to make the assumption. Rather, use theory to assess whether it is a good assumption. If there were any possibility of this assumption being violated, then you need to design a model to address the problem.

When we learn how to assess a model in Chapter 6, the concepts underlying Assumption **A5** will be relevant and will be put in much simpler terms than a conditional expectation of the error term.

Table 2.4 sums up these assumptions and how reasonable they are. The optimal strategy for honest research is to assume nothing. All of the conditions presented in assumptions **A2–A5** pose potential problems. It is the responsibility of the researcher to assess whether it is a problem, make corrections if so, and admit the possibility that there still could be this problem if it is not addressable.

Table 2.4 A summary of regression assumptions, how reasonable they are, and what action to take

Assumption	Is it a reasonable assumption?	Action to take if violated
A1. $E(\varepsilon) = 0$	It's an automatic property	N/A
A2. ε is independently and identically distributed	Depends on the situation (see Section 6.6.3)	Easy fix if not so, in Chapter 6
A3. ε is normally distributed	Yes, in most cases	Might need to change model, or require stronger levels of significance to conclude that the empirical relationship is real
A4. Homoskedasticity $\mathrm{var}(\varepsilon \mid X) = \mathrm{var}(\varepsilon)$	No (see Section 6.6.2)	Easy fix that should almost always be applied
A5. For key X variable, X_1, $E[\varepsilon \mid X_1, X_2] = E[\varepsilon \mid X_2]$	No (see Section 6.4)	Methods from Chapter 8 (if they can be applied)

2.11 Calculating standardized effects to compare estimates

Let's consider an analysis on the Peasant Rebellion in Romania in 1907. Chirot and Ragin (1975) analyzed what factors determined the intensity of the rebellion across counties. The variables were:

- *Intensity* of the rebellion (the dependent variable), which captures the number of deaths, the amount of violence, and the spread of the rebellion;
- *Inequality*, measuring a Gini Coefficient for land-owning;
- *Commerce*, measuring the percentage of land devoted to the production of wheat, which was the main cash crop;
- *Tradition*, measured as the illiteracy rate, signaling the lack of progress and new ideas;
- *Midpeasant*, which indicates the percentage of rural households that owned between 7 and 50 hectares.

The model produces the following regression equation:

$$\widetilde{intensity} = -12.91 + 1.14 \times inequality + 0.12 \times tradition + 0.09 \times commerce - 0.003 \times midpeasant$$

Of course, we need to consider how precise the estimates are and whether they are statistically significant, but that type of exercise will wait until Chapter 5.

But, does the regression equation mean that *inequality* has the strongest relationship with the intensity of the rebellion? It does not because we need to take into consideration the amount of variation in each of the X variables.

In particular, what is often estimated or calculated is a **standardized effect** (even though it is not necessarily an "effect"). This statistic removes the units from both the X and Y variables, using the estimated standard deviations of the variables ($\hat{\sigma}_X$ and $\hat{\sigma}_Y$), so that the magnitude of different estimates can be compared.

From the equation from earlier:

$$Y = \beta_0 + \beta_1 X_1 + \beta_2 X_2 + \varepsilon \tag{2.19}$$

Table 2.5 Standardized effect sizes of determinants of the Romanian Peasant Rebellion

	Standard deviation	Coefficient estimate (dep. var. = intensity)	Standardized effect estimate
Intensity	1.77		
Inequality	0.11	1.14	0.07
Tradition	3.86	0.12	0.26
Commerce	11.92	0.09	0.61
Midpeasant	17.38	0.003	0.03

the standardized effect of a given variable, say X_1, is:

$$\text{Standardized effect} = \left(\hat{\sigma}_{X_1}\right) \star \left(\frac{\hat{\beta}_1}{\hat{\sigma}_Y}\right) \tag{2.22}$$

Table 2.5 shows the estimated standardized effects for the factors determining the intensity of the Romanian Rebellion. The variable with the largest standardized effect size, *commerce*, has the second-lowest coefficient estimate. The interpretation for *commerce* is that a 1 standard deviation increase in *commerce* is associated with a 0.61 higher standard deviation in *intensity*. In contrast, *inequality*, which has the largest coefficient estimate in the model, has the second-lowest estimated standardized effect.

2.12 Causal effects are "average effects"

When a result from a regression model is relayed to a non-statistical person, sometimes a response will be some anecdote of a case in which a person had the treatment but didn't enjoy/suffer the predicted outcome. For example, someone may say that his son completed four years of college and earns only $30,000 so the monetary benefit to a college education can't be very high. Or, one may respond to a study showing that exercise reduces the probability of getting cancer by referring to a friend who exercised vigorously six days per week and still got cancer, so the study can't be true.

Remember that we live in a probabilistic world. Almost nothing is certain, predetermined, or fully explainable by a set of factors. Any regression coefficient estimate is based on how two variables move together, **on average**. It is not an absolute relationship (or effect) for everyone.

In our education–income example, the coefficient estimate indicates how income moves with an extra year of schooling, on average. This will be based on some groups of people for whom income is not much higher with more years-of-schooling (e.g., low-AFQT people – as you will see in Section 4.3) and others for whom each year of schooling is associated with much higher income. And, the average schooling–income relationship will be affected by some levels of years-of-schooling that are associated with fairly low advantages in income and other levels of years-of-schooling (e.g., college years) associated with much greater income advantages.

If a regression were convincing in its ability to isolate causality of the key explanatory variable, then the coefficient is an estimate of the **average effect**. If our education–income regression were convincing in this way, then the regression coefficient estimate would indicate how much we believe a year of schooling increases income, on average. Of course, there will be cases such as Bill Gates who became, for a long time, the richest person in the world with just 14 years-of-schooling. And, I'm sure there are Ph.D.s out there (with 21+ years-of-schooling) who are waiters making $25,000 or less in Boulder, Colorado. So, there are exceptions and outliers.

In the same vein, exercise would probably have varying effects on the probability of cancer for different people. Some people will have a genetic predisposition to get cancer, so exercise may have a smaller effect on their probability of getting cancer. For others, who perhaps have been exposed to environmental toxins or who may not have a healthy diet, exercise may have a larger effect on the probability that they get cancer. Assuming the model is correct and the estimates are unbiased, the coefficient estimate would represent the estimated *average effect* of exercise on that probability of getting cancer, across the population.

In some cases, there may be opposing effects of some treatment on a population. For example, a divorce or separation may have negative effects on some children but positive effects on other children, perhaps those from households having much discord. *The average effect may be estimated to be close to zero, even though many children are truly negatively affected and others are positively affected.*

Example: the contribution of teachers to children's achievement

My wife recently shared with me a blog article about myths on what affects children's academic achievement.[4] Myth #1 was that "Teachers Are the Most Important Influence on a Child's Education." To back up the argument that this is a myth, the author said:

> [R]esearch indicates that less than 30 percent of a student's academic success is attributable to schools and teachers. The most significant variable is socioeconomic status, followed by the neighborhood, [and] the psychological quality of the home environment.

The blogger and the authors of the book the blogger was citing (Berliner and Glass, 2014) were apparently making a common mistake of attributing a general finding to each case. On average, the blogger might be right that these other factors are more important. But, my guess is that there are hundreds of thousands of cases per year in which the teacher was indeed the most important factor in a child's educational achievement that year and perhaps in years to come.

The first person that comes to my mind is . . . my wife Jennifer, who for several years taught 6th grade in a school largely comprised of first-generation children of Mexican immigrant farm workers. Most of these children had no support from home for their education. They rarely had parents encouraging them to read. My wife, a natural in the classroom, was remarkable at generating curiosity in these children. For many of these children, their 6th grade teacher was the most important influence on their learning in 6th grade (and perhaps beyond).

So, the "less-than-30%" figure is an average contribution of teachers. That figure reflects the effects of some teachers who contribute nothing to students' achievement beyond what the children's parents and environment contribute and other teachers who deserve full credit (or blame) for a child's success (or lack thereof).

2.13 Causal effects can change over time

> A nickel ain't worth a dime anymore.
>
> — Yogi Berra

Historically, when the price of oil has increased, profits of U.S. companies tend to decrease, as production and delivery costs are higher. This tended to cause the stock market to decrease. But, 2015 and 2016 had a different pattern, as the stock market tended to decrease with *decreases* in oil prices. The difference is likely due to the economy becoming less dependent on oil, delivery of many services being done online, and oil companies becoming a larger share of U.S. companies in the stock market.

The lesson from this is that economic relationships change over time, as the nature of the economy changes. Another good example is that the effects of increases in state tax spending or tax rates could change over time. Perhaps 50 years ago, spending went to, on average, more investments that lowered the cost of conducting business (e.g., building roads and public-transportation systems), whereas today spending may go more towards less productive investments (e.g., bridges to nowhere).

Similarly, relationships between many socio-economic factors can change over time. Parental divorces may have had more harmful effects on children 30 years ago when divorce was less frequent and more of a stigma. Today, the increased prevalence of divorce may help children cope, as they are more likely to have friends having similar experiences.

Thus, it is important to keep in mind that estimated effects from the past may not still be relevant. This is reason #831 for why social science research is less accurate than research in the hard sciences.

2.14 A quick word on terminology for regression equations

I propose we leave math to the machines and go play outside.

– Calvin (of Calvin and Hobbes)

CALVIN AND HOBBES © Watterson. Reprinted with permission of
ANDREWS MCMEEL SYNDICATION. All rights reserved.

When using a Multiple Regression Model, it is common to write a regression equation as the following:

$$Y_i = X_i \beta + \varepsilon_i \tag{2.23}$$

where X_i is, now, a vector for individual i, representing multiple explanatory variables. The equation can be represented in Linear-Algebra form in the following equation, where each row represents one of the n observations:

$$
\begin{bmatrix} Y_1 \\ Y_2 \\ \cdot \\ \cdot \\ \cdot \\ Y_n \end{bmatrix}
=
\begin{bmatrix} 1\ X_{11}\ X_{21} \ldots X_{K1} \\ 1\ X_{12}\ X_{22} \ldots X_{K2} \\ \cdot \\ \cdot \\ \cdot \\ 1\ X_{1n}\ X_{2n} \ldots X_{Kn} \end{bmatrix}
\times
\begin{bmatrix} \beta_0 \\ \beta_1 \\ \beta_2 \\ \cdot \\ \cdot \\ \beta_k \end{bmatrix}
+
\begin{bmatrix} \varepsilon_1 \\ \varepsilon_2 \\ \cdot \\ \cdot \\ \cdot \\ \varepsilon_n \end{bmatrix} \tag{2.24}
$$

$$
\begin{array}{ccccc}
n \times 1 & & n \times K & K \times 1 & n \times 1 \\
Y & = & X & \times\ \beta & +\ \varepsilon
\end{array}
$$

In Linear Algebra, the multiplication of two matrices involves transposing each row of the first matrix and multiplying it by the matching entry in the second matrix. Thus, for a product of the two matrices, X and β, the number of columns in the first matrix (K) has to equal the number of rows in the second matrix (K). For observation 1, the equation comes out to:

$$Y_1 = \left(1 \times \beta_0 + X_{11} \times \beta_1 + X_{21} \times \beta_2 + \ldots + X_{K1} \times \beta_K\right) + \varepsilon_1 \tag{2.25}$$

And, the product of the ($n \times K$) and ($K \times 1$) matrix becomes an ($n \times 1$) matrix, one entry for each observation. This means that the ($n \times 1$) matrix on the left-hand side of the equation is the sum of two ($n \times 1$) matrices on the right-hand side. Note that one could not write $\beta \times X$, as the number of columns in β (1) does not equal the number of rows in X (n). As a result, the notation we would use to represent the product of the X variables and the β coefficients is $X\beta$.

Sometimes, in describing a regression model, a single key explanatory variable (say, X_1) is separated from the rest, as follows:

$$Y_i = \beta_1 X_{1i} + X_{2i}\beta_2 + \varepsilon_i \tag{2.26}$$

If it is just a single variable in X_1, then the product of the variable and coefficient is often represented with the coefficient first, as I have had it so far: $\beta_1 \times X_1$ or $\beta_1 X_1$.

What is important is that the proper representation of the product of β_1 and X when X represents a set of variables is: $X_i\beta_1$. I will represent sets of X variables, henceforth, as a vector. (Note that I do not follow the convention of using bold for vectors, as I do not want to draw extra attention to the vectors, which are typically a minor set of variables in the equations in this book, representing a set of control variables rather than the key X variable or the treatment.) Other than one brief mention in Section 8.4, *this is the last thing you need to know about Linear Algebra in this book.*

Note that when a generic X is used to represent a set of variables in the Multiple Regression Model, the intercept (β_0) is left out from the equation, just for the sake of brevity or standard practice, even though the intercept is almost always included in regression models (unless specified otherwise). This is because, as in equation (2.24), the constant term (the column of 1s) is typically included.

Hereafter, in Multiple Regression Models in which one component of an equation represents a vector (or set) of several variables, I will assume that the model includes the intercept term and leave the intercept term out of the equations. For equations in which each component of the equation represents just one variable, I will continue to use the intercept term, β_0.

Lastly, note that Linear Algebra is how computers estimate most regressions. This means that the study of theoretical regression analysis and the study of Advanced Econometrics rely more on Linear Algebra. This is where most of the advances in regression analysis come from. For the purposes of almost all of us, we do not need to use it. (I have gone my whole career without much consideration of Linear Algebra or Calculus.)

2.15 Definitions and key concepts

2.15.1 Different types of data (based on unit of observation and sample organization)

There are several different ways that data could be organized. This may have implications for the existence of pitfalls (Chapter 6) and what methods are available for addressing the pitfalls (Chapter 8).

Unit of observation: individual vs. aggregate data

The **unit of observation** indicates what an observation represents, or who/what is the subject. One dimension by which data can be organized is individual entities vs. aggregated data. Individual entities are often an individual or a family, but it could be an organization or business – e.g., a baseball team, with the variables of interest being wins and total payroll. Aggregated data are averaged or summed typically at some geographical or organizational level, such as class-level or school-level data. The data at the aggregate level may be some averaged value for everyone in a classroom (such as a test score) or a state (such as the average years-of-schooling or the proportion of the adult population with a high-school diploma in that state).

Sample organization

There are five main types of organization for a sample. They are as follows.

1. **Cross sectional data.** This is the standard type of data that is used. It involves taking a sample of all entities (an individual or, say, a state) at a given period of time.
2. **Time-series data.** This is based on one entity over many time periods. An example of this could be quarterly earnings per share for one company over time.
3. **Panel data.** This is a combination of cross-sectional and time-series data. It involves multiple entities observed at two or more periods each.
4. **Multiple cross-sectional periods.** This has multiple years (as with panel data), but the subjects are different each year.
5. **Survival data.** This is somewhat similar to panel data in that it involves multiple time periods for each person or entity, but the dependent variable is a variable that turns from 0 to 1 if some event occurs, at which point the person is dropped from the sample. For example, in an examination of what causes divorces, a couple will be in the data for each year of marriage until a divorce occurs or until the end of observation for the couple. If they get divorced, they are no longer in the sample of couples "at risk" for getting divorced.

A common problem with cross-sectional data is that there are many alternative stories that can contribute to a correlation beyond the causation. For example, if one were to examine how class size affects student achievement (which we presume would be negative), then the mechanisms that could contribute to the empirical relationship would include, among others: (1) a true causal effect of class size on student achievement; (2) correlation due to common factors, such as wealth of a school district; and (3) randomness creating incidental correlation by chance. If there were not adequate data to address the common factors, then the common factors, in this case, would likely contribute negatively to the association between class size and student achievement, perhaps overstating any causal effect. The contribution of incidental correlation towards the estimated effect could be positive or negative.

Having panel data on children or teachers would provide a more accurate estimate of the causal effect of class size. This allows a researcher to hold constant the child's or teacher's average test scores, allowing for an estimate of how children's achievement with a certain class size compares to their achievement with different class sizes. Plus, this often reduces the role of incidental correlation.

A similar problem occurs with time-series data. For example, it would be very difficult to estimate the effects of tax rates on economic growth in a country. If we examined this for the 1990s and 2000s in the United States, we would observe much higher growth rates with higher tax rates, as real GDP growth was higher after tax rates increased in 1993. In this case, there is likely incidental correlation: the strong-economic growth generated by the internet boom occurred after President Clinton's tax increases of 1993. It is doubtful that the higher tax rates caused the internet boom.

How can you address this?

You can't . . . with national data. There is no way to address the incidental correlation!

However, having panel data of state-level tax rates and economic growth *may* provide more accurate estimates. Panel data generally has the major advantage in that it can hold constant the entity and the time period. It would control for the national effects of the internet boom. This will be discussed in more detail in Chapter 8.

2.15.2 A model vs. a method

Mixing up the concept of a model vs. a method is an issue that doesn't bother me much, but it could be an important distinction. A regression model can be distinguished by what variables are in the equation and how the explanatory variables describe the outcome. For example, the explanatory variables could describe the outcome linearly or quadratically. The following are various models:

$$Y_i = \beta_0 + \beta_1 X_{1i} + \varepsilon_i$$
$$Y_i = \beta_0 + \beta_1 X_{1i} + \beta_2 X_{2i} + \varepsilon_i$$
$$Y_i = \beta_0 + \beta_1 X_{1i} + \beta_2 \left(X_{1i}\right)^2 + \varepsilon_i$$

The method is how the equation can be estimated. This could be from regular OLS, or it could be from a Weighted Least Squares method (Chapter 3). Or, there are other possible methods that could be used, as will be covered in Chapters 8 and 9. So, a model is characterized by an equation. A method indicates how the model is estimated. And, a given model can be estimated with various methods.

2.16 Chapter summary

Figure 2.8 demonstrates, through a story, many of the key points of this chapter. But, more formally, here are descriptions of some of those important points.

- Regressions indicate the statistical relationship between variables. They indicate how some outcome variable moves, on average, when other variables change, holding other variables in the model constant.
- The objective of most regression models is to identify causal relationships, in contrast with just correlational relationships. That is, we are often interested in how some treatment variable (X) affects an outcome variable (Y).
- To conclude causality with any adequate degree of certainty, we need to rule out other causes of two variables having a statistical association.
- The Multiple Regression Model attempts to rule out the influence of other factors by including them in the regression.

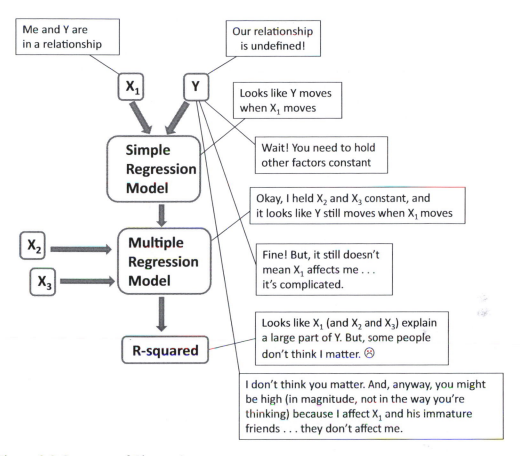

Figure 2.8 Summary of Chapter 2

Exercises

1. Suppose that, in a particular city, a regression of prices of homes sold in the prior year (*price*) on the number of bedrooms (*bedrooms*) and square feet (*sqft*) yields the following regression model:

$$\widehat{price} = 100,000 + 45,000 \times bedrooms + 10 \times sqft$$

   a. Interpret the coefficient estimate on *sqft*.
   b. If a home had 2 bedrooms and was 1500 square feet, what would the predicted price be?
   c. If that home had a selling price of $170,000, what would be the residual?
   d. How would you interpret the residual?
   e. What is a possible reason for the residual being what it is?

2. From the book's website, use the data set, **foxnewsdata**. (The data come from DellaVigna and Kaplan 2007). With an observation being a town that did not have Fox News in its cable–channel lineup in 1996 and that is from one of 28 states that are covered, regress the 1996-to-2000 change in vote share for the Republican presidential candidate among all votes for either the Democratic

or Republican candidate (*r_vote_share_ch*) on the changes in the male and Hispanic share of the population (*male_ch* and *hisp_ch*). Do this for those with at least 2000 votes for 1996 (*votes1996*). (Note that this model excludes the key explanatory variable for this data, *foxnews*, which is a dummy variable. We will discuss dummy variables in the next chapter and then add in *foxnews* to the model in the exercises.) Answer the following questions.

    a.   Interpret the coefficient estimate on *male_ch*.

    b.   For a town with *r_vote_share_ch* = 0.1, *male_ch* = −.1, and *hisp_ch* = 0.2, what is the predicted value of the dependent variable and the residual?

    c.   Interpret the predicted value and the residual.

    d.   Interpret the R^2.

    e.   Which of the explanatory variables has the larger standardized effect?

3.   From the book's website, use the data set, **Romanian_rebellion**. (The data come from Chirot and Ragin 1975). Estimate four separate models, with intensity (of the rebellion) as the dependent variable. Include just one of the four explanatory variables (*inequality, tradition, commerce, midpeasant*) in each model. Which explanatory variable explains the greatest amount of variation in *intensity*? How did you arrive at your answer?

Notes

1 The NLSY is provided by the Bureau of Labor Statistics, U.S. Department of Labor. The NLSY started with 12,686 youth in 1979, aged 14 to 22. It has followed them since, asking questions on labor-market outcomes, demographics (marital history), and many other factors (Bureau of Labor Statistics, 2014).

2 To protect the confidentiality of respondents, the NLSY top-codes income data. Their method is to assign respondents in the top 2% of income values the average for that group. Due to our sample restrictions leaning the sample towards higher-earners (e.g., males and having positive income), 3.9% of the respondents in our sample are in the top-coded group. The cut-off is $145,000, and they are assigned an income of $265,933 (Bureau of Labor Statistics, 2014).

3 You can also examine methods the coaches used: Jackson had his players read Zen; Popovich taught his players about the background cultures of each of his international players – such as the discrimination experiences of point guard Patty Mills's people from the Torres Strait of Australia – which served towards helping players understand and respect each other. Popovich's players generally liked each other and were objectively unselfish; not so for Jackson's players.

4 http://tinyurl.com/pyb6zna

References

Berliner, D., & Glass, G. (2014). *50 Myths & lies that threaten America's public schools*. New York: Teachers College Press.

Bureau of Labor Statistics, U.S. Department of Labor. (2014). *National Longitudinal Survey of Youth 1979 cohort, 1979–2012 (rounds 1–25)*. Columbus, OH: Center for Human Resource Research, The Ohio State University.

Chirot, D., & Ragin, C. (1975). The market, tradition and peasant rebellion: The case of Romania. *American Sociological Review*, 40(4), 428–444.

DellaVigna, S., & Kaplan, E. (2007). The Fox News effect: Media bias and voting. *The Quarterly Journal of Economics*, 122(3), 1187–1234.

Frost, J. (2014). How important are normal residuals in regression analysis? *The Minitab Blog*. (Available at http://blog.minitab.com/blog/adventures-in-statistics-2/how-important-are-normal-residuals-in-regression-analysis, accessed December 28, 2017).

<table>
<tr><td>3</td><td></td></tr>
</table>

3 Essential tools for regression analysis

> You better cut the pizza in four pieces because I'm not hungry enough to eat six.
>
> —Yogi Berra

This chapter introduces a few necessary tools for regression analysis. The first one (on dummy variables) is a method of characterizing yes/no indicators or qualitative factors. The second set of tools is based on allowing for non-linear relationships between the X variables and the Y variable. This may produce a better fit of the data or better characterize the relationship between an X and Y variable. Finally, there is a discussion on weighted regression models, which are used when certain observations (e.g., larger states, compared to smaller states) should have greater importance in a regression.

3.1 Using binary variables (how to make use of dummies)

So far, we have dealt with variables that are quantitative in nature: income, years-of-schooling, and AFQT score. For these variables, a higher vs. lower value of the variable has meaning in terms of being better or worse or there being more or less of something.

But, sometimes there are variables that are qualitative in nature. These variables could be based on categories or based on a yes/no classification. Examples could include:

- Gender,
- Race/ethnicity,
- Occupation,

- Type of college,
- Whether a hospital patient receives a certain treatment,
- Whether a registered Republican voted for Hilary Clinton,
- Whether a person used heroin.

To incorporate qualitative factors into a regression, the qualitative variable needs to be converted into one or a series of **dummy variables**, which take on the value of either 0 or 1. Dummy variables are also sometimes referred to as **dichotomous**, **indicator**, and **binary** variables.

When creating the dummy variables, all categories cannot be included in the regression model. Rather, there needs to be a "reference category" (also call "reference group" or "excluded category"). For example, for a yes/no classification (e.g., whether a patient receives a medical treatment), the two categories are boiled down to one variable (say, T, for "treatment") coded as follows:

- $T = 1$ if the person receives the treatment;
- $T = 0$ if the person does not receive the treatment (the reference category).

The reference category is "not receiving the treatment" or $T = 0$. There cannot be another variable for "not receiving the treatment." In an example on a categorical variable, if we were trying to control for the type of college a person graduated from, we may want to use "4-year public university" as the reference category. The college-type variables may then include:

- $C_1 = 1$ if the person graduated from a 4-year private university; $= 0$ otherwise;
- $C_2 = 1$ if the person graduated from a 4-year liberal arts college; $= 0$ otherwise;
- $C_3 = 1$ if the person graduated from a 2-year community college; $= 0$ otherwise;
- $C_4 = 1$ if the person graduated from some other type of college (e.g., music college); $= 0$ otherwise.

Everyone would have a value of 1 for exactly one of the variables, C_1 to C_4, with the exception of those who went to a "4-year public university" – the reference group – who have a value of 0 for all four of the variables. *The coefficient estimates on the college-type variables would be how the outcomes for people having graduated from the given type of college compare to the outcomes for people in the reference category, holding the other factors constant.*

There is one exception to the rule that there needs to be a reference category. When a model is specified to not have an intercept, then all categories of a qualitative variable could be included in the model. The coefficient estimates on each category would represent what the expected value of Y would be for that category if the other X variables were all 0 – that is, the intercept for each category. But, this is a rare type of model.

To demonstrate how to set up and interpret sets of categorical variables, I took the 2004 NLSY data (on 2003 income), and I added variables for "Black" and "Hispanic" to equation (2.21). This is based on the available classification in the NLSY (Bureau of Labor Statistics, 2014). For simplicity of interpretation, I classified those who are both Black and Hispanic as just Black. Thus, the racial/ethnic categorization would be:

- Black,
- Hispanic,
- Non-Hispanics of races other than Black (the reference group).

The regression model gives the following equation:

$$\left(\widehat{income}\right)_i = -32{,}984 + 5704 \times \left(educ\right)_i + 304 \times \left(AFQT\right)_i - 7815 \times \left(Black\right)_i - 1642 \times \left(Hispanic\right)_i \quad (3.1)$$

The coefficient estimate on *Black* of −7815 indicates that, after controlling for the other variables included in equation (3.1), Blacks earn an estimated $7815 less than non-Hispanic people of other races. It is not that Blacks earn $7815 less than non-Blacks. Rather, it is $7815 less than the reference group of "non-Hispanics of races other than Black." Likewise, Hispanics are estimated to earn $1642 less than "non-Hispanic people of races other than Black," after controlling for the other factors.

Whereas the examples here use dummy variables for representing qualitative data, dummy variables can also be used to represent quantitative data. For example, one may want to characterize the AFQT score in categories rather than in linear format. Thus, instead of (or in addition to) using the AFQT score, one could use dummy variables for each AFQT quartile – excluding one quartile as the reference group.

Be mindful of the proper interpretation based on the reference group

As stated above, the coefficient estimate should be interpreted as a comparison to the reference group. You can set up the dummy variables to give the reference group that you want.

Consider an alternative specification for education, using *highest degree* earned. For the sake of simplicity, let's limit the sample to the 2393 respondents in our NLSY sample who had at least a high-school diploma (Bureau of Labor Statistics, 2014). A "college degree" refers to having a 4-year college degree as one's highest degree, while a "graduate degree" involves having a Master's, Doctoral, or professional degree. Figure 3.1 shows the average income by each group, plus the average for the first two categories combined, which is weighted towards the "High school" average because a larger share of the sample has just a high-school diploma.

The estimated income premium for a graduate degree depends on what the reference group is. Estimating a model just with a dummy variable for having a graduate degree produces the following equation (with other variables such as the AFQT score excluded for simplicity):

$$\left(\widehat{income}\right)_i = 52{,}623 + \mathbf{63{,}790} \times \left(graduate\ degree\right)_i \quad (3.2)$$

Note that the intercept ($52,623) is the average income for the first two groups. The $63,790 estimate is the difference between those with a graduate degree and all others, which is $116,413 − $52,623. Thus, without assigning those with just a high-school degree to a separate category, they are counted in the reference group along with those with a college degree. This is an important point worth repeating: **For a set of dummy variables, any group not assigned to a category is part of the reference group.**

Including a control for "having one's highest degree being a college degree" makes the reference group the one excluded group not part of one of the categories included, which is comprised of those with just a high-school diploma:

$$\left(\widehat{income}\right)_i = 45{,}429 + 35{,}471 \times \left(college\ degree\right)_i + \mathbf{70{,}984} \times \left(graduate\ degree\right)_i \quad (3.3)$$

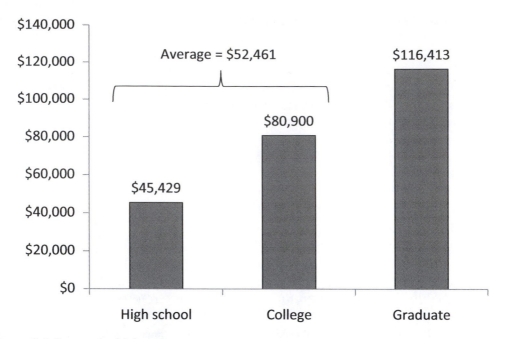

Figure 3.1 Income by highest degree

Source: Bureau of Labor Statistics, 2014 (n = 2363).

The intercept is now the "High school" average. The $70,984, sure enough, is the difference, in Figure 3.1, between the $116,413 (for those with a graduate degree) and the $45,429 for those with just a high-school diploma. And, it follows, the $35,471 coefficient estimate is the difference between the $80,900 (for those with a college degree being the highest degree earned) and the $45,429.

An alternative setup could use "has a college degree" rather than "highest degree is a college degree," which gives the regression equation:

$$\left(\widehat{income}\right)_i = 45,429 + 35,471 \times \left(\textit{has a college degree}\right)_i + \mathbf{35,514} \times \left(\textit{graduate degree}\right)_i \qquad (3.4)$$

This is the same as (3.3) except that the coefficient estimate of $35,514 on the graduate degree is now relative to those with a college degree ($116,413 − $80,900, with rounding). This is because those with a graduate degree (all of whom have a college degree also) have the $35,471 for the college degree contributing to the predicted value, so the coefficient estimate on *graduate degree* is now what is over and above those with a college degree.

3.2 Non-linear functional forms using OLS

3.2.1 Combining variables for interaction effects

In the research on how divorce affects children, the conventional wisdom is that divorce is harmful to children, but you have a theory that divorce would not be as bad and may actually help children if it gets them away from a dysfunctional situation with high levels of conflict. How can you examine whether divorce effects on children are different for those in such families?

One option is to estimate separate models for families with a high level (H) vs. a low level (L) of conflict. Let's set up the model as follows. Consider a sample of children whose parents were married, as of say, 2010, and we observe them again in 2014, with some of the children having experienced a parental divorce. The models would be the exact same for the two groups, but with different subscripts for the variable names and coefficient estimates:

$$\text{High-level of conflict families}: \quad Y_{iH} = X_{iH}\beta_{1H} + \beta_{2H}D_{iH} + \varepsilon_{iH} \quad\quad (3.5a)$$

$$\text{Low-level of conflict families}: \quad Y_{iL} = X_{iL}\beta_{1L} + \beta_{2L}D_{iL} + \varepsilon_{iL} \quad\quad (3.5b)$$

where:
- "H" and "L" subscripts refer to the families with "high" and "low" levels of conflict, respectively;
- Y is the outcome for child i, measured as the change in test score from 2010 to 2014;
- X is a set of control variables;
- D is an indicator (dummy variable) for having one's parents divorce between 2010 and 2014.

The test to examine whether children from high-conflict families have different effects of divorce from that for children from low-conflict families would be a comparison of the coefficient estimates, $\hat{\beta}_{2H}$ and $\hat{\beta}_{2L}$. The expectation would be that $\hat{\beta}_{2H}$ would be less negative than $\hat{\beta}_{2L}$ (or even positive) – that is, any adverse effects of the divorce may be lower or non-existent for children from high-conflict families, and the divorce effects may even be positive.

An alternative method is to use **interaction effects**, which would involve combining all children, from both high- and low-conflict families, into one model, as follows:

$$Y_i = X_i\beta_1 + \beta_2 D_i + \beta_3 H_i + \beta_4 (D_i \times H_i) + \varepsilon_{iH} \quad\quad (3.6)$$

where H is an indicator (dummy variable) for being in a high-conflict family. The interaction term is $D \times H$, which has the "divorce" dummy variable being interacted with the "high-conflict" dummy variable. This variable equals 1 only if the child's parents divorced and the family is "high conflict." The estimated effects of a divorce would be calculated as:

$$\frac{\Delta Y}{\Delta D} = \hat{\beta}_2 + \hat{\beta}_4 \times H \quad\quad (3.7)$$

For children from low-conflict families, the estimated divorce effect would be $\hat{\beta}_2$ (because $H = 0$). For children from high-conflict families, the estimated divorce effect would be $\hat{\beta}_2 + \hat{\beta}_4$ (because $H = 1$). Either or both variables in the interaction could be a non-dummy variable.

The test for whether the divorce effects are different for high-conflict vs. low-conflict families would be based on the value of $\hat{\beta}_4$. If there were evidence that the effect of a divorce on children's test scores was different for high-conflict vs. low-conflict families, then the level of conflict would be a **moderating factor** for this effect.

The advantages of using the interaction effect (equation 3.6) instead of separate regression equations (3.5a and 3.5b) are that:

- It is a more direct test of differences in the estimate across the two models rather than comparing two coefficient estimates;
- It produces more precise estimates for all variables, as it has a larger sample than separate models.

The disadvantages are that:

- It does not produce a direct estimate of the effect of divorce for children from high-conflict families – rather, you have to add the two estimates ($\hat{\beta}_2 + \hat{\beta}_4$) and the standard error for the hypothesis test may need to be calculated manually;
- It is constraining $\hat{\beta}_1$, the estimates on other X variables, to be the same for the two groups – the low-conflict and the high-conflict samples.

These considerations need to be weighed when determining whether to use interaction effects or separate models. The standard in such a situation is to use interaction effects, but of course, both methods could be used.

Box 3.1   Discrimination as a self-fulfilling prophecy

A great example of interactions comes from Glover et al. (2017), who examine how differently minority cashiers at a grocery-store chain in France perform when they work a shift with a manager who has greater bias against minorities. If minority cashiers did work less productively in the presence of managers with greater bias, then any initial discrimination would tend to be self-fulfilling or self-confirming. This would be an important finding because the normal assumption in studies on discrimination is that any bias by an employer does not affect worker productivity.

The model is the following:

$$Y_{ist} = \beta_0 + \beta_1 \times (minority)_i \times (bias)_{ist} + \beta_2 \times (bias)_{ist} + \delta_i + X_{ist}\beta_3 + \varepsilon_i$$

where:

- Y = one of four dependent variables (for worker i on shift s in time period t):
  - Dummy variable for whether the worker is absent on a given day;
  - Minutes worked in excess of schedule;
  - Articles scanned per minute;
  - Time between customers;
- *minority* = whether the cashier is a minority;
- *bias* = bias measure for the shift manager (based on an "implicit association test") for worker i's shift s in time period t;
- minority × (*bias*) = interaction of the two variables;
- X = a set of other factors (which are not terribly important);
- δ_i = a set of controls for each cashier.

The coefficient estimate on *bias* will indicate how the level of bias in managers affects the productivity of non-minorities, as it is possible that managers with more bias have other characteristics that motivate performance differently from that for managers with less bias. The coefficient estimate on the interaction (*minority* × *bias*) then estimates how minorities' outcomes respond to greater-bias managers, compared to non-minorities.

There is a little more to the model, but its complexity is minimal. I will discuss the results in Section 11.1. But, as a quick preview, there is indeed evidence for, in this setting, discrimination being self-fulfilling.

3.2.2 Logarithmic forms of variables

So far, all of the quantitative variables have been the actual values rather than any transformed value. This means that, for any value of X:

$$\beta = \frac{\Delta Y}{\Delta X} \tag{3.8}$$

whether that is holding constant other factors or just part of a Simple Regression Model. This indicates how the variable Y changes, on average, with a one-unit change in variable X.

In some cases, we may be interested in percent changes in X and/or Y rather than the changes in the actual values. When a variable is transformed to its natural logarithm, it becomes interpreted as a percentage change.

Table 3.1 shows four cases of what are called functional forms, which vary based on whether or not the X and Y variables are transformed to their natural logarithm. In some fields, an elasticity is often

Table 3.1 Interpretations based on logarithmic forms of the X and Y variables

Functional form	Model	Interpretation	Formula for β_1
Linear	$Y_i = \beta_0 + \beta_1 X_i + \varepsilon_i$	The change in Y associated with a one-unit increase in X	$\dfrac{\Delta Y}{\Delta X}$
Linear-log	$Y_i = \beta_0 + \beta_1 \ln(X_i) + \varepsilon_i$	The change in Y associated with a one-percent increase in X.	$\dfrac{\Delta Y}{\%\Delta X}$
Log-linear	$\ln(Y_i) = \beta_0 + \beta_1 X_i + \varepsilon_i$	The percentage change in Y associated with a one-unit increase in X.	$\dfrac{\%\Delta Y}{\Delta X}$
Log-log	$\ln(Y_i) = \beta_0 + \beta_1 \ln(X_i) + \varepsilon_i$	The percentage change in Y associated with a one-percent increase in X. (This is also called the **elasticity**.)	$\dfrac{\%\Delta Y}{\%\Delta X}$

Note: While the models here are based on the Simple Regression Model, the same interpretation holds with Multiple Regression Models.

calculated, which uses the log-log functional form and is interpreted as the percentage change in Y associated with a one-percentage-point increase in X:

$$\frac{dY}{dX} \times \frac{X}{Y} \text{ or } \frac{\%\Delta Y}{\%\Delta X}$$

Box 3.2 How income regressions are typically estimated

When there are regressions with income, earnings, or the wage rate as the dependent variable, the dependent variable is typically transformed to its natural logarithm. This helps reduce problems of heteroskedasticity (Section 6.6.2). And, a percent change is more interpretable across years and different price levels. The coefficient estimate, $\hat{\beta}_1$, from the equation:

$$ln(income) = \beta_0 + \beta_1 \times (years\text{-}of\text{-}schooling) + \varepsilon$$

represents the estimated percent change in income associated with one extra year of schooling. Despite this being the convention, I will continue to use just "income" instead of "ln(income)" for the sake of simplicity in conveying the key concepts.

3.2.3 Quadratic and spline models

There are many situations in which there could be non-linear relationships of the explanatory variable on the outcome. Imagine that you are a professor and you want to examine how much studying affects test scores in your class. Somehow, you get students to truthfully answer how many hours they studied for the midterm and you match that to the students' grades. My guess is that you would probably get a relationship similar to the following in Figure 3.2, which is based on data I made up.

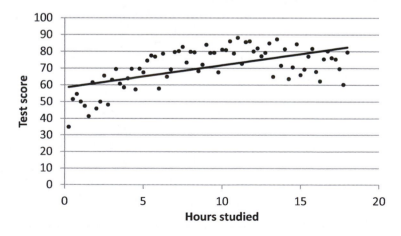

Figure 3.2 Notional example of study hours and test score

This relationship demonstrates a basic and simple economic concept: diminishing returns. There are likely strong returns to those first few hours of studying, as the students review the core material. But, as they study more and more, they are probably being less productive. Maybe they are re-reading things, and maybe they are just losing concentration from too much studying.

Let's say that you use a regression analysis and make the assumption that hours studied (H) has a typical linear effect in test score (Y), as follows:

$$Y_i = \beta_0 + \beta_1 H_i + \varepsilon_i \tag{3.9}$$

I inserted the estimated equation resulting from the regression in Figure 3.2. It looks like $\hat{\beta}_1$ would understate the effects of studying for low numbers of hours studied, as seen by the slope of the trend line being lower than the general slope for the data points. And, $\hat{\beta}_1$ would overstate the effects of hours studied for higher values of hours studied. There are two alternative models that could provide for a better fit of the data.

First, there is a **quadratic model** that adds the square of hours studied, as follows:

$$Y_i = \beta_0 + \beta_1 H_i + \beta_2 H_i^2 + \varepsilon_i \tag{3.10}$$

Of course, one could use a higher-order polynomial than a quadratic model (a 2nd-order polynomial). For example, a 3rd-order polynomial would add a cubed-H variable. This will be more accurate for predicting the test score, but it will make it more difficult to answer the question of whether and how hours studied affects the test score.

Second, you can use what is called a **spline function**, in which you allow H to have a different linear effect at different levels of H. We can see from Figure 3.2 that around 8 hours of studying is when the benefit of studying appears to level off and maybe decrease. Thus, you can estimate the separate marginal effects of "an hour of studying up to 8 hours" and "an hour of studying beyond 8 hours." The model is the following:

$$Y_i = \delta_0 + \delta_1 \times I(H_i \geq 8) + \delta_2 \times (H_i \text{ up to } 8) + \delta_3 \times \left[(H_i \text{ beyond } 8) \times I(H_i \geq 8) \right] + \varepsilon_i \tag{3.11}$$

where $I()$ is an indicator function, taking the value of 1 if the expression is true and 0 otherwise. The interpretation on the coefficients would be the following:

- δ_0 would be the intercept, or the expected score for someone with 0 hours of studying.
- δ_2 measures how much scores move, on average, with a one-unit change in hours studied between 0 and 8 hours of studying; those who studied more than 8 hours would all have a value of 8 for the variable (H_i up to 8) and would not contribute to this estimate.
- δ_3 measures how much scores move, on average, with a one-unit change in hours studied of more than 8; those who studied less than 8 hours would have a 0 for the variable (H_i beyond 8) and would not contribute to the estimate of δ_3.
- δ_1 would be any difference in the expected score at the spline point, $H = 8$, based on the spline for (H_i beyond 8) compared to the spline for (H_i up to 8).

The results of the three models are the following:

Linear: $\quad\quad\quad \hat{Y}_i = 58.4 + 1.3 \times H_i$ $\quad\quad\quad\quad\quad\quad\quad\quad\quad\quad (R^2 = 0.340) \quad (3.12)$

Quadratic: $\quad \hat{Y}_i = 42.3 + 6.6 \times H_i - 0.3 \times H_i^2$ $\quad\quad\quad\quad\quad (R^2 = 0.675) \quad (3.13)$

Spline: $\quad\quad \hat{Y}_i = 44.5 - 0.3 \times I(H_i \geq 8) + 4.6 \times (H_i \text{ up to } 8)$

$\quad\quad\quad\quad\quad\quad - 0.8 \times \left[(H_i \text{beyond } 8) \times I(H_i \geq 8) \right] \quad\quad (R^2 = 0.667)$ $\quad\quad (3.14)$

To demonstrate how the data work for the spline model, a value of $H = 2$ would mean, rounding the coefficient estimates, that:

- $(H \text{ up to } 8)$ would have a value of 2 and contribute $4.6 \times 2 = 9.2$ to the predicted test score.
- $(H \text{ beyond } 8) \times I(H \geq 8)$ would have a value of 0 and contribute $-0.8 \times 0 = 0$ to the predicted test score.
- $I(H \geq 8)$ would be 0, so would not contribute to the predicted score.
- Combined with the constant of 44.5, the predicted score would be 53.7.

A value of $H = 15$ would produce:

- $(H \text{ up to } 8)$ would have a value of 8 and contribute $4.6 \times 8 = 36.8$ to the predicted test score.
- $(H \text{ beyond } 8) \times I(H \geq 8)$ would have a value of 7 and contribute $-0.8 \times 7 = -5.6$ to the predicted test score.
- $I(H \geq 8)$ would be 1, so it would contribute $(-0.3) \times 1 = -0.3$ to the predicted score.
- Combined with the constant of 44.5, the predicted score would be 75.4.

Figure 3.3 shows the predicted values for the three models of (3.12–3.14). One interesting result is that the slopes for the spline and the quadratic models are greater than that for the linear model up to 8 hours, and the slopes of those two are lower than that for the linear model after about 8 hours. And, these two models appear to fit the data better, as can be seen in the R^2's for equations (3.12–3.14). What also is striking is that the linear model will tend to overstate the predicted test score for those on the ends ($H = 2$ or 15) and understate the score around the center of the distribution ($H = 8$).

How do you know if you need to model non-linear effects? You could look at basic plots to observe the nature of the relationship. Alternatively, you could base it on theory. Is there any reason to believe that the effects of the explanatory variable on the outcome would be different for different values of the variable? For example, one would expect different returns to schooling for primary vs. secondary vs. college years-of-schooling. One could imagine that each level of schooling provides different skill sets that are rewarded differently in the workplace. Or, simply, the theory of diminishing returns would suggest a reduced return to greater years-of-schooling.

All of this said, just because the X variable could have varying effects on Y at different levels of the X variable does not mean it needs to be reported this way. Researchers may want to know the average effect of the X variable on Y. They may just want one number, not a series of numbers. In this case, just estimating the average linear effect of the X variable on Y may be all that is needed. But, it may still be worth mentioning its non-linear effects.

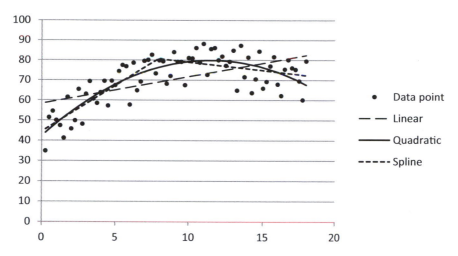

Figure 3.3 Predicted values for the linear, quadratic, and spline models

---

Box 3.3   Does heat bring out voters?

In a thought-provoking article, Van Assche et al. (2017) estimate the effects of temperature on voting participation rates. The idea is that hot temperatures can elicit pro-social behaviors (not just the anti-social behaviors we normally associate with high temperatures). They use aggregated, (U.S.) state-level data for the presidential elections from 1960 to 2016. There were several explanatory variables, but the key explanatory variable was the average temperature on election day. The results indicated that a 1°C increase in the state's average high temperature on election day was associated with a 0.14% increase in the voter participation rate, on average. (This was statistically significant at the 5% level.) This provides some support for their theory for the effects of hot weather.

But, might there have been a better way to characterize the temperature data? What is driving the result? Going from normal to hot temperatures? Or, maybe going from bone-chilling-freezing temperatures to just cold temperatures? There probably are not many places in the U.S. that have hot days around election day, in early November. So, the effect may have been coming from the lower end of the temperature distribution – comparing the cold election days to the bone-chilling-freezing election days – and not have had anything to do with "heat."

How could the data have been characterized? Perhaps there could have been a spline function, with separate slopes at, say (using Fahrenheit): (1) −50° to 20°, (2) 20° to 70°, and (3) 70° or higher. The slope on the latter group would more test the authors' theory, and it would rule out the alternative explanation that it could just be people not wanting to vote in freezing weather (which could include snow).

3.3 Weighted regression models

The standard regression model treats each observation the same in terms of its weight (importance) in the calculation of the regression equation. For example, if studying how serving in Iraq affected the likelihood of an Army soldier suffering from post-traumatic stress disorder (PTSD), there is no reason to give any set of soldiers greater weight in the model than a different set of soldiers.

But, there are many situations in which each observation should not be counted the same. Some of these reasons include:

- Some surveys, including the NLSY, over-sample from particular sub-populations – e.g., by race or income levels. This means that the data are not going to be nationally representative. The NLSY provides sampling weights to indicate how representative a respondent is of the nation's general population.
- The unit of observation, if aggregated, may be based on different-sized populations. For example, if examining how state tax rates affect average state employment growth, one may want to give greater weight to larger states (e.g., California and Texas) than to smaller states (Wyoming and Vermont).
- An analysis of corporations may be more relevant if the larger corporations are given more weight in the model than smaller corporations.

The fix for this is quite simple in most statistical packages and often involves simply indicating the sampling-weight variable one would wish to apply to the observation. Applying weights to OLS would be considered the **Weighted Least Squares** method. But, practically any method (some of which you will learn in Chapter 9) can apply different weights to different observations.

As an example, let's consider the relationship between the state unemployment rate and state marijuana use among teenagers (12–17-year-olds), which comes from the National Survey on Drug Use and Health (NSDUH). This is a preview of an issue that will be examined with more detail in Chapters 6 and 8. Let's consider a simple cross-sectional model. The NSDUH provides two-year averages for teenage marijuana use at the state level. So, let's take 2009–10, which had the highest unemployment rates of the Financial Crisis. And, let's average the state unemployment rate over those two years. So, the dependent variable and explanatory variable are:

- MJ = Percentage of 12–17-year-olds in the state using marijuana in the past 30 days (2009–10).
- UR = Average unemployment rate in the state in 2009–10.

The issue at hand is how states should be weighted. If no sample weights were used, then this analysis would treat Wyoming (with a population less than 500,000 in 2010) the same as California (with almost 34 million people). However, to weight the sample based on population would make states like Wyoming meaningless for the model. Weighting by the 2010 population would mean that the 10 most-populous states would have 54% of the weight in the model, while the 10 least-populous states would have 0.3% weight in the model. Alternatively, some use the square root of the population, which would produce weights of 38% for the top-10 states and 8% for the bottom-10 states, which seems more reasonable. However, there is no theory for determining which of these weighting schemes (no weights, population, or square-root-of-population) is optimal.

I estimate the model all three ways: (1) weight all observations equally (i.e., not indicating any weights); (2) weight observations by the square root of the 2010 population; and (3) weight by the 2010 population.

The results are in Table 3.2. The pattern is that the coefficient estimate is more positive the more that the state's populations determine the weight of the observations. And, the R^2 increases, so the

Table 3.2 A comparison of models using various weighting schemes

Weight	Regression equation	R^2
None	$\widehat{MJ} = 9.597 + 0.205 \times UR$	0.022
Square root of state's 2010 population	$\widehat{MJ} = 8.971 + 0.244 \times UR$	0.035
State's 2010 population	$\widehat{MJ} = 7.961 + 0.373 \times UR$	0.092

Sources: National Survey of Drug Use and Health; Bureau of Labor Statistics.

population weights help explain more variation in the model, at least for this case. This analysis suggests the possibility that greater unemployment rates lead to greater marijuana use. But, there are many potential problems here, which we will learn about in Chapter 6. And, it is uncertain which of these three models is optimal, or if there is another weighting scheme better than these.

3.4 Chapter summary

This chapter presented some important tools for conducting regression analysis. Dummy variables can be used to represent qualitative factors or different levels of quantitative factors so as not to limit a model to having a linear effect. Further methods for estimating non-linear effects of factors include spline, quadratic, and logarithmic functional forms of models. And, interactions of variables allow a variable to have different effects (or contributions) based on the values of other factors. Finally, weighted models can be used when certain observations should have greater importance in a model, such as when using grouped data with different-sized groups. This could produce a better-fitting model.

Exercises

1. With the Fox News data (**foxnewsdata**) and from the regression in Question #2 in Chapter 2, add in three variables: *foxnews* = dummy variable for whether the town had the Fox News channel made available between 1996 and 2000; *group3* = dummy variable for whether the town had the variable *votes1996* between 5000 and 9999; *group4* = dummy variable for whether the town had the variable *votes1996* at least 10,000. (Note that this model may not be holding constant all relevant factors, and so the coefficient estimate on *foxnews* may be a biased estimate of the true causal effect of the adoption of Fox News.)
   a. Interpret the coefficient estimate on the variable, *foxnews*.
   b. Interpret the coefficient estimate on the variable, *group3*.
   c. Based on the regression model estimates, if *group3* were instead a dummy variable for "at least 5000 voters in 1996" then what would be the new coefficient estimate on *group4*? Explain why this is the case.
2. Repeat the regression from Question #1, but weight it by *votes1996*. What are some of the more notable differences in results between this regression and the regression in #1?
3. Add to the regression from Question #2: *male2000* (share of the town's population in 2000 that is male) and the interaction of *foxnews* and *male2000*. Interpret the coefficient estimate on the interaction and its statistical significance.

4. From Question #2, estimate a spline for how the change in the population share of Hispanics in the town affects the outcome (*r_vote_share_ch*) differently for negative and positive values of *hisp_ch*. Interpret the different estimates for these two variables.
5. Use the data set **oecd_gas_demand**, which comes from Baltagi and Griffin (1983).[1] Regress the (natural) logarithm of gas consumption per car (*lgaspcar*) on the logarithms of income per capita (*lincomep*), real motor gasoline price (*lrpmg*), and the stock of cars per capita (*lcarpcap*) and dummy variables for years 1961 to 1978 (using 1960 as the reference year).
    a. Interpret the coefficient estimate on the variable, *lrpmg*.
    b. Interpret the coefficient estimate on the variable for year 1975.

Note

1   The data source is: https://vincentarelbundock.github.io/Rdatasets/datasets.html, accessed July 10, 2018.

References

Baltagi, B. H., & Griffin, J. M. (1983). Gasoline demand in the OECD: An application of pooling and testing procedures. *European Economic Review*, 22(2), 117–137.

Bureau of Labor Statistics, U.S. Department of Labor. (2014). *National Longitudinal Survey of Youth 1979 cohort, 1979–2012 (rounds 1–25)*. Columbus, OH: Center for Human Resource Research, The Ohio State University.

Glover, D., Pallais, A., & Pariente, W. (2017). Discrimination as a self-fulfilling prophecy: Evidence from French grocery stores. *The Quarterly Journal of Economics*, 132(3), 1219–1260.

Van Assche, J., Van Hiel, A., Stadeus, J., Bushman, B. J., De Cremer, D., & Roets, A. (2017). When the heat is on: The effect of temperature on voter behavior in presidential elections. *Frontiers in Psychology*, 8, 929. (Available at www.frontiersin.org/articles/10.3389/fpsyg.2017.00929/full, accessed July 10, 2018).

4 What does "holding other factors constant" mean?

Yakka foob mog. Grug pubbawup zink wattoom gazork. Chumble spuzz.
— Calvin (of Calvin and Hobbes), when asked to explain either Newton's First Law of Motion or "holding other factors constant" in his own words

There are many points in regression analysis that are often misinterpreted. Some of these include the interpretation of coefficient estimates on dummy variables being relative to a particular reference group (Chapter 3) and statistical significance or insignificance (as you will see in Chapter 5). In this chapter, the main focus is on one of the most fundamental, yet least understood concepts in regression analysis: "holding other factors constant." This is the basis for proper modeling and choosing the optimal set of control variables.

Regression models are meant to indicate how various factors determine an outcome. Regressions are "models" because we are trying to, well, *model* or simulate how an outcome is determined. When we say we want to **hold some factor constant**, we want to tweak the model so that one explanatory variable moves without the other factor moving with it. For example, when estimating the effects of schooling on income, we want to design a model in which we compare people with different levels of education without those differences being accompanied by differences in inherent intelligence and other things that typically come with higher levels of schooling (but are not a product of schooling). We want to hold constant those other factors as educational levels vary. This should help us get closer to the true causal effect of a year of schooling.

But, there are going to be times in which you do want to allow factors to move with the injection of a treatment into the model. Think of a weather model that is trying to predict how a Nor'easter will affect New York's weather. A Nor'easter – with the most famous one being the 1991 storm that had a book and movie depicting it, both titled *The Perfect Storm* – is a storm coming from the North Atlantic Ocean that typically hits New England before making its way to New York. Boston weather can affect New York weather, so one may argue that we should "hold constant" Boston weather. But, if we were to do so, our model would not capture how the storm would affect New York weather, as it would miss any effects coming from Boston.

In this chapter, I use a few approaches to describe what "holding other factors constant" means. (This is also known as *ceteris paribus*, which may have come from Latin, meaning "all other things equal" or from French, meaning "Don't put all of those damn things in my coffee at once so that I know what particular ingredients make it perfect.")

4.1 Case studies to understand "holding other factors constant"

Case 1: Making a better chocolate-chip cookie

Let's say you want to test whether adding cinnamon to your chocolate-chip cookies makes them tastier. There are two simple methods to make a control and treatment group:

(A) Make two separate batches from scratch, one with cinnamon (the treatment batch) and one without cinnamon (the control batch).
(B) Make one batch, divide the batch in two, and add cinnamon to one (the treatment batch) and not the other (the control batch).

Which method is better? Why?

I would choose method B. When comparing the treatment to the control batch, we would want nothing else to be different between the two batches other than the inclusion of cinnamon. That is, we want to **hold constant** all other factors that could vary with whether cinnamon is added. In method A, when building two different batches from scratch, there might be slight variations in the amount of butter, sugar, chocolate, and other things that affect the taste of the cookies. In method B, since it comes from the same batch, the other ingredients, if mixed well, are in the same proportions, so they are being held constant. Thus, unless you are a well-experienced cookie maker and can get the ingredients nearly exactly the same in both batches (with method A), method B should be more reliable than method A because it does a better job at holding the other factors constant.

Case 2: How much should lemon trees be watered?

Let's say that we are interested in determining how the amount of water affects the production from lemon trees. Consider these details:

• On Day 1, you plant 50 baby lemon trees that appear to be the same.
• Half are planted in the good-soil part of the yard.

- Half are planted in the bad-soil part of the yard.
- Upon planting the trees, you randomly assign each tree 1 of 10 different amounts of water that the tree is then given weekly for 5 years – each of the 10 water amounts will be given to 5 trees.
- Assume that trees are covered when it rains so that the only water they receive is what you give it.

The setup for the model would be:

- Dependent variable: Number of lemons the tree produces in the 5th year (L);
- Key explanatory variable: Amount of weekly water (W);
- Possible control variables:
  - Indicator variable for being in the "good soil" part of the yard (G);
  - The height of the tree has at the start of the 5th year (H) – this could be measured in feet or meters or any other unit.

The important issue is what control variable(s) should be used. That is, what factor(s) should we hold constant and what factor(s), if any, should we allow to change as the amount of water changes.

I think most of us would agree that we would want to control for the indicator on being in the "good soil" part of the yard (G). Even though the amount of water is randomized, for this small sample of 50 trees, it is quite likely that the randomness would not make it even for how many trees watered a given amount are in the good vs. bad soil. Thus, we want to hold constant the "good soil" factor so that this would not vary when we allow the amount of water to vary, just as we do not want the amount of other ingredients to vary as we add cinnamon to our cookies.

Do we also want to control for the height of the tree at the beginning of the 5th year (H)? This comes down to whether, in our model, we want the height to be allowed to change or to be held constant when the amount of water changes.

We are injecting a treatment of the amount of water into this model of lemon-tree production. In the model, we want to see how lemon production changes as the amount of water varies. I would argue that part of the reason why the amount of water could affect the number of lemons produced by the tree is that it affects how large the tree grows. If we were to hold constant the height (i.e., not allow it to change as the amount of watering changes), then we are factoring out part of the watering effect. We would not capture the full effect of the watering on how many lemons are produced.

To demonstrate this, let's consider Figures 4.1a (*not* controlling for the height) and 4.1b (controlling for the height), along with the accompanying Table 4.1 describing the differences. Figure 4.1a demonstrates the mechanisms for how the amount of water (W) affects the number of lemons (L):

- Mechanism M1 is that the water affects the height (H), which in turn affects the number of lemons;
- Mechanism M2 is that the water affects the overall health of the tree in other ways besides the height, or "other indicators of health" for the tree, which again affects the number of lemons.

(I use an oval for the "other indicators of health" because it is unobserved, unlike the other variables.)

The height and the "other indicators of health" are considered **mediating factors**, which are factors through which the key X variable affects the dependent variable. Mediating factors are products of the key X variable that, in turn, affect the dependent variable.

$$L_i = \beta_0 + \beta_1 W_i + \beta_2 G_i + \varepsilon_i$$

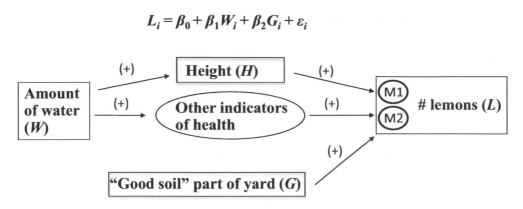

Figure 4.1a Flow chart showing mechanisms for lemon-tree example when excluding "height"

$$L_i = \beta_0 + \beta_1 W_i + \beta_2 G_i + \beta_3 H_i + \varepsilon_i$$

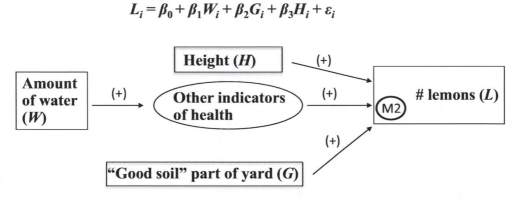

Figure 4.1b Flow chart showing mechanisms for lemon-tree example when including "height"

In Figure 4.1a, the estimate for β_1 in the equation at the top of the figure will capture both mechanisms M1 and M2 because both the height and "other indicators of health" are allowed to change when the amount of water changes. That is, neither the height nor any other indicator of the tree's health is held constant.

In contrast, in Figure 4.1b, $\beta_3 H_i$ is added to the model. This means that the model is effectively making it so that when the amount of water (W) is higher, the height (H) does not change (or, is held constant), as seen by the lack of an arrow from "water" to "height." Thus, β_1 would no longer capture mechanism M1 since there is no longer an effect of the amount of water on the height. This would be equivalent to, in the weather model above, holding constant the weather in Boston when estimating how the Nor'easter will affect weather in New York City.

We would expect both M1 and M2 to be positive, as all effects (how watering affects the height and other health indicators, and how those factors affect the number of lemons) should be positive in this case (assuming there is no over-watering). Thus, β_1 in the model in Figure 4.1b, which just captures mechanism M2, would likely understate the full effect of watering a tree. (This assumes that more water, on average, is good for the health and production of the tree. We may be able to improve

Table 4.1 A summary of the two cases for the lemon-tree example

	$L_i = \beta_0 + \beta_1 W_i + \beta_2 G_i + \varepsilon_i$ *(Figure 4.1a)*	$L_i = \beta_0 + \beta_1 W_i + \beta_2 G_i + \beta_3 H_i + \varepsilon_i$ *(Figure 4.1b)*
Is the variable H (height) included in the model? That is, is it held constant?	No	Yes
In the model, does H vary with the amount of water (W)?	Yes	No (it's held constant)
What mechanisms are captured by β_1 (the coefficient on W)?	M1 and M2	Just M2
What is the interpretation of β_1?	How the # lemons is affected by the amount of water	How the # lemons is affected by the amount of water beyond the mechanism of increasing the height of the tree
Is this the full causal effect of the amount of water?	Yes	No

the estimate of the optimal amount of water by using a quadratic model, with W and W^2. But, I use the linear model for simplicity.)

Note that, in both figures, the variable for being in the "good soil" part of the yard (G) is not part of the mechanisms for how the amount of water affects the number of lemons (i.e., G is not a mediating factor), as it has its own effect in the model and is not affected by how much water the tree is given (W). The difference between whether we include the height (H) and the indicator for being in the "good soil" part of the yard (G) is that the height is part of the effect of how much water the tree gets, while being in the "good soil" part of the yard is not a product of how much water the tree gets, but *may* be correlated with the amount of water.

The main lesson is that:

- We control for the factors we want to not change as the key explanatory variable varies.
- We do not control for the factors we want to allow to change when the key explanatory variable changes. (These are typically mediating factors, or variables that are products of the key explanatory variable and affect the dependent variable.)

What is the difference in interpretation of β_1 for the two models? As indicated in Table 4.1:

- β_1 in the model in Figure 4.1a tells us how the amount of lemons produced varies with the amount of water, holding constant whether the tree is in the "good soil" part of the yard.
- β_1 in the model in Figure 4.1b tells us how the amount of lemons produced varies with the amount of water, holding constant being in the "good soil" part of the yard and the height of the tree. Or, how the amount of water affects the number of lemons by affecting aspects of the tree's

health other than the height. This is not informative on how water affects the number of lemons produced, as it is only part of the effect we want.

As you are probably thinking, the model in Figure 4.1a gives the full effect of the water given, and the model in Figure 4.1b gives only part of the effect, as any effect through how water affects the height is held constant and not captured in the estimated effect of the amount of water.

Case 3: An example with domino chains

This would not be a typical regression one would do, as it certainly does not speak to a world problem, but it may do a good job of highlighting what a model is and what happens when you hold a factor constant. Imagine that you set up 10 simple domino chain reactions, with a length of 5 dominos each. The data on the 10 domino chains are in Table 4.2, with an observation number and five variables.

The situation is as follows:

- We want to know what the causal effect of tipping the first domino (D_1) is on the probability of the last domino falling (D_5). Theoretically, it should be a 1-to-1 relationship, so the causal effect of D_1 should be 1.0. But, I've introduced a few errors.
- Observations 1–3 go as planned, with the first domino being tipped $(D_1 = 1)$ and the last domino eventually falling $(D_5 = 1)$.
- Observations 4 and 5 had a miscue, with the first domino being tipped, but the error occurring before the third domino for observation 4 and after the third domino for observation 5.
- Observations 6–10 had the first domino never being tipped $(D_1 = 0)$, and so the last domino did not fall $(D_5 = 0)$ – I'll let you imagine reasons for why the first domino did not get tipped, but in my mind, it had something to do with people being on their cell phones.

Table 4.2 Notional data on dominos chains to understand "holding other factors constant"

Observation number	First domino got tipped (D_1)	2nd domino fell (D_2)	3rd domino fell (D_3)	4th domino fell (D_4)	Last (5th) domino fell (D_5)
1	1	1	1	1	1
2	1	1	1	1	1
3	1	1	1	1	1
4	1	1	1	0	0
5	1	1	0	0	0
6	0	0	0	0	0
7	0	0	0	0	0
8	0	0	0	0	0
9	0	0	0	0	0
10	0	0	0	0	0

This situation is also depicted in the top panel of Figure 4.2. Each arrow represents the causal effect of a one–unit change in the source variable on the variable being pointed at:

- Tipping the first domino always results in the second domino falling (whereas the second domino never falls when the first domino does not), so the causal effect is 1.0.
- The third domino falls 80% of the time (4 of 5 times) that the second domino falls, so the causal effect is 0.8.
- The fourth domino falls 75% of the time (3 of 4 times) that the third domino falls, so the causal effect is 0.75.
- The fifth domino falls each time (3 of 3 times) that the fourth domino falls, so the causal effect is 1.0.

Whereas the effect of water on lemon-tree production had multiple mechanisms, there is only one mechanism for how the first domino tipping affects whether the last domino tips. That mechanism simply has the first domino tipping the second, which tips the third, which tips the fourth, which then tips the fifth. So, D_2, D_3, and D_4 are mediating factors for the effect of D_1 on D_5.

Note that the coefficient on tipping the first domino, in the top panel, is 0.6, which is the product of the four values of the arrows: $1.0 \times 0.8 \times 0.75 \times 1.0 = 0.6$.

This value of 0.6 is the correct causal effect of D_1 on D_5. This is a difference in means for the value of D_5 when $D_1 = 1$ vs. $D_1 = 0$, as would be the case with any regression with having just a dummy variable for the explanatory variable, as described in Section 3.1. And so, the mean value of D_5 equals zero when $D_1 = 0$, and it equals 0.6 when $D_1 = 1$.

Now, what would happen if we controlled for one of the mediating factors? In the bottom panel, we control for D_3 (whether the third domino fell) by including it as a control variable.

This would make it so, as D_1 varied in the sample (or, changed in the model), D_3 would not be allowed to vary because it would be held constant. In the model, that breaks the chain, and so D_2

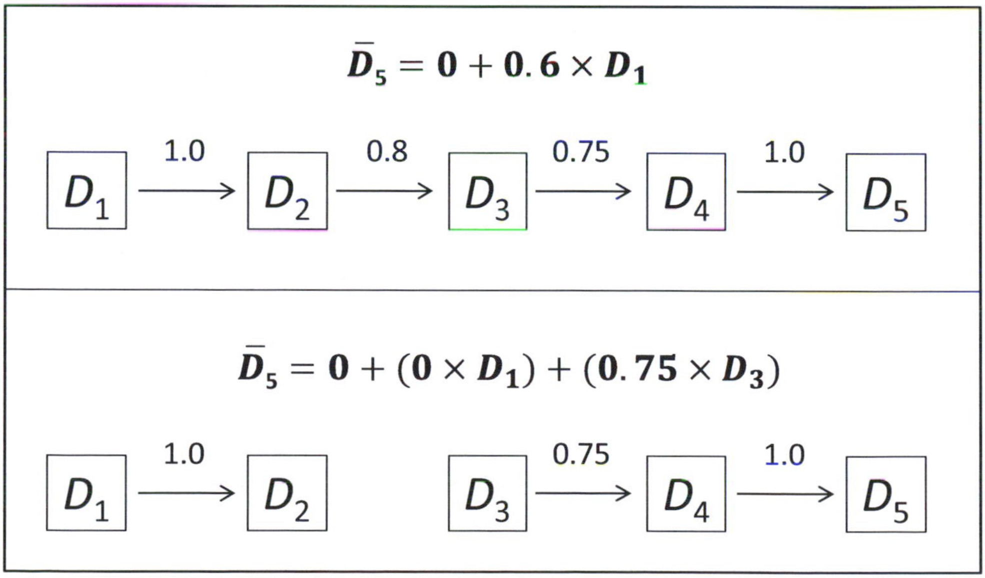

$$\bar{D}_5 = 0 + 0.6 \times D_1$$

$$D_1 \xrightarrow{1.0} D_2 \xrightarrow{0.8} D_3 \xrightarrow{0.75} D_4 \xrightarrow{1.0} D_5$$

$$\bar{D}_5 = 0 + (0 \times D_1) + (0.75 \times D_3)$$

$$D_1 \xrightarrow{1.0} D_2 \qquad D_3 \xrightarrow{0.75} D_4 \xrightarrow{1.0} D_5$$

Figure 4.2 Mechanisms for how tipping the first domino affects whether the last domino falls

changing does not affect D_3. And, that means that the final domino would not fall as a result of the initial tip of the first domino.

And, the regression model would now be:

$$\hat{D}_5 = 0 + 0 \times D_1 + 0.75 \times D_3.$$

This understates the true causal effect of D_1 on D_5. It should be 0.6.

Also, note that the coefficient on D_3 is the product of the causal effects in the mechanism for how D_3 affects D_5: $0.75 \times 1.0 = 0.75$.

We have controlled for part of the reason why D_1 affects D_5. This is similar to controlling for the height of the lemon tree. We no longer are estimating the true causal effect. We need to be careful what we actually want to hold constant.

4.2 Using behind-the-curtains scenes to understand "holding other factors constant"

Figures 4.3a and 4.3b provide a flow chart to demonstrate a different approach to understanding "holding other factors constant" (and to demonstrate what a coefficient estimate represents). In Figure 4.3a, we start in the box at the top right, marked with as Box A. This is a Simple Regression Model, regressing *income* on *educ* (a simpler variable name for years-of-schooling). The question is, "What does the estimate on *educ* (β_1) capture?"

In the box marked B, I list four things that tend to move with one additional year of schooling. That is, if we were to compare people with, say, 14 years-of-schooling (two years of college) to those with 13 years-of-schooling, we would expect to see these four factors, on average, to be different for the two sets of people. Let's assume for the sake of the story here that this is a complete list of things that tend to change with an additional year of schooling, even though we know that there are other factors we've discussed earlier. The variables for these four factors are Z_1 to Z_4, and we will say that the average changes in factors Z_1 to Z_4 associated with one more year of schooling are, correspondingly, values a_1 to a_4. So, the Zs are variables, and the as are changes in the value of the Z variables.

Note that the list of factors that move with an additional year of schooling includes both things that result from more schooling (greater workplace skills and more network connections) and factors that preceded a person's education (innate intelligence and motivation).

All four of these factors that are associated with years-of-schooling probably have some effect on income, and we will say that if we had a model estimating the simultaneous effects of these factors (Z_1 to Z_4) on income (as in Box C), we would obtain coefficients δ_1 to δ_4, which are also shown in the arrows (marked by the circled C) from the four factors in Box B to *income*. I call this a "notional model" in Box C because it is going on behind the curtains and probably cannot be estimated given that most of the factors are unobservable/non-quantifiable.

(As with the domino example, and elsewhere in the book, think of the arrows as the effect of a one-unit increase in one variable on the variable it is pointing to. If multiple arrows are going towards one variable, then it is the causal effect of one variable, holding the other variables constant.)

We now can see how β_1 is determined. In Box D,

$$\beta_1 = a_1\delta_1 + a_2\delta_2 + a_3\delta_3 + a_4\delta_4$$
$$\text{M1} \quad \text{M2} \quad \text{M3} \quad \text{M4}$$

(4.1)

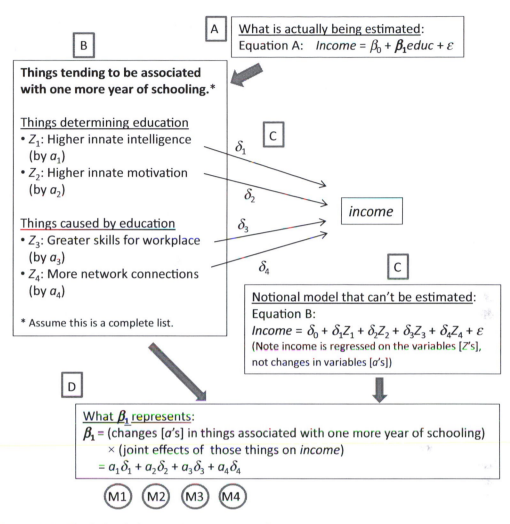

Figure 4.3a The behind-the-curtains operations of a regression

That is, β_1 is the sum of the products of how much the factors change (on average) with one more year of schooling (a_1 to a_4) and how each factor simultaneously affects income (the coefficients in the notional model, δ_1 to δ_4) – again, coefficients that cannot be accurately identified. These four products ($a_1\delta_1$ to $a_4\delta_4$) represent the four mechanisms as to why income tends to vary with an additional year of schooling. These mechanisms are labeled M1 to M4 in the figure and equation (4.1). In reality, there are likely many more than just four Z factors and four mechanisms, but we're trying to keep it simple here.

Is the β_1 in Box D what we want? Does it represent the causal effect of schooling?

Probably not. We want the estimated effect of schooling (β_1) to capture the effects of things that are products of schooling and that affect income (greater skills and more network connections). These would be captured by mechanisms M3 and M4. But, we do not want β_1 to include the mechanisms of things that occurred before the schooling took place (innate intelligence and motivation), or M1 and

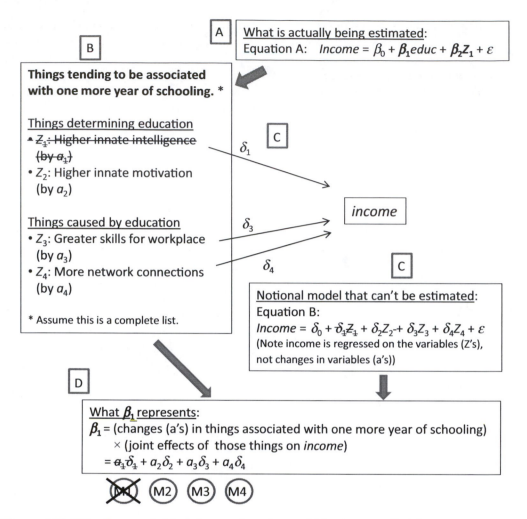

Figure 4.3b What happens behind the curtains when variables are controlled for

M2. This means that we want to design the model so that, as years-of-schooling varies in the sample, workplace skills and network connections are allowed to vary, but innate intelligence and motivation are *not* allowed to vary – i.e., are held constant. And, this would be simply done, if data were available, by including the variables for innate intelligence and motivation (Z_1 and Z_2) in the model, thereby holding them constant.

Holding innate intelligence and motivation constant would make it so that β_1 would just capture the effects from what an additional year of schooling results in, not what one more year of schooling is a marker of, or:

$$\beta_1 = a_3\delta_3 + a_4\delta_4 \qquad (4.2)$$

Note that this is similar to the lemon-tree example from above. Just as we wanted the things affected by watering to be allowed to change as the amount of water changed, we want to allow the things resulting from additional schooling to vary as the years-of-schooling varies. We would not want to include these products of schooling as control variables so that β_1 captures their effects. You are probably thinking that this is counter-intuitive: we need to exclude the factor from the model so that its effects are captured by the estimated effect of the key explanatory variable.

Now, let's hold a factor constant and see what happens. Let's now say that we have data on innate intelligence (Z_1), so we include that variable in the model but not any variable for innate motivation. How does the estimate of β_1 change? This is represented in Figure 4.3b. Note that the model in Box A now includes Z_1 as an explanatory variable. This means that innate intelligence is "held constant" in the model. And, that means that, in Box B, innate intelligence, as measured linearly by Z_1, no longer changes, on average, with an additional year of schooling.

It is possible and even likely that years-of-schooling would still be associated with some effect of innate intelligence beyond the linear effect of Z_1 on *income* – that is, maybe there is a non-linear effect of innate intelligence on income. But, for the sake of the argument, let's say that we adequately held innate intelligence constant so that, in equation (A) and in Box D, higher innate intelligence is no longer associated with differences in the years-of-schooling.

In turn, in Box C, the notional (behind-the-curtains) model no longer includes the effects of Z_1. (This means that the other δ coefficients may change – e.g., δ_2 in Figure 4.3b would likely be different from δ_2 in Figure 4.3a, as these are simultaneous effects that would depend on the correlation of the Z variables. We'll get more into that in a moment.) And then, in Box D, we see that β_1 no longer captures the effect of Z_1. Mechanism M1 is now eliminated from β_1.

Have we isolated the causal effect? Not yet. There is still the influence of innate motivation, as:

$$\beta_1 = a_2\delta_2 + a_3\delta_3 + a_4\delta_4 \tag{4.3}$$

Consider what would happen if we also had data on innate motivation and some measure of skills for the workplace and were to control for all of those factors (Z_1 to Z_3). In that case, the estimated effect of a year of schooling would be:

$$\beta_1 = a_4\delta_4 \tag{4.4}$$

This would merely be the effect of a year of schooling on income through the mechanism of creating better network connections. This would no longer tell us how much more income a person would expect to receive from one more year of schooling.

And, if we were to control for all four factors (Z_1 to Z_4), then β_1 would be zero, as no factor of income would be allowed to vary when years-of-schooling changes. All mechanisms, M1–M4, would be eliminated.

Let me add a little complexity for a more realistic situation. Some of the Z variables are likely correlated. For example, Z_1 and Z_2 (if we think of "innate" as measured before any formal schooling begins) may be positively correlated, as having greater innate intelligence may stimulate greater motivation or *vice versa*. This would mean that, in Figure 4.3b:

- In Box A, β_2 may partly pick up the effects of innative motivation (Z_2) – in addition to the effects of Z_1, which means that
- In Box B, a_2 may now be lower (than its corresponding value in Figure 4.3a) because Z_2 is partly being controlled for due to being correlated with Z_1;

- Also, in Box C, δ_2 may be higher (than in Figure 4.3a), as it would capture the effects of innate intelligence (this is a preview of omitted-variables bias, which you will see in Section 6.4.2);
- And so, M2 may be different from what it was in Figure 4.3a – it would be lower from a lower a_2 but higher from a higher δ_2.

The mechanisms are notional, and they give guidance on why we may find certain effects. Quantifying these mechanisms would be extremely difficult. It would require excellent data on all variables involved with all mechanisms and no potential biases (from Chapter 6).

The general concept described in this sub-section is a bit controversial, as opinions may vary on this – probably because it is misunderstood. But, if we want to know how years-of-schooling affects income, we do not want to hold constant the factors that are products of additional schooling and could affect income, such as the occupation the person has, and even whether the person is married.

4.3 Using dummy variables to understand "holding other factors constant"

Another approach to understanding "holding other factors constant" is to consider what happens when dummy variables are included in a model. Let's separate the sample into four groups based on quartiles for the AFQT score – these are quartiles for the sample rather than for the national distribution. If we include variables for the AFQT quartile – instead of the AFQT score itself, as in equation (2.21) – then we get:

$$\left(\widehat{income}\right)_i = -34,673 + \mathbf{5742} \times \left(educ\right)_i + 5177 \times \left(afqt2\right)_i + 13,787 \times \left(afqt3\right)_i + 26,761 \times \left(afqt4\right) \quad (4.5)$$

where *afqt2*, *afqt3*, and *afqt4* are the second, third, and fourth quartiles – with the first (the lowest) quartile excluded as the reference category. I will now demonstrate how the estimated effect of years-of-schooling (*educ*) is calculated.

Let's first see what happens when we separate the sample into the quartiles of the AFQT score:

$$\text{1st quartile}: \quad \left(\widehat{income}\right)_i = 17,592 + \mathbf{1261} \times \left(educ\right)_i \quad (4.6a)$$

$$\text{2nd quartile}: \quad \left(\widehat{income}\right)_i = 10,106 + \mathbf{2659} \times \left(educ\right)_i \quad (4.6b)$$

$$\text{3rd quartile}: \quad \left(\widehat{income}\right)_i = -18,594 + \mathbf{5618} \times \left(educ\right)_i \quad (4.6c)$$

$$\text{4rd quartile}: \quad \left(\widehat{income}\right)_i = -71,224 + \mathbf{9838} \times \left(educ\right)_i \quad (4.6d)$$

By separating the sample into sub-samples based on their AFQT score quartile, we are, to some extent, controlling for the AFQT score (aptitude). The estimated effects of years-of-schooling (*educ*) are no longer capturing differences *across* quartiles of the AFQT score. Rather, the estimates are based on within-quartile income comparisons of people with different levels of schooling. However, the coefficients on *educ* may still reflect the effects of differences in AFQT score *within* the quartiles. Thus, we are far from perfect here, but we are getting closer to comparing a similar set of people. Instead of comparing apples to oranges, perhaps we are comparing Fuji to Granny Smith apples.

The estimates on *educ* vary widely across these quartiles. This may be partly due to differences across quartiles in where most of the variation lies for the *educ* variable (see Section 2.6); the higher quartiles probably have more variation in college years. Note that this does not necessarily mean that the causal effects of schooling are greater for college years. Instead, it could partly reflect that, at the college years-of-schooling, more schooling is a stronger indicator of other attributes that contribute to economic success, such as inherent intelligence and determination, compared to other levels of schooling.

This is where it gets kind of neat. When categories are controlled for with dummy variables, the coefficient estimate on *educ* is the average of the within-category coefficient estimates on *educ*, weighted by the product of:

- The number of observations in each category;
- The variance of *educ* in each category.

More formally, if you want to see the equation version of this, the coefficient estimate, $\hat{\beta}_1$, on some variable X_1, when controlling for a categorization of groups marked by g, would be the following equation (which is a slight variant of one presented by Gibbons et al. [2014]):

$$\hat{\beta}_1 = \sum_g \hat{\beta}_{1g} * \left[\frac{\Pr(g) \times \mathrm{var}(X_1 \mid g, X_2)}{Z} \right] \qquad (4.7)$$

where:
- $\hat{\beta}_{1g}$ is the coefficient estimate on X_1 for group g in the categorization;
- $\Pr(g)$ is the percentage of observations in group g, or, the probability that a given observation is in group g;
- $\mathrm{var}(X_1 | g, X_2)$ is the variance of X_1 in group g, conditional on all other variables, as represented in X_2; (In our case, there are no other variables.)
- Z is the sum of $\Pr(g) \times \mathrm{var}(X_1 | g, X_2)$ across groups. (Including this in the denominator scales the bracketed part, the "weight," so that the weights sum to one across all groups.)

Just so you believe me, I'll show the calculations in Table 4.3:

- Column (2) indicates the number of observations in each group – due to a limited set of values for AFQT score (100) and natural variation producing a non-even distribution, the groups are not quite equally sized when split into quartiles.
- Column (3) has the coefficient estimate on *educ* for each quartile, from equations (4.6a–d).
- Column (4) has the proportion of the observations in the particular AFQT quartile (group). This is the probability that an observation is in group g: $\Pr(g)$.
- Column (5) has the variance of *educ* within each quartile.
- Column (6) is the numerator of the weight in brackets in equation (4.7).
- Column (7) divides the weight in column (6) by the sum of the weights (4.1152) so that they sum to 1.0.
- Column (8) multiplies the coefficient estimate in column (3) by the final weight in column (7). The sum of these is the weighted average of the coefficient estimates within each quartile.

Note that the weighted average of the coefficient estimates, **5742**, is the same as that from equation (4.5), when all groups are included in the model and there are dummy variables to control for the AFQT quartile. This demonstrates the point made above, that

Table 4.3 Demonstrating coefficient estimates in the presence of dummy variables

(1)	(2)	(3)	(4)	(5)	(6)	(7)	(8)
AFQT Quartile	Number of observations	$\hat{\beta}_{1g}$	Pr(g)	Variance of years-of-schooling	Weight numerator (4) × (5)	Final weight	$\hat{\beta}_{1g}$ × final weight
1	688	1261.607	0.2482	3.344	0.8300	0.2017	254.5
2	692	2659.185	0.2496	2.935	0.7328	0.1781	473.5
3	693	5618.352	0.2500	4.243	1.0608	0.2578	1448.3
4	699	9838.401	0.2522	5.915	1.4916	0.3625	3566.1
	2772				4.1152	1.0000	5742.3

Source: Bureau of Labor Statistics, 2014.

including a set of dummy variables in a model to control for groups effectively makes it so the coefficient estimate on the key X variable is the average of the within-group coefficient estimates on that X variable, with the average weighted by the share of observations and the variance of that X variable within each group. When the AFQT quartile is controlled for (i.e., held constant), no longer does the coefficient estimate on *educ* capture comparisons of people across-AFQT-quartiles. Rather, the coefficient estimate on *educ* is the weighted average of coefficient estimates from four models in which the AFQT quartile does not change.

This means that the model is designed so that, as years-of-schooling varies, AFQT quartile does not vary.

What if the AFQT is used linearly rather than by quartile (or other quantile) groups, as in equation 2.19 in Section 2.9? I don't know of any smooth and simple formula that could be used. But, the general idea is the same. The linear effect of the AFQT score is effectively factored out of the income variable before we see how years-of-schooling affects income. But, it is not that clean, as the AFQT effect comes after the education effect (or association) is factored out (simultaneously). Incidentally, in a situation like this, applied researchers would tend to prefer using quantiles for AFQT scores (perhaps more granulated than using quartiles) because of likely non-linear effects of the AFQT score.

The straightforward interpretation of equation (4.7) applies when there is only one explanatory variable (*educ*) other than the categorization (AFQT category). If other explanatory variables were added, then the same concept would apply, but the interpretation would be a little different. For example, if we were to add a dummy variable for being "Black" into the model, the interpretation of the coefficient estimate on *educ* would be:

The average of the within-AFQT-quartile coefficient estimates on *educ*, weighted by the share of observations in each quartile and by the within-quartile variance of *educ* after factoring out the effect that "Black" has on income.

or

The average of the coefficient estimates on *educ* for the two groups of Blacks and non-Blacks, weighted by the share of observations in the two groups and by the within-group variance of *educ* after factoring out the effect that the AFQT quartile has on income.

Let us consider one more example, this time with two dummy variables as the explanatory variables to explain income (Y) – whether a person has a college degree (*CollDeg*) and whether a person is Hispanic. The use of two dummy variables like this allows us to see in a table who is compared to whom. The regression equation is:

$$Y_i = \beta_0 + \beta_1 \times (CollDeg)_i + \beta_2 \times (Hispanic)_i + \varepsilon_i \tag{4.8}$$

This model would probably not produce the true causal effect of having a college degree or of being Hispanic, as it remains unlikely that the college degree is randomly assigned. Nevertheless, the model produces our "estimates" of these effects. And so, we are estimating the effect of having a college degree, holding Hispanic constant; and, we are estimating the effect of Hispanic, holding college degree constant.

Let's consider who is being compared to whom, based on the average incomes for each group, as defined in Table 4.4. For β_1, since *Hispanic* is being held constant, we are comparing the average incomes for those with and without a college degree within each *Hispanic* category. Thus, we have two comparisons: ($\bar{Y}_C$ to $\bar{Y}_A$) and ($\bar{Y}_D$ to $\bar{Y}_B$). The estimate for β_1 would then be a weighted average of the differences in average incomes, with the weights being based on the percentage of observations in the non-Hispanic and Hispanic groups and the variance of *CollDeg* in each group – see equation (4.7) above. Note that, given the groups that are being compared to each other, the value of the *Hispanic* variable does not change as we go from a value of 0 to 1 for *CollDeg*. That is, in the comparisons determining the estimated effect of *CollDeg*, we are not comparing across Hispanic and non-Hispanic groups. Thus, *Hispanic* is "held constant."

Likewise, since *CollDeg* is held constant, the estimate for β_2 is based on the weighted average of the difference in average incomes between: ($\bar{Y}_C$ and $\bar{Y}_A$) and ($\bar{Y}_D$ and $\bar{Y}_B$). And, in our comparisons, as we vary whether a person is Hispanic, we are holding constant whether they have a college degree.

Note that when we say we are holding the variable *Hispanic* constant, it does not mean that we are only including Hispanics or only including non-Hispanics. Rather, the value of *Hispanic* does not change as we, effectively, change *CollDeg* in the model and see how average income changes.

Okay, I lied. One more example . . . since this is such a neat thing. Suppose that we wanted to estimate the effect of Obama's presidency (2009–16) on "Real GDP Growth" (Y) in the 2000s, but factoring out the influence of the Financial Crisis (*FC*), which we will say, for the sake of the exercise, occurred in 2008–09. Let's say we have 16 observations: 2001–16.

$$Y_i = \beta_0 + \beta_1 \times (Obama)_i + \beta_2 \times (FC)_i + \varepsilon_i \tag{4.9}$$

I must note that it would be extremely difficult to accurately estimate the effect of Obama's presidency, as there are many influences on economic growth in the Obama and non-Obama (Bush) years that are beyond the influence of his presidency or Bush's presidency (e.g., September 11 for Bush and the lingering effects of the Financial Crisis for Obama). These would be examples of omitted-variables bias, which you will see in Chapter 6.

Table 4.4 Average income for each group

	Hispanic = 0	Hispanic = 1
CollDeg = 0	$\bar{Y}_A$	$\bar{Y}_B$
CollDeg = 1	$\bar{Y}_C$	$\bar{Y}_D$

Table 4.5 Average real GDP growth (and defined years) for each group

	$FC = 0$	$FC = 1$
Obama = 0 (Bush years)	$\bar{Y}_A(2001-07)$	$\bar{Y}_B(2008)$
Obama = 1	$\bar{Y}_C(2010-16)$	$\bar{Y}_D(2009)$

Table 4.5 shows the comparisons that would occur. The estimated Obama effect would be based on comparisons of average growth rates for the 2010–16 period to the 2001–07 period and for 2009 to 2008. It would be weighted based on the percentage of observations in each *FC* period (87.5% in the *FC* = 0 period, and 12.5% in the *FC* = 1 period) and the variance of the variable *Obama* in each group (which actually would be the same, since the average value of *Obama* in each *FC* period [0 or 1] would be 0.5). So, we know we are holding the Financial Crisis constant because the estimated Obama effect is not based on any comparisons from the non-*FC* period to the *FC* period.

4.4 Using Venn diagrams to understand "holding other factors constant"

One other useful approach for understanding this concept was given by Peter Kennedy (1992) in his book, *A Guide to Econometrics*. Consider Figure 4.4. In the Simple Regression Model, on the left, the top circle represents the variation in the outcome variable, *Y* (income), and the bottom circle represents the variation in the variable X_1, years-of-schooling. We can think of the R^2 as B/(A + B), or the portion of the variation in *Y* that can be explained by variation in X_1. Recall that R^2 does not speak to the slope of the line, just how much variation in *Y* can be explained by variation in X_1. But, it is the common variation of *Y* and X_1 (area B) that determines the coefficient on X_1, based on how *Y* changes, on average, with a one–unit change in X_1.

In the Multiple Regression Model, the AFQT score (the aptitude measure) is added. Now, the R^2 would increase to (F + G + H)/(E + F + G + H), which adds area H to the R^2 from the simple model. There is common variation in schooling and the AFQT score that helps explain income (area G). That part is now thrown away for determining the coefficient estimates because it is not certain whether it is the schooling or the AFQT score that is affecting income. So, the part of variation in schooling that identifies the coefficient estimate on schooling is area F, which is variation in years-of-schooling that occurs without any variation in the AFQT score. This is "the estimated effect of years-of-schooling on income, holding constant the variation in the AFQT score." Likewise, the variation in the AFQT score in area H would identify the coefficient estimate on AFQT score. In most cases, the estimated effect of schooling on income would be closer to the true causal effect by controlling for AFQT score.

4.5 Could controlling for other factors take you further from the true causal effect?

This is an excellent question! Two sentences ago, I said "*in most cases*, the estimated effect of schooling on income would be closer to the true causal effect" because it is possible that including a measure of intelligence (or another factor) would take you further away from the true estimate. There are several

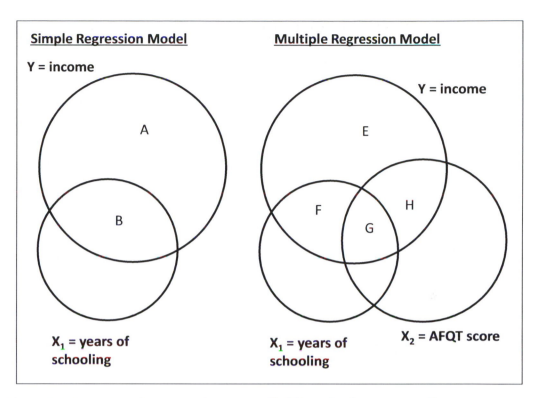

Figure 4.4 Using Venn diagrams to demonstrate "holding other factors constant"

possible causes of this. One of these comes from Section 4.2, in which the true estimate for the effect of a year of schooling on income was:

$$\beta_1 \;=\; a_3\delta_3 \;+\; a_4\delta_4 \tag{4.2}$$

which are the two mechanisms of schooling affecting income by increasing workplace skills and network connections, after factoring out the innate intelligence and motivation that tend to come with an extra year of schooling (assuming we could control for these factors). I said that if we were to somehow control for workplace skills as well, we would then get:

$$\beta_1 \;=\; a_4\delta_4 \tag{4.4}$$

which would take us further away from the true effect from equation (4.2).

A second reason why adding a control variable could take you further away from the true causal effect could be from reducing the smaller of the positive and negative biases. That is, there may be positive and negative biases affecting a coefficient estimate, which I will describe in Chapter 6. In a situation in which the negative biases were to dominate the positive biases (so that there is a net negative bias), eliminating a positive bias would increase the net negative bias.

Of course, quantifying these biases is near impossible. Thus, in cases in which there are plausible positive and negative biases, it is difficult to determine whether eliminating one bias (such as by controlling for an important factor) would bring the estimate closer to or further from the true causal effect. But, in cases in which the bias almost certainly goes in one direction, adjusting for one of the biases is likely to bring you closer to the true causal effect. Generally, adding controls likely, but not necessarily, gets you closer to the true estimate.

4.6 Application of "holding other factors constant" to the story of oat bran and cholesterol

Let's apply the concept to an example from our list of regression topics from Section 1.1: "how does oat-bran consumption affect cholesterol levels?" This was an issue back in the late 1980s, when cholesterol was considered one of the leading causes of heart disease. Researchers noticed that oat-bran consumption was associated with lower cholesterol levels. They probably created some graph that looked something similar to the notional one I create below in Figure 4.5, in which each point represents one person's cholesterol level and reported oat-bran consumption. And, they likely found the best-fitting line for the data to be downward-sloping, as this one is. And, they probably argued from this that oat bran *reduces* cholesterol.

What is wrong with this conclusion? The problem is that we probably cannot rule out other reasons why those who consume more oat bran have lower cholesterol. I can think of two such general reasons:

1. Eating oat bran may replace other high-cholesterol breakfast foods. My guess is that people who eat oat bran (often in the form of oatmeal) probably are not eating Egg McMuffins, bacon, or sausage for breakfast. This would mean that any cholesterol-neutral food would be associated with lower cholesterol if it replaced high-cholesterol food.
2. It probably is not random who eats oat bran. People who eat oat bran tend to be health-conscious, so they likely tend to exercise regularly and avoid eating Big Macs or Loco-Mocos (a Hawaiian double cheeseburger with bacon and two fried eggs on top). So, it is possible that the negative

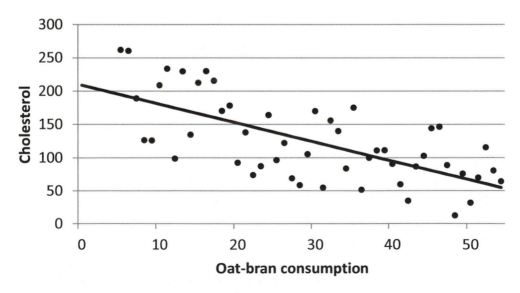

Figure 4.5 Notional scatterplot of oat-bran consumption and cholesterol

association we see between oat bran and cholesterol – meaning that when one is higher, the other is generally lower – is due to oat bran being a marker for other healthy behaviors.

Before we conclude that oat bran *causes* lower cholesterol, we need to rule out these other possible explanations. This means that we need to make sure that variation across people in the amount of oat-bran consumption occurs in isolation and not with variation in other dietary or health-conscious behaviors. To address these issues from a simple model of equation (4.10) below (representing Figure 4.5), we could attempt to hold these factors constant by adding variables representing breakfast food, other dietary characteristics, and exercise to the model, in equation (4.11):

$$Y_i = \beta_0 + \beta_1 X_{1i} + \varepsilon_i \tag{4.10}$$

$$Y_i = \beta_0 + \beta_1 X_{1i} + \beta_2 X_{2i} + \beta_3 X_{3i} + \beta_4 X_{4i} + \varepsilon_i \tag{4.11}$$

where:
- Y = cholesterol;
- X_1 = oat-bran consumption per week;
- X_2 = sausage and bacon servings per week;
- X_3 = Big Macs and Loco-Mocos per week;
- X_4 = days exercising per week.

The estimated effect of oat bran on cholesterol, $\hat{\beta}_1$, would probably be smaller (less negative) in equation (4.11). In (4.10), when oat bran is higher, there is probably less sausage/bacon/Big-Mac/Loco-Moco consumption and probably more exercise. But, in (4.11), when oat bran is higher, the amount of sausage/bacon/Big-Mac/Loco-Moco consumption and exercise stays the same . . . because they are held constant. Technically, controlling for these factors might not take the factor of Big Macs and Loco-Mocos out of the oat-bran–cholesterol relationship if there were non-linear effects of these factors on cholesterol levels. Using more detail to represent these factors could do a better job of controlling for these factors.

Still, we need to ask ourselves whether there are any unobservable factors we are missing. Also, are we accurately identifying "breakfast food" with our variable for sausage and bacon servings or "health consciousness" with our variables for Big-Mac and Loco-Moco consumption and the number of days per week a person exercises? Are we adequately holding constant the other factors that could move with oat-bran consumption?

My guess is that there are probably many people who do not eat Big Macs or Loco-Mocos who still have poor dietary habits. We need to consider many other aspects of a diet. And, we would probably need to consider other aspects of exercise. So, how confident could we be that we have controlled for all other explanations for the negative relationship between oat bran and cholesterol? It is uncertain, as it is quite conceivable that other explanations remain. That is, there could be *omitted-variables bias* in that "omitted" factors could contribute to both a person's oat-bran consumption and cholesterol levels, thus causing them to be correlated. This is one of the key pitfalls of regression analysis that I will discuss in Chapter 6.

This story is also emblematic of an often-ignored truth in regression analysis:

In observational studies, in contrast with randomized trials, controlling for observable characteristics only takes you so far in addressing alternative explanations. The unobserved reasons why someone receives a treatment or why a subject has a certain value of the key X variable (e.g., amount of oat bran consumption) may greatly impact the estimated association between the key X variable and the dependent variable.

In these cases, special methods will be needed. Chapter 8 will introduce some of those methods.

4.7 Chapter summary

- "Holding other factors constant" means that, in the model, as one key factor changes, the other factor does not change so its effects on the outcome do not occur. This aims to isolate the effect of the key factor on the outcome.
- Controlling for groups within some categorization (with dummy variables) means that the overall coefficient estimates are based on within-group relationships between the explanatory variables and the dependent variable. This is what tells you that the group is held constant as the key explanatory variable changes.
- When estimating causal effects, not all factors should be held constant, particularly factors that occur after the key explanatory variable.

Exercises

1. Consider the regression model from Chapter 2, Question #1,

$$\widehat{price} = 100,000 + 45,000 \times bedrooms + 10 \times sqft$$

If you observed home prices listed for 1000-square-foot homes and for 3000-square-foot homes (without any other information), why would the difference in average home price between the two sets of homes likely be more than $20,000 (which is $10×2000, with 2000 being the difference between 3000 and 1000)? Why would this be different from what the regression indicates?

2. Consider the Fox News case from the Chapter 3 exercises, in which we estimated how the adoption of Fox News into a town's cable-TV channels affects Republican vote share. Set up a notional model, similar to Figure 4.1a, that has: (a) at least one mediating factor that should not be controlled for (similar to the height of the lemon tree); and (b) one variable that is not a mediating factor and should be controlled for (similar to the variable for the "good soil part of the yard").

3. Design a behind-the-curtains regression model (similar to Figure 4.3a) on a research topic of your choice that aims to estimate the causal effect of some factor on an outcome. Include at least one mediating factor for the key explanatory variable and at least one variable that determines the key explanatory variable and affects the outcome.

4. With the data on the book's website, **income_coll_hisp_data**, regress *income* on *coll* and *hisp* (for the purpose of estimating the effect of a college degree on income, holding constant whether the person is Hispanic). Create a table similar to Table 4.3 to demonstrate how the coefficient estimate on *coll* is based on the weighted average of the coefficient estimates on *coll* for the two groups identified by the variable, *hisp*.

References

Bureau of Labor Statistics, U.S. Department of Labor. (2014). *National Longitudinal Survey of Youth 1979 cohort, 1979–2012 (rounds 1–25)*. Columbus, OH: Center for Human Resource Research, The Ohio State University.

Gibbons, C. E., Serrato, J. C. S., & Urbancic, M. B. (2014). Broken or fixed effects? (No. w20342). National Bureau of Economic Research.

Kennedy, P. (1992). *A guide to econometrics*, 3rd edition. Boston: MIT Press.

<table>
<tr><td>5</td><td>

Standard errors, hypothesis tests, p-values, and aliens
</td></tr>
</table>

Sometimes I think the surest sign that intelligent life exists elsewhere in the universe is that none of it has tried to contact us.

– Calvin (of Calvin & Hobbes)

If a researcher wants to know the percentage of the population who would support Donald Trump for reelection, she would take a random sample from the population of voters and calculate the percentage. If the researcher were to take a different random sample from that population, there would likely be a different percentage supporting Trump. While some things in the world are certain (e.g., Trump tweeting by 6:00am after being insulted publicly), sampling from a population is not one of those things. There will inevitably be **sampling error**, represented by differences in the characteristics of a sample relative to the population from which it is drawn. The more observations there are, assuming the sampling is random and representative of the voting population, the less sampling error there would be and the more certain the researcher can be on her estimate of the extent of support for Trump's reelection.

In regression analysis, there is a similar story for coefficient estimates. One sample of people would give us one answer for how some outcome (Y) moves with an explanatory variable (X). Another sample would give a different answer. Having more observations would reduce sampling error and get you closer to the true relationship.

Even if you have data on the entire population for which you are attempting to make inferences, having a larger set of observations will provide more precise estimates for any empirical relationships. Consider the analysis from Section 2.7 on the relationship between payroll and wins for baseball teams. There were 30 observations. With so few observations, even though it was the entire population of teams, random events can play large roles in determining how many wins a team has. Such events may include an unexpected star emerging on a low-paying team, contributing to more wins than would be expected. Or, perhaps a few stars on a high-paying team get injured, leading to fewer wins than would be expected for the team. With more observations, the random events average out to be similar for low- vs. high-payroll teams, so the estimated relationship would be more precisely estimated.

In this chapter, we build from what you learned in Chapter 2 by determining, given the data, what the likely range of possible values for the coefficient estimates are, or how accurate the estimates are for how the variables move together. And, we will discuss the necessary statistics to conduct hypothesis tests for whether some factor is indeed related to the outcome.

5.1 Setting up the problem for hypothesis tests

Let's say that you want to explore the theory that the anti-bullying campaigns that today's teenagers are exposed to affect their empathy. In particular, you want to test whether current teenagers have a different level of empathy from the historical population of teenagers. Suppose you have a random sample of 25 teenagers. And, let's say that there is a questionnaire with a multitude of questions that are combined to give a standardized score on empathy that has, in the historic population of teenagers, a normal distribution with a mean of 100 and a standard deviation of 15. From your sample of current teenagers, let's say that you find that their average empathy score is a little higher than the historical average, with an average of 104. So, you want to conduct a hypothesis test to see whether there is evidence confirming the contention that current teenagers do indeed have a different level of empathy from the historical teenage average. (Note that I am initially testing for a *different level* and not a *higher level* of empathy. We will consider directional hypothesis testing later on.)

The test is really about how certain we can be to rule out randomness giving you the sample statistic that is different from 100, the historical mean. Randomness pervades our life. Randomness in getting the right coach can dictate the difference between making it or not in professional sports. For a student growing up in poverty, randomness in the teacher she gets could determine academic and financial success in life. Randomness on questions you are guessing on when taking the SAT could determine whether you get into your desired college, which could change the course of your life. Randomness could mean the difference between life and death on the battlefield. And, randomness can determine who you marry.

In statistics, randomness in outcomes can affect the empirical relationships between variables. The more observations there are, randomness will tend to have a smaller role in those relationships, and we can better gauge whether any relationships observed are real (whether large, small, or zero). And, randomness dictates the sample that you get when you draw from a larger population. The higher mean level of empathy in the sample of current teenagers means that either:

- They do have the same mean empathy level as the historical population of teenagers, and it was random variation that caused this sample of 25 teenagers to have a mean level of empathy that is 4 points off from the population mean of 100; or
- Current teenagers indeed have a different mean empathy level from the historical population of teenagers.

We want to determine whether the difference is large enough that we can rule out, with an adequate level of certainty, that the mean of current teenagers is still 100 and randomness is giving us the sample mean of 104. This would allow us to conclude that current teenagers do indeed have a significantly different empathy level from the historical teenage population.

The test procedures are:

1. Define the hypotheses:

    Null hypothesis: H_0: mean empathy of current teenagers = μ = 100

    Alternative hypothesis: H_1: mean empathy of current teenagers = $\mu \neq 100$

2. Determine the standard error of the estimate. To keep the calculations simpler for the sake of the exercise, let's assume that the sample of current teenagers have the same standard deviation (σ) of empathy of 15 as in the historical population – this allows us to use the normal distribution rather than the Student's t-distribution (if we didn't know the true standard deviation). The standard error of the mean is equal to: $\frac{\sigma}{\sqrt{n}} = \frac{15}{\sqrt{25}} = 3$. (See Appendix Section A.3) Note that sometimes the sample standard deviation (s) is used instead of the population standard deviation (σ), depending on whether σ is known.

3. Determine how certain you want to be for the test by establishing a statistical significance level. Most people use 95% certainty, which translates into a 5% (statistical) significance level. This would say that, if the null hypothesis were true, you allow a 5% chance that the random sample you have would show that the alternative hypothesis was true. That is, if the null hypothesis were true, you would make the wrong conclusion 5% of the time. (This does not say that that there is a 5% chance that the conclusion is wrong, as it just speaks to what happens if the null hypothesis were true.)

4. Starting with the assumption that the null hypothesis is true (the mean empathy for current teenagers is 100), determine whether 104 is different enough from the hypothesized value of 100 that we can rule out (with a high degree of certainty) that randomness gave us the sample mean (104) this far from the hypothesized value of 100. If so, we can *reject* the null hypothesis and *accept* the alternative hypothesis. We can see this graphically in Figure 5.1. In this figure, we make the safe assumption that there is a normal distribution for the current teenagers given that the underlying population has a normal distribution.

In Figure 5.1, I shade in the **rejection regions**, which mark the parts of the distribution of mean scores that would make us "reject" the null hypothesis that current teenagers have the same empathy as the rest of the population. They represent the "unlikely-to-occur" ranges. In this case, I make the rejection region represent 5% of the area under the curve, split between the left and right tails of the

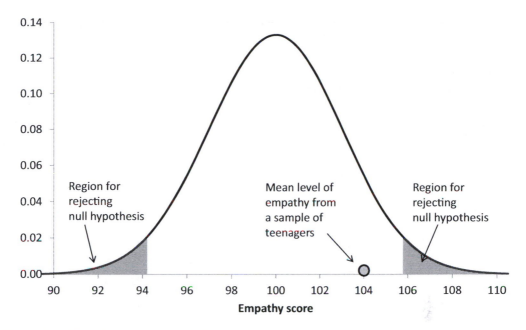

Figure 5.1 Hypothesis test example for a sample mean

distribution. So again, we would accept a 5% chance of being wrong if the null hypothesis were true. The critical values defining the rejection regions are:

$$100 \pm 1.96 \times 3 = 94.12, \ 105.88$$

(The value 1.96 is the z value that leaves 0.025 in each tail, or 0.05 total area or probability in the rejection regions. This comes from the standard normal distribution, as described in Appendix Section A.2. The value 3 is the standard error for the mean as calculated above.)

The teenagers' sample mean (104) is not in one of those rejection regions, so the sample mean is not far enough away from 100 that we can rule out randomness producing a different mean empathy level from that of the historical population. Thus, we cannot conclude that current teenagers have a different mean level of empathy. Note that we do not conclude that current teenagers have the same mean level of empathy, as we cannot prove a null hypothesis.

This was a two-sided test, formally testing whether current teenagers have a *different* mean level of empathy from the historical population. Alternatively, you could do a one-sided test, testing whether current teenagers have *higher* empathy than the population. In this case, the hypotheses would be:

$$H_0 : \mu \leq 100$$
$$H_1 : \mu > 100$$

The critical value would be: $100 + 1.645 \times 3 = 104.935$. (The z value of $+1.645$ is the z value that leaves all 0.05 in the right tail in the standard normal distribution.) Again, we could not conclude that current teenagers have a higher empathy level than the historical population of teenagers.

There is always the possibility that the conclusion of the test could be wrong. The two types of errors will be discussed in more detail in Section 5.2.7. Briefly, they are:

- Type I error (False Positive) – current teens have the same level of empathy as historical teens, but random sampling happens to produce a level of empathy that is significantly different from the historical value of 100.
- Type II error (False Negative) – current teens do have a different level of empathy, but we are not able to detect a statistically significant difference.

The reason for going through this exercise is that the same concepts are used to determine if randomness can reasonably be ruled out for a coefficient estimate to be different from zero or different from a particular number.

5.2 Hypothesis testing in regression analysis

5.2.1 The four steps

Hypothesis tests from regression analyses involve a similar set of four steps, as outlined above:

1. Define the hypotheses for a coefficient, with the most common being:
   Null hypothesis : $H_0 : \beta_i = 0$
   Alternative hypothesis: $H_1 : \beta_i \neq 0$
2. Determine the standard error of the coefficient estimate (typically produced by the statistical program).
3. Determine how certain you want to be for your test.
4. Starting with the assumption that the null hypothesis is true ($\beta_i = 0$), test whether the coefficient estimate, $\hat{\beta}_i$, is far enough from 0, given the standard error, to rule out (with the chosen level of certainty) that randomness gave us this estimate. If so, we can be fairly confident that some actual meaningful empirical association caused the coefficient estimate to be different from 0. Simultaneously, you can determine how confident you can be that the coefficient estimate is different from 0. (That said, it is debatable how confident we can be, as you will see in Section 5.3 below.)

With regression analysis, the Student's t-distribution is used. The Student's t-distribution (or, just t-distribution) is very much like the *standard normal* distribution, but it is a little wider. With samples of around 100 or more, the Student's t-distribution gets pretty close to the standard normal distribution. While one should have some understanding of reading a Student's t-distribution, statistical programs typically indicate the significance and certainty levels.

5.2.2 Standard errors

Let's consider the case with several explanatory variables from the income model we have been working with. Tables 5.1 and 5.2 show the results of a model with a dependent variable of 2003 income, as reported in the 2004 survey, using the original data set **income_data**. Table 5.1 shows the output from Stata, while Table 5.2 shows the R output. Note that there are differences in the output that is produced, with Stata giving a more complete picture (in my mind).

From Table 5.1, the top panels have overall regression statistics – the top-left three numbers (under SS) are *ExSS*, *RSS*, and *TSS*. The R^2, in the top-right panel, is 0.210. In the bottom panel of the table, the variables used in the model are listed. The variable definitions are:

- *income* (the dependent variable) = the person's income in 2003;
- *educ* = years-of-schooling completed;
- *afqt* = AFQT percentile;
- *ageyears* = age in 2003;
- *black* = 1 if the respondent is Black; = 0 otherwise;
- *hisp* = 1 if the respondent is Hispanic; = 0 otherwise;
- *mom_hs* = 1 if the respondent's mother completed at least 12 years-of-schooling; = 0 otherwise;
- *mom_coll* = 1 if the respondent's mother completed at least 16 years-of-schooling; = 0 otherwise;
- *dad_hs* = 1 if the respondent's father completed at least 12 years-of-schooling; = 0 otherwise;
- *dad_coll* = 1 if the respondent's father completed at least 16 years-of-schooling; = 0 otherwise.

Note that the variables for highest-grade-completed of the mother was missing for 808 respondents (6.4% of the initial 12,686 respondents), and the highest-grade-completed of the father was missing for 1806 respondents (14.2%). For the sake of keeping the observations for this exercise, I did the technically incorrect thing of merely giving these observations 11 years-of-schooling (meaning, they

Table 5.1 Stata output for regression of 2003 income on various factors

Source	SS	df	MS	Number of obs = 2772
				F(9, 2762) = 81.43
Model	1.47E+12	9	1.63440E+12	Prob > F = 0.0000
Residual	5.54E+12	2762	2.00710E+10	R-squared = 0.2097
Total	7.01E+12	2771	2.531.40E+10	Adj R-squared = 0.2071
				Root MSE = 44,800

income	Coef. estimate	Standard error	t value	[p-value]	[95% Conf. Interval]	
educ	5119	461	11.10	0.000	4215	6023
afqt	250	43	5.76	0.000	165	335
age	753	386	1.95	0.051	−4	1510
black	−6868	2331	−2.95	0.003	−11439	−2298
hisp	−76	2517	−0.03	0.976	−5012	4859
mom_hs	2025	2158	0.94	0.348	−2206	6256
mom_coll	2135	3638	0.59	0.557	−4999	9269
dad_hs	996	2126	0.47	0.639	−3173	5165
dad_coll	14840	3011	4.93	0.000	8936	20744
_cons	−59671	17699	−3.37	0.001	−94377	−24966

Source: Bureau of Labor Statistics, 2014.

Table 5.2 R output for regression of 2003 income on various factors

From summary() command

Residuals:

Min	1Q	Median	3Q	Max
−106269	−22127	−6816	9387	242031

	Estimate	Std. Error	t value	[p-value]
(Intercept)	−59671	17699	−3.37	0.001
educ	5119	461	11.11	< 2.00E−16
afqt	250	43	5.76	0.000
ageyears	753	386	1.95	0.051
black	−6868	2331	−2.95	0.003
hisp	−76	2517	−0.03	0.976
mom_hs	2025	2158	0.94	0.348
mom_coll	2135	3638	0.59	0.557
dad_hs	996	2126	0.47	0.639
dad_coll	14840	3011	4.93	0.000

Residual standard error: 44800 on 2762 degrees of freedom
Multiple R-squared: 0.2097, Adjusted R-squared: 0.2071
F-statistic: 81.43 on 9 and 2762 DF, p-value: < 2.2E − 16

From confint() command
(lower and upper bounds of 95% confidence intervals)

	2.5%	97.5%
(Intercept)	−94377	−24966
educ	4215	6023
afqt	165	335
ageyears	−4	1510
black	−11439	−2298
hisp	−5012	4859
mom_hs	−2206	6256
mom_coll	−4999	9269
dad_hs	−3173	5165
dad_coll	8936	20744

Source: Bureau of Labor Statistics, 2014.

would have a 0 for the educational variables of having a high school diploma or college degree). In Section 12.2, I discuss a better option for dealing with missing data.

The first number in each row represents the coefficient estimate on the given variable. The second number is the **standard error** of the given coefficient estimate. The standard error is a measure of how accurate the coefficient estimate is. Often standard errors are reported in studies in parentheses next to or under a coefficient estimate.

From the Appendix of Background Statistics Tools, an "estimator" is the best guess we have for what the true population estimate is. The coefficient estimate in a regression is an estimator as well. There is inevitably randomness in the estimate due to two major sources: (1) often having just a sample of the population; and (2) the outcome itself being subject to randomness. The **standard error** is the standard deviation of the sampling distribution for the coefficient estimate.

In some sense, the coefficient is a random variable in the population. For example, being Hispanic wouldn't affect income the same for all Hispanics. What would be estimated, if proper controls were included, would be an average causal effect of being Hispanic for the selected sample (Section 2.12). If we were to select a different sample, we would likely obtain a different estimated Hispanic effect.

The second major source of randomness comes from the unexpected and random things affecting outcomes. A student may be sick and perform worse on an exam than would be expected. An incorrect referee call can determine who wins a basketball game. A judge wavering between giving a score of 5.3 or 5.4 can determine who wins a gymnastics competition. As the outcome changes with these random events, the coefficient estimates linking explanatory variables to these outcomes will change. The more random the outcome is (marked by not being explained well by the set of explanatory variables), the greater would be the standard errors.

The formula for the standard error on a coefficient estimate on variable, X_j, is the following:

$$SE\left(\hat{\beta}_j\right) = \frac{\hat{\sigma}}{\sqrt{\sum\left(X_j - \bar{X}_j\right)^2 \times \left(1 - R_j^2\right)}} \quad (5.1)$$

where:

- $\hat{\sigma}$ is the Standard Error of the Regression or Root Mean Square Error (Section 2.5 and equation (2.16));
- R_j^2 is the R^2 from a regression of the variable X_j on the other X variables and a constant.

Note that, if there were no other X variables in the model other than X_j, then the second quantity in the numerator would be equal to one and would just disappear.

From the formula for the standard error of the coefficient estimate, we can determine that the following main factors would be associated with a *lower* standard error (which is always better) for some variable, X_j:

- A larger sample size (n is in the denominator in the formula for $\hat{\sigma}$ in equation (2.16));
- A smaller standard deviation in Y;
- A larger standard deviation in X_j (which gives more variation to explain Y);
- Less variation in X_j explained by the other X variables (which leads to a greater effective variation in X_j and allows the relationship between X_j and Y to be more easily separated from the relationships between other X variables and Y).

So, by reducing the Standard Error of the Regression, $\hat{\sigma}$, adding control variables reduces the standard error for the coefficient estimate on a given explanatory variable, X_k, provided the new variables are not too highly correlated with X_k. Of course, as you learned in Chapter 4 and will see again in Chapter 6, there are other factors that need to be considered before adding more control variables.

Perhaps a useful way to think about what affects the standard error is using the Venn diagrams, in which the size of the circle represents the variation in the variable. In Figure 5.2, the two diagrams are

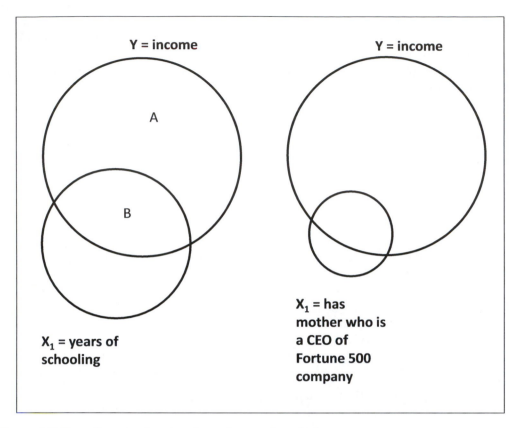

Figure 5.2 Venn diagrams showing determinants of standard errors

the one from Figure 4.4 on schooling and income and a new model that is trying to determine the effect on income from the variable, X_1, having a mother who is a CEO of a Fortune 500 company. Note that the circle for X_1 is much smaller for "having a CEO mother," which is the case because hardly anyone in the population has a mother who is a CEO of a Fortune 500 company, and so the variation in this variable would be small. Furthermore, compared to "years–of–schooling," less of the variation in Y is explained by "having a CEO mother." These forces would probably cause the standard error to be much larger for the coefficient estimates on "having a CEO mother" than for "years–of–schooling."

Sometimes, the standard error needs to be adjusted given the nature of the data or the model being used. I will discuss these issues and corrections in Section 6.6.

Box 5.1 Why macroeconomists are so bad at predicting recessions

Economists in the November 2007 Philadelphia Federal Reserve's Survey of Professional Fore-casters predicted 2008 GDP growth of 2.5% and estimated just a 3% chance of a recession.[1]

What makes this laughable is that this occurred just *one month before the Great Recession / Financial Crisis officially began.*

On a related note, in the Summer of 2015, I had a foul-shooting contest with LeBron James. The final score was:

LeBron:	60 of 68
Me:	56 of 68

Why did we shoot 68 free throws? (LeBron wondered the same thing.) You will see in a moment.

Can one conclude from this contest that LeBron is a better free throw shooter? Some may say yes, but a statistician would say that there are not enough observations to make such a conclusion, particularly given the small difference in our shooting percentages.

Now, imagine trying to predict a recession. Decent macro-economic data has been collected since 1947. Thus, there were only **68** years of good data on the economy (at the time of my imaginary contest with LeBron). In that time, there had only been 11 recessions. With so few observations, the standard errors on the coefficient estimates would be very large for any variable used to predict recessions because of the larger role that randomness has in smaller samples. Thus, it would be difficult to identify things that lead to a recession.

Referring back to an earlier point (Section 2.13), the economy has changed: a shift from manufacturing to technology, more energy-efficient technologies and vehicles, more financial instruments to spread risk which could stabilize (or destabilize) the economy, etc. Thus, what caused recessions in the past might be very different from what would cause a recession today. In the same vein, what helped stave off recessions in the past may be different from what helps stave off recessions today. In other words, causal effects can change over time. And, next time, I might beat LeBron.

5.2.3 t-statistics

The observed **t-statistic** or **t-stat** ($t_{observed}$ or t_o) for a coefficient estimate is simply:

$$t_o = \frac{coefficient\ estimate\left(\hat{\beta}\right)}{standard\ error\left(SE\left(\hat{\beta}\right)\right)} \tag{5.2}$$

In rare cases, the hypothesized value for the null hypothesis will be some number other than zero. In those cases, the numerator for the t-stat would be the coefficient estimate minus the hypothesized value.

The t-stat is the statistic that is used to test whether the coefficient estimate is statistically significant. This is the third number in each row in Table 5.1 (for Stata). As an example, the t-stat for the years-of-schooling variable (*educ*) is, rounding, 5119.4/461.0 = 11.10.

Note that, similar to the transformation to Z for the standard normal distribution (which I discuss in the Appendix Section A.2), the t-stat transformation involves subtracting out the hypothesized value (which is normally zero) and dividing by the standard error. And so, the t-stat is similar to the Z value in that it represents the number of standard errors away from zero that the coefficient estimate is. The more standard errors away from zero it is, the more certainty we can have that the true population parameter is not zero.

An important ingredient for the t-stat (for hypothesis tests) is the degrees of freedom. The number of **degrees of freedom** indicates the number of values that are free to estimate the parameters, which equals the number of observations minus the constraints (parameters to be estimated). Having more parameters to estimate reduces the freedom of variables to help explain other variables even though they should explain the other variables more accurately. The definition is:

$$\text{Degrees of freedom} = n - K - 1 = n - k$$

where
- n = sample size;
- K = # explanatory variables;
- $k = K + 1$ = # parameters to be estimated (the explanatory variables and the constant).

While computer programs typically indicate the degrees of freedom, you may need to calculate it in order to conduct manual tests or to construct confidence intervals, as demonstrated below.

In the next two sections, we apply the standard errors and the t-distribution in order to conduct the hypothesis tests and calculate p-values and confidence intervals. This would be appropriate as long as the error terms were normally distributed or at least approximately normally distributed (Assumption A.3 from Section 2.10). In cases in which the error terms were not normally distributed, these calculations would be incorrect. A simple solution to address the possibility of miscalculations due to non-normal error terms would be to require higher levels of significance to make certain conclusions. This will be discussed in more detail in Section 6.8.

5.2.4 Statistical significance and p-values

In a criminal trial, the hypotheses a jury weighs are:

- Null H_0 : The defendant is innocent.
- Alternative H_1 : The defendant is guilty.

The jury needs to determine if there is enough evidence to reject the null hypothesis with a high level of certainty (i.e., beyond a reasonable doubt) and accept the alternative hypothesis that the defendant is guilty. The jury does not need to establish that the null hypothesis is true, that the defendant is innocent.

Two-sided hypothesis tests

To test for the significance of a coefficient estimate, formally, you would start with the hypotheses, as in Section 5.2.1 above:

- Null H_0 : $\beta_i = 0$.
- Alternative H_1 : $\beta_i \neq 0$.

Just as in a criminal trial, we aim to test whether the null hypothesis can be disproven beyond a reasonable doubt. That is, we aim to test whether the coefficient estimate is far enough away from zero to conclude that it is **"statistically significant"** or **"significantly different from zero,"** signifying that the true coefficient is likely not zero. We do not aim to prove that the null is true (that $\beta_i = 0$).

With the t-stat, the statistical significance of a coefficient estimate can be determined. Note the language: *It is not a variable but rather it is the coefficient estimate that is statistically significant or insignificant.*

The test for significance for a coefficient estimate involves comparing the t-stat to critical values on the Student's t-distribution. As with the example with the mean level of empathy from a sample of current teenagers above, if the t-stat is beyond one of the critical values, in one of the tails of the distribution, then we can conclude that it is unlikely that randomness caused the estimate to be that far away from zero. We would then conclude that the coefficient estimate is statistically significant.

Figure 5.3 shows the rejection regions for the hypothesis test, based on having a 5% significance level. That is, the rejection regions are defined so as to have the probability of rejecting a true null hypothesis of 5%. To determine the critical t value ($t_{critical}$ or t_c) that defines the rejection regions, you can easily find online calculators to do this, or, in Excel:

- Use the command T.INV.2T (two-tail test).
- Plug in 0.05 for a 5% level of significance (or 0.01 for a hypothesis test based on a 1% level of significance).
- Plug in "degrees of freedom" = $n - K - 1 = 2772 - 9 - 1 = 2762$.

(This is for the coefficient estimate in Tables 5.1 and 5.2, with nine explanatory variables.)

- It should give you a critical value of $t_c = 1.9608$.

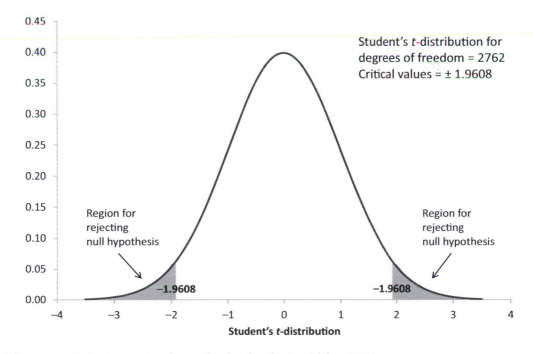

Figure 5.3 Rejection region for Student's t-distribution (d.f. = 2762)

And, one would reject the null hypothesis (that the coefficient estimate equals 0) if the *t*-stat were in the rejection region of greater than 1.9608 or less than −1.9608.

Based on the rejection regions, we can conclude from Tables 5.1 and 5.2 that *educ, afqt, black, dad_coll,* and the constant term have coefficient estimates different from zero (using the 5% significance level). That is, we can reject the null hypothesis at the 5% level for these four variables and the constant term. Note that the *t*-stat for *ageyears* is 1.95, which is close to the critical value, but not quite there. And, the other variables (*hisp, mom_hs, mom_coll,* and *dad_hs*) all have *t*-stats with an absolute value below 1.9608. Thus, their coefficient estimates are statistically insignificant. The critical values for significance at the 1% level would be ±2.578. These four variables (*educ, afqt, black,* and *dad_coll*) have *t*-stats exceeding these critical values, as well. Thus, they are also significant at the 1% level. Normally, we do not have to look up these critical values, as most statistical programs will indicate the statistical significance for us, as Stata does above, with the p-value.

The **p-value** indicates the likelihood that, if the true coefficient were actually zero, random processes (i.e., randomness from sampling or from determining the outcomes) would generate a coefficient estimate as far from zero as it is. In Tables 5.1 and 5.2, note how the larger the *t*-stat (t_o) is, the lower the p-value is, meaning that it is less likely that random processes would produce such a value if the null hypothesis ($\beta_i = 0$) were true.

These calculations are similar to equation (A.18) in the Appendix, in which we estimate the probability of obtaining a sample mean for IQ at least 2 standard deviations from the mean. Here we are calculating how likely it would be, if the null hypothesis were true that the population coefficient were zero, that we would obtain an estimate that is a certain number of standard errors away from zero. That "number of standard errors" would be the absolute value of the *t*-stat. And so, the calculation for, say, *mom_coll*, with a *t*-stat (expanding the decimal places) of 0.587, would be:

$$\text{p-value} = \Pr\left(|t| > 0.587\right) = \Pr\left(t < -0.587\right) + \Pr\left(t > 0.587\right) \tag{5.3}$$

Because the distribution is symmetrical, we just need to calculate one of the probabilities on the right-hand side and double it. The second term on the right-hand side equals 0.2786, so the p-value would be 0.557, which is indeed what Tables 5.1 and 5.2 indicate.

The relationship between the p-value and statistical significance is the following:

- (p-value < 0.10) = (statistical significance at the 10% level).
- (p-value < 0.05) = (statistical significance at the 5% level).
- (p-value < 0.01) = (statistical significance at the 1% level).
- . . . and so on.

Based on the results, we can determine that the following variables have coefficient estimates that are statistically significant at the 1% level (i.e., p-values less than 0.01): *educ, afqt, black,* and *dad_coll*. That is, we can be pretty certain of the patterns that, *holding the other factors constant*, people with more schooling, a higher AFQT score, and a father with a higher level of education have higher income, while those who are Black have lower income, holding these other factors constant. The coefficient estimate on "age" has a p-value of 0.051. This means that it is not significant at the 5% level. However, it is significant at the 10% level. Remember, we have *not* made the case that these are causal effects. We need some theory and stories to sort through the alternative explanations before concluding whether any of these are causal effects or possibly related to each other for other reasons.

The coefficient estimates on Hispanic, the two variables for mother's education, and the variable on father's college degree are statistically insignificant, as the p-values are above 0.10, which is considered the maximum p-value for even weak statistical significance.

All this said, the p-value does not indicate how certain one can be that a given estimate signifies a real empirical relationship between an explanatory variable and the outcome. As I will discuss in Section 5.3, there are many problems with using the p-value, despite it being the standard statistic used to gauge how confident we can be on an empirical relationship.

Furthermore, people tend to put too much weight on the primary thresholds of statistical significance – 5% and 10%. Researchers tend to label an estimate with a p-value of 0.049 to be a "significant predictor," but an estimate with a p-value of 0.051 to be a "weakly significant predictor," or "insignificant predictor." As you can see, there is little difference between how significant they are, so randomness or bias could cause the difference in significance.

Finally, let me note that, if two or more explanatory variables are highly correlated, they may be sharing any "effect" or empirical relationship with the dependent variable. This may cause the variables to, individually, have statistically insignificant coefficient estimates even though collectively they are significantly related to the dependent variable. One option in such a situation is to exclude one or more of the correlated explanatory variables to see if the one remaining in the model has a significant coefficient estimate. A second option is to test the joint significance of the coefficient estimates. I will demonstrate this "joint significance test" test in Section 5.2.6.

One-sided hypothesis tests

While most tests on statistical significance are based on two-sided tests, the more appropriate test may be one-sided. This should be used when it is clear, theoretically, that an X variable could affect the outcome only in one direction. For example, we can be pretty certain that, on average and holding all the other factors constant, Blacks will get paid less than Whites and older people would be paid more than younger people at least for the age range of our data (38 to 46). Thus, we can form a hypothesis test on whether the coefficient on the variable, *black*, is negative and that on the variable, *ageyears*, is positive. Making the test one-sided makes it easier to reject the null hypothesis (which may not be a good thing).

For *ageyears*, the hypotheses would be:

- $H_0: \beta_i \leq 0$.
- $H_1: \beta_i > 0$.

In contrast with the procedures for the two-sided test in Figure 5.3, the rejection region for this one-sided test will be entirely in the right tail of the *t*-distribution. To find the critical value that defines the rejection region for a hypothesis test, based on having a 5% significance level, in Excel:

- Use the command T.INV (one-tail test) – this is a left-tail test, so you may have to reverse the sign.
- Plug in 0.05 for a 5% level of significance (or 0.01 for a hypothesis test based on a 1% level of significance).
- Plug in "degrees of freedom" = 2762.

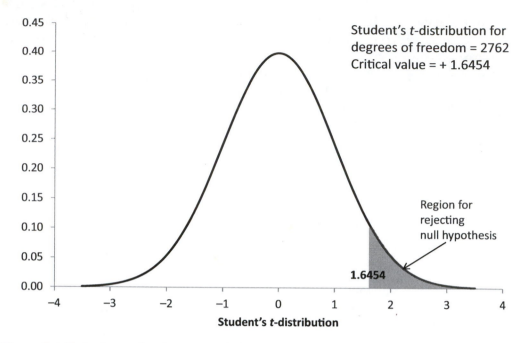

Figure 5.4 Rejection region for a one-sided hypothesis test, Student's *t*-distribution (d.f. = 2762)

- It should give you $t_c = -1.6454$.
- Reverse the sign to $t_c = 1.6454$, since it is a right-tailed test and the *t*-distribution is symmetric.

You would then compare the *t*-stat on the coefficient estimate on the variable, *ageyears*, with that critical value of 1.6454. The graphical representation of this test is Figure 5.4. The *t*-stat on *ageyears* is 1.95 (from Tables 5.1 and 5.2), so it now lies in the rejection region, and we can reject the null hypothesis that the true coefficient on *ageyears* is less than or equal to zero and accept the alternative hypothesis that age is positively related to income, holding the other factors constant.

Pretty much all researchers (me included, including in the last sub–section) make the wrong official interpretation of two–sided tests. We would take, say the coefficient estimate and *t*-stat (−3.13) on *black* from Tables 5.1 and 5.2 and conclude: "being Black is associated with significantly lower income than non-Hispanic Whites (the reference group)." But, the proper interpretation is "being Black is associated with significantly different income from non-Hispanic Whites."

The reason why people make this incorrect interpretation and why it is okay is that, if it passes a two–sided test, then it would pass the one–sided test in its direction as well. This is because the rejection region for a one–sided test would be larger in the relevant direction than for a two–sided test. So, the two–sided test is, in fact, a stricter test.

5.2.5 Confidence intervals

Confidence intervals indicate the interval which you can be fairly "confident" that the value of the true coefficient lies in. Assuming that the sample is randomly drawn from the population of interest, a 95% confidence interval (the standard percentage) is the one in which you can be 95% confident that the true coefficient estimate lies in that interval. This does not mean that we can be 95% confident that the true *causal effect* lies in that interval, as this requires that the coefficient estimate is unbiased as an estimate of the causal effect.

The formula for a confidence interval for the true population value of a coefficient, β, in a given model is:

$$\hat{\beta} \pm t_c \times \text{SE}\left(\hat{\beta}\right) \text{ or } \left[\hat{\beta} - t_c \times \text{SE}\left(\hat{\beta}\right), \hat{\beta} + t_c \times \text{SE}\left(\hat{\beta}\right)\right] \tag{5.4}$$

where
- α = the significance level;
- t_c = the critical value from the Student's t-distribution giving $\alpha/2$ in each tail, based on degrees of freedom = $n - K - 1$ (n = # observations; K = # explanatory variables);
- $\text{SE}\left(\hat{\beta}\right)$ = standard error on the coefficient estimate for β.

This means that:

$$Pr\left[\beta \text{ is in } (\hat{\beta} - t_c \times SE\left(\hat{\beta}\right), \hat{\beta} + t_c \times SE\left(\hat{\beta}\right)\right] = 1 - \alpha \tag{5.5}$$

To determine the critical t value, use the same method as outlined above (in Section 5.2.4). So, from Table 5.1, the 95% confidence interval for the coefficient estimate on *ageyears* would be:

$$752.8 \pm 1.9608 \times 386.2 = (-4.4, 1510.1)$$

Note that the interval includes zero. In fact there is a relationship between statistical significance (for two-sided hypothesis tests) and confidence intervals:

- [Significant at the 5% level (p < 0.05)] ↔ [95% confidence interval does not include 0]
- [Insignificant at the 5% level (p > 0.05)] ↔ [95% confidence interval includes 0]

In Tables 5.1 and 5.2, the 95% confidence intervals for *educ*, *afqt*, and the other variables with estimates with p < 0.05 do not include zero.

Confidence intervals do not receive the credit and use that they should. A coefficient estimate is typically just the central and best guess on the true estimated effect or association. But, the confidence interval has much more information, as it indicates the range of likely values. This is especially important for estimates that are only borderline statistically significant, as an estimated large effect could have a small and inconsequential effect within the realm of possibilities.

For example, the best guess for the association between *ageyears* and *income* is an extra $780 per year. But, an estimate as low as $0 is in the "plausible" range, as it is within the 95% confidence interval.

5.2.6 F-tests for joint hypothesis tests and overall significance

The hypothesis tests so far have dealt with one coefficient estimate. But, one may be interested in whether a set of variables is collectively statistically significant. Likewise, one may want to understand whether all the explanatory variables together in a model have statistical significance – something that the R^2 statistic, by itself, does not indicate. Both tests use the F-distribution.

Joint hypothesis tests

The formal hypothesis test, for four variables, $X_1 - X_4$, would be:

- $H_0: \beta_1 = \beta_2 = \beta_3 = \beta_4 = 0$ (for corresponding explanatory variables X_1, X_2, X_3, X_4).
- H_1: one of the β's does not equal 0.

This joint hypothesis test (sometimes called the Chow/Wald test) involves calculation of the F-statistic, which is:[2]

$$F_{n-k}^{k-1} = \frac{\left(\sum \hat{\varepsilon}_{RR}^2 - \sum \hat{\varepsilon}_{UR}^2\right) / m}{\left(\sum \hat{\varepsilon}_{UR}^2\right) / (n-k)_{UR}} \tag{5.6}$$

where:
- $\sum \hat{\varepsilon}_{UR}^2$ is the Sum of Squared Residuals in the unrestricted regression (UR), in which all variables are included;
- $\sum \hat{\varepsilon}_{RR}^2$ is the Sum of Squared Residuals in the restricted regression (RR), in which variables X_1, X_2, X_3, and X_4 are excluded from the model (assuming there is at least one other explanatory variable that remains);
- m is the number of variables being excluded (four, in this case);
- $(n - k)_{UR}$ is the degrees of freedom in the original unrestricted regression, with n being the sample size and k being the number of explanatory variables (K) plus one.

As an example of the joint hypothesis test, let's consider the four variables on parents' education in Table 5.1 in Section 5.2.2. Estimating the original model, with all four parents' education variables, produces an RSS of (5.5436e + 12) or (5.5436×10^{12}). The model without those four variables produces an RSS of (5.6190×10^{12}). Thus, the F-statistic is:

$$F_o = \frac{\left(5.6190 \times 10^{12} - 5.5436 \times 10^{12}\right) / 4}{\left(5.5436 \times 10^{12}\right) / (2772 - 9 - 1)} = \frac{0.018885 \times 10^{12}}{0.0020007 \times 10^{12}} = 9.40 \tag{5.7}$$

The critical F value at the 5% significance level, with degrees of freedom of 4 (m) in the numerator and 2762 ($n - K - 1$) in the denominator, is 2.375. This can be determined in Excel with the function, F.INV.RT (using 0.05 probability and 4 and 2762 as the degrees of freedom). Given that the F-statistic of 9.40 exceeds the critical value of 2.375, we can reject the null hypothesis and conclude, at the 5% significance level, that the variables are jointly significant. If we wanted to calculate a p-value, we use the Excel command F.DIST.RT, and plug in the test statistic of 9.40 and the degrees of freedom, which should give you 0.00000015. If we were to just test the mother's education variables, we get an F-statistic of 0.67, which is statistically insignificant.

Thus, we would say that all the coefficient estimates on the four parents' education variables are jointly significant, but the coefficient estimates on the two mother's education variables are not jointly significant.

Overall-significance test

For overall significance, the hypothesis test would be:

$H_0: \beta_1 = \beta_2 = \dots \beta_K = 0$ (for a model with K explanatory variables $X_1, X_2, \dots X_K$).
H_1: one of the β's does not equal 0.

With $k = K + 1$ (number of parameters to be estimated equals number of explanatory variables plus one), the test statistic is:

$$F_{n-k}^{k-1} = \frac{(ExSS)/(k-1)}{(RSS)/(n-k)} = \frac{R^2}{(1-R^2)} * \frac{(n-k)}{(k-1)} \tag{5.8}$$

This would actually be the same as equation (5.6) above if all of the variables were being tested in equation (5.6). In the original model from Table 5.1, the regression output automatically gives the test statistic, with $K = 9$ (nine variables) of $F(9, 2792) = 81.43$, which is easily statistically significant, with a p-value of zero.

The overall-significance test is not that common a test. Most regressions that see the light of day would have some significant coefficient estimates, which is a good sign that the overall regression has significance. Furthermore, the test itself has minimal bearing on any of the four main objectives of regression analysis. I rarely see the overall-significance test in published research studies.

The joint hypothesis test is also rare, but it has more value. This is particularly the case when there are two variables that are highly correlated. They may be individually statistically insignificant (due to splitting explanatory power for the dependent variable), but they may be collectively or jointly significant.

Tests for linear combinations of variables

In some cases, one may want to test whether two coefficients are equal. From a regression equation

$$Y = \beta_1 X_1 + \beta_2 X_2 + \beta_3 X_3 + \varepsilon_i$$

one could test whether $\beta_2 = \beta_3$. This would be equivalent to the test for whether $\beta_2 - \beta_3 = 0$.

Under the null hypothesis (that $\beta_2 - \beta_3 = 0$):

$$\left(\hat{\beta}_2 - \hat{\beta}_3\right) \sim Normal\left(0, Var\left(\hat{\beta}_2 - \hat{\beta}_3\right)\right) \tag{5.9}$$

$$\text{with } Var(\hat{\beta}_2 - \hat{\beta}_3) = Var(\hat{\beta}_2) + Var(\hat{\beta}_3) - 2 \times Cov(\hat{\beta}_2, \hat{\beta}_3).$$

The test for this would then use the Student's t-distribution:

$$t_o = \frac{\left(\hat{\beta}_2 - \hat{\beta}_3\right)}{SE\left(\hat{\beta}_2 - \hat{\beta}_3\right)} \tag{5.10}$$

with the same degrees of freedom as with the test for a single parameter $(n - K - 1)$.

Note that if one were testing whether $\beta_2 + \beta_3$ equaled some value, the variance of the distribution would be $Var(\hat{\beta}_2 + \hat{\beta}_3) = Var(\hat{\beta}_2) + Var(\hat{\beta}_3) + 2 \times Cov(\hat{\beta}_2, \hat{\beta}_3)$.

5.2.7 False positives and false negatives

As Jay Leno alluded to (in Chapter 1), a good portion of research will be wrong. Many of the reasons that will be given in Chapter 6 have to do with modeling and data problems, or the pitfalls of regression analysis. But, even with a perfectly executed regression (i.e., without any pitfalls or biases), the wrong conclusion may result from any hypothesis test. We can classify incorrect conclusions from hypothesis tests into two categories:

- **Type I error** (false positive), in which the null hypothesis is true, but it is rejected. In practice, this means that one factor has no significant relationship with the outcome, but the regression mistakenly finds statistically significant evidence for a relationship. In a criminal trial, this would be convicting an innocent defendant. (The "positive" term in "false positive" refers to a non-zero relationship – not necessarily a positively correlated relationship.)
- **Type II error** (false negative), in which the null hypothesis is false (the factor is related to the outcome), but the regression does not find evidence for a statistically significant estimate. In a criminal trial, this would be acquitting a guilty defendant. (The "negative" term refers to no empirical relationship – not a negatively correlated relationship.)

Conventionally, the probability of a Type I error (a false positive), typically labeled as α, would be the significance level at which one is using to test the coefficient estimate. Typically, 5% is used, so 5% would be the probability of a Type I error. However, as you will see in Section 5.3, the conventionally used probability of a Type I error (the significance level) can severely understate the true probability of a Type I error. That is, there are many more false positives in the research world than has been conventionally thought.

Calculating the probability of a Type II error, typically labeled β, is more complicated. It requires an alternative hypothesis for the coefficient estimate. I will spare you the calculation – it's ugly – but this probability will be lower if:

- The alternative hypothesis for the population coefficient is further from zero;
- The probability of a Type I error (α) is larger.

Many proposals to obtain research grant funding require a calculation of **statistical power** (or, just "power") for reasonable coefficient estimates. The power of a model is the probability that a model rejects the null hypothesis if the null hypothesis is false – that is, what is the probability that, if there were a real empirical relationship of some size, the model would capture that relationship with statistical significance. The power of a model is the opposite of a Type II error (power = $1 - \beta$). Such calculations are somewhat arbitrary and involve many assumptions, such as the size of a given effect, but a power of 0.80 is typically considered adequate.

5.2.8 Statistical vs. practical significance

With enough observations, standard errors decrease and the likelihood of a coefficient estimate being statistically significant increases. But, just because it is statistically significant does not mean that the estimated effect is meaningful. That is, it may not be practically significant.

A good example comes from Box 8.1 in Section 8.1. I describe Pope and Schweitzer's (2011) study on whether professional golfers' strategy is subject to "loss aversion," a cognitive bias that people go to costly efforts to avoid a loss. The "loss" in this situation would be a score worse than par – bogey or worse. So, loss aversion would mean that the golfers try harder for a par putt than for a birdie or eagle putt because missing a par putt would put them in "the domain of losses." Of the eight models in their Table 3, I personally prefer column (4), and I'll describe why in Box 8.1. One practically and economically significant result is that players are less likely to make a birdie or eagle putt than a par putt by about 3–4 percentage points, holding constant the distance and many other factors. This does suggest that they play it too safe on the birdie putts particularly to avoid getting bogey (a relative loss). But, another result is that players have a higher probability of making a putt for bogey by 0.3 percentage points. This estimate is statistically significant ($p < 0.01$), but I would call it practically insignificant. It means that any difference in effort or risk for bogey putts causes one extra made putt every 300 or so bogey putt attempts. Given that the median player has less than 3 bogeys per round, this result appears not to be practically important, despite its statistical significance.

The opposite is that, when there are too few observations, standard errors are higher, making it difficult to detect statistical significance. Thus, there could be a meaningful estimated effect that is unbiased but is deemed insignificant because the standard errors are too high. This would be a "false negative," or Type II error.

Box 5.2   Do we really know who the best hitters in baseball are each year?

Can there be a case in which something is not statistically significant but is perceived to be practically significant? Think of baseball batting crowns, which go to the player with the highest batting average in each (American and National) league. The player who has the highest batting average in a league is considered to have a *practically significant* advantage because they are crowned the best hitter in the league. But, it is very rare that the difference between the batting champion and the runner-up is *statistically significant.*

For a 0.350-hitting batting champion (35 hits for every 100 at-bats), assuming 600 at-bats, the runner-up would need a batting average of less than 0.323 (at least 0.027 lower) for us to be able to conclude that the batting champion was indeed the better hitter. (This, of course, assumes that other factors are the same between the top hitters, including opponent-pitcher quality.) In the past 25 years, only 4 of the 50 batting champions (two in each league) have beaten the runner-up by a statistically significant margin (at the 5% level). This would just be 1.5 more times than the expected 2.5 times that it would occur (in 50 instances) just by chance or a Type I error, if the top two hitters had exactly the same batting skills every year. So, batting champions are crowned even though we are rarely certain that they are indeed the best hitters in a given year.

5.3 The drawbacks of p-values and statistical significance

A thousand phenomena present themselves daily which we cannot explain, but where facts are suggested, bearing no analogy with the laws of nature as yet known to us, their verity needs proofs proportioned to their difficulty.

– Thomas Jefferson

The main statistic to determine how certain one can be that an observed empirical relationship is real has been the p-value or significance level. In the last several years, however, there has been increased criticism of using p–values. *The p-value, as it turns out, is not an objective indicator of whether the estimate you find is different from the hypothesized value (typically zero).*

As described above, the p–value indicates the likelihood that, if the coefficient were actually zero, random processes would generate a coefficient estimate as far from zero as it is. But, whereas most perceive this to mean that the probability that the statistical relationship is real is one minus the p–value, the actual probability the statistical relationship is real requires extra information. John Ioannidis (2005) argued that the probability that a research finding is true depends on three important pieces of information:

• The *prior* probability that there is an effect or relationship (pretty nebulous, eh?);
• The **statistical power** of the study (which depends on the probability of a false negative and requires an alternative hypothesized value);
• The significance of the coefficient estimate.

The p–value is based just on the last one.

Regina Nuzzo (2014) demonstrated how these *prior* probabilities matter. She calculated the probability that an estimated relationship is real for a given p–value, given various levels of the prior probability. Table 5.3 shows her calculations.[3]

• A p–value of 0.05 is usually the standard for determining statistical significance and is typically interpreted as there being 95% certainty that the empirical relationship is real. But, the calculations show that if the prior probability is a toss–up (i.e., a 50% chance that there is a non-zero relationship between two variables), then a p–value of 0.05 indicates that there is only a 71% chance that there is a real empirical relationship.
• A p–value of 0.01, which is usually considered very strong evidence, is only correct 89% of the time for a toss–up. (This blew my mind when I read about this! This conventionally used indicator of "strong evidence," a p–value less than 0.01, actually does not meet the criteria for "weak evidence," which is typically 90% certainty.) And, for a long–shot (such as whether a newly developed drug could affect certain medical conditions), an estimate that is significant at even the 1% level has less than a 1-in-3 chance of being correct. Wow!!

Let me demonstrate the problem with some real data. It has been shown that, from 1999 to 2009, the number of films Nicolas Cage appeared in for a given year was highly correlated with the number

Table 5.3 The probability that an estimated relationship is real for various p–values and prior probabilities

	Prior probability of an effect	*p-value for estimate*	*Probability that the effect is real*
"Long-shot"	5%	0.05	11%
	5%	0.01	30%
"Toss-up"	50%	0.05	71%
	50%	0.01	89%
"Good-bet"	90%	0.05	96%
	90%	0.01	99%

Source: Nuzzo (2014).

of people who drowned in a swimming pool in the U.S., with a correlation coefficient of 0.67.[4] A regression using the 11 observations gives:

$$(\#\ pool\ \overset{\frown}{drownings}) = 87.1 + 5.8 \times (\#\ Nicolas\ Cage\ movies)$$

The coefficient estimate of 5.8 has a p-value of 0.025.[5] The conventional method would say that we can conclude at the 5% level of significance (i.e., with greater than 95% certainty, or more precisely, 97.5% certainty) that the number of Nicolas Cage movies is empirically related to the number of pool drownings. But, it would be misguided to think that there was a causal effect or a systematic empirical relationship occurring. His movies are not *that* bad!

The problem is that we could do the same for the top 1000 actors/actresses, and we would get some statistically significant relationship (at the 5% level of significance) for about 5% of them – this is a Type I error, as described in Section 5.2.7. I'd bet my Nicolas Cage movie collection (even *Moonstruck*) that his movies do not cause drownings. Rather, Nicolas Cage just happens to be one of those 50 or so out of 1000 for the 1999–2009 period; and without looking at the data, I'd bet my Kevin Bacon movie collection on him being one also. (There are two interpretations of my willingness to make the Kevin Bacon bet.)

To account for the likelihood that 5% of actors/actresses would have a significant coefficient estimate by chance, the prior probability that there is a relationship needs to be accounted for. If we were to do so, then we would probably come to the correct conclusions, which I am guessing is that the number of films for any actor/actress in a year is not empirically related, in any meaningful way, to the number of drownings.

A related problem that also casts doubt on the p-value is that null hypotheses are almost always false – almost everything is related statistically by a non-zero amount. Many of these relationships are so small that they are meaningless, but with a large enough sample, p-values would indicate significance and null hypotheses would be rejected. (This is where the statistical significance vs. practical significance issue comes into play.) What this suggests is that, with larger samples, the p-value thresholds for determining significance should be lower.

Does all of this mean that the typical approach of using p-values, called the "frequentist approach," is no longer any good? Probably not. I doubt it's going away anytime soon. The resistance to changing approaches is that once you introduce the prior probability, as is needed in the new approach, the statistical testing becomes subjective. There would no longer be the nice objectiveness of the current standard of using p-values.

What is the best approach given these issues?

This lesson indicates that we should heed the (Carl) Sagan Standard, that "extraordinary claims require extraordinary evidence." This is in line with the Thomas Jefferson quote to open this section. Unfortunately, there is no straightforward solution to this problem. One large problem is that any calculation of the true probability that an empirical relationship is real requires some assumptions on the prior probabilities of various magnitudes of the relationship. Instead of going down this path, what many researchers do these days is an "informal Bayesian approach," which involves:

- Using p-values of 0.01 as the benchmark, and being skeptical of results with p-values of 0.10 or 0.05 unless they are backed by strong prior probabilities of there being a relationship.

- Lowering those p-value thresholds when sample sizes are very large. Unfortunately, no one has come up with a theoretically backed rule of thumb on what thresholds to use.
- Using many robustness checks to determine if the results stand up to alternative specifications. For example, add or cut some control variables to see if the main estimates remain statistically significant. A problem with this is that the alternative specifications would likely be highly correlated with the "best" model.
- Focusing on practical significance as well as economic significance.
- Being cautious with interpretations. When significance is not strong (e.g., a p-value greater than 0.01), then perhaps the most that can be said is that the data "support the theory." A typical interpretation of "strong evidence" may be misleading.

5.4 What the research on the hot hand in basketball tells us about the existence of other life in the universe

A friend of mine, drawn to the larger questions on life, called me recently and said that we are all alone – that humans are the only intelligent life in the universe. Rather than questioning him on the issue I have struggled with (whether humans, such as myself, should be categorized as "intelligent" life), I decided to focus on the main issue he raised and asked how he came to such a conclusion. Apparently, he had installed one of those contraptions in his backyard that searches for aliens. Honestly, he has so much junk in his backyard that I hadn't even noticed. He said that he hadn't received any signals in two years, so we must be alone.

While I have no idea whether we are alone in the universe, I know that my curious friend is not alone in his logic. A recent *Wall Street Journal* article made a similar logical conclusion in an article with some plausible arguments on why humans may indeed be alone in the universe. But, one of those arguments was based on the "deafening silence" from the 40-plus year Search for Extraterrestrial Intelligence (SETI) project, saying that this is strong evidence that there is no other intelligent life (Metaxas, 2014). Never mind that SETI only searches our galaxy (of the estimated 170-plus billion galaxies in the universe) and that for us to find life on some planet, we have to be aiming our SETI at that planet (instead of the other 100 billion or so planets in our galaxy) at the same time (within the 13.2 billion years our galaxy has been in existence) that the alien geeks on that planet are emitting strong-enough radio signals in our direction (with a 600-plus-year lag for the radio signals to reach us). It may be that some form of aliens sent radio signals our way 2.8 billion years ago ~~(before they went extinct after eliminating their Environmental Protection Agency)~~, and our amoeba-like ancestors had not yet developed the SETI technology to detect the signals.

The flawed logic here, as you have probably determined, is that lack of evidence is not proof of non-existence. This is particularly the case when you have a weak test for what you are looking for.

This logic flaw happens to be very common among academics. And, one line of research that has been subject to such faulty logic is that on the hot hand in basketball. The "hot hand" is a situation in which a player has a period (often within a single game) with a systematically higher probability of making shots (holding the difficulty of the shot constant) than the player normally would have. The hot hand can occur in just about any other sport or activity, such as baseball, bowling, dance, test-taking, etc. In basketball, virtually all players and fans believe in the hot hand, based on witnessing players such as Stephen Curry go through stretches in which they make a series of high-difficulty shots. Yet, from 1985 to 2009, plenty of researchers tested for the hot hand in basketball by using various tests to essentially determine whether a player was more likely to make a shot after a made shot (or consecutive made shots) than after a missed shot. They found no evidence for the hot hand. Their conclusion was "the hot hand is a myth."

But then a few articles, starting in 2010, found evidence for the hot hand. And, as Stone (2012), Arkes (2013), and Miller and Sanjurjo (2018) show, the tests for the studies in the first 25 years were pretty weak tests for the hot hand because of some modeling problems, one of which I will describe in Box 6.3 in the next chapter.

The conclusions from those pre-2010 studies should not have been "the hot hand is a myth," but rather "there is no evidence for the hot hand in basketball." The lack of evidence was not proof of non-existence of the hot hand. Using the same logic, in the search for aliens, the lack of evidence is not proof of non-existence, especially given that the tests have been weak.[6] I'd bet my friend's SETI machine that the other life forms out there, if they exist, would make the proper conclusions on the basketball hot hand (and that they won't contact us until we collectively get it right on the hot hand).

5.5 What does an insignificant estimate tell you?

The basic reason why the lack of evidence is not proof of non-existence is because there are alternative reasons for the lack of evidence. As mentioned earlier, when a jury in a criminal trial deliberates on whether a defendant is guilty, the jury is not directed to conclude that the defendant has been proven innocent. Rather, they are supposed to determine whether there is significant evidence (beyond a reasonable doubt) that indicates the defendant was guilty. Thus, one reason why a defendant may be found "not guilty" is that there was not enough evidence.

The same concept is *supposed to* be used for statistical analysis. We are often testing whether a coefficient estimate is different from zero. Let's say we are examining how class size affects students' test scores. And, let's say that we find an insignificant estimate on class size. In a recent study of mine (Arkes 2016), I list four general possible explanations for an insignificant estimate:

1. There is actually no effect of the explanatory variable on the outcome in the population.
2. There is an effect in one direction, but the model is unable to detect the effect due to a modeling problem (e.g., omitted-variables bias or measurement error – see Chapter 6) biasing the coefficient estimate in a direction opposite to the actual effect.
3. There is a small effect that cannot be detected with the available data due to inadequate power – i.e., not a large enough sample given the size of the effect.
4. There are varying effects in the population (or sample); some people's outcomes may be affected positively from the treatment, others' outcomes may be affected negatively, and others' outcomes may not be affected; and the estimated effect (which is the average effect) is insignificantly different from zero due to positive and negative effects canceling each other out or being drowned out by those with zero effects.

So, what can you conclude from the insignificant estimate on the "class size" variable? You cannot conclude that class size does not affect test scores. Rather, as with the hot hand and the search for aliens, the interpretation should be: "There is no evidence that class size affects test scores."

Unfortunately, a very common mistake made in the research world is that the conclusion would be that there is no effect. This is important for issues such as whether there are side effects from pharmaceutical drugs or vaccines. The lack of evidence for a side effect does not mean that there is no effect, particularly if confidence intervals for the estimates include values that would represent meaningful side effects of the drug or vaccine.

All that said, there are sometimes cases in which an insignificant estimate has a 95% or 99% confidence interval with a fairly narrow range and outer boundary that, if the boundary were the true population parameter, it would be "practically insignificant" (see Section 5.2.8 above). If this were the case and the coefficient estimate were not subject to any meaningful bias, then it would be safe to conclude that "there is no meaningful effect."

Sometimes, there could be hidden information behind an insignificant estimate. Consider the fourth reason for the lack of a significant estimate: that different segments of the population could experience different effects of a treatment. An important issue in the world of military manpower is how servicemen and servicewomen are affected by hostile deployments, which are basically deployments that involve being put in danger from an enemy combatant. Of great concern to the military is how hostile deployments affect the probability that someone reenlists. For some who do not like danger, a hostile deployment could reduce the probability of reenlisting. However, for others, a hostile deployment might be exciting or give them more of a sense of protecting the country. For these latter types, a hostile deployment could increase the probability of reenlistment. It is possible that, when estimating the effects of a hostile deployment, these negative and positive effects cancel each other out. Thus, the hidden information could be that there are real effects (in one or both directions), but the model is unable to capture those effects.

In some cases, the counteracting positive and negative effects are not important, as a researcher may be interested only in the average effect. For example, the military might be more concerned with how reenlistment rates would be affected. But, it would be incorrect to conclude from an insignificant estimate that a hostile deployment has no effect, in part, because it very well could affect people, but just in opposing directions.

Let me also note that a statistically significant estimate may also be subject to some of these issues/interpretations from the list above. Any estimate (insignificant or significant) is potentially subject to modeling problems (reason #2). Inadequate power could mean that a significant estimate still has wide confidence intervals that include numbers that would indicate a practically insignificant relationship between variables (reason #3). And, a significant estimate in one direction could be mitigated, to some extent, by a counteracting effect in the other direction for some segment of the population (reason #4).

In sum, in Section 2.8, I discussed how there could be a correlation without causation. What I have discussed in this section is an example of there being causation without a correlation, or at least without an observed or statistically significant correlation. One variable may have a causal effect on another variable, but inadequate data or modeling problems may preclude the detection of any correlation, or opposing effects may cancel each other out.

5.6 Statistical significance is not the goal

As we conduct research, our ultimate goal should be to advance knowledge. Our goal should not be to find a statistically significant estimate. Advancing knowledge occurs by conducting objective and honest research.

A statistically *insignificant* coefficient estimate on a key explanatory variable is just as valid as a *significant* coefficient estimate. The problem, many believe, is that an insignificant estimate may not provide as much information as a significant estimate. As described in the previous section, an insignificant estimate does not necessarily mean that there is no meaningful relationship, and so it could have multiple possible interpretations. If the appropriate confidence intervals for the coefficient were narrow (which would indicate adequate power), the methods were convincing for ruling out modeling problems, and the effects would likely go in just one direction, then it would be more reasonable to conclude that an insignificant estimate indicates there is no meaningful effect of the treatment. But, meeting all those conditions is rare, and so there are multiple possible conclusions that cannot be distinguished between.

As mentioned in the previous section, a statistically significant estimate could also be subject to the various interpretations of insignificant estimates. But, these are often ignored and not deemed as important, to most people, as long as there is statistical significance.

Statistical significance is valued more, perhaps, because it is evidence confirming, to some extent, the researcher's theory and/or hypothesis. I conducted a quick, informal review of recent issues of leading economic, financial, and education journals. As it has been historically, almost all empirical studies had statistically significant coefficient estimates on the key explanatory variable. Indeed, I had a difficult time finding an insignificant estimate. This suggests that the pattern continues that journals are more likely to publish studies with significant estimates on the key explanatory variables.

It is unfortunate that insignificant estimates are not accepted more. But, hopefully, this book will be another stepping stone for the movement to be more accepting of insignificant estimates. I personally trust insignificant estimates more than significant estimates (except for the hot hand in basketball).

The bottom line is that, as we conduct research, we should be guided by proper modeling strategies and not by what the results are saying.

5.7 Chapter summary

Figure 5.5 summarizes the main points of this chapter. Standard errors are important for indicating how precise your coefficient estimates are. The standard errors from your regression will help to produce a range of likely values (confidence intervals) as well as hypothesis tests and significance indicators (p-values) for the coefficient estimates.

However, the standard approach to using p-values has been called into question. The true probability that a given estimated relationship is real depends on, among other things, its size relative to the standard error and the prior probability that such an empirical relationship could exist. But, it is impossible to objectively calculate these probabilities.

The best approach is to reduce the p-value threshold for what constitutes "strong evidence" for an empirical relationship (particularly when the sample size gets larger), focus on practical significance as well as statistical significance, and be cautious about interpretations on significance.

Another common misinterpretation is for an insignificant effect. Often, an insignificant effect is interpreted as "there is no effect," whereas the more appropriate interpretation would be that "there is no evidence for an effect." Furthermore, there could be hidden information behind an insignificant estimate. Given that a coefficient estimate represents an average effect or association, it is possible that a given treatment positively affects (or is positively associated with) the outcome for some people and negatively affects others. Distinguishing between these positive and negative effects could be quite fruitful for better understanding the research issue.

Exercises

1. Borrowing from Table 8.5 in Chapter 8, consider the regression model:

$$\widehat{MJ} = \hat{\beta}_0 + \hat{\beta}_1 * (UR)$$

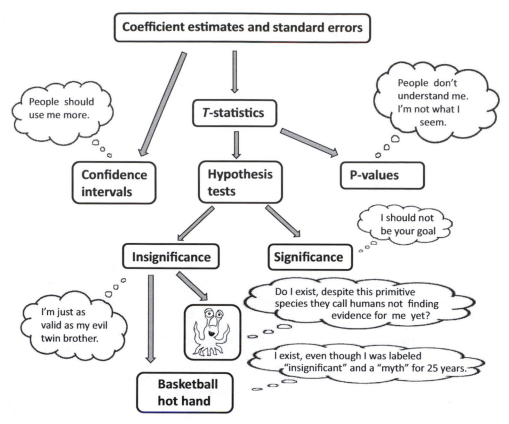

Figure 5.5 Summary of Chapter 5

Credit: Abigail Soong

where *MJ* is the past-month-marijuana-use rate for 12–17-year-olds in a state in 2009–10, *UR* is the average state unemployment rate for 2009–10, and there are 51 observations (50 states plus DC). The results are the following, with the standard errors in parentheses below the coefficient estimate:

$$\widehat{MJ} = 8.971 + 0.244 * (UR)$$
$$(1.406) \quad (0.148)$$

a. Give the formal null and alternative hypotheses for whether the variable *UR* has a coefficient that is different from zero.
b. Give the formal null and alternative hypotheses for whether the variable *UR* has a positive coefficient.
c. Calculate the *t*-stat for the coefficient estimate on *UR*.
d. Determine the critical values for the two-sided test on that coefficient for tests at the 1%, 5%, and 10% levels. Is the coefficient estimate statistically significant at those levels?
e. Determine the critical value for the one-sided hypothesis test (at the 5% significance level) on that estimate to test if it is positive. What is the conclusion of the hypothesis test?
f. Calculate the 95% confidence interval for the coefficient estimate on *UR*.

2. Use **foxnewsdata**. For cities and towns with at least 2000 voters in 1996 (*votes1996*), regress *r_vote_share_ch* on:
   - *foxnews,*
   - *male_ch,*
   - *hisp_ch,*
   - *black_ch,*
   - *coll_ch,*
   - *pop_ch,*
   - *income_ch.*
      a. Which coefficient estimates are statistically significant at the 1, 5, and 10% levels?
      b. Test for the joint significance of *coll_ch* and *pop_ch*.

3. Suppose that some researcher, with nothing else better to do, were to estimate a model for each of the 500 baseball players with the most plate appearances in 2017. The model is:

   (*# lightning strikes in the U.S. that night*) = $\beta_0 + \beta_1 *$(*# hits player had in game that day*) $+ \varepsilon$

   The researcher is surprised to find that seven of the 500 players had a statistically significant estimate of β_1, with a p-value below 0.01 – four were positive and significant, and three were negative and significant. Thus, this researcher concluded that four players generate so much excitement with their hits that it must change the weather and produce lightning.
      a. What is wrong with this conclusion?
      b. What other information needs to be considered before concluding that there is a real empirical relationship between the number of hits for these players and the number of lightning strikes?

4. Suppose that some researchers regressed, for graduating high-school seniors, "high-school-GPA" on "tablet-use-in-high-school" and found an insignificant estimate on "tablet-use." What are three reasons why "tablet-use" may indeed affect GPA, despite the finding of this research?

5. Based on the available evidence, is there intelligent life elsewhere in the universe?

Notes

1 Research Department, Federal Reserve Bank of Philadelphia (2007). Survey of Professional Forecasters, November 13, 2007. https://www.philadelphiafed.org/-/media/research-and-data/real-time-center/survey-of-professional-forecasters/2007/spfq407.pdf, accessed October 23, 2018.

2 With large samples, this F-test is equivalent to a χ^2 test in which the observed F-stat (F_o) multiplied by the number of restrictions (*m*) is distributed χ^2 with *m* degrees of freedom:

$$F_0 * m = \frac{\left(\sum \hat{\varepsilon}^2_{RR} - \sum \hat{\varepsilon}^2_{UR}\right)}{\dfrac{\left(\sum \hat{\varepsilon}^2_{UR}\right)}{(n-k)_{UR}}} \sim \chi^2(m)$$

3 These are complicated calculations that require a few assumptions. In a private email conversation with the author, I was told that conservative assumptions were made.

4 www.tylervigen.com/, accessed July 10, 2018.

5 This regression was based on a simple cross-sectional regression. A more complicated time-series model (borrowing methods from Chapter 10) produces a coefficient estimate on the number of Nic Cage movies of 6.0, with a p-value of 0.012 – i.e., it's ever more strongly significant.

6 Now, scientists are arguing for the possibility that there are multi–verses – other universes. Maybe, in a Bizarro World in a different universe, Bizarro Me is an NBA star and Bizarro LeBron James is a geeky sports fan writing a book about regressions.

References

Arkes, J. (2013). Misses in "hot hand" research. *Journal of Sports Economics*, 14(4), 401–410.

Arkes, J. (2016). On the misinterpretation of insignificant coefficient estimates. SSRN Working Paper. (Available at http://papers.ssrn.com/sol3/papers.cfm?abstract_id=2821164, accessed July 10, 2018).

Bureau of Labor Statistics, U.S. Department of Labor. (2014). *National Longitudinal Survey of Youth 1979 cohort, 1979–2012 (rounds 1–25)*. Columbus, OH: Center for Human Resource Research, The Ohio State University.

Ioannidis, J. P. (2005). Why most published research findings are false. *PLoS Medicine*, 2(8), e124. doi:10.1371/journal.pmed.0020124

Metaxas, E. (2014). Science increasingly makes the case for god. *Wall Street Journal*, December 25, 2014. (Available at www.wsj.com/articles/eric-metaxas-science-increasingly-makes-the-case-for-god-1419544568, accessed July 10, 2018).

Miller, J. B., & Sanjurjo, A. (2018). Surprised by the hot hand fallacy? A truth in the law of small numbers. *Econometrica*, forthcoming.

Nuzzo, R. (2014). Statistical errors. *Nature*, 506(7487), 150–152.

Pope, D. G., & Schweitzer, M. E. (2011). Is Tiger Woods loss averse? Persistent bias in the face of experience, competition, and high stakes. *The American Economic Review*, 101(1), 129–157. (Available at http://faculty.chicagobooth.edu/devin.pope/research/pdf/Website_Golf.pdf, accessed July 10, 2018).

Stone, D. F. (2012). Measurement error and the hot hand. *The American Statistician*, 66(1), 61–66.

6 What could go wrong when estimating causal effects?

If the world were perfect, it wouldn't be.

— Yogi Berra

Box 6.1   A regression is like a glass of beer

On the rare occasions in graduate school when we weren't neck-deep in proofs, my friends and I would drink beer on the terrace at the Student Union on the shore of Lake Mendota in Madison, Wisconsin. One day, I had a half-filled cup of beer. I held up my cup, and told my friends, "This . . . is a good regression." I then poured the contents of the pitcher into my beer, causing beer to spill onto the table and giving me a mostly foam glass of beer. In response to their query on what the heck I was doing wasting all that beer, I said, "This is what happens when you put too many variables into your regression." If my friends were not so upset over the spilt beer, I would have explained that important information becomes lost as you add more variables, and the meaning of the estimates on the existing variables becomes "foamier." Deciding on the best set of variables in a regression model is an art, as is pouring a glass of beer.

So, doesn't it seem magical that a computer can take the data you input and produce all of these regression results indicating how the dependent variable moves with each explanatory variable, holding the other explanatory variables constant? Well, it's not that magical after all. You see, the secret is that there are little green elves inside the computer doing these calculations. These remarkably error-free and fast-computing creatures are concerned about one thing: *how* the variables move with each other, holding other factors constant. We don't pay the green elves enough for them to give a hoot about *why* the variables move (or don't move) together, whether it is due to a causal effect of X on Y (as you may hypothesize), a causal effect in the other direction of Y on X, common factors creating a correlation, incidental correlation (think Nic Cage from Chapter 5), or some other explanation. We have to figure out the "why" ourselves. We need to determine how certain we can be that the coefficient estimate is representative of the causal effect of an X variable on the Y variable (or lack thereof), if that is our objective. This should depend on whether alternative explanations for the relationship between the X and Y variables can be ruled out.

Thus, the ultimate question for research is the following: **Is there an alternative explanation to the estimated relationship between the X and Y variables representing a causal effect or lack thereof?** The main focus of this chapter is on six of the most likely sources of **alternative explanations** to regression results. They are presented based on six relatively straightforward BIG QUESTIONS on issues that could bias the coefficient estimate, which in turn could bias a hypothesis test. These are the questions to ask when assessing your own research or when scrutinizing others' research. This is not a complete list of alternative explanations. But, these BIG QUESTIONS form a fairly general set of issues that can explain most of the things that could bias coefficient estimates when estimating causal effects.

Before getting into the main things that could go wrong (the BIG QUESTIONS), I will define the problem and set up the problem in terms of estimating the causal effect of some treatment. And, besides the discussion on the BIG QUESTIONS, this chapter also includes a discussion on the strategies for the best set of control variables to include in a model. In addition, there is a discussion of problems with standard errors. While of less significance than biased coefficient estimates, biased standard errors could still affect any hypothesis tests, just as biased coefficient estimates could. Potential issues from sample problems are also discussed.

6.1 How to judge a research study

As you judge others' research studies or assess your own, there are three criteria that should be used, in order of importance:

1. How credible is the study based on the research design being able to rule out alternative explanations for the evidence?
2. To the extent that there are alternative explanations for the evidence, how forthright and complete is the study in terms of acknowledging these alternative explanations (i.e., remaining limitations)?
3. How well does the study put the research in the proper context with existing research?

How credible is the study?

An empirical study generally provides some quantitative evidence to test for a theory and makes conclusions on the theory based on the evidence – with the conclusions often being on a causal effect. The criterion of "how credible the study is" should be based on the extent to which there are any plausible alternative stories to the empirical evidence. Is there another story (competing with the hypothesized theory) that could produce the same empirical evidence? How likely is that alternative story vs. the hypothesized theory? The more likely that an alternative story can explain the evidence, the less credible the study would be.

How forthright and complete is the study?

If the study has some credibility (in terms of the alternative stories not being too likely to explain the evidence), then the study should also be judged on how careful, forthright, and complete it is in terms of acknowledging the remaining limitations. Sometimes, the alternative explanations are very minor, which is the case with randomized control trials. But, sometimes they are distinct possibilities for what could be creating the empirical evidence. When this occurs, the researchers should be forthright and complete in accounting for all of the plausible stories. This is important for two main reasons:

- So that peer reviewers (for a journal) and the public reading the research have all the information to make their own judgment on the credibility of the findings.
- So that a proper perspective is put on the research findings.

The unfortunate thing is that, if peer reviewers do not do diligent jobs of contemplating the alternative stories, then the less forthright and complete the authors are, the more likely an article is to get published. What this means is that we should not necessarily trust a study just because it is published or because it is published in a high-quality journal. The peer reviewers may just have missed some obvious alternative explanations that the authors neglected to mention (accidentally or not).

How well is the research put in the proper context?

A study should indicate any prior literature on the specific research issue. If there is no or minimal prior research on the specific issue, then any research on a related topic should be noted. If the results of the given study differ from prior studies, then efforts should be made to theorize why there could be a difference. This will be covered in more detail in Chapter 12.

The rest of this chapter

This chapter focuses on identifying what alternative stories there could be, with the heart of the chapter being Section 6.4 on what could bias the coefficient estimates. This will help towards identifying:

- The strengths and weaknesses of prior research (to give the proper context for the current study),
- What alternative stories need to be addressed in the current study,
- What alternative stories remain potential limitations of the current study.

6.2 Exogenous (good) variation vs. endogenous (bad) variation

The first three BIG QUESTIONS in Section 6.4 deal with non-random explanatory variables. Many explanatory variables will have sources of variation that are exogenous (good) and other sources of variation that is endogenous (bad). Table 6.1 summarizes the differences between the two sources of variation.

The key is whether there is any part of the variable that is correlated with the error term. That is, is the explanatory variable correlated with unexplained factors that could explain the dependent variable? If so, then the coefficient estimate would pick up those effects.

Consider the empirical relationship we have dealt with on how years-of-schooling affects income. The sources of variation in years-of-schooling could include:

1. A part based on the student's aptitude/intelligence, effort, motivation, and expected benefit from schooling;
2. A part based on contributions from one's parents, including their education, assistance (financial and other), and encouragement;
3. A part based on luck in guesses on college entrance exams.

The first two parts could be correlated with the error term, as these factors could not just affect years-of-schooling, but also the amount of income a subject eventually receives. Variation in years-of-schooling from these sources would be *bad variation*. In contrast, variation in years-of-schooling from luck (or lack of luck) in guesses on college entrance exams could be more random, and this luck would theoretically be uncorrelated with the error term. Thus, they may create *good variation* in the years-of-schooling.

As we estimate how years-of-schooling affects income, we want there to only be **exogenous variation** in the years-of-schooling variable, which is variation that is unrelated to the dependent variable, income. That is, we want to design the model so that years-of-schooling varies without variation in other factors that affect income (such as intelligence). If there were any **endogenous**

Table 6.1 Exogenous and endogenous variation in an explanatory variable

	Exogenous (random) variation	*Endogenous (non-random) variation*
What is it?	The contribution to the value of the variable that is not affected by the dependent variable or factors that could also affect the dependent variable that are unaccounted for	The contribution to the value of the variable that depends on the dependent variable or factors of the dependent variable that are unaccounted for
What does the prefix mean?	Exo = external/outside	Endo = within/inside
Relationship with error term (ε)	Uncorrelated	Correlated
Is it good or bad variation for estimating causal effects?	Good variation	Bad variation

(bad) variation in the years-of-schooling variable (that is correlated with uncontrolled-for factors that could affect income), the coefficient estimate on years-of-schooling would capture the effects of those other factors, such as innate intelligence and aptitude and parents' education. Note that parents' education is not in the subject's control, but it still could cause problems because it could affect both years-of-schooling and income. Unless the endogenous (bad) variation could be removed from the years-of-schooling variable (or controlled for), we would not be able to obtain an unbiased estimate of the effect of schooling on income. If the explanatory variable were endogenous, this would violate Assumption **A5** from Section 2.10 in that the error term would contain the effects of factors that are correlated with the key explanatory variables.

6.3 Setting up the problem for estimating a causal effect

The classic model in quantitative research is to examine the effect of some treatment on an outcome. The treatment could be the conventional meaning of a treatment for, say, some medical condition. Or, the treatment could refer to any other intervention or even a choice by a person. And, whereas the treatment is often considered a dummy variable (for whether the subject had exposure to the treatment), it could also be a quantitative variable representing different levels of exposure to the treatment (such as years-of-schooling). For the sake of this current discussion, it is easier to think of the treatment as a yes/no situation. These could include:

- Experiencing a parental divorce,
- Drinking alcohol as a teenager,
- Meditating.

What researchers would typically be interested in is the **Average Treatment Effect** (ATE) on an outcome, or the average effect of the treatment on a given outcome in the relevant population. That is, if the treatment were assigned to everyone in the relevant population, how would a given outcome change, on average? This is equivalent to: if a random person were to be assigned the treatment, how would we *expect* his/her outcome to change?

To understand the difficulty in estimating the ATE, let's define the following:

- $T = 1$ if the person received the treatment; $T = 0$ otherwise;
- $Y_i(1)$ = the outcome for person i if he/she *received the treatment;*
- $Y_i(0)$ = the outcome for person i if he/she *did not receive the treatment.*

The treatment effect for individual i would be: $Y_i(1) - Y_i(0)$. And, the ATE would be the average of everyone's treatment effect:

$$ATE = \sum_{i=1}^{N} \frac{\left[Y_i(1) - Y_i(0)\right]}{N} \qquad (6.1)$$
$$= E\left(Y_i|\, Treatment\right) - E\left(Y_i|\, No\,treatment\right)$$

where N is the number of people in the population.

Unfortunately, we only observe people in either the treatment or the non-treatment state; we cannot observe the counterfactual for any given person. Incidentally, this is the reason for why we rarely can know whether some government policy/investment (a tax increase, Obamacare, the Iraq War, the Bridge to Nowhere) was beneficial in the long run. We will never know what the counterfactual outcomes would have been.

Given that we do not know the counterfactual for each person, what a model would typically estimate for the treatment effect would be:

$$\hat{\beta} = \left\{E\left[Y_i(1|\, T = 1)\right] - E\left[Y_i(0|\, T = 0)\right]\right\} \qquad (6.2)$$

= Average outcome	− Average outcome
for those who	for those who
receive the	do not receive the
treatment	treatment
(Treatment group)	(Control group)

This would provide a decent estimate of the ATE only if the two sets of people (those receiving and not receiving the treatment) were similar in all relevant characteristics other than whether they received the treatment. This would be more likely to occur if assignment to the treatment were random, such as in a randomized control trial (RCT), and the sample were large enough so that there were no big differences between the two groups due to random variation (or bad luck for the researcher).

Recall the example we had back in Section 4.1 on how to test whether adding cinnamon improves your chocolate-chip cookies. We wanted to make sure that, when cinnamon varies among the cookies (in that some cookies have it and some don't), nothing else varies. That is, the amount of chocolate, butter, sugar, etc. should be the same in the cinnamon and non-cinnamon sets of cookies so that we know that any differences in taste are attributable to the presence of cinnamon.

In our situation, we want to make sure that there are no differences in the treatment and control groups that could affect the outcome. That would be necessary for us to attribute any differences between the two groups to the treatment itself. Obviously, there will be many individual differences between those in the two groups. But, that would be okay if the two groups, on average, were similar in the other factors that could affect the outcome. As mentioned above, random assignment to the treatment and an adequate sample size would present such a scenario. This would make it so the treatment was exogenous to the dependent variable.

The problem is that most treatments are not randomly assigned, but rather have an endogenous component. Families that end up divorcing are, on average, different in meaningful ways from families that remain intact. People who choose to use illicit drugs often have non-random reasons for doing so. In these cases, the treatment is probably not the only thing that is different between the treatment and control group. These things that are different could include observable characteristics (e.g., parents' education), but it would also, almost certainly, include unobserved or non-quantifiable characteristics. And so, other (unobservable) factors are not held constant, as we estimate the effects of these treatments (divorce and drug use) on various outcomes. These could present alternative stories to why the estimated treatment effect is what it is, other than it being the causal effect.

The same idea would apply if the key explanatory variable were a non-dummy variable, such as years-of-schooling or the unemployment rate. Those with different values of the key X variable must be similar to each other, on average, holding the other factors constant. Otherwise, we cannot attribute the change in outcome related to a change in the key X variable to being a product of the key X variable itself.

The non-randomness (endogeneity) of the treatment represents one source of the several problems of regression analysis in trying to estimate the true causal effect of a treatment. Problems can arise for various reasons, which I will cover in the next section. Here is a preview of the problems (BIG QUESTIONS) that will be described in the next section, in relation to the setup above:

- The outcome itself, or something highly correlated with the outcome, could determine whether the person is assigned the treatment (**reverse causality**).
- Some unobserved factor may affect both the outcome and the probability of being assigned the treatment. Thus, part of the difference between the treated and non-treated population could be from the omitted factor (**omitted-variables bias**).
- Someone may choose to receive the treatment because they believe it will strongly benefit him/her (**self-selection bias**).
- The data are faulty in that people are not coded correctly as to whether they received the treatment (**measurement error**).
- Some **mediating factor** for *why* the treatment affects the outcome or some **other outcome may be included as a control variable**, causing the estimated treatment effect to only capture a part of the effect of the treatment.

6.4 The BIG QUESTIONS for what could bias the coefficient estimate

6.4.1 BIG QUESTION 1: *Is there reverse causality?*

No one goes there nowadays. It's too crowded.

–Yogi Berra

Reverse causality deals with the simple question of "which came first?" or "what caused what?" Sugar or the sweet tooth? The rude teenager or the overbearing parent? The E! Network or the Kardashians? The Chicken McNugget or the Egg McMuffin?

Reverse causality is a situation in which the dependent variable (Y) affects an explanatory variable (X). Or, something closely tied with the dependent variable affects an explanatory variable. This would mean that any empirical relationship between two variables, even when holding other factors constant, could be partly to fully attributable to Y affecting X rather than what we aim to estimate – how X affects Y.

Let's say that you are examining whether marijuana use affects the probability that a person experiences depression. Perhaps marijuana affects the brain in some physical fashion, making a person more susceptible to depression. Or, perhaps marijuana use effectively relieves anxiety, which can help a person be more social, which in turn helps to relieve depression symptoms. The model would be the following:

$$Y_i = X_i\beta_1 + \beta_2 \times (MJ_i) + \varepsilon_i \tag{6.3}$$

where:

- Y = a measure of depression;
- X = a set of exogenous factors you control for;
- MJ = some measure of marijuana use.

Assuming that you had a random sample, would you consider the estimate on β_2 to be a good indicator of how much using marijuana *affects* the extent of depression? Figure 6.1 demonstrates the problem. You aim to test the value of C, which we'll say is the effect of a one-unit increase in marijuana use on the extent of depression. But, as shown with the dashed line labeled D, there could be **reverse causality**. That is, a person's depression (the outcome) could affect whether they use marijuana (the key X variable), even after controlling for other determinants of marijuana use and depression. Perhaps some depressed people use marijuana to self-medicate (Harder et al. 2006). If that effect, D, were positive, then the reverse causality would contribute positively towards the coefficient estimate. That is, the coefficient estimate, $\hat{\beta}_2$, would capture both C and D, not just the effect you want, C – *remember that the coefficient estimate indicates how the variables move together, regardless of the direction of causality.* Thus, it is possible that the true effect, C, might be zero (that marijuana use does not affect the extent of depression), but, the positive reverse causality may be giving the impression that there is a positive effect of marijuana use on depression. Regardless of the true effect of C, the estimate would probably not be trustworthy, as it would be upwardly biased in this situation, provided that D is positive.

If there were reverse causality, we would say that marijuana is **endogenous** to depression in that it is determined within the model. *This means that marijuana use is not random with respect to depression.* And, this means that, unlike our cinnamon-cookie case back in Section 4.1 (in which we had cinnamon be the only relevant thing different between two batches of cookies), marijuana use is not the only relevant thing that is different across people with different levels of marijuana use, as some underlying depression may already exist. In terms of the assumptions of the Multiple Regression Model, **A5** would be violated because the error term (representing the unexplained propensity to suffer from depression) would be higher for those who use marijuana.

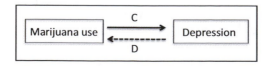

Figure 6.1 A demonstration of reverse causality with marijuana use and depression

Reverse causality can rarely be proven. In this marijuana-depression example, it is virtually impossible to determine which is causing which because the effects in both directions (C and D in Figure 6.1) could be the same sign. But, there are situations in which your model may provide strong evidence for reverse causality. Consider a problem a student had explored: whether omega-3 consumption affects depression. In that situation, the effect of omega-3's on the probability of depression should be zero or negative, as it is unlikely that omega-3's would increase the likelihood of depression. And, the reverse causality should be positive, if anything, as having depression could lead to higher omega-3 consumption to help medicate the depression. In this case, the desired effect and the reverse causality worked opposite to each other. Thus, when the student estimated a positive coefficient estimate on omega-3 consumption, she had some evidence for the reverse causality dominating any negative causal effect of omega-3's on depression. When the likely causal effect is opposite in sign to the expected reverse causality and the coefficient estimate is of the sign consistent with reverse causality, then this suggests that your estimate is affected by reverse causality.

Demonstrating reverse causality with an exogenous world and an endogenous world

I created two worlds today. I created an Exogenous (good) World that is free from reverse causality or any other issue with non-random key explanatory variables. And, I created an Endogenous (bad) World, which does have reverse causality.

The research issue for these worlds is how much confidence affects students' achievement test scores. The potential reverse causality is that greater performance on a test (or a better understanding of the material, which is closely tied with the test score) could increase a student's confidence.

In these two worlds, I created 1000 observations (500 of Type A students and 500 of Type B students – with no connection with the standard labels for personality types). And, I created two variables: measures of the student's confidence and the test score (for a given subject). I first randomized student confidence levels and the test score as standard normal variables, meaning that they are normalized to have a mean of zero and each unit is a standard deviation.

For both worlds, I then added in the causal effects and reverse causality, as seen in Figure 6.2. Recall that the value of the arrow represents how much a one-unit increase in the source variable affects the value of the variable that is being pointed at. The traits are:

- For Type A:
  - Each standard deviation in confidence causes an increase in their test score by 0.5 standard deviations.
  - There is no reverse causality, as the test score does not affect their confidence.
- For Type B:
  - Confidence has no effect on their test score.
  - In the Endogenous World (but not the Exogenous World), there is reverse causality, as each standard deviation in their test score causes an increase in their confidence by 0.8 standard deviations.

So, there is reverse causality in the Endogenous (bad) World, but not in the Exogenous (good) World. We can presume that the confidence would be measured before the test and for Type B's, it is a marker

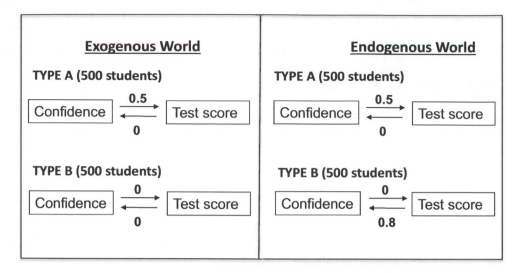

Figure 6.2 Demonstrating reverse causality in Exogenous and Endogenous Worlds

for how well prepared they were for the test. A non-creator of this world would not know whether and by how much confidence was affected by the test score for Type A's or B's. Out of simplicity for the exercise, I created these worlds to have those subject to reverse causality (Type B's) be separate from those whose scores are affected by confidence (Type A's).

When some researchers (who don't know these relationships I've created) come in and attempt to estimate the causal effect of confidence on test scores, they hopefully will estimate the average causal effect in the population. In both worlds, that average effect would be the average of the effect for Type A's (0.5) and for Type B's (0.0), which comes to 0.250. Note that this does not mean that the coefficient estimate would be exactly 0.250 because of the random component to the test score.

In the Exogenous World, it is likely that the researchers will find a coefficient estimate on *confidence* close to that 0.250, as there is no reverse causality (nor other problem) affecting their estimates. However, in the Endogenous World, there should be a positive bias from the reverse causality, so we would expect the researchers to find a coefficient estimate on *confidence* to be considerably higher than 0.250.

Table 6.2 shows the results of the model. (Note that if I were to allow Excel to re-randomize the variables, I would get numbers that are a little different, but they should follow the same general patterns.) In the Exogenous World, the estimated effect on *confidence* (0.272) is indeed close to 0.250 – less than one standard error away. However, in the Endogenous World, as would be predicted, the estimate (0.492) is upwardly biased from the true causal effect. As the Supreme Benevolent Creator of this world, I know this to be the case. But, the researcher/reader wouldn't know how much of that 0.492 was a causal effect of confidence on test scores versus the consequences of reverse causality.

This is also a good example of a case in which the R^2 is not relevant. One may look at these two worlds and conclude that the model is better in the Endogenous World because it has an R^2 that is almost five times higher than that in the Exogenous World. But, the higher R^2 is attributable to a reverse causality that hinders the model from estimating the true causal effect.

In the Endogenous World I created, the reverse causality is positive, which is the same direction as the actual causal effect. And so, the estimated effect is exaggerated. However, if I introduced a reverse causality that moved in a direction opposite to the main causal effect, then the estimated effect would

Table 6.2 Demonstration of the biases from reverse causality

	Exogenous (good) World	Endogenous (bad) World
	Test score	Test score
Confidence	0.272	0.492
	(0.034)	(0.025)
Constant	−0.044	−0.039
	(0.033)	(0.029)
R^2	0.060	0.279
Number of observations	1000	1000

be understated. The bias would be in the negative direction, causing the estimated effect of the key X variable to be less positive or even negative. Furthermore, the R^2 would likely decrease unless the reverse causality was quite large relative to the causal effect of the key X variable.

What to check for: reverse causality

The check for reverse causality is to ask whether the outcome or something closely tied to the outcome could affect an explanatory variable, particularly the key explanatory variable.

Box 6.2 Testing for what's more important in the NFL: running or passing

A big topic in football is whether the running (rushing) game or passing game is more import- ant. But, the debate has historically been one-sided. The great coach and famous commentator, John Madden, would often argue that it is the running game, usually citing some statistic, for example, that a given team has a 7–2 win-loss record when their main running back rushes for 100 yards.

For years, I wanted to yell at the television: "RUSHING YARDS IS ENDOGENOUS." That is, teams run the ball more (and pass less) when they are winning. It helps preserve the ball and run the clock down. Thus, having a 100-yard rusher could be more of a *marker for winning* than a cause of winning. So, if you are estimating how having a rushing and passing advantage increases the probability of winning, you would set up a model, perhaps in terms of the home team, as follows:

$$Y = \beta_1 (Rush) + \beta_2 (Pass) + X\beta_3 + \varepsilon$$

where
- Y = whether the home team won;
- *Rush* = a measure of the rushing advantage of the home team over the visiting team;

- *Pass* = a measure of the passing advantage of the home team over the visiting team;
- *X* = Other factors, including controls for the teams playing.

Figure 6.3 demonstrates the problem. You want to estimate the causal effects represented by the solid lines, A and C. But, potential reverse causality, represented by the dashed lines (B and D), could affect the estimates. In particular, the coefficient estimate on rushing advantage ($\hat{\beta}_1$) would capture both A (the true causal effect) and B (the endogenous part of the relationship between rushing advantage and the probability of winning). It is likely that B > 0. That is, as the probability of winning increases, teams will generally rush the ball more. So, $\hat{\beta}_1$ would be biased upwards.

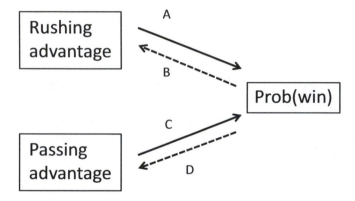

Figure 6.3 Reverse causality in football

The estimate for C ($\hat{\beta}_2$) would capture both C and D, regardless of the direction of the causality. D would likely be negative – teams pass less as their chance of winning increases – so the estimate of C would be biased downwards.

The key to eliminating such biases, as I will discuss in Chapter 8, is to eliminate the endogenous part of the explanatory variables that is subject to reverse causality (or any other bias). My solution in this case is to use first-half statistics (on rushing yards, passing yards, and other factors) to predict the eventual winner rather than full-game statistics, as teams typically would not change strategies in the first half based on a lead or deficit (Arkes 2011). That is, hopefully first-half statistics are exogenous, containing only good variation.

Using full-game statistics produced results consistent with the conventional argument: controlling the rushing game was associated with a higher probability of winning, but no evidence for having a passing advantage mattering. However, these results were subject to the biases mentioned above. Using first-half statistics reversed the results, so there was strong evidence that controlling the passing game increased the probability of winning, but there was no evidence that controlling the rushing game mattered, on average. These results were more credible because they were less subject to reverse causality.

Maybe if this whole regression-book thing doesn't work out, I can be a football commentator.

6.4.2 *BIG QUESTION 2: Is there omitted-variables bias?*

I never blame myself when I'm not hitting. I just blame the bat and if it keeps up, I change bats.

−Yogi Berra

Omitted-variables bias is like getting blamed for (or credited with) something that you didn't do because it happened in your vicinity or on your watch. Perhaps you were the Admiral in charge of Navy recruiting during the dot-com boom, and you got fired because the Navy did not meet its recruiting goal, even though no one (not even the Dos Equis most-interesting-man-in-the-world guy) would have met the goal given how strong the economy was. Or, you are the coach of the U.S. Olympic basketball team and you lead them to the gold medal. You get honored as a great coach, even though there is so much talent on the team that they could have won without a coach. Or, you are a baseball superstar, and you are in the middle of a slump. You can't pinpoint any intangible factor causing the slump (such as your concentration or randomness), so you blame the one tangible thing that is in plain sight: your bat.

The idea in all of these examples is that the blame or accolades you (or the bat) receive is partly for something that is "correlated" with your position but is not your doing. This is the concept behind omitted-variables bias: the estimated causal effect of some observable factor on an outcome is picking up the effects of some other factor that is correlated with the observable factor but is not accounted for.

More formally, let's say that you are interested in how some key variable, X_1, affects some outcome, Y. Consider a Simple Regression Model:

$$Y_i = \beta_0 + \beta_1 X_{1i} + \varepsilon_i \tag{6.4}$$

Omitted-variables bias, also called **unobserved heterogeneity**, occurs when some other variable, X_2:

- Is not included in the model,
- Affects the outcome Y, and
- Is correlated with X_1 (not solely due to X_1 affecting X_2).

If these conditions apply, then β_1 in equation (6.4) would not just capture the effects of X_1, but also reflect to some extent the effects of X_2. Thus, it would be a biased predictor of the causal effect of X_1 on Y. In other words, X_1 would be blamed for (or credited with) the variation in X_2 that happens to come along with a one-unit increase in X_1 and its effects on Y. And, this presents an alternative story (to the "causal effects" story) for why the coefficient estimate, $\hat{\beta}_1$, is what it is.

Let's think back to our discussion of "holding other factors constant" and Figures 4.3a and 4.3b back in Section 4.2 (pages 69–70). From equation (A) in Figure 4.3a,

$$income = \beta_0 + \beta_1 \times educ + \varepsilon,$$

the coefficient estimate for β_1 was determined based on how several factors move with years-of-schooling (*educ*) and how those factors then simultaneously determine income. And those factors included two that determine the level of schooling (innate intelligence and innate motivation) and two that are the product of schooling (skills for the workplace and network connections).

Without adequate controls for innate intelligence and motivation, there would be omitted-variables bias because innate motivation and innate intelligence:

- Are not included in the model,
- Affect income, and
- Are correlated with years-of-schooling (not because years-of-schooling affects them).

This would mean that the years-of-schooling would be incorrectly credited with the effects of innate motivation and intelligence on income.

We would say that years-of-schooling is not random in the population, as certain relevant factors cause some people to obtain more years-of-schooling. The assumption on the Multiple Regression Model that is being violated, again, is **A5** because the error term would be correlated with the amount of schooling the person obtains.

In contrast, not controlling for workplace skills and network connections does not present an omitted-variables bias problem because they are correlated with years-of-schooling *because* the number of years-of-schooling affects them and not *vice versa*. (This is similar to the lemon-tree and dominos problems from Section 4.1 and will be discussed further in BIG QUESTION 5 below.)

We can also draw a connection with the cinnamon-chocolate-chip-cookie example from Section 4.1; the idea was to make one batch, stir well, and then split it and add cinnamon to one of the batches. This way, the only thing that changes between the two batches is the cinnamon. In contrast, if separate batches were made from scratch and cinnamon were added to one of the batches, then there could be omitted-variables bias because taste differences due to any differences in the two batches in the amount of sugar, chocolate, or butter would be attributable (positively or negatively) to the cinnamon.

There are two main types of omitted-variables bias:

- **Spurious correlation** between the key explanatory variable and the dependent variable. The two variables would be correlated with each other by the nature of things, due to having a common factor. This is the case of the unobserved variable (X_2) affecting both the key X variable (X_1) and the outcome (Y).
- **Incidental correlation** between the key explanatory variable and an omitted factor. The correlation would just be by coincidence and not by any deterministic or systematic relationship.

Omitted-variables bias, in most cases, is something that cannot be proven to be the case. Rather, one must think about whether omitted-variables bias may be affecting their estimates. Omitted-variables bias would be a concern if there were a reason why there could be a systematic spurious correlation between the key X variable and the dependent variable or if there were the possibility that there is incidental correlation between the key X variable and omitted variables. I will now give examples of the two types of omitted-variables bias.

Examples of omitted-variables bias from spurious correlation

Let's refer back to the oat bran example from Section 4.6. You are interested in how oat-bran consumption affects cholesterol levels. The problem is that oat-bran consumption is probably correlated with many other factors that could affect cholesterol, represented broadly by the non-quantifiable concept of "concern for healthy living." This could include such factors of health as the amount of Big Macs and Loco-Mocos the person eats, the amount of bacon-and-egg breakfasts the person has, and how much the person exercises. In the almost-certain case that "concern for healthy living" is not fully captured by the variables included in the model, the estimated effect of oat bran would capture, to some extent, the effects of "healthy living" on cholesterol levels. So, oat-bran consumption would be unduly credited with the effects of healthy living.

Figure 6.4 shows a graphical representation of the problem. There are three variables, with the two in rectangles being observed and the circled one being unobserved. You are interested in **A**, which is the causal effect of a one unit increase in oat-bran consumption on cholesterol. The "concern for healthy living" would probably also have an effect on your cholesterol, and we will call that effect, **C**, which is likely negative. Omitted-variables bias is only applicable here if:

1. You do not have data to adequately control for "concern for healthy living";
2. "Concern for healthy living" affects cholesterol; and
3. "Concern for health living" is correlated with oat-bran consumption by affecting oat bran.

And, in this case, it would likely be **spurious correlation** between the key X variable (oat-bran-consumption) and the outcome (cholesterol) that is causing omitted-variables bias because "concern for healthy living" tends to systematically lead to both eating more oat bran and having lower cholesterol. So, oat-bran consumption and cholesterol have a common factor.

Again, we would say that *oat-bran consumption is not random in the population*, even after controlling for other factors. Certain unobserved factors cause people to eat more or less oat bran, and it is quite conceivable that such factors may affect cholesterol in other ways. That is, as the amount of oat bran varies in the population, so do other factors of cholesterol.

Another example of omitted-variables bias from spurious correlation comes from a 2012 study, in the highly respected *New England Journal of Medicine*, that found a very strong correlation (0.791) between a country's per-capita chocolate consumption and the number of Nobel Laureates (Nobel prize winners) per capita (Messerli 2012). The correlation was highly significant, with $p < 0.0001$. The author notes that this is consistent with the idea that the flavonoids in chocolate improve cognitive functioning so much that it creates more Nobel Laureates. While the author recognized that

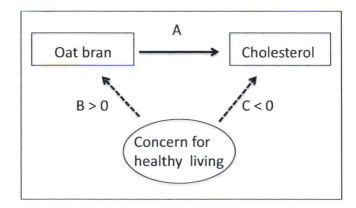

Figure 6.4 Omitted-variables bias for the relationship between oat bran and cholesterol

correlation does not mean causation, he argues there is no common factor to chocolate and Nobel Laureates. But, the alternative explanations for this could include the fact that chocolate is a luxury good that is eaten more in richer countries, which tend to have better educational systems. So, the key omitted factors here would be variables representing the wealth of the country, the effects of which seem to be incorrectly credited to the chocolate.

Example of omitted-variables bias from incidental correlation

President Bush (the first one), along with Congress, raised the top marginal income tax rate from 28% to 31% in 1991. President Clinton and Congress then raised the top tax rate to 39.6% in 1993. We normally think that tax-rate increases lead to lower GDP growth and higher unemployment rates, but the economy started a long expansion after Bush's first tax hike, and continued strongly after Clinton's tax increase, up until the 2001 recession, which is the record for the longest period in U.S. history without a recession.

If we expand the data to the 1991–2017 period and test this a bit more formally, the general pattern from the 1990s is confirmed. Time-series regressions, which include lags of the dependent variables, are presented in Table 6.3. (I am getting ahead of myself, as I will cover time-series models in Chapter 10.) The model consists of:

- Dependent variable = annual national unemployment rate or real GDP growth rate;
- Key explanatory variable = top marginal income tax rate;
- Control variables = 1-year-lagged unemployment rate or real GDP growth rate.

Table 6.3 Likely biased (from omitted-variables bias) estimates of top marginal tax rates on the unemployment rate and real GDP growth rate, 1991–2017

	(1)	(2)
	Dependent variable = unemployment rate	Dependent variable = real GDP growth rate
Top marginal tax rate	−0.177***	0.120
	(0.058)	(0.122)
	[−0.297, −0.057]	[−0.131, 0.372]
1-year lagged unemployment rate	0.763***	
	(0.106)	
1-year lagged real GDP growth rate		0.334
		(0.206)
Constant	7.982***	−2.847
	(2.377)	(4.323)
Observations	27	27
R^2	0.752	0.220

Note: Standard errors in parentheses. 95% confidence intervals for key explanatory variables are in brackets. *** $p < 0.01$, ** $p < 0.05$, * $p < 0.1$.

The results show that the top tax rate has a significant estimated negative association with the unemployment rate ($p < 0.01$, as indicated by the stars on the coefficient estimate), but an insignificant positive association with the real GDP growth rate. Each percentage point of the tax rate is associated with an estimated 0.18-percentage-point *lower* unemployment rate. The estimate on the tax rate in the unemployment-rate model (and the insignificant one for the other model) are opposite to what most would have predicted – that higher tax rates hinder economic growth.

Are these coefficient estimates representative of the causal effects? It is always possible that the higher tax rates helped towards balancing the budget and that contributed to a stronger economy. But, the more likely explanation for these estimates is that events unrelated to but *incidentally correlated* (or occurring) with the tax rates were stronger determinants of the strength of the economy. The internet boom of the 1990s (which likely would have occurred regardless of the tax rate) was likely what led to the strong GDP growth, and it just happened to occur in a high-tax-rate period. The Financial Crisis of 2008 and its aftermath, also likely not affected by the tax rate, occurred in a relatively low-tax-rate period, after the second President Bush (and Congress) lowered tax rates. Thus, the tax rate and the major factors of GDP growth (e.g., the internet boom) were likely just incidentally correlated. And, this caused the coefficient estimate on the tax rate to pick up the effects of the internet boom, the September 11 attacks, the Financial Crisis, and all other events that affected the economy. In a sense, in the regression, the low tax rates get unfairly blamed for the effects that September 11 and the Financial Crisis had on the economy, and the high tax rates get inappropriately credited with the effects of the internet boom. Thus, the **incidental correlation** is causing omitted-variables bias. And, it is reason #854 why macro-economic outcomes are so difficult to correctly model and predict, as there are too many moving parts, many of which are unobservable or difficult to quantify. I will present a method to improve such models on tax-rate effects in Section 8.1, when discussing fixed effects.

Omitted-variables bias from incidental correlation is common when an aggregated measure is used. For example, suppose that one is examining the effects of the state unemployment rate on some outcome (say teenage pregnancies). There are naturally going to be differences across states in the outcome due to non-economic factors that are not observable or quantifiable. The coefficient estimate on the state unemployment rate would pick up the effects of these unobservable/non-quantifiable factors since there would likely be some incidental correlation with the unemployment rate. Thus, there would probably be omitted-variables bias here. If there were multiple observations per state (i.e., panel data), then one could control for the state with dummy variables or fixed effects (as done below in Section 6.4.6, but described in detail in Section 8.1), which would address this problem to some extent.

How to determine the direction of omitted-variables bias

Let's return to the oat-bran-cholesterol example. For the sake of the argument, let's say that, "concern for healthy living" has a positive effect on oat-bran consumption, represented by **B** in Figure 6.4. And, let's assume that healthy living causes lower cholesterol levels, represented by **C**. The product of effects **B** (positive) and **C** (negative) would be negative. This means that the omitted factors contribute negatively to the estimated causal effect of oat-bran consumption on cholesterol, **A**. Thus, the bias for the estimated effect (**A**) would likely be in the negative direction, perhaps creating a correlation without there being causation. That is, it is possible that oat bran has no effect on cholesterol (**A** = 0), but the omitted-variables bias produces a negative relationship observed between oat bran and cholesterol. Again, this is an alternative story (to the "causal effects" explanation) for why there would be a negative relationship between oat-bran consumption and cholesterol.

The formula for omitted-variables bias

Let's go back to the generic case, building off of equation (6.4):

$$Y_i = \beta_0 + \beta_1 X_{1i} + \varepsilon_i \tag{6.4}$$

and add in X_2 (and using δ's instead of β's):

$$Y_i = \delta_0 + \delta_1 X_{1i} + \delta_2 X_{2i} + u_i \tag{6.5}$$

This is a notional model that, most of the time, couldn't be estimated because X_2 is unobserved. Let's create one more notional model of regressing X_2 on X_1:

$$X_{2i} = \lambda_0 + \lambda_1 X_{1i} + v_i \tag{6.6}$$

The omitted-variables bias for β_1 in equation (6.4) is $\delta_2 \times \lambda_1$. Basically, the bias on β_1 will be the product of: (1) how much X_2 moves with a one-unit change in X_1; and (2) how much Y moves with a one-unit change in X_2, holding X_1 constant in the notional model of (6.5). This is equivalent in theory to **B** × **C** in the oat-bran-cholesterol example.

As an example (in which we do have the omitted variable), let's take equations (2.4b) and (2.21), expanding to 3 or 4 decimal places for the relevant coefficient estimates,

$$\left(\widehat{income}\right)_i = -54{,}299 + 8120.978 \times \left(educ\right)_i \tag{2.4b}$$

$$\left(\widehat{income}\right)_i = -34{,}026 + 5394.537 \times \left(educ\right)_i + 367.4847 \times \left(afqt\right)_i \tag{2.21}$$

and add the equivalent of equation (6.6),

$$\left(\widehat{AFQT}\right)_i = -55.165 + 7.419 \times \left(educ\right)_i \tag{6.7}$$

In equation (2.4b), the magnitude of the omitted-variables bias on the coefficient estimate on *educ*, when *afqt* is excluded, equals:

$\delta_2 \times \lambda_1 = 7.419 \times 367.4847 = 2726.44$, which is exactly equal (other than rounding) to the difference in coefficient estimates on *educ* from equations (2.4b) and (2.21): 8120.978 − 5394.537.

Again, the amount of omitted-variables bias would be how much *afqt* changes (on average) with a one-unit increase in *educ* (7.419) times how much income increases (on average) with a one-unit increase in *afqt* (367.4847), holding *educ* constant.

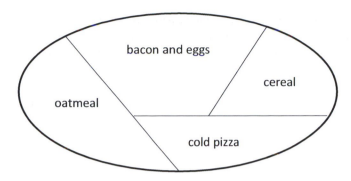

Figure 6.5 What people eat for breakfast

Omitted-variables bias from improper reference groups

Omitted-variables bias could also describe the bias resulting from improperly designed reference groups. Consider the example again of oat bran (or oatmeal) and cholesterol, and consider Figure 6.5, which indicates what the population eats for breakfast. In the following regression:

$$Cholesterol = X\beta_1 + \beta_2 \times (oatmeal\ consumption) + \varepsilon, \tag{6.8}$$

if X did not include other things for breakfast people eat, the model would be comparing the oatmeal people to the bacon-and-eggs and the cold-pizza people. So, it would be possible that oatmeal did not affect cholesterol, but it looks like it did because oatmeal people are being compared to people consuming high-cholesterol foods. In light of omitted-variables bias, bacon-and-eggs would be negatively correlated with oatmeal and would positively affect cholesterol, and so β_2 would be biased negatively.

What would the optimal reference group be? It would be whichever breakfast is most likely to be cholesterol-neutral. I'm guessing the cereal would be the best one in this case, although it could still be problematic to the extent that milk affects cholesterol.

The same concept could apply to estimating the effects of wine consumption on health. The reference group of no wine could include alcohol-abstainers, as well as heavy consumers of beer and hard alcohol. If these variables (beer and hard-alcohol consumption) were not included, the estimated effects of wine consumption could pick up the effects of not being big beer and hard-alcohol drinkers.

When is there no omitted-variables bias?

Omitted-variables bias does not occur if there is no connection between the omitted factor and the key explanatory variable. The truth is that everything is correlated to some extent. But, as long as any such correlation is very low, then there should not be any meaningful omitted-variables bias. The problem is that we mostly do not observe the omitted variables, so the determination of whether there is possibly a correlation needs to be based on theory or stories.

Omitted-variables bias is also not a problem if the omitted factor is a mediating factor, or a product of the key X variable. This was the case with the height variable in the lemon-tree example in

Section 4.1. The height of the tree would be correlated with the key X variable (the amount of water) and would affect the outcome (number of lemons produced). However, the height is a product of the amount of water given to the tree, so it does not present an omitted-variables bias problem. And, in the domino-chain example in that same section, the variable for the third domino falling (D_3) would be correlated with the variable for the first domino falling (D_1) and would affect whether the last domino fell (D_5). But, because D_3 is a product of D_1, it is not an omitted-variables bias problem.

What is quasi-omitted-variables bias?

This is a term that I just made up as I wrote this, but it explains the case well. **Quasi-omitted-variables bias** occurs when a control variable that is included to avoid or reduce omitted-variables bias has a biased coefficient estimate itself. This means that its effects are not correctly accounted for, and so it might under-explain the outcome, causing more of its positive and negative effects to load onto the coefficient estimate on the key explanatory variable. Alternatively, it could over-explain the outcome, leaving less of an effect for the key explanatory variable to have.

Let's suppose that, in estimating the effects of schooling on income, the only variable causing omitted-variables bias is the AFQT score. And, let's suppose that you then add AFQT score as a variable. But, let's say that AFQT score has an upwardly biased coefficient estimate for some reason. This would mean that, for the combination of the positively correlated "years-of-schooling" and "AFQT score," more of the effect of these two factors is being loaded onto AFQT score than should be the case, which means that less of the load would fall on the years-of-schooling variable. This would likely contribute a negative quasi-omitted-variables bias to the estimated effect of schooling. Thus, even though the AFQT score is controlled for, there is still some *quasi-omitted-variables bias* affecting the estimated effect of schooling.

How omitted-variables bias can describe reverse causality

Reverse causality can often be described using omitted-variables bias. Consider the issue on examining how marijuana affects depression, one could apply omitted-variables bias in that the factors leading to depression could cause both marijuana use and depression. Even though almost all cases could fall under omitted-variables bias, the concept of reverse causality is still important because it may sometimes describe a problem more efficiently or with more clarity.

What to check for: omitted-variables bias

To check for omitted-variables bias, ask whether there is some factor not included in the model that could affect or be incidentally correlated with *both* the key explanatory variable *and* the outcome. That is, when the key X variable changes, is there anything else that could affect Y, is not controlled for, and is not a product of the key X variable? Variables that affect the outcome and are not correlated with the key X variable (or are caused by the key X variable) do not create omitted-variables bias.

6.4.3 *BIG QUESTION 3: Is there self-selection bias?*

> When you come to a fork in the road, take it . . . rather than choosing your path randomly, as this will vex academic researchers who aim to estimate the causal effects of your choices.
> — paraphrasing Yogi Berra

There are various forms of what is called "selection bias." I will address "sample-selection bias" below in Section 6.7. Here, I focus on **self-selection bias** (sometimes called just selection bias).[1] This occurs when the following two conditions occur:

- The subject can, to some extent, select him-/herself into a category (i.e., choose a value) for the key explanatory variable, or that the category/value the person gets is at least partly determined by certain characteristics of the person; and
- The reason(s) for that choice or determination of the key explanatory variable are related to the individual benefits or costs of that factor on the dependent variable.

Consider the following example, in Table 6.4, based on a sample of two people: Charlie (who wants to work in Silicon Valley for Google or Facebook) and David (who wants to do construction or some other manual labor). The big tech firms in Silicon Valley typically do not consider people for programmer jobs if they do not have a college degree, so Charlie needs to go to college to land such a job and would be handsomely rewarded if he does so. David, on the other hand, would receive much less of a benefit for going to college; maybe a college degree would boost his earnings a little by increasing the likelihood that he will have a management job for whatever manual labor he wants to do.

The Average Treatment Effect we hope to estimate would be $50,000, the average of the effects of $80,000 for Charlie and $20,000 for David. However, the likely scenario would be that Charlie gets his college degree and David does not because the expected effect of college on his income may not be worth the costs of college for David. And so we would observe $120,000 for the person who went to college and $40,000 for the person who did not go to college, translating to an estimated $80,000 effect of college. Thus, we would be overstating the true average effect of college on income (which was $50,000) because the person who chose college did so for expecting to receive the larger effect.

In this case, assignment to different levels of education is not random, but rather tied to something that would have implications for their future earnings potential. Of course, people do not always know what the effect of college would be for them, but many people have a sense of how their income potential would be affected based on what type of career they plan on pursuing.

More generally on this issue of the effects of years-of-schooling on income, there is a distribution of individual effects, and people choose the level of schooling for which their individual net benefit is

Table 6.4 An example for self-selection bias

	Charlie (likes to work with computers)	David (likes to get his hands dirty)
Income without a college degree	$40,000	$40,000
Income with a college degree	$120,000	$60,000
Effect of college	$80,000	$20,000

maximized (considering the individual costs of schooling as well). Thus, the benefit of schooling (or average effect) for those who actually acquire more schooling is likely higher than the average effect for those who have less schooling. This contributes to a positive bias on the estimated effect of schooling on income.

As another example, consider the effects of marijuana use on income and on depression as follows:

$$Y_i = X_i\beta_1 + \beta_2 MJ_i + \varepsilon_i \tag{6.9a}$$

$$D_i = X_i\beta_1 + \beta_2 MJ_i + \varepsilon_i \tag{6.9b}$$

where
- Y = income;
- D = a measure of the extent of depression;
- MJ = a measure of marijuana use;
- X = a set of demographic variables.

The effects of marijuana use on these outcomes would likely be different across the population. Let's say that the distribution of the effects of marijuana use on income in the population is as it is depicted in Figure 6.6. The actual distribution is not important, but depicting it as a normal distribution makes it easier to understand the concept. Regardless of the distribution, what we aim to estimate is $\overline{\beta}_2$, which is the average causal effect of marijuana use on income. The zero just orients us, and it has no bearing on what direction the bias is in. But, what it says is that, in this notional world, a few people would have higher income as a result of marijuana use (perhaps marijuana reduces their anxiety, or perhaps they work for a marijuana dispensary, and using marijuana helps them better understand the product they are selling). However, most people have some negative or near-zero effect of marijuana use on income.

Self-selection bias would occur if those who have a greater benefit (or lower cost) of marijuana use, in terms of income gained or lost, were more likely to use marijuana than those with less benefit (or greater costs) of marijuana use. Assuming that there is a connection between actual effects of marijuana use on income and expected effects by individuals, those to the right of $\overline{\beta}_2$ (i.e., those who benefit from marijuana use or have low costs) would probably be more likely to use marijuana

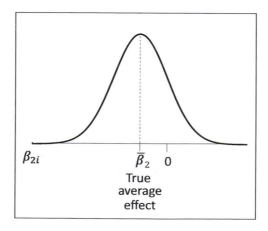

Figure 6.6 A demonstration of self-selection bias

than those who have an effect to the left of $\bar{\beta}_2$. This would mean that the more positive effects of marijuana use would be realized, which contributes towards a positive bias on the estimated effect of marijuana use on income, $\bar{\beta}_2$ in equation (6.9a).

Now consider the effects of marijuana use on depression. And, suppose that the distribution of effects looks similar to what we had in Figure 6.6, in that some people would have marijuana use increase depression (perhaps having a physiological effect on the brain), but most would have marijuana use reduce depression (perhaps reducing anxiety). (Note that I have no idea what the distribution of effects truly looks like and whether marijuana could reduce or increase depression symptoms.)

Again, as long as there is a connection between expected effects of marijuana on depression and the actual effects, those who have an effect to the *left* of $\bar{\beta}_2$ would be more likely to use marijuana. This means that the more negative effects would be realized, which would cause the estimated effect to be negatively biased, in contrast to the prior example.

The direction of the bias comes down to whether the outcome was good or bad:

- For the outcome of income (which is good), the bias was positive.
- For the outcome of depression (which is bad), the bias was negative.

Note that the direction of the bias does not depend on whether the average causal effect is positive or negative. The direction of the bias just depends on whether higher values of the outcome are perceived as good or bad by the subjects. Furthermore, keep in mind that self-selection bias is one bias that is likely on top of other biases rather than just an isolated bias. That is, self-selection bias occurs when the key X variable is not randomly determined, which would likely be associated with other problems, such as omitted-variables bias.

Consider another example on the optimal assignment of military recruiters. Military personnel assigned as recruiters can typically request their duty locations, and many often request locations near their family or where they grew up. Being back at home may positively affect productivity if the recruiter has old contacts or if the recruiter would be more trustworthy to potential recruits, being from the neighborhood, than other recruiters would be. On the other hand, for some people, being back home could negatively affect productivity because the recruiter spends more time with family and his/her homies. A service, say the Army, may be interested in estimating how assigning recruiters to their home county, on average, affects their productivity as a recruiter, or the number of contracts they get. So, the Navy may estimate the following model:

$$C_i = X_i \beta_1 + \beta_2 H_i + \varepsilon_i \tag{6.10}$$

where
- C = # contracts (or recruits) for a given recruiter in a given time period;
- X = a set of characteristics of the recruiter and the location;
- H = an indicator for being assigned to one's home county.

Self-selection bias would apply if those who believed they could be more effective back home (relative to other areas) were more likely to request to be sent to their home county. In contrast, the ideal situation for the researcher would be that recruiters are assigned to their home county regardless of their individual causal effect, β_{2i}. But, the likely situation is that there is some self-selection bias in that those actually assigned to their home county likely have a higher β_{2i} than the average effect in the population of recruiters, $\bar{\beta}_2$. We can think of it as more people with an above-average β_{2i} have the "home-county" variable turned to 1 (instead of 0) than those with below-average β_{2i}'s. And so, we're observing more of the effects for those with higher β_{2i}'s. This means that the estimated effect in equation (6.10) would likely overstate the true average causal effect, or the expected improvement in productivity if they placed all recruiters or a random set of recruiters in their home county.

Here is another example. In the medical/pharmaceutical field, a common endeavor is to attempt to determine the effect of some intervention (e.g., a treatment or procedure) on a health outcome for people with a certain condition, say migraines. A naïve approach would be to estimate the following model, for, say, the effects of the procedure treatment:

$$Y_i = X_i\beta_1 + \beta_2 T_i + \varepsilon_i \tag{6.11}$$

where Y is the health outcome (extent of migraines), X is a set of factors that may affect the outcome, and T is the treatment.

There could be self-selection bias here because it would not necessarily be random as to who gets the procedure done (the treatment). It could be that the people who suffer the most from migraines and, thus, would have the most to gain (in terms of reduced intensity of migraines), are more likely to choose to do the procedure. And so, the average β_2 in the set of those volunteering for the treatment would likely be more negative (reduced migraine pain) than the average β_2 in the population. So, the estimated effect would likely be downwardly biased relative to the true $\bar{\beta}_2$, which we do not know.

The bias here is based on the determination of who receives the treatment, not who is in the sample. The latter is a case of sample-selection bias (Section 6.7).

This is one of the reasons why health researchers try to use randomized control trials. In such a trial, they use a sample of those who choose to do the treatment and then randomize, from that group, who actually receives the treatment. Of course, precautions would need to be made for placebo effects as well.

What to check for: self-selection bias

The key question here is whether the subject, to some extent, can "choose" the value of the key explanatory variable (the treatment) and whether the subject determines the value of the treatment variable based on the benefits/costs of the treatment.

6.4.4 BIG QUESTION 4: Is there significant measurement error?

I usually take a two-hour nap from one to four.

–Yogi Berra

Measurement error bias occurs when an explanatory variable is measured with error. It causes the estimated effect of the explanatory variable on the outcome to be biased, with the bias usually being in the direction towards zero.

Causes of measurement error

Just like humans have flaws, most data have errors (but not always due to human errors). Here are several examples where one might experience a non-trivial amount of measurement error.

- In surveys, respondents may lie about a sensitive topic such as health, unlawful behaviors, or the bad things that they eat.
- Respondents in surveys may not remember their experiences correctly – e.g., people may not remember how much marijuana they smoked in the past year.
- Coders for surveys may mis-code the data.
- The data may not accurately represent the concept of interest. For example, diagnosing depression or post-traumatic-stress-disorder (PTSD) is often based on just a few questions, and so the algorithm likely incorrectly diagnoses some cases and fails to diagnose others.

Note that, in the last bullet on measuring depression or PTSD, the data may indeed be coded perfectly and the respondents may have told the truth on the questions that are used for a diagnosis. But, the measurement error would come from the questions not accurately identifying whether a person has PTSD.

Consequences of measurement error

Suppose that the average income for those without and with a college degree is as depicted in Figure 6.7. On average, those with a college degree earn $40,000 more than those without a college degree.

Now suppose that a random sample of people with a college degree were mis-assigned to the non-college-degree group. Assuming that this sample of the mis-assigned is fairly representative of the college-degree group, this would raise the average income for the non-college-degree group. This would reduce the difference in average income between the two groups. Conversely, let's say that part of the non-college-degree group is mis-assigned to the college-degree group. This would likely lower the average income of the college-degree group, again reducing the difference.

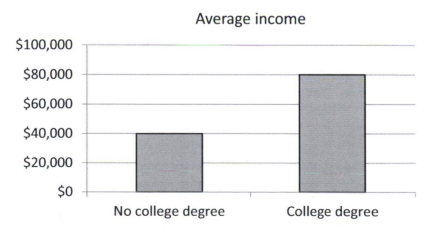

Figure 6.7 Notional example to demonstrate measurement error

This demonstrates the effects of an explanatory variable being measured with error. It typically causes the coefficient estimate to be attenuated towards zero. If the explanatory variable were a variable with many possible values (such as years-of-schooling) rather than just a dummy variable, the same concept applies: the mis-classification from measurement error would typically cause a bias towards zero in the coefficient estimate on the variable.

Let's use some actual data to test for the effects of measurement error. In Table 6.5, I show the results of two models:

- Column (1) is the same as the Multiple Regression Model from Figure 5.2 in Section 5.2.2, except that "college degree" is used instead of "years-of-schooling";
- Column (2) is the same except that I switched the "college degree" assignment for a randomly selected roughly 10% of the sample. That is, for about 10% of the sample, I set the college-degree variable equal to 1 if it was originally 0 and *vice versa*.

Table 6.5 Regression models demonstrating the effects of measurement error

	Dependent variable = income in 2003	
	(Model 1)	(Model 2)
College degree	29,361***	16,938***
	(2510)	(2119)
AFQT score	315***	423***
	(40)	(38)
Age	703*	460
	(384)	(388)
Black	−4,309*	−2,451
	(2278)	(2297)
Hispanic	370	1,176
	(2495)	(2526)
Mother has a HS diploma	3,420	3,520
	(2149)	(2176)
Mother has a college degree	1,391	4,182
	(3631)	(3662)
Father has a HS diploma	890	1,644
	(2123)	(2149)
Father has a college degree	13,983***	16,875***
	(2996)	(3014)
Constant	−83	5,810
	(16,403)	(16,596)
Observations	2,802	2,802
R-squared	0.213	0.193

Note: Standard errors are in parentheses.

*** $p < 0.01$, ** $p < 0.05$, * $p < 0.1$.

Source: Bureau of Labor Statistics, 2014.

What we see is that the coefficient estimate on "college degree" is reduced significantly: from $29,361 to $16,938. Thus, the measurement error in the college-degree variable is causing a bias in the coefficient estimate towards zero. (Note that if you try to replicate this with the code on the book's website, you will obtain different numbers due to the randomization, but the general story should be the same.)

But that is not all that happens. Note that the other coefficient estimates change as well. In particular, the one variable that has a very strong positive association with schooling, *afqt*, has a much higher estimate when measurement error is added into the college-degree variable. This is likely because the *afqt* variable is now picking up the variation in income that the college-degree variable is failing to do because of the measurement error. The same is true for the other factors that are likely positively correlated with having a college degree. **This demonstrates that measurement error bias, as with other biases, can affect all estimates (creating quasi-omitted-variables bias), not just the estimate on the variable causing problems.**

There was undoubtedly measurement error in the existing data, before I added my own measurement error. The important point is this: *Added to any other biases, measurement error will typically contribute to a downward-in-magnitude bias on the coefficient estimate.*

That said, there are cases in which measurement error could cause an upward-in-magnitude bias. This would occur if, in this case, those without a college degree but mis-coded as having a college degree had higher income, on average, than the true college-degree people. Alternatively, this could result from those "with a degree" coded incorrectly as "not having a college degree" having lower average income than the true non-degree people.

More generally, the bias from measurement error can be in any direction if there is what is called *differential measurement error*, which occurs when:

- The measurement error in a given X variable is related to the value of the X variable; or
- The measurement error in one X variable is correlated with another X variable.

Consider an analysis using as an X variable the number of times a person used marijuana in the past year. Assuming everyone tells the truth (to the best of their knowledge), someone who had used marijuana between zero and two times would likely remember how many times they used marijuana. But, someone who had used marijuana more often may not be able to remember, perhaps thinking that it was somewhere in the range of 15–25 times. In this situation, the bias in the estimated effect of the amount of marijuana use on an outcome could be positive or negative.

So, the general rule is:

- If the error in an explanatory variable is uncorrelated with the value of the explanatory variable or other explanatory variables (*non-differential measurement error*), then the likely direction of the bias is towards zero.
- If there is a reason to believe that there could be non-zero correlation between the error in the explanatory variable and the value of that or other explanatory variables, then the direction of the bias from measurement error is in an uncertain direction that needs significant efforts to calculate.

A researcher should assess whether any error in a given explanatory variable would naturally be greater at certain values of that variable. For something like marijuana use in the past year, there probably would be greater measurement error at certain values. For other variables, such as how many children one has, the value would be planted well in people's minds, and so the error should not be that different across the number of children.

Can bias from measurement error be corrected for?

There have been various attempts at correcting for measurement error. The most common methods have been summarized well in Guolo (2008) and Carroll et al. (2006). Unfortunately, all methods rely on many assumptions about the relationship of the error with the other explanatory variables. They also result in higher standard errors. Furthermore, these methods are computationally intensive, which makes it questionable whether it's worth the unknown benefit of improved estimates.

Theoretically, the instrumental-variables method that will be introduced in Chapter 8 could address the problem of measurement error. But, it is a rare option, as it requires a variable that affects the key explanatory variable and has no other effect on the outcome. You will see more on this later.

Measurement error in the dependent variable

Measurement error in the dependent variable is much less problematic. In fact, it results in no bias in the estimated effect of the explanatory variables as long as the reason for the measurement error is unrelated to the explanatory variable. To see why this is the case, consider again Figure 6.7. Let's suppose that 10% of the people lie and add an average of $5,000 to their income. As long as there is not too large of a discrepancy between the two groups in the propensity to lie, then the averages for both groups would increase by about $500, and the difference in their average income should stay about the same.

The one effect that measurement error in the dependent variable may have is that the standard errors on the coefficient estimates become larger. But, there would need to be relatively large measurement error for a relatively large share of the sample for there to be a meaningful effect on the coefficient estimates.

What to check for: measurement error

Check if there could be non-trivial error in the survey response or the coding of the explanatory variable. Or, consider whether the explanatory variable is imperfect in representing the intended concept.

Box 6.3   The hot hand in basketball: 25 years of measurement error

As discussed in the Preface, the inspiration for this book came from incorrect interpretations of results from research on the "hot hand" in basketball – I fully recognize that this sounds like a strange motivation. I described back in Section 5.4 that the "hot hand" is a period of elevated performance in which a person has a higher-than-normal probability of making a shot. It is often called "being in the zone" or "*en fuego*." The hot hand can show up in any sport, but it is most known in basketball, where a player gets in a groove and plays well above his/her normal playing level. I played a ton of basketball in my youth. I had regular experiences with the "hot hand" . . . not nearly as often these days, unfortunately.

Anyway, I couldn't believe my eyes when I discovered that all published research on this topic claimed that the hot hand in basketball was a "myth." That is, whenever we see someone hit several shots in a row, these authors argue, it is just part of random variation, just as we would get several instances of 6 or so heads or tails in a row if we flip a coin enough times. As my friend, Dan Stone, pointed out, this conclusion implies that there can be no improved performance from temporary increases in confidence. So, according to these researchers, the 100% of basketball players and coaches and 90% of basketball fans who believe in the hot hand are wrong and are committing the common human fallacy of seeing patterns in data that are actually random. This was such a great story that it has shown up in many pop-economics books (~~even a few by perhaps chocolate-deprived Nobel-prize-winning economists~~). Even an almost Fed-Chairman-nominee lectured the Harvard basketball team that the hot hand didn't exist (Brooks 2013).

So, I had to figure out what was wrong with their research. First, I combined all players into one model to generate greater power (rather than the prior studies examining one player at a time). I found a small hot-hand effect with free throw data (Arkes 2010) – that players were 3 to 5 percentage points more likely to make a second of two free throws if they hit their first free throw.

But, a real break-through came mostly from Daniel Stone (2012) and partly from an article of mine (Arkes 2013) building off of Stone's work. Stone demonstrated that *measurement error* caused by the mis-assignment of players into the hot or normal state causes the estimated hot-hand effects to be severely under-estimated. That is, the "hot" state may have been indicated in the research by hitting one's last shot or last few shots. But, a person with the hot hand will not necessarily hit every shot. So, sometimes a person is "hot" but classified as "not hot" and *vice versa*. (The data may be coded correctly but not reflect the intended concept, "hot hand," accurately.) In Arkes (2013), I simulated a world with a hot hand occurring regularly and demonstrated how the prior research, given their methods and sample sizes, severely understated the hot-hand effect and would have had a very low probability of detecting a significant effect for the hot hand. Importantly, what this also implied was that the small hot-hand effect I found with free throw data in 2010 (which was also subject to the same measurement error) is likely representative of a much larger hot-hand effect. Further biases related to the Gambler's Fallacy were recently identified by Joshua Miller and Adam Sanjurjo in a fascinating article (Miller and Sanjurjo 2018), in which they demonstrate that, if you take all "heads" in a finite sequence of coin flips, the probability that the following flip is a "heads" is less than 50%. They actually reverse the result from the seminal hot-hand study by Gilovich et al. (1985), using that study's data to demonstrate that correcting for the Gambler's-Fallacy bias leads to significant hot-hand effects.

So, as mentioned in Section 5.4, the proper interpretation of the prior research should not have been, "the hot hand is a myth." Rather, it should have been, "We found no evidence for the hot hand."

What a delicious irony here! *The original researchers (and Nobel Prize winners) who claimed that basketball players and fans were mistakenly seeing patterns in data that are actually random were actually the ones making the error, concluding randomness in data that are almost certainly patterned.* (And, good thing that the near-Fed-Chairman-nominee didn't become the Fed Chairman.)

6.4.5 BIG QUESTION 5: *Are there mediating factors used as control variables?*

I wouldn't have hit so many homers if I hadn't hit the ball so hard.

– notional Yogi Berra quote

Why mediating factors should be excluded

This is the underappreciated star of regression pitfalls. Even though it is quite straightforward, it is often overlooked. And, without taking it into account, the regression will likely produce biased estimates of the true causal effects. This is a mistake few researchers are conscious of and something you won't see in other textbooks, at least as of this writing.

Recall from earlier discussions:

- From Section 6.4.2, omitted-variables bias is not a problem if the omitted factor is a product of the key explanatory variable.
- In the lemon-tree example from Section 4.1 and Figures 4.1a and 4.1b (on "holding other factors constant"), we did not want to control for the height on the tree, as that was part of the reason why the amount of water affected how many lemons the tree produced.
- In the domino-chain example from Section 4.1 and Figure 4.2, as we aimed to estimate how tipping the first domino affected whether the last domino fell, we did not want to hold constant whether the third domino fell. That too was part of the mechanism we wanted to capture.
- From Section 4.2 and Figures 4.3a and 4.3b, when you control for a variable (holding it constant), in the model it is no longer part of the reason why the outcome moves with the key explanatory variable. And, it was argued, we wanted to hold constant factors that determined schooling, but we did not want to hold constant things that resulted from more schooling (workplace skills and network connections). We wanted these latter factors to be allowed to change in the model as years-of-schooling changed.

The BIG QUESTION in this section formalizes the concept of not controlling for factors that are products of the key explanatory variable. To see an example, let's consider a case that comes from one of my publications (Arkes 2007). In that study, I examined what happens to teenage drug use when the unemployment rate increases. From the more recent NLSY (starting in 1997, Bureau of Labor Statistics, 2015), I had individual-level data of teenagers from all states, over several years, during their teenage years. I specified the model as follows:

$$Y_{it} = X_{it}\beta_1 + \beta_2 UR_{it} + \varepsilon_{it} \tag{6.12}$$

where Y is the measure of teenage drug use, UR is the state unemployment rate for year t. The vector X would include a set of demographic variables, year dummy variables, and state dummy variables. This is equivalent to using state and year fixed effects, which will be covered in Section 8.1.

When writing this article, I conceived of several mechanisms for how a higher unemployment rate could lead to a change in teenage drug use. They are represented in Figure 6.8, which is similar in nature to Figures 4.1a and 4.1b. The first set of arrows on the left represent how an increase in the unemployment rate (by one percentage point) would affect three mediating factors.

Recall from Chapter 4 that mediating factors (also called "intervening factors" or "mechanism variables") are factors through which the key explanatory variable affects the dependent variable. For example, in the lemon-tree example, the tree's height was a mediating factor for how watering affected the number of lemons the tree produced.

The second set of arrows represents how one-unit *increases* in those mediating factors would affect teenage drug use. *Decreases* in the mediating factors would cause the opposite effect. A **mechanism** would be a full reason why a change in the unemployment rate caused a change in teenage drug use, represented in Figure 6.8 as a full pathway, or one set of the left and right arrows. There are three mechanisms, labeled with circled M1, M2, and M3. For example, mechanism "M1" represents how the unemployment rate affects teenage drug use through effects on teenage income. Mechanism "M1" is assumed to be negative because it is a product of a negative effect of the unemployment rate on teenage income and a positive effect of teenage income on teen drug use. That is, according to my theory, a higher unemployment rate will lead to less teen drug use from any effects the unemployment rate has on teenage income.

The mechanisms and the likely sign of the effect are that a higher unemployment rate would:

- M1: reduce teenage income, making drugs less affordable ➔ reducing drug use (NEGATIVE EFFECT);
- M2: lead to greater free time and boredom, creating more opportunity to use drugs or greater motivation to use drugs to add excitement to their life ➔ increasing drug use (POSITIVE EFFECT);
- M3: increase the number of drug sellers, which makes drugs more available and perhaps easier to obtain ➔ increasing use (POSITIVE EFFECT).

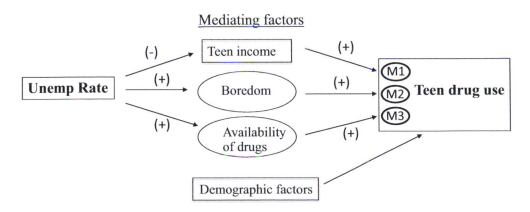

Figure 6.8 Demonstration of mediating factors

In Figure 6.8, teenage income is in a rectangle because it is often observable, while boredom and availability are in ovals because they cannot be measured easily. Also in the figure is a rectangle for "demographic" variables (e.g., gender and race/ethnicity). These are *not* part of the mechanism for how the unemployment rate would affect teenage drug use, as they probably would not be affected by the unemployment rate.

The classic definition for omitted-variables bias from all textbooks I have seen implies one should control for these mediating factors (particularly teenage income) because they are correlated with the unemployment rate and they likely affect the outcome. But, changes in teenage income represent part of the reason why the unemployment rate affects teenage drug use.

If we estimated equation (6.12), which does not include the teenager's income (or any proxy for boredom or availability), then the estimate for β_2 would capture the effects of the unemployment rate on teenage drug use from all three mechanisms (M1 to M3) plus any other mechanisms that I may not have conceived of.

In this case, assuming the model has no other biases, the estimate for β_2 would be an unbiased estimate of the "*full effect*" – or, how teenage drug use should move if the unemployment rate were to increase by 1 percentage point, holding constant the demographic factors (X). This is likely the estimate that you want.

As for identifying each of the six effects (the six arrows) that are part of the mechanisms, that would be very difficult to accurately identify for many reasons – e.g., not any available data or reverse causality for teenage income and drug use. But, we do not have to be concerned about those if you are interested in the *full effect* for β_2.

At the beginning of this sub-section, I said many researchers were not aware of this issue. And, here is an example of why I say this. When I submitted this article for publication, a referee at the well-respected journal where it is now published said that I needed to include the teenager's income in the model. I responded that I cannot do that. Let's look at what would have happened to the model if I had controlled for teenage income.

The model would be the following:

$$Y_{it} = X_{it}\beta_1 + \beta_2 UR_{it} + \beta_3 \left(teenager's\ income\right)_{it} + \varepsilon_{it} \qquad (6.13)$$

This model is represented in Figure 6.9. Teenage income now has its own separate effect outside of the unemployment-rate effect. **Thus, in the model, when the unemployment rate changes, boredom and availability would increase (not that we observe it), but income would not change because it is being "held constant."** This means that drug use would change from the increases in boredom and availability, but not from changes in income. So, the unemployment-rate effect would only capture the other two mechanisms, M2 and M3. The interpretation of the estimate for β_{2a} in equation (6.13) would now be: how a 1-percentage-point increase in the unemployment rate affects teenage drug use, after holding constant teenage income (and the other factors represented in X). It would no longer represent the "full effect" of the unemployment rate or how teenage drug use moves with the unemployment rate.

Is the new coefficient estimate on the unemployment rate ($\hat{\beta}_{2a}$) interesting? Maybe . . . if you want to gauge the size of those other effects. But, from a practical standpoint, it is not as interesting or relevant as the "full effect" of the unemployment rate on teenage drug use.

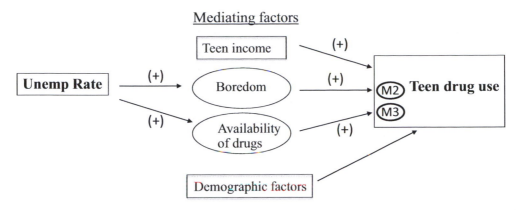

Figure 6.9 What happens if one controls for a mediating factor

In what direction would the estimated unemployment-rate effect be biased? Because the teen-income mechanism (M1) contributed towards a negative effect of the unemployment rate on drug use, eliminating this mechanism from the unemployment-rate effect would cause a positive bias on the estimate – i.e., we would be eliminating a negative mechanism, causing the estimate to increase. Thus, if I had followed the referee's suggestion, I would have only estimated a *partial effect* of the unemployment rate on teen drug use rather than the *full effect*.

(The term "partial effect" [used here to contrast with the "full effect"] is also used when describing coefficient estimates in a Multiple Regression Model. A "partial effect," like a partial derivative, is the effect of some variable on the outcome while holding other factors constant. I personally believe that using those terms here – in the context of capturing a "full causal effect" as opposed to only "part of a causal effect" – is a better use of those terms in regression analysis.)

Note that even if the coefficient estimate were higher in equation (6.13), as we may expect, it would still be a partial effect because it does not include every mechanism. Yes, a partial effect can be larger than a full effect if the excluded mechanisms are in the opposite direction of the net effect of the other mechanisms.

In the income-schooling case, controlling for the AFQT score likely got us closer to the true causal effect of schooling. In this case, controlling for teenage income likely takes us away from the true causal effect, as it gives just a partial effect instead of the full effect.

Mediating factors vs. omitted-variables bias

Someone may argue that not controlling for teenage income would cause omitted-variables bias. However, recall that I said back in Section 6.4.2 that omitted-variables bias is not a problem if the key explanatory variable is affecting the omitted variable and not *vice versa*. That is the case here with the key explanatory variable (the state unemployment rate) and the omitted variable (the teenager's income). So, omitted teenage income should not be a concern because the only reason that the teen-ager's income would be correlated with the unemployment rate is because the unemployment rate affects teenage income.

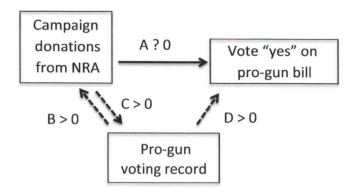

Figure 6.10 The effect of campaign donations on voting behavior

However, there are other situations in which it would not be as clear as to whether to control for some variable. Take the case in Figure 6.10, a political-science issue, in which you want to estimate the effects of campaign donations from the National Rifle Association (NRA) on the probability that a Congressman votes for a certain pro-gun legislative bill.

The issue is whether a Congressman's "pro-gun voting record" should be included as a control variable. Excluding the variable would present a potential omitted-variables bias problem because the Congressman's voting record, which proxies for views on guns, could lead to NRA campaign donations and the eventual vote on the current bill. However, including "pro-gun voting record" would mean that you may only be estimating a "partial effect" rather than the "full effect" of NRA campaign donations on the probability of the "yes" vote because the campaign donations could increase their pro-gun leanings (which the pro-gun voting record represents).

So, what do you do? The best thing to do is:

1. Acknowledge the dilemma in your article;
2. Estimate the model both with and without "voting record";
3. If the estimated effect of "NRA campaign donations" is similar with and without "voting record" included, then you probably are okay;
4. If the estimated effect of "NRA campaign donations" is different with "voting record" included vs. not included, then you should report both, or perhaps explore further, if data are available, what precedes what in terms of donations and voting record.

Summary

Summing up, a necessity for capturing the true causal effect is that mediating factors must be excluded from the model. Or, you can say that any variable that could be affected by the key X variable needs to be excluded from the model. In the first example above, the question would be: "Does the model exclude variables that are affected by the unemployment rate?" Rather than having to think of the mechanisms, the simple check would be to look at the existing control variables and determine whether any could be a product of the key X variable.

What to check for: mediating factors

If there is a variable included in the model that is a product of the key explanatory variable (or that is determined after the key explanatory variable), then take that variable out of the model. If you are assessing another model, just think of the obvious variables that could be part of non-trivial mechanisms of how the key explanatory variable affects the outcome.

6.4.6 *BIG QUESTION 6: Are there any outcome variables used as control variables?*

> Congratulations. I knew the record would stand until it was broken.
>
> —Yogi Berra

Seems like a no-brainer, eh? That's what I thought. In fact, I wouldn't have even included it here had it not been done in a series of articles, mostly published in well-respected journals. Made me wonder about the research game and how people decide what to publish. I won't single out any specific article. But, if you investigate articles on how state tax rates affect state economic growth, you will find that most articles on this topic included outcome variables as control variables. This was to make the regression model consistent with a theoretical model, but it results in biased estimates, typically leading to an understatement of the true effect.

Let me demonstrate this point by borrowing from a model I will be using in Chapter 8 on this topic. Again, rather than singling anyone out, I use mostly my own data that I compiled. Table 6.6 shows the effects of state income tax rates on the growth rate in Gross State Product (the state version of Gross Domestic Product) for three models:

- Model (1) has just state and region-year-interacted dummy variables as control variables, as well as a few other tax rates (indicated in the Notes section of the table);
- Model (2) adds state employment growth as an explanatory variable;
- Model (3) further adds growth in real personal income per capita for the state as an explanatory variable.

These two variables that are added in Models (2) and (3) are outcomes in themselves. That is, growth in state employment and real personal income per capita are likely, to some extent, products of the tax rate.

The important result here is that the coefficient estimates on the key X variable, "maximum marginal income tax rate," are reduced in magnitude as the outcome variables are added into the model, in Models (2) and (3). And, the reason is that the outcomes included as control variables are soaking up a good part of the variation in the outcome. There is less of an effect that the tax rates can have with more of the variation in the outcome being explained.

The logic on the interpretation here is similar to that for mediating factors. In Model (3), we are now estimating the effect of the state tax rate on growth in Gross State Product beyond any effects

Table 6.6 The effects of state tax rates on Gross State Product growth (n = 1440), 1980–2009

	Dependent variable = growth rate in Gross State Product		
	Model (1)	*Model (2)*	*Model (3)*
Maximum marginal income tax rate	−0.366*** (0.140) [−0.640, −0.092]	−0.295** (0.133) [−0.556, −0.034]	−0.142 (0.117) [−0.371, 0.087]
Employment growth		0.762*** (0.069)	0.536*** (0.062)
Real personal income per-capita growth			0.770*** (0.042)

Note: The sample includes the lower 48 states for 30 years (1980 to 2009). ***, **, and * indicate statistical significance at the 1, 5, and 10 percent levels. Standard errors are in parentheses. 95% confidence intervals are in brackets. Models also include state and region-year-interacted dummy variables. In addition, they include maximum corporate income tax, sales tax, and long-term capital gains tax rates.

that state tax rates have on employment and income growth – not exactly an interesting or useful concept. The more useful regression would be Model (1), which tells us how Gross State Product changes with a 1-percentage-point increase in the tax rate, holding state and region-year constant.

What to check for: using outcome variables as control variables

The check for whether there are any outcome variables is the same as that for mediating factors. You determine if any control variable could be a product of the key explanatory variable(s). If so, depending on how important the mechanism is, you are probably not estimating the full causal effect. So, the best practice is to drop the variable from the model.

6.5 How to choose the best set of control variables (model selection)

> Regressions are 90% avoiding biases, and the other half is choosing the best set of control variables.
>
> – paraphrasing Yogi Berra

In this section, I discuss another highly misunderstood topic: choosing the optimal set of control variables. This is often called **model selection**. Recall that control variables are those that are included in a model to help identify the true causal effects of the key explanatory variables (or the key empirical relationships for other regression objectives). Opinions vary widely on the criteria for choosing the right set of control variables. Poor choices in choosing control variables contribute to the plethora of incorrect research results. I will lay out criteria here that mostly follow from the discussion so far, particularly from the BIG QUESTIONS in Section 6.4. The criteria are:

1. Theory suggests that the *control variable* could affect the outcome *and* the key explanatory variable(s), or the *control variable* addresses a likely source of omitted-variables bias due to incidental correlation.
2. The *control variable* is not a product of the key explanatory variable and is not an outcome itself.
3. The coefficient estimate on the *control variable* is not in an inconceivable direction or of an inconceivable magnitude.
4. The *control variable* is not too highly correlated with the key explanatory variable.
5. The *control variable* does not violate these BIG QUESTION criteria:
    *   It is not affected by the outcome (reverse causality);
    *   People do not select into different values of the *control variable* based on expectations of the effects of that variable on the outcome (self-selection bias).

The first criterion is the basis for including any control variable. If the variable should not affect the outcome or is not possibly correlated with the key explanatory variable, then there is no need to control for the variable. The second criterion just speaks to whether the control variable would be a mediating factor for the key explanatory variable or an outcome itself (BIG QUESTIONS 5 and 6).

The third criterion is a bit controversial. The idea here is that, for a variable that could only have a positive effect (if any), according to theory, a few non-representative outlying observations could cause a coefficient estimate to be negative. The incorrect estimate may exacerbate any bias from *quasi-omitted-variables bias*. The important part of this criterion is being certain that the coefficient estimate cannot conceivably be in the direction it is. Also, if a variable has an inconceivably large estimated effect, then give some thought as to whether this apparently overstated estimate would affect other estimates and whether it is best to exclude the variable from the model. This is part of the "art" in regression modeling.

For the fourth criterion, if a control variable were too highly correlated with the key explanatory variable or would not allow much independent variation in the key explanatory variable, then it would be difficult to generate precise effects of the key explanatory variable. The effects of the key explanatory variable would be split between the key variable and other factors that almost always move with the variable. A good example is in Section 6.6.1, below, on the discussion on multicollinearity.

For the fifth criterion, if a control variable were subject to reverse causality or self-selection bias, then the coefficient on it may absorb too much of the variation in the dependent variable, leaving less to be explained by the key explanatory variable, or it could create quasi-omitted-variables bias. This is like BIG QUESTION 6 in that part of the outcome is being controlled for. This could contribute to greater bias in the estimated effect of the key explanatory variable.

Whereas reverse causality and self-selection bias in a control variable cause problems for estimating the causal effect of some key X variable, violations of the other BIG QUESTIONS are not important for a control variable. If a control variable were subject to omitted-variables bias or measurement error, it does not mean that the variable should not be included, as it would still likely reduce any bias. Omitted-variables bias on the control variable can actually be a good thing, as it could capture the effects of other important variables that could be correlated with the key explanatory variable.

In addition, a variable that has measurement error still could provide value to the model in helping to control for an important factor. Any bias from measurement error should just change the magnitude of the coefficient estimate without changing its sign. Thus, the explanatory power it has would likely still help towards reducing omitted-variables bias for the key explanatory variable, which most of the time would bring the estimate closer to identifying the causal effect of interest. That said, a biased estimate on the control variable may result in quasi-omitted-variables bias for the key explanatory variable, but less bias than one would get without controlling for that variable. Finally, it is also okay if a control variable has its own mediating factor as another control variable, as it would just provide more information.

There may be some potential control variables that satisfy some of the criteria but not all. This is where judgment needs to be used to determine which violation of the BIG QUESTIONS causes the least bias.

One criterion that some believe should be used is that the variable has to be statistically significant. I do not use this criterion because of what we learned in Section 5.5 about how an insignificant estimate does not mean that the variable has no effect/association. Regardless of the significance, the coefficient estimate is usually the best guess on the contribution of the variable in explaining the outcome. Furthermore, an insignificant coefficient estimate still imparts information, provided it satisfies the third criterion above on the estimate being conceivable.

Also, many use as a guide some goodness-of-fit measure. We saw R^2 and Adjusted R^2 back in Section 2.5, with higher values being indicative of a better fit of the model. There is also the Akaike Information Criterion (AIC), the corrected AIC (AICc), and the Bayesian Information Criterion (BIC). I will leave details on these measures to Chapter 10 on time-series models, but the lower values are the better fits. These are the criteria that are usually considered when one discusses "model selection." But, these should not be used to decide if a control variable should be included in a model or not, as the set of criteria described above is more useful. However, these other criteria could help in deciding how to best characterize a key explanatory variable or a control variable. For example, these criteria may speak to whether, in order to provide a better fit of the data, a certain variable should be represented in a quadratic form, as a spline, or as a set of dummy variables for various values of the variable.

Table 6.7 Criteria to use and not to use for determining what *control variables* to include

Criteria to use	*Criteria* not to use
• Could affect both the outcome and key explanatory variable or could address omitted-variables bias from incidental correlation; • Is not a product of the key explanatory variable (a mediating factor or an outcome); • Does not have a coefficient estimate that is inconceivable in direction or magnitude; • Is not subject to reverse causality or self-selection bias; • Is not too closely correlated and simultaneously determined with the key explanatory variable.	• Whether it is subject to omitted-variables bias; • Whether it has measurement error; • Whether it is a mediating factor for another control variable (not for the key X variable); • Whether it is significant; • Whether it affects the goodness-of-fit (R^2, Adjusted R^2, AIC, BIC) . . . except for choosing how to characterize variables.

Table 6.7 provides a summary table of what criteria to use and not to use when determining whether to include or exclude control variables for the objective of estimating causal effects. When it says "not to use" the criteria, it means that this should not be a consideration.

6.6 What could bias the standard errors and how do you fix it?

The 6 BIG QUESTIONS above dealt with issues in a model that could move the *coefficient estimate* away from the true causal effect of a variable. Having a biased coefficient estimate would, of course, affect any hypothesis test and confidence interval for how one variable affects another. The validity of hypothesis tests and accuracy of confidence intervals could also be affected by whether the *standard errors* are properly and efficiently estimated. Some aspects of a model or the data could lead to a bias (an overstatement or understatement) of the true standard errors; and some strategies may be able to reduce the bias in the standard errors.

While addressing such biases is important, keep in mind that the biases on standard errors tend to be (although are not always) minor relative to most biases on the coefficient estimates. Getting the standard errors right doesn't help much if you are off-target on the coefficient estimate.

6.6.1 Multicollinearity

Multicollinearity is a situation in which having explanatory variables that are highly correlated with each other causes the coefficient estimates to have inflated standard errors. **Perfect multicollinearity** occurs when one X variable is an exact linear transformation of another X variable or set of X variables – the R^2 would equal 1.000 if that X variable were regressed on the other X variable(s). When this occurs, the model is unable to distinguish between the effects of the two-or-more variables. Either the model will not run, or it will run and just not be able to estimate the coefficients for at least one of the collinear variables.

One other consequence of high multicollinearity, not mentioned in other textbooks (to my knowledge), is that it could bias the coefficient estimate for the key explanatory variable if the multicollinearity is so high that it leaves little independent variation in that variable. If the key X variable and a control variable were so highly correlated so that the key X variable rarely moves independently of the other, then the coefficient estimate on the key X variable would likely be highly sensitive to a single outlier. That said, if the control variable clearly preceded the key X variable, then it would be important to control for that variable to avoid omitted-variables bias.

We will now consider two sets of highly correlated X variables:

- How years-of-schooling affects income (with AFQT score as a potential control variable);
- How the state unemployment rate affects alcohol consumption (with state personal-income-per-capita as a potential control variable).

Case 1: How years-of-schooling affects income

Figure 6.11 shows two different Venn diagrams to demonstrate the problem of multicollinearity. In the left diagram, years-of-schooling and the AFQT score are somewhat correlated, but still leave a good amount of independent correlation between income and education (area F) to identify the effect. In the diagram on the right, years-of-schooling and the AFQT score are much more highly correlated,

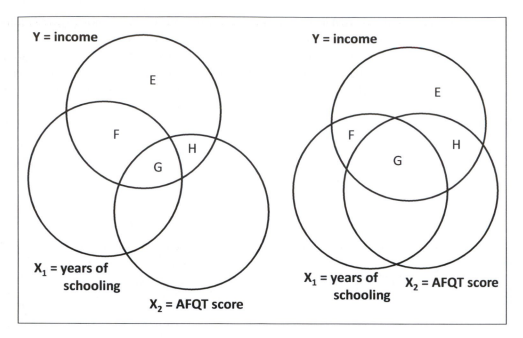

Figure 6.11 Using Venn diagrams to demonstrate multicollinearity

causing area F to be much smaller. That is, less of the variation in income can be explained by years-of-schooling, independently of the AFQT score. We saw in Chapter 5 that this would lead to a larger standard error on the coefficient estimate on education.

Let's consider one situation of this with the results of our schooling-income models, as shown in Table 6.8. There are three models. The first two just have years-of-schooling or AFQT separately, and the third model has both variables as explanatory variables. Note that the standard errors for the coefficient estimates on both variables are larger by more than 25% in the third model, with both variables included. This demonstrates the concept from Figure 6.11, that including in the model a

Table 6.8 Demonstrating the effects of multicollinearity (dependent variable = 2003 income)

	(1)	*(2)*	*(3)*
Years–of–schooling	8,121***		5,395***
	(347)		(436)
AFQT score		651***	368***
		(29)	(37)
Constant	−55,043***	25,390***	−34,765***
	(4,693)	(1,558)	(5,038)
Observations	2,772	2,772	2,772
R–squared	0.165	0.150	0.195

Note: Standard errors in parentheses.

*** $p < 0.01$, ** $p < 0.05$, * $p < 0.1$.

Source: Bureau of Labor Statistics, 2014.

control variable that is highly correlated with the key explanatory variable causes the standard errors to be larger for the key explanatory variable.

This does not mean that the AFQT score should not be included, as excluding it would likely cause omitted-variables bias. In this case, the benefits of including the AFQT score (reducing the bias on the estimated effect of years-of-schooling) likely outweigh the costs (higher standard error on the years-of-schooling estimate). Typically, reducing the bias in the coefficient estimate is more important, so variables should be included if they would reduce omitted-variables bias. And, in this situation, it is likely that, despite the high correlation, years-of-schooling does move independently of the AFQT score.

Case 2: How the state unemployment rate affects alcohol consumption

A different situation presents itself if the key explanatory variable is so highly correlated with another variable that its effects get confounded and (possibly) partly captured by the other variable. Consider the following analysis of how "the strength of the economy" affects alcohol use (Ruhm and Black 2002). A weak economy could increase alcohol use as people have more time to drink and may be depressed from being unemployed; but a weak economy could reduce income and stress from working too much, which could reduce drinking. Thus, the causal effect could go in either direction. Table 6.9 shows results from two models that Ruhm and Black estimated on the log of the number of drinks, with only the coefficient estimates on the key X variables being presented.

In Model (1), the authors just include the unemployment rate as the measure of the strength of the economy. In Model (2), they add state personal income per capita (PI/C). As you can see, the significant coefficient estimates (having t-stats between 4 and 7) all point to the result that the number of drinks is lower in a weaker economy and higher in a stronger economy.

Multicollinearity occurs here because, in Model (2), both the unemployment rate and PI/C are included at the same time, and they are likely highly negatively correlated with each other. As a result of the inclusion of PI/C, the standard error on the unemployment-rate estimate increases a little. But, more importantly in this case, the coefficient estimate on the unemployment rate is reduced in magnitude from -0.313 to -0.231.

So, which estimate is better, -0.313 or -0.231? It depends on the question you are asking. For Ruhm and Black, who were interested in whether drinking increases or decreases in bad economic times, either model is correct. And, Model (2) gives even stronger support for the evidence from Model (1).

Table 6.9 Results on how the economy affects alcohol use – from Ruhm and Black (2002)

	Model (1)	Model (2)
State unemployment rate	−0.0313	−0.0231
	(0.0048)	(0.0052)
State personal income per capita (PI/C)		0.0537
		(0.0080)

Note: The dependent variable is the log of the number of drinks in the prior month. Standard errors are in parentheses. Also included in the models are controls for personal characteristics, state, state-specific time trends, beer taxes, and month.

However, let's say that the question you are asking is: "How does the amount of drinking change if the state unemployment rate were to increase by 1 percentage point?" In this case, the best strategy (in my view) would be to exclude PI/C. The unemployment rate typically does not move on its own. Rather, it usually moves with other economic variables. So, controlling for PI/C would give an estimate that represents: "How a one-percentage-point increase in the unemployment rate affects the number of drinks a person has beyond any effect that PI/C has." This is similar to a "partial effect" that occurs with the inclusion of a mediating factor (BIG QUESTION 5) in that the partial effect usually does not tell you anything useful. The difference, however, is that this situation involves coinciding variables rather than variables coming in a specific sequential order.

So, if you wanted to estimate the effect of the unemployment rate, you would not want to hold PI/C constant because the model would effectively hold constant part of the unemployment-rate effect.

One situation in which you do not have to be concerned with multicollinearity is if it occurs for two or more control variables (and not the key explanatory variable). Again, the more relevant information from control variables that are included in the model, the less omitted-variables bias there would be for the key explanatory variable.

What to check for: multicollinearity

Just for the key explanatory variable, consider whether there is another variable that it is highly correlated with so that there would not be adequate independent variation to allow for relatively precise estimated effects. If so, exclude the variable if it does not present a non-trivial omitted-variables bias problem.

6.6.2 Heteroskedasticity

One of the assumptions for the Multiple Regression Model in Section 2.10 was **A4**: the model has **homoskedasticity** in that the error terms have the same variance, regardless of the values of X or the predicted value of Y. That is, $var(\varepsilon \mid X) = var(\varepsilon)$, for all explanatory variables. A violation of this assumption would be called **heteroskedasticity**, which occurs when the variance of the error term is not the same at all values of a given X variable or set of X variables. Some say the word "heteroskedasticity" comes from the Greek terms of "hetero" (meaning different) and "skedasis" (meaning dispersion); another theory says it comes from French, meaning "On Thursdays, I like to let the barista choose how to prepare my coffee, and I'm okay with the wider variance in quality."

Figure 6.12 shows a notional example of what homoskedasticity would look like between the AFQT percentile and income. Note that there is a relatively consistent distribution of values of income across the whole range of the AFQT percentile scores. And so, with a line going through the middle of these data, the spread of the residuals would probably be generally similar at different values of the AFQT score.

Now, I show, in Figure 6.13, the true data from the NLSY, with just a small partly random sample to make the graph tractable. In this case, the distribution of income is much narrower for low percentiles for the AFQT score than for higher percentiles. This is heteroskedasticity. The pattern makes sense, as those with lower aptitude would tend to have a narrower range of economic opportunities.

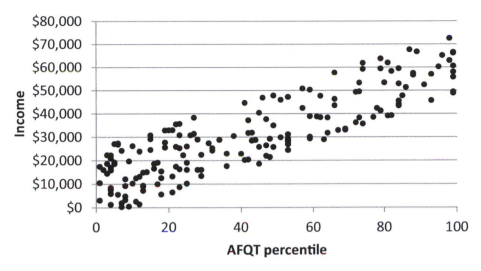

Figure 6.12 A notional example of homoskedasticity

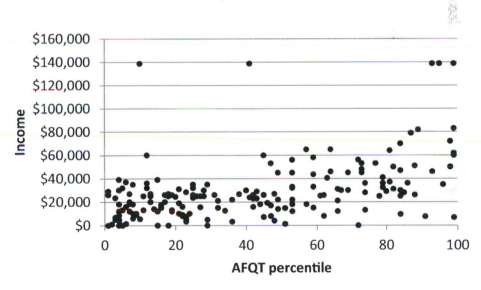

Figure 6.13 A sample of real data on AFQT and income, demonstrating heteroskedasticity
Source: Bureau of Labor Statistics, 2014.

Heteroskedasticity causes biased standard errors in regression models. This occurs because, at the values of the X variable where there is greater variation in the *Y* variable, we have less certainty on where the central tendency is. But, we assume that we have the same certainty as for the other values for the X variable. With the variation greater at some values of the X variable, the weight should be less for those observations to calculate the standard errors due to the greater uncertainty in the value of *Y*. So, the estimated standard errors would be biased estimators of the true population standard deviation of the coefficient. Given that the estimated standard errors are biased, any hypothesis tests would be affected. (Heteroskedasticity does not bias the coefficient estimates.)

The correction is simply to use **robust standard errors**, also known as Huber–White estimators. This allows the standard errors to vary by the values of the X variables. The equation for the robust standard errors is highly mathematical, so in the spirit of the book, I will leave it out. In research, it is typically adequate to just mention that you are using robust standard errors; showing the equations is typically not necessary.

Table 6.10 shows, from our basic model of regressing *income* on *educ* and *afqt*, the **Breusch–Pagan tests** for heteroskedasticity with respect to the predicted value of income, years-of-schooling, and AFQT score. All are statistically significant (with p = 0.000), providing strong evidence for heteroskedasticity for each case. In Model (2), I show the heteroskedasticity-corrected model. Note that the coefficient estimates do not change with the correction. It is just the standard errors that change. For *educ*, there is a large increase in the standard error, but that for *afqt* has a small decrease.

In most cases, the direction of the bias on the standard errors is downwards, so **robust standard errors** (those corrected for heteroskedasticity) are usually larger. Corrected standard errors will be smaller in the atypical cases in which there is wider variation in the error terms for the central values of an explanatory variable than for the extreme values. This could occur if, say, most low-education people have a small variance in their income (due to being mostly blue-collar workers), most high-education people have a small variance (perhaps being mostly white-collar workers), and those with a middle amount of education have higher variance because they could get on either a blue-collar or white-collar career track.

Given the simplicity of the test and of the correction for heteroskedasticity in most statistical programs, it is worth doing the test and making the correction when there is

Table 6.10 The correction for heteroskedasticity (n = 2772)

	Dependent variable = income	
	(1)	*(2)*
	No correction for heteroskedasticity	*With a correction for heteroskedasticity*
Years-of-schooling (*educ*)	5395	5395
	(436)	(531)
AFQT score (*afqt*)	367	367
	(37)	(36)
Tests for heteroskedasticity:		
heteroskedasticity with respect to the predicted value of income	$\chi^2(1) = 782.60$, p = 0.000	
heteroskedasticity with respect to *educ*	$\chi^2(1) = 718.04$, p = 0.000	
heteroskedasticity with respect to *afqt*	$\chi^2(1) = 544.23$, p = 0.000	

Note: The standard errors are in the parentheses.

Source: Bureau of Labor Statistics, 2014.

even a small possibility of heteroskedasticity. However, just as an insignificant estimate on a variable does not indicate that the variable is not related to the dependent variable, an insignificant test for heteroskedasticity does not prove that there is no heteroskedasticity. The best approach may be to do a visual inspection of the data.

If you find yourself assessing another study and do not have the data, then consider the issue theoretically. You do not have to think about whether the error terms would have a different variance for different values of each explanatory variable. Rather, just focus on the key explanatory variable(s).

Note that correcting for heteroskedasticity is important, but the egregiousness from not correcting for heteroskedasticity is fairly small compared to the egregiousness from having a poorly specified model or having a meaningful BIG QUESTION violation.

Also, note that different statistical programs might produce different standard errors from the correction for heteroskedasticity, due to slightly different methods. In particular, the two programs I used, Stata and R, generate different standard errors with the corrections. (There are discussions of these discrepancies on the internet.) The differences are typically small enough that it would not matter which one is correct, but that is not the case all of the time. This is another situation, adding to the Bayes critique of p-values, in which extra care needs to be used when interpreting p-values.

What to check for: heteroskedasticity

Focus on the key explanatory variable and inspect the data to determine whether the variance in the residuals is systematically higher for a certain part of the distribution of the key explanatory variable. Or, think theoretically whether the variance of the error terms could be different for different values of the X variable. If so, use robust standard errors.

6.6.3 Correlated observations or clustering

Imagine that, in a school of 10 classes of 30 students each, 5 of the classes are randomly selected to have a new-math program that is given to all students in those 5 classes. You then estimate a model as follows:

$$Y_{ic} = X_{ic}\beta_1 + \beta_2 T_c + \varepsilon_{ic} \tag{6.14}$$

where
- Subscript i refers to student i;
- Subscript c refers to class c;
- Y is the math score growth in the given year;
- X is the student's other characteristics;
- T_c is the treatment of having the new-math program for class c.

So, 150 students get the new-math program, and 150 students receive the old program. Are the 150 students randomized? Not exactly. Really, only 5 of 10 entities were randomized – the classes. Randomizing 5 of 10 classes is not as powerful as randomizing 150 of 300 students would be, in part because there is a greater likelihood that there are non-trivial differences between the classes in terms of teacher quality or overall student aptitude when 5 of 10 are chosen randomly. If we chose 150 students of 300 randomly (and held constant the teacher), then there would likely be fewer differences between the randomly selected treatment and control groups in factors that could affect the outcome.

It is likely that at least one of the 10 teachers is really good or really bad. So, the effectiveness of, say, a really good teacher will have effects that vary with the treatment and are not held constant. Thus, if we observe one child in a class with a positive residual, then we would expect others in that class to be more likely to have a positive residual than a negative residual – the students in that class would tend to benefit from the good teacher, beyond the effect of the treatment. Thus, the error terms for observations would tend to be positively correlated for people from a particular class. And, this means that the effective sample size would be much less than 300.

In this situation, we would say that there is "**clustering**" at the class level. Another way to look at this is that we have violated one of the original assumptions of the regression model – that the error terms have to be independently and identically distributed across observations (Assumption **A2**). Because of this violation, the standard errors would need to be corrected. The reason for this is that the "effective sample size" is lower because, with a sample size of N, there are not N independent observations. The bias is typically that the standard errors are lower than they should be, so the correction results in larger standard errors.

Sometimes, there may be some vagueness over how to specify the clusters (i.e., the potentially correlated sets of observations). Moulton (1990) argues that one should cluster at the level of the aggregated explanatory variable. For example, with a key explanatory variable being the annual state unemployment rate, the cluster would be specified at the state-year level. This would mean that everyone observed from a state in a given year would be allowed to have correlated error terms. Pepper (2002), on the other hand, argues that the clusters should be specified at the highest level possible. Thus, people would be clustered at the state (or, perhaps year) level, or two sets of clusters at the state and year level.

The correction is typically pretty simple in most statistical packages. It basically involves an indication that observations should be allowed to be correlated based on the value of a particular variable that you stipulate.

What to check for: correlated observations

Think of whether certain observations could have correlated error terms. Are there people, perhaps from the same family or the same geographical area, who would likely have similar unobserved influences on their outcomes?

6.7 What could affect the validity of the sample?

In some cases, the sample for a regression includes the whole population that is being evaluated. But, in most cases, a sample is just that – a sample of the intended population that you are attempting to describe. For example, a clinical trial for a cancer procedure would be intended for the population of patients for a particular cancer. Sometimes, it may be vague. For example, in the payroll-wins analysis for baseball that I performed in Section 2.7, the sample included the whole population of the 30 Major League Baseball teams for the 2013 season, but it was a sample of all baseball-team-seasons.

When you only have part of a population, the important question is whether the sample is representative of the intended population. Are the baseball teams of 2013 representative of the population of baseball teams in other relevant years (and the future for which we aim to make inferences) in regards to the issue examined. Obviously, if the sample is non-representative, then making inferences on the population is questionable.

There are three main causes of samples being non-representative of the intended population. The first is **sample-selection bias**, which occurs when the sample is non-random due to subjects (observations) being selected for the sample based on some factor related to the outcome. Note that *self-selection bias* (Section 6.4.3) is that people are selecting themselves into a certain value of an explanatory variable, whereas *sample-selection bias* is selecting oneself or being selected into a sample for a reason connected to the outcome.

Consider researchers who want to examine the impact of a pharmaceutical drug to treat a certain medical condition. They need approval of subjects to participate in the study. Who is going to participate? It would probably tend to be those who were more concerned about the toll of the health condition, which may not be a random sample of people with the medical condition. Even though the researchers may design a valid randomized experiment among the study volunteer subjects, there may still be sample-selection bias based on who volunteers. And, this would matter if the drug had different effects on mild versus severe forms of the medical condition.

A second cause for non-representative samples is attrition bias in longitudinal surveys, which are surveys that track people over time. **Attrition bias** occurs when those who stay in the sample are different from those who leave or stop responding (or "attrite"). The reasons for attriting from a longitudinal survey could be positive or negative: they might attrite due to being homeless, being too busy in an important job, moving overseas due to a good job offer, or escaping authorities for tax evasion. So, if you were estimating the effects of schooling on income with longitudinal data, the estimate may not be representative of the population parameter if the schooling-income pattern is different for attriters than for those still in the sample at the time the data are used.

A third cause of non-representative samples is strategic sampling for a survey, where certain parts of the population (e.g., minorities) may be oversampled. This may be for the purpose of ensuring that there are enough observations for separate analyses of particular sub-population groups. Strategic sampling occurs often in social science surveys. But, the surveys often provide sampling weights, which can typically be applied to regression models to make it nationally representative – see Section 3.3.

While the latter cause of non-representative samples can be addressed with sample weights (when available), the other two causes of non-representative samples are not easily addressed. One method that has been used is the Inverse Mills Ratio – also known as the Heckman correction (Heckman 1979). But, this method requires an identifying variable that affects sample inclusion, but not the outcome, as well as data on non-participants in the sample. Because such an identifying variable is very difficult to find, it is rare that adequate corrections can be made in the case of sample-selection or attrition bias.[2]

One other (less prevalent) cause of non-representative samples is that the period of analysis may not be relevant for making inferences about what would happen today. For example, in examining the effects of a divorce on children's adjustment, an analysis of data from 30 years ago (when divorce was less frequent) may not be relevant for today, as there would likely be less stigma with being from a divorced home due to the greater prevalence.

What to check for: non-representative samples

Is some factor causing the sample to be different in nature from the population for which you are trying to make inferences? Typical causes include sample-selection bias, attrition bias, and strategic sampling for a survey.

6.8 What model diagnostics should you do?

None! Well, most of the time, none. This is my view, and others (including your professor) may have valid reasons to disagree. But, here is the argument why, in most cases, there is no need to perform any model diagnostics.

The two most common model diagnostics that are conducted are:

- Checking for heteroskedasticity,
- Checking for non-normal error terms.

One problem is that the tests are not great. The tests will indicate whether there is statistically significant evidence for heteroskedasticity or non-normal error terms, but they certainly cannot prove that there is not any heteroskedasticity or non-normal error terms.

Regarding heteroskedasticity, your regression probably has heteroskedasticity. And, given that it is costless and painless to fix, you should probably include the heteroskedasticity correction.

Regarding non-normal error terms, recall that, due to the Central Limit Theorem, error terms will be approximately normal if the sample size is large enough (i.e., at least 200, at worst, and perhaps only 15 observations would suffice). However, this is not necessarily the case if: (1) the dependent variable is a dummy variable; and (2) there is not a large enough set of explanatory variables. But, a problem is that the test for non-normality (which tests for skewness and kurtosis) is highly unstable for small samples.

Having non-normal error terms means that the t-distribution would not apply to the standard errors, so the t-stats, standard levels of significance, confidence intervals, and p-values (Section 5.2) would be wrong. The simple solution for cases in which there is the potential for non-normal errors is to require a lower p-value than you otherwise would to conclude that there is a relationship between the explanatory and dependent variables.

I am not overly concerned by these matters because any errors (particularly due to non-normal error terms) are small potatoes when weighed against the Bayes critique of p-values (Section 5.3) and the potential biases from BIG QUESTION violations. If you have a valid study that is pretty convincing in terms of the BIG QUESTIONS and low enough p-values in light of the Bayes critique, having non-normal error terms would most likely not matter.

One other diagnostic would be to check for outliers having large effects on the coefficient estimates. This would likely not be the case with dependent variables that have a compact range of possible values, such as years of education or academic achievement test scores. But, it could be the case with dependent variables on individual/family income or corporate profits/revenue, among other things. In these situations, it could be worth a diagnostic check of outliers for the dependent variables or the residuals. One could estimate the model without the big outliers to see how the results are affected. Of course, the outliers are supposedly legitimate observations, so any results without the outliers are not necessarily more correct. The ideal situation would be that the direction and magnitude of the estimates are consistent between the models with and without the outliers.

Outliers, if based on residuals, could be detected by residual plots. Alternatively, one potential rule that could be used for deleting outliers is based on calculating the **standardized residual**, which is the actual residual divided by the standard deviation of the residual – there is no need to subtract the mean of the residual since it is zero. The standardized residual indicates how many standard deviations away from zero a residual is. So, an outlier rule could be to delete observations with the absolute value of the standardized residual greater than some value, say, 5. With the adjusted sample, one would re-estimate a model to determine how stable the main results are, and perhaps deleting more outliers in the new model.

6.9 Make sure your regression analyses/interpretations do no harm

A series of studies in the 1990s, based on a longitudinal study of 122,000 nurses, found that women who take estrogen supplements are just one-third as likely to have a heart attack as those not taking estrogen. As a result of these studies, millions of women were prescribed estrogen by their doctors.

Meanwhile, some medical researchers, appropriately, wanted to confirm this result with clinical randomized trials. And, in these trials, the original results did not hold up. In fact, the research showed that taking estrogen *increased* the risk of heart disease, breast cancer, and other maladies.

What went wrong with the original research?

It is uncertain, but when the treatment is not assigned randomly – i.e., people can choose to have (or self-select into) the treatment – then any connection between the treatment and some outcome may, instead of reflecting a causal effect of the treatment, be more of a marker of the things that cause people to choose the treatment. So, in the original studies, the factors that contributed to women having Estrogen Replacement Therapy, perhaps having an active sex life or better health insurance, may be what were associated with the lower probability of heart disease.

As a result of the original research, millions of women were being put at risk, and some researchers estimated that this may have caused tens of thousands of women to die prematurely or suffer a stroke or breast cancer.[3]

So, extending Whelan's (2013) thoughts on the proper use of regression analysis (on not letting your regression kill anyone):

Make sure your interpretations of your (or someone else's) regression do no harm.

My alter-ego believes that anyone conducting regression analysis that gets out in the public domain should have to take some *hippo-statistical oath* that they try to do no harm. Personally, I think that is a really corny name for an oath.

Nevertheless, if there are concerns about whether your research is truly capturing a causal effect, make sure those concerns are loud and clear, especially if people's well-being is at stake!

The initial estrogen studies constituted legitimate research. The researchers found a pattern in the data. It may have just been a correlation rather than causation. But, the researchers didn't know that, and it was worth reporting and generating attention for the issue, which precipitated the clinical trial.

At least some of the initial researchers were clear that this was an observational study and clinical trials were needed. (It is important to acknowledge the shortcomings of a study so people who do not understand regression analysis would not make over-reaching conclusions, especially when lives are at stake.) It should have been incumbent on the media and the doctors prescribing estrogen to have better understood these caveats and understood that there were explanations for the results alternative to there being a causal effect in the direction indicated.

. . .

Wait! There is BREAKING NEWS! I may have been wrong . . . or, the research may have been wrong. While I was waiting on reviewers to recommend to the publisher whether this book was worth publishing, new research has come out that says that, after 18 years, those taking estrogen had no greater risk of death (from any cause) than those taking the sugar pill (Manson et al. 2017). In fact, for those who started taking estrogen in their 50s, there was a slight reduction in the probability of death. Please don't take this to mean you should start estrogen in your 50s (especially guys). Dissect the research first. Note the confidence intervals on the estimates. I have not fully dissected this research myself.

6.10 Applying the BIG QUESTIONS to studies on estimating divorce effects on children

It has been estimated that 50% of all children born to married parents experience their parents divorcing by age 18 (Fagan and Rector 2000). Divorces (and separations) can be quite harmful to children. Immediate effects could be that their academic achievement is affected, which could then have lasting effects on their future academic and economic success. Any subsequent co-parenting conflict or instability from later parental relationships and marital transitions could cause further problems for children. All that said, divorces could be helpful for some children whose families have so much conflict that the parents divorcing may help foster a more peaceful upbringing.

Many researchers have attempted to estimate the effects of a divorce on children's outcomes. This is not easy, as it is not random which parents end up divorcing. But, if researchers can accurately assess how children are affected, this could help inform policymakers on whether resources should be used to keep families together, and it may help families decide whether they should break apart.

I have alluded to this research issue several times in this book. Now, I will apply the lessons from the BIG QUESTIONS to the analysis of how divorces affect children's outcomes.

The basic model would be some form of:

$$Y_i = X_i\beta_1 + \beta_2 D_i + \varepsilon_i \tag{6.15}$$

where:
- Y is some outcome for a child (academic achievement, behavior problems, substance use);
- D is an indicator (dummy) variable for the parents being divorced;
- X is a set of other factors that could help towards estimating the true causal effect of the divorce.

The variables in X would represent factors that could affect both whether parents may divorce and the child's academic achievement. This could include demographic or socio-economic factors, such as parents' income and education.

One concern would be making sure the reference group ("no parental divorce") is what you want. This group could theoretically include those children who always lived in a single-parent household. They technically do not experience a parental divorce, and so their outcomes may not be the ones to compare to those experiencing a divorce, as this would not speak to the policy issues described above.

One way to address this could be to classify children whose parents were never married to be in a separate category, so there would be three categories (the reference group of parents being married, parents are divorced, and parents never married). Or, one could start with a sample of children whose parents were initially married so that the results would speak to the policy issue of how the divorce affects children. There is also the possibility of a remarriage of a parent. Perhaps, this could be ignored, and the focus would be on the divorce of the child's biological parents, with the remarriages (after a divorce) being part of the overall effect of the initial divorce.

What I describe next are all of the potential BIG QUESTION violations that would need to be addressed to properly estimate the causal effects of a divorce on children.

Reverse causality: This is probably minor enough so that it would have minimal effects on the estimated effect of a divorce, but it is possible that the child's academic or behavioral problems could lead to greater tension for the parents, which increases the likelihood of a divorce.

Omitted-variables bias: This is likely the most applicable and important BIG QUESTION for this issue. There are many potential factors that could affect both the probability that the parents divorce and the child's outcomes. Such factors could include: family income, the level of dysfunction in the family, the intensity of parental arguments, and parental substance abuse. To the extent that these factors were not controlled for, they would likely contribute to a bias in the estimated effect of the divorce in the direction of divorce being more harmful (e.g., a negatively biased effect of divorce on academic achievement).

Self-selection bias: The idea behind self-selection bias is that the parents may choose whether to divorce partly based on how they believe it would affect the child. If the parents believe that their child(ren) would suffer from a divorce, the parents may make an extra effort to avoid a divorce. On the other hand, if the conflict is so great that the divorce would likely make for a better environment for the child(ren) or if the parents believe they could have a seamless divorce without too much co-parenting conflict, then they would be more likely to divorce. Basically, the divorce is not random, and it may be partly dictated by what the expected effect would be on the child. Of course, parents may not know exactly how their child would be affected and some parents may make this choice regardless of how their children would be affected, but assuming that there is some connection between parents' beliefs and the reality for how children would be affected, there could be self-selection bias, contributing, in this case, towards "beneficial effects" (i.e., divorce improving the child's outcomes). Thus, the harmful effects of a divorce could be understated.

Measurement error: What may be the consequential event for children is the separation, and this may occur long before an actual divorce. Sometimes, surveys ask parents about separation dates. But, often parents are just asked about the divorce. It is possible that some parents may answer survey questions based on the separation date rather than the divorce date. But, it is difficult to know which parents do this. If there is any appreciable measurement error, it would likely contribute to a bias towards zero.

6.11 Applying the BIG QUESTIONS to nutritional studies

It is difficult to go onto your favorite news website without seeing the results of a new study on what foods or vitamins contribute to or help prevent certain illnesses. Or, there may be studies that say that certain foods are not as harmful as we had thought. What does John Ioannidis, the Greek doctor/ medical-researcher mentioned in Chapter 1, say about these studies? According to Freedman (2010), Ioannidis says, **"Ignore them all."**

Well, maybe that's going too far. Or, maybe it isn't. I won't single out any particular study, but just discuss them in general. Let's think about all of the potential problems with such studies and the questions to ask. First, the benefits or harms from foods could take years to surface. Most nutritional studies have not tracked people very long. Thus, there may not be enough variation in the outcomes to identify the effects.

Second, people routinely misreport their food/nutrition intake. Or, for long-term retrospectives studies, it is doubtful that people can remember what they would typically eat. This means that there would be significant measurement error, which would likely bias the estimates towards zero (BIG QUESTION 4).

Third, eating certain foods is not random, and estimated effects of certain foods may be subject to omitted-variables bias (BIG QUESTION 2). The things that determine how much of certain kinds of foods people eat are likely correlated with other factors that affect people's health. As with the oat bran example, people who tend to eat oat bran may be less health-conscious and more likely to eat several Big Macs or Loco-Mocos per week. Thus, diet is not assigned randomly.

Fourth, researchers can design the reference group (or equivalently, what other factors to control for) so as to maximize an effect. For example, from the oat-bran/cholesterol issue from earlier, eaters of bacon and sausage (high-cholesterol foods) may eat less oat bran because they are having their bacon/sausage instead. Thus, it would be easier finding a significant difference in cholesterol levels across different levels of oat-bran consumption if bacon and sausage were part of the reference group. Factoring out the bacon/sausage eaters from the reference group (which could be done by controlling for bacon/sausage consumption) would provide a more appropriate comparison group.

Fifth, if you examine enough types of food/nutrition and enough types of illnesses, there will undoubtedly be some significant relationships. In fact, if food had no effect on any illness, then about 5% of different types of food would, by randomness, be significantly related (positively or negatively) to a given illness at the 5% significance level. These factors need to be considered when evaluating statistical significance – see Section 5.3.

Sixth, consider who funded the research. If the dairy industry funded a study on the effects of milk consumption, I can guess what it would say. I doubt the funder would allow a bad result to be published. (Coincidentally, I find myself eating cheese as I write this.)

Ioannidis (2013) noted the extremely poor results from replicating nutritional research claims with randomized trials. He notes how difficult it is to accurately measure nutritional intake. And, he notes that while the new randomized trials have been promising, we need to significantly increase the size of these studies to tens of thousands in order to obtain any meaningful results.

So, if you can't trust these studies, what can you do? Best thing to do may just be to use common sense. What types of foods do obese people tend to eat more of than other people? Does a certain type of food taste unnatural (think of some sweeteners in diet soft drinks)? If pesticides kill insects, is it reasonable to conclude that it would be harmless to humans? Would variety be better than eating the same types of food (for different nutrients and to avoid too much of something that may be bad for you)?

6.12 Chapter summary: a review of the BIG QUESTIONS

This chapter focuses on the main objective of regression analysis: estimating the causal effect of a treatment on an outcome. The general story of this chapter is:

- Regressions indicate how two variables move together, after holding other factors constant.
- There are many reasons why two variables could move together (or not move together), other than due to the causal effect of the treatment on the outcome (or lack of any effect).
- The BIG QUESTIONS present some of these common reasons . . . these are the pitfalls that could bias an estimate of the causal effect.
- And, these are the pitfalls that need to be considered as you select the optimal set of control variables to use in a model.
- These are also the pitfalls that need to be considered when assessing the soundness of other studies and when properly assessing how likely it is that your estimates represent the true causal effect.
- Chapter 8 will demonstrate some methods to address some of these biases or pitfalls.
- To the extent that the biases cannot be addressed, it is important to acknowledge this so that readers can properly judge a study.
- There are also potential problems with standard errors that would need to be addressed to conduct proper hypothesis tests and create proper confidence intervals. But, these are typically small potatoes compared to the biases on the coefficient estimates.

Table 6.11 summarizes the BIG QUESTIONS, along with what someone should check for to determine if it is a problem. In addition, Table 6.11 shows my own judgment, for each BIG QUESTION, on how egregious a typical violation would be and how frequently a violation occurs, both on a 0–100 scale. While this is somewhat for fun and just reflects my own experiences, it is meant to give a crude guide on what issues occur most often and are most problematic in regression analyses. The egregiousness of a modeling problem, of course, depends on the extent of the problem, as there could be mild or major violations. And, of course, the frequency of the problem depends on the area and topic of study.

If there were only two takeaways you receive from this entire book, I would hope they would be:

1. The hot hand in basketball is real and not a myth, as many famous economists, statisticians, psychologists, authors, and Nobel Prize winners continue to argue.
2. Whenever you hear a research finding from a friend or on the news, before believing it, you would ask yourself "Is the explanatory variable random?"

Having non-random explanatory variables is likely the most important and most common thing that could go wrong in a research study trying to determine causality. So, someone may say that using marijuana leads to an increase in the probability of getting arrested for non-drug-related crimes. You should ask whether it is random who uses marijuana. Even though marijuana use is becoming more prevalent, there are still certain characteristics that determine marijuana use, and it is easy to imagine that some of those characteristics could contribute to an increased likelihood of getting arrested for other crimes. Thus, arguing that smoking marijuana *causes* a person to get arrested is shaky, unless the researchers somehow address the non-randomness problem.

Table 6.11 A summary of the 6 BIG QUESTIONS

BIG QUESTION	What to check for	Egregiousness	How often it is a problem in the literature
NON-RANDOM EXPLANATORY VARIABLES			
1. Is there reverse causality?	Does the outcome affect an X variable?	100	20
2. Is there omitted-variables bias?	Does some omitted factor affect both the key X variable and the outcome? Or, might there be incidental correlation between the key X variable and some other factor that affects Y?	85	85
3. Is there self-selection bias?	Did the subject choose or get assigned to the key X variable by some means that is related to the personal benefits or costs of the X variable?	80	65
DATA ISSUES			
4. Is there significant measurement error?	Is there non-trivial error in the coding of the explanatory variable? Or, is the X variable imperfect in representing the intended concept?	55	45
MODELING ISSUES			
5. Are there mediating factors (mechanism variables) in the model?	Is there is a variable included in the model that is a product of the key X variable (or determined after the key X variable)?	45	20
6. Are there any outcome variables (or other variables that could be a product of the key explanatory variable) used as control variables?	Is any control variable a product of the key X variable(s)?	85	10

It is rare that an analysis will come out of an overall assessment 100% clean. In survey data, there is often some degree of measurement error, perhaps due to people mis-reporting parts of their life such as substance use or income. There may be omitted variables that you cannot do anything about. Also, in some cases, fixing some problems may create other problems.

In Chapter 8, I will introduce several methods of addressing the issues related to non-random explanatory variables – generally the most egregious of pitfalls. Sometimes, the fix is near perfect . . . other times, it just improves the model but still may leave doubt.

Not being able to perfectly address some of the BIG QUESTIONS does not mean that you should automatically throw away or discount the research. Rather, you would want to take into account how much it violates the issue and how egregious a problem that specific BIG QUESTION turns out to be.

As an example of how much of a violation there is, on the issue of how the state unemployment rate affects adult alcohol use, it is possible that there is reverse causality by alcohol use affecting the unemployment rate by negatively impacting the employability of workers. But, this is probably a tiny effect.

In other cases, the problem is much larger, such as the issue of how drug use affects depression, for which reverse causality could dominate the estimate on how the two variables move together. It is important to understand that in such cases in which the inherent problems are so large, the problem would need to be addressed for the research to have any credibility.

Alternatively, you could call the relationship you are analyzing a "*correlation*" or an "*association*" that suggests the possibility of a causal effect. Hopefully, your analysis would be considered a stepping stone for further efforts to better capture the causal effect rather than anything that would guide policy.

LAST POINT: When conducting research, do the responsible thing and acknowledge all potential biases and pitfalls of the research. Be careful with your interpretations. If many pitfalls remain, use more modified language such as "the evidence in this analysis *supports* the theory that . . ." rather than "the evidence *proves*" or "the results *provide strong evidence for*" the theory. And, add the necessary caveats. Remember: **Make sure your interpretations do no harm.**

Exercises

1. Explain how the Yogi quote in Section 6.4.3 relates to BIG QUESTION 3 on self-selection bias.
2. Explain how the Yogi quote in Section 6.4.6 relates to BIG QUESTION 6 on including outcomes as control variables.
3. Which of these is more likely to suffer from self-selection bias? Explain.
   Case 1: Estimating how participating in a voluntary meditation program affects an 11th grader's GPA.
   Case 2: Estimating how having an unemployed father affects an 11th grader's GPA.
4. Which of the following would be more likely to suffer from reverse causality? Explain.
   Case 1: With observational (non-experimental) data, estimating how meditation affects blood pressure.
   Case 2: With observational (non-experimental) data, estimating how blood-pressure medicine affects the likelihood of getting the flu.
5. Which of the following is more likely to suffer from bias due to measurement error? Explain.
   Case 1: Estimating how a person's reported cocaine use affects their income.
   Case 2: Estimating how the number of murders per capita in a county affects the county unemployment rate.
6. Which of the following control variables would be more likely to cause bias due to being a mediating factor for estimating the effect of class size on 6th grade student math achievement? Explain.
   Control variable 1: The amount of parental help on homework.
   Control variable 2: The amount of individual time with the teacher.
7. Consider the following model estimating peer effects in marijuana use among teenagers:

$$MJ_i = \beta_1 * \left(Peer\text{-}MJ \right)_i + X_i \beta_2 + \varepsilon_i$$

where *MJ* is a measure of the person's marijuana use, *Peer-MJ* is a measure of the marijuana use of the person's peers, and *X* is a set of demographic factors.

  a. Describe why and how (i.e., in what direction) reverse causality could bias the estimate for β_1.
  b. Describe why and how omitted variables bias could affect the estimate for β_1.
  c. Describe why and how self-selection bias could affect the estimate for β_1.
  d. Describe why and how measurement error could bias the estimate for β_1.

 8. A research finding was recently given on one of those "health-advice" radio shows: "Those who are more optimistic at the start of a week have a better week." The host then said that you can make your week better if you are optimistic at the start of the week. Critique this conclusion.

 9. Researchers have found that those who drink more wine live longer. Describe how omitted-variables bias could be the basis for an alternative explanation of the results to the theory that drinking more wine tends to lengthen people's lives.

10. Consider the following model to estimate the effects of certain foods on health for a sample of 60-year-olds:

$$health60_i = \beta_0 + \beta_1 * (bb)_i + \beta_2 * (bigmacs)_i + X_i\beta_3 + \varepsilon_i,$$

where:

health60 = a measure of health at age 60;
bb = average annual pounds of blueberries eaten over the past 30 years;
bigmacs = average annual number of Big Macs eaten over the past 30 years;

  a. If *X* were just a set of demographic variables, what are two likely BIG QUESTION violations for β_1 and β_2?
  b. Based on the rules for deciding what control factors to include in a model (Section 6.5), indicate whether the following potential control variables ("should be excluded," "should be included," or "could be included or excluded") and explain why:
  i. A measure of health at age 50;
  ii. Average days of exercise over the past 30 years;
  iii. Racial/ethnic indicator variables;
  iv. Of one's 5 best childhood friends, the number who regularly ate Big Macs.

11. Consider the following model to estimate the effect of college quality on income (among a sample of 40-year-old college graduates):

$$\ln(\text{income})_i = \beta_1 \times (CQ)_i + \beta_2 \times (SAT)_i + \beta_3 \times (C\_SAT\_AVG)_i + X_i\beta_4 + \varepsilon_i,$$

where

CQ = person *i*'s college quality;
SAT = person's SAT score;
C_SAT_AVG = college's average SAT of incoming students;
X = demographic characteristic.

  a. Describe how omitted-variables bias could affect the estimate for β_1.
  b. Describe how self-selection bias could affect the estimate for β_1.

c. Describe why there could be heteroskedasticity in this model.

d. Describe how there could be correlated error terms in this model.

12. Is the hot hand in basketball a real phenomenon?

13. In the movie, *Saving Private Ryan*, one of the soldiers said to another, something like, "The best way to fall asleep is trying to stay awake." Use one of the BIG QUESTIONS to critique this statement.

Notes

1 Let me note here that some people (particularly those writing on Wikipedia) have tried to take the term "self-selection bias" and make it mean the same thing as "sample-selection bias." I am taking the meaning back to its original form, as the term "self-selection bias" better describes the source of bias described in this sub-section.

2 The Heckman correction requires having data on subjects that do not make the final sample – e.g., for attrition bias, those who were in the earlier surveys but not the primary-analysis sample. Let's say that the primary-analysis sample is for 2008. The procedure involves first modeling the probability that the person is in the 2008 sample. It then calculates a propensity to be in the 2008 sample based on the explanatory variables. Next, it includes that propensity variable in the final regression for the 2008 sample. Unfortunately, this model is highly volatile with respect to variables included. Furthermore, to achieve any reasonably valid results, the model requires having an "identifying" variable that: (1) explains whether the person is in the 2008 sample; and (2) has no independent effect on the outcome. It is quite rare to find such an "identifying" variable.

3 Sarrel, P. M., Njike, V. Y., Vinante, V., & Katz, D. L. (2013). The mortality toll of estrogen avoidance: an analysis of excess deaths among hysterectomized women aged 50 to 59 years. *American Journal of Public Health*, 103(9), 1583–1588 (Available at www.nytimes.com/2007/09/16/magazine/16epidemiology-t.html?pagewanted=all&_r=0, accessed July 10, 2018).

References

Arkes, J. (2007). Does the economy affect teenage substance use? *Health Economics*, 16(1), 19–36.

Arkes, J. (2010). Revisiting the hot hand theory with free throw data in a multivariate framework. *Journal of Quantitative Analysis in Sports*, 6(1).

Arkes, J. (2011). Is controlling the rushing or passing game the key to NFL victories? *The Sport Journal*, 14(1), 1–5.

Arkes, J. (2013). Misses in "hot hand" research. *Journal of Sports Economics*, 14(4), 401–410.

Brooks, D. (2013). The philosophy of data. *New York Times*, February 4. (Available May 9, 2013 at www.nytimes.com/2013/02/05/opinion/brooks-the-philosophy-of-data.html, accessed July 10, 2018).

Bureau of Labor Statistics, U.S. Department of Labor. (2014). *National Longitudinal Survey of Youth 1979 cohort, 1979–2012 (rounds 1–25)*. Columbus, OH: Center for Human Resource Research, The Ohio State University.

Bureau of Labor Statistics, U.S. Department of Labor. (2015). *National Longitudinal Survey of Youth 1997 cohort, 1997–2013 (rounds 1–16)*. Columbus, OH: Center for Human Resource Research, The Ohio State University.

Carroll, R. J., Ruppert, D., Stefanski, L. A., & Crainiceanu, C. M. (2006). *Measurement error in nonlinear models: A modern perspective*. London: CRC Press.

Fagan, P. F., & Rector, R. (2000). The effects of divorce on America. *World and I*, 15(10), 56–61.

Freedman, D. H. (2010). Lies, damned lies, and medical science. *The Atlantic*. November 2010 issue. (Available at www.theatlantic.com/magazine/archive/2010/11/lies-damned-lies-and-medical-science/308269/, accessed July 10, 2018).

Gilovich, T., Vallone, R., & Tversky, A. (1985). The hot hand in basketball: On the misperception of random sequences. *Cognitive Psychology*, 17(3), 295–314.

Guolo, A. (2008). Robust techniques for measurement error correction: A review. *Statistical Methods in Medical Research*, 17(6), 555–580.

Harder, V. S., Morral, A. R., & Arkes, J. (2006). Marijuana use and depression among adults: Testing for causal associations. *Addiction*, 101(10), 1463–1472.

Heckman, J. (1979). Sample selection as a specification error. *Econometrica*, 47(1), 153–161.

Ioannidis, J. P. (2013). Implausible results in human nutrition research. *British Medical Journal* 347, f6698.

Manson, J. E., Aragaki, A. K., Rossouw, J. E., Anderson, G. L., Prentice, R. L., LaCroix, A. Z., . . . Lewis, C. E. (2017). Menopausal hormone therapy and long-term all-cause and cause-specific mortality: The Women's health initiative randomized trials. *Journal of the American Medical Association*, 318(10), 927–938.

Messerli, F. H. (2012). Chocolate consumption, cognitive function, and Nobel Laureates. *New England Journal of Medicine*, 367(16), 1562–1564.

Miller, J. B., & Sanjurjo, A. (2018). Surprised by the hot hand fallacy? A truth in the law of small numbers. *Econometrica*, forthcoming.

Moulton, B. R. (1990). An illustration of a pitfall in estimating the effects of aggregate variables on micro units. *The Review of Economics and Statistics*, 72(2), 334–338.

Pepper, J. V. (2002). Robust inferences from random clustered samples: An application using data from the panel study of income dynamics. *Economics Letters*, 75(3), 341–345.

Ruhm, C. J., & Black, W. E. (2002). Does drinking really decrease in bad times? *Journal of Health Economics*, 21(4), 659–678.

Stone, D. F. (2012). Measurement error and the hot hand. *The American Statistician*, 66(1), 61–66.

Whelan, C. (2013). *Naked statistics: Stripping the dread from the data*. New York and London: W. W. Norton and Company.

7 | Strategies for other regression objectives

7.1 Strategies for forecasting/predicting an outcome
7.2 Strategies for determining predictors of an outcome
7.3 Strategies for adjusting outcomes for various factors
7.4 Summary of the strategies for each regression objective

> You've got to be very careful if you don't know where you are going, because you might not get there.
>
> −Yogi Berra

Recall from Section 2.2 that the four main objectives of regression analysis are:

- Estimating causal effects,
- Determining predictors of an outcome,
- Forecasting an outcome,
- Adjusting outcomes for various factors (to gauge relative performance).

Chapter 6 focused on the pitfalls of and modeling strategies for the first of these objectives, estimating causal effects. For the other objectives of regression analysis, the pitfalls and modeling strategies are different, as the BIG QUESTIONS from Chapter 6 do not apply to each regression objective. (Things that could go wrong in regard to the standard errors and the validity of the sample apply to all four objectives.) This chapter will offer general guidelines that will work most of the time when using regressions for objectives other than estimating causal effects.

7.1 Strategies for forecasting/predicting an outcome

Let us go back to the lemon-tree example from Section 4.1. To properly estimate the causal effect of water on the number of lemons, we decided that we did not want to control for the height of the tree, as this would be a mediating factor and doing so would prevent us from estimating the full effect of watering. This would violate BIG QUESTION 5.

But, what if the farmer wanted to give a potential produce buyer an estimate of how many lemons she can produce each month? The height of the trees could provide important predictive power, and so estimating a regression with height as an explanatory variable would likely help generate a more accurate forecast of the number of lemons her trees will produce than a model that does not control for the height of the tree. This example demonstrates that the strategy for what control variables to include in the model depends on what the objective of the regression is.

This characterizes one of the other objectives of regression analysis: to **forecast** or **predict** some outcome. Do not confuse this with the next regression objective of **determining predictors**, which is figuring out what factors are the best determinants of a dependent variable. Rather, for this regression objective, the goal is to get as accurate a prediction as possible of the dependent variable. And so, it does not matter if one does not estimate the true causal effect of certain factors.

There are many cases in which a forecast is needed. In logistics, parts suppliers may want to forecast the demand for various parts of a machine or vehicle that would be needed for repairs. Sports teams may want to forecast attendance for various visiting teams so they can set a more profitable ticket price or stock enough beer. Google may want to forecast how much space people will use on their Google Drive cloud space. The U.S. Army may want to forecast how many soldiers will attrite in their first year of service. And, an insurance company may want to predict the probability that a given customer will get in a car accident in a given year.

Some of these examples involve time-series variables, which we will see in Chapter 10. But, forecasts and prediction could also be based on cross-sectional analyses, with multiple subjects and multiple explanatory variables.

This is how it would work for the insurance company. The insurance company would have some historical data on its customers that is something like the following:

- Y = whether the person got in an accident in a given year;
- X_1 = number of accidents the person had in the last 10 years;
- X_2 = years-of-schooling;
- X_3 = age;
- X_4 = income;
- X_5 = a dummy variable equal to 1 if the person had a white-collar job.
  (A more developed model could use a set of dummy variables for many different types of jobs.)

Note that X_1 (number of accidents in the last 10 years) would likely be a statistically significant determinant of having an accident, but I suspect it would still be a weak overall predictor in that it would not explain many accidents that occur. If the company were estimating the causal effects of a year of schooling on the probability of an accident, then it would exclude X_4 and X_5 from the model, as these variables could be mediating factors for years-of-schooling. That is, part of the reason why more schooling (likely) leads to a lower probability of an accident is that it increases a person's income and the probability that a person obtains a white-collar job (and perhaps the value of their car, which could affect how careful they are). Thus, including these variables in the model would prevent the estimation of the full effect of schooling on income.

But, the causal effect of schooling on the probability of an accident is not of concern to the insurance company. The company is only interested in the best guess for a customer's probability of getting into an accident. Thus, it would include X_4 and X_5 in the model.

The forecast, or predicted probability of an accident, for a particular person would be $\hat{Y}_i$, or what is obtained by multiplying the $\hat{\beta}$'s by the value of the associated X variables and summing them together, as in equation (7.1), as follows:

$$\hat{Y}_i = \hat{\beta}_0 + \hat{\beta}_1 X_{1i} + \hat{\beta}_2 X_{2i} + \hat{\beta}_3 X_{3i} + \hat{\beta}_4 X_{4i} + \hat{\beta}_5 X_{5i} \qquad (7.1)$$

What BIG QUESTIONS matter?

In forecasting/prediction, the objective is to obtain the most accurate prediction of $\hat{Y}$. Given that forecasting regressions are not concerned with estimating causal effects, most of the BIG QUESTIONS are not applicable. For example, the existence of omitted-variables bias (BIG QUESTION 2) just means that the included observable variable is picking up part of the predictive power of the omitted variables on the outcome. It does not mean that the forecast would be biased in any way due to the unobserved variable.

Similarly, including mediating factors (such as the height of the lemon tree) for some key explanatory variable can be good because they have potential explanatory power for the outcome. Again, it does not matter that the model would only be estimating the partial effect of a key explanatory variable.

Generally, when forecasting is the goal of the regression analysis, throwing in the kitchen sink of explanatory variables is a good strategy to follow, with a few caveats:

- The variables should be easily obtainable for people to plug values of the variables into the model (multiplying them by the coefficient estimates) so that the outcome can be predicted in the future, if having continual forecasts is a goal.
- Variables subject to reverse causality should be avoided because it would then be forecasting the outcome with something that is a function of the outcome itself. Thus, it would be ideal that all variables are determined before the outcome. This implies that other outcomes should not be included as explanatory variables if they are concurrently determined or determined after the dependent variable is determined.

These simple rules make forecasting an outcome one of the easiest in terms of avoiding biases. That said, recall the lesson from Section 2.13, that effects can change over time. That is, you must make a leap of faith that the determination of the outcome in the future will follow a similar set of rules as what happened in the past. While lemon-tree production probably does not change how it follows the rules of nature, attrition in the first term for Army soldiers very well could structurally change with the economy or military environment changing.

Just to quickly review, here are how the BIG QUESTIONS play out for forecasting analyses:

- **Reverse causality:** This is the most important BIG QUESTION that causes problems for forecasting.
- **Omitted-variables bias:** Not a problem. This can be good in that one factor captures the effects of other factors.
- **Self-selection bias:** Not a problem.
- **Measurement error:** Measurement error in a variable could lead to a less accurate forecast of the outcome, but it should not lead to a biased forecast. Moreover, it will likely be a more accurate forecast with the variable that is subject to measurement error included in the model than it would be without the variable.

- **Mediating factors as control variables:** Not a problem because the more variables included, the better the forecast will be.
- **Outcomes as control variables:** This is okay (as with mediating factors) in cases in which the outcome-as-a-control-variable occurs before the dependent-variable outcome. But, it is a problem if the outcome-as-a-control-variable is determined concurrently or after the dependent-variable outcome.

How accurate is the forecast?

I am certain that for over a century, researchers on the stock market have searched for predictors of stock-market performance. They often found legitimate results for what factors helped to forecast stock-market performance in whatever period they were examining. But, that often does not translate into what subsequently happened in the stock market.

If one of these researchers includes enough variables, he/she will certainly find some things to have significant relationships with stock-market performance. Some such relationships could be by chance (Type I errors); some could be real relationships that were specific for the period studied; and some could be real relationships that are persistent over time. To increase confidence for whether any significant relationship is real and persistent, they would need to test how well the model predicts the outcome with new data. Unfortunately, one has to wait for new data to emerge (more stock-market returns for a few years, perhaps), or one would need to do an **out-of-sample prediction** by leaving part of the sample out of the forecast model and then seeing how well the forecast model predicted stock-market performance in the out-of-sample data. Of course, in that situation, you'd need to hope that the relationship continues beyond the out-of-sample period and into the future.

Whether using in-sample data, out-of-sample data, or new data, one option to determine the accuracy of the forecast is to calculate the **average forecast error**, which is the average of the absolute values of the difference between the actual outcome and the forecasted/predicted outcome:

$$\text{Average forecast error } = \sum_{i=1}^{n} \left| Y_i - \widehat{Y_i} \right|$$

The common statistic, however, is the **root mean square (forecast) error (RMSE or RMSFE)**, which penalizes a model more (in terms of greater error) for larger forecast misses. The statistic is simply:

$$\text{RMSFE } = \sqrt{\sum_{i=1}^{n} \left(Y_i - \widehat{Y_i} \right)^2}$$

In theory, these statistics might be used for model selection. Perhaps some variable contributes little to reducing RMSFE and so it may be dropped to help simplify the forecast model, or to reduce the costs of data collection.

7.2 Strategies for determining predictors of an outcome

Sometimes, a researcher may want to avoid a complex forecast model and simply want to know:

- Whether a certain factor predicts an outcome,
- How well a certain factor predicts an outcome,
- What the best predictors for an outcome would be.

Suppose that a high-school counselor wants to know to what extent a parental divorce could be an indicator for students dropping out of high school. This may help them know how much they need to monitor students who experience a parental divorce. The counselors would not be concerned with how much the divorce itself affected the likelihood that a given student drops out. Rather, they would want to know how good a predictor experiencing a parental divorce would be for whether a student drops out.

If we were attempting to estimate the causal effect of a parental divorce, then we would have difficulty because the divorce may be reflective of other factors, such as conflict at home or parental substance use, so there could be omitted-variables bias. But, if we were just trying to find a predictor for dropping out, then it would be okay that the parental divorce reflected these other factors. There likely would not be good data for conflict at home or parents' substance use, so the tangible variable of "parental divorce" may be a useful predictor that captures some of these unobservable factors. Thus, we do not have to worry about omitted-variables bias when determining predictors.

As another example, suppose that you wanted to know what factors predicted suicide. You have some interesting data on life events, such as becoming unemployed and whether the person takes anti-depressants. If you were interested in whether "becoming unemployed" predicts suicide, you may not want to hold other factors constant. It comes down to whether you are interested in:

- Does unemployment predict the probability of suicide? or
- Does unemployment predict the probability of suicide beyond any predictive power that taking anti-depressants (and other factors) have?

In some cases, you may be more interested in the first case – whether unemployment predicts suicide, unconditional on other factors. This would mean that the best strategy would be to not hold ANY other factors constant. This wouldn't be as sexy as a regression with many controls, but it may be more informative.

To demonstrate the logic behind the best strategies for determining predictors, let's explore, with the NLSY, what factors predict "health status at age 50" for females (Bureau of Labor Statistics, 2014). When respondents reached ages 40 and 50 in the NLSY survey, they were asked to rate their health status on a 1 to 5 scale, with the choices being: poor (1), fair (2), good (3), very good (4), and excellent (5). In Table 7.1, I present the results from several regressions examining factors of "health status at age 50."[1] The model in column (1) includes the full set of explanatory variables. Columns (2) to (5) then include just one of the explanatory variables at a time.

Let's address the issue of whether being Black is a significant predictor of health-at-50 (relative to the reference group of non-Blacks). In column (1), when all variables are included, being Black has an insignificant coefficient estimate. Thus, one may conclude that there is no evidence that race predicts health at age 50. But, is this correct? In column (3), for which the variable for Black is the only explanatory variable, it has a strongly significant coefficient estimate. Note also that the AFQT score is a relatively stronger predictor when it is the only explanatory variable – in column (5) – than in the full model in column (1).

So, what is going on here? Why is being Black understated as a predictor in column (1)? And, how would we answer the question of whether race significantly predicts health at age 50?

The basis for the answer comes from column (2). Note that the R^2 is 0.300 from just the one variable of health-at-age-40 as an explanatory variable, not much below the R^2 of 0.317 in column

Table 7.1 Predicting health status at age 50 for females

	(1)	(2)	(3)	(4)
Health status at age 40	0.537***	0.577***		
	(0.017)	(0.017)		
Black	–0.055		–0.299***	
	(0.038)		(0.043)	
AFQT	0.005***			0.010***
	(0.001)			(0.001)
Constant	1.234***	1.252***	3.422***	2.937***
	(0.065)	(0.062)	(0.024)	(0.032)
Observations	2849	2849	2849	2849
R-squared	0.317	0.300	0.017	0.077

Note: Standard errors are in parentheses. Standard errors are corrected for heteroskedasticity.

***$p < 0.01$, **$p < 0.05$, *$p < 0.1$.

Source: Bureau of Labor Statistics, 2014.

(1) when all variables are included. This means that this one variable, health-at-40, is sopping up a significant amount of variation in health-at-50, leaving less variation to be explained by the rest of the variables.

Deciding what variables should be included in the model when searching for predictors of an outcome should be based on whether one is interested in:

- How much a certain variable predicts the outcome, or
- How much a certain variable predicts the outcome, after controlling for other factors.

We can make two statements regarding the relationship between years-of-schooling and health-at-50:

- Health-at-50 is significantly worse for Black females than non-Black females.
- There is no evidence that health-at-50 is significantly worse for Black females, once health-at-40 and the AFQT score are controlled for.

Whether to control for other factors depends on which of these is more interesting. In most cases, the second statement (from both sets of bullets above) has little value.

When determining predictors of an outcome, most people in the research community would be more interested in the model that controls for everything. But, this makes it a horserace with the odds favoring the variables that are less correlated with other variables. Thus, there could be one factor that is indeed the best predictor, but it is highly correlated with a few other factors, causing its predictive power to be spread out to those other variables. We would have the second-bulleted interpretation above, which is pretty nebulous. And, we would then be unable to determine how well it alone predicted the outcome.

Personally, for determining predictors of an outcome, I'm more inclined towards the models that keep it as simple as possible and include just:

- One explanatory variable at a time,
- One set of dummy variables representing one concept (e.g., racial/ethnic groups), or
- One interaction of explanatory variables.

Note that, if there were just dummy variables as potential predictors, this strategy would be equivalent to estimating a series of differences in the means for different groups (e.g., Black vs. non-Black). But, the regression method offers a simpler and quicker method.

Note also that those who use such information (such as the counselor trying to determine which teenagers might be at risk for dropping out) may not have the capabilities and knowledge to run a regression or to combine the effects of multitudes of predictors. Thus, it would probably be best to know which factors acting *alone* are the best predictors of dropping out. Or, perhaps they may want to know what combination of two factors were the best predictors.

How do you determine what the best predictor is? It is not just the variable with the largest-in-magnitude coefficient estimate for two reasons. First, the scale of the explanatory variable needs to be considered (see Section 2.11). Second, the variation in the explanatory variable will determine how well the variable predicts the outcome. For example, if we were trying to find the best predictor for a teenager having a baby before age 18, one variable that probably has high predictive ability for the outcome is a dummy variable for "having an older sister who had two babies before age 18." But, this would apply to such a small percentage of the sample that it would not be effective for predicting whether the subject has a baby herself.

Perhaps the best indicators would be the R^2 and Root Mean Square Error (RMSE), as introduced in the prior section. Of course, to label one variable as the winner for being the best predictor, it would need to be well above others in R^2 or well below others in RMSE in order to take the prize. Small differences in R^2 could be from natural sampling variation rather than one predictor being stronger.

Regarding the 6 BIG QUESTIONS, they are not all important for the objective of "determining predictors," largely because it is not important to estimate the true causal effect of any factor. The following is how they should be considered for analyses attempting to determine predictors:

- **Reverse causality:** This should be avoided because you would be predicting the outcome with itself (because the explanatory variable is a product of the outcome with reverse causality).
- **Omitted-variables bias:** Not a problem. In fact, you may want the predictor to capture unobservable factors, as it would give a variable greater predictive power.
- **Self-selection bias:** This is also okay, as with omitted-variables bias.
- **Measurement error:** This would be a problem because measurement error in an explanatory variable could lead to an understatement for how well the variable can predict the outcome. However, it does not mean that the variable should not be considered as a predictor.
- **Mediating factors as control variables:** This would be a problem because it would take away from the predictive power of the explanatory variable.
- **Outcomes as control variables:** Same as with mediating factors.

7.3 Strategies for adjusting outcomes for various factors

The unadjusted life is not worth comparing.

– paraphrasing Socrates

Main approaches

When we want to determine how strong the performance was for a team, a worker, a student, a business, etc., just comparing the outcome itself may be a flawed approach as subjects may have different conditions or environments that make success simpler or more difficult. The concept of *adjusting outcomes* involves factoring out influences that reflect determinants of performance other than the actions of the subjects being compared. This allows one to estimate how subjects performed relative to what would be expected.

This is the concept behind the new statistic used in basketball of "real–plus–minus," which is a player's average impact on net points per 100 offensive and defensive possessions. The "real" part is that it factors out the real–plus–minus of the teammates and opponents who were on the court at the same time as the player (based on how much time they shared the court with that player).

There are two main approaches to this regression objective:

1. Adjust for all factors in a model by simply using the residual.
2. Adjust for a subset of the factors in a model by subtracting out the influence of just that subset of factors. This would be done if the model necessitates extra variables.

The simpler approach, obviously, is the first one of using the residual. Relative performance (RP) would be:

$$RP_i = \hat{\varepsilon}_i = Y_i - E[Y \mid X_i] = Y_i - \hat{Y}_i \qquad (7.2)$$

However, sometimes there are explanatory variables in the regression that should not be adjusted for. These variables may be in the model to help isolate the causal effect of some key variables that are being adjusted for. For example, suppose that Y is regressed on four variables, X_1 to X_4,

$$Y_i = \beta_0 + \beta_1 X_{1i} + \beta_2 X_{2i} + \beta_3 X_{3i} + \beta_4 X_{4i} + \varepsilon_i \qquad (7.3)$$

but you want to condition on just two of the variables, X_1 and X_2. Relative performance would be:

$$RP_i = Y_i - (\hat{\beta}_1 X_{1i} + \hat{\beta}_2 X_{2i}). \qquad (7.4)$$

Examples

Let's consider two examples, one for each approach.

Example 1: Payroll and wins in baseball

This example from earlier is based on the idea that simply comparing wins or championships for, say, the Oakland A's to that of the New York Yankees does not speak to which team was more effective because they are on completely different levels for payrolls. It must be much easier to win if you can spend the annual GDP of France in payroll every year, compared to other teams that are hamstrung in how much payroll they can afford. If we adjust for payroll, we can get a measure for relative performance (or payroll-adjusted performance). We may simply run a regression of the number of wins in a season on the payroll and use the residual. Thus, from the following regression from Section 2.7:

$$\widehat{wins} = 71.24 + 0.09 \times (payroll\ in\ \$millions) \tag{2.17}$$

we would calculate:

$$relative\ wins = \hat{\varepsilon}_i = Y_i - \hat{Y}_i$$
$$= Y_i - [\hat{\beta}_0 + \hat{\beta}_1 \times (payroll)_i] \tag{7.5}$$
$$= Y_i - \left[71.24 + 0.09 \times (payroll)_i\right]$$

A nice feature of using the residual is that the average residual equals zero. Thus, a positive residual means that performance was better than expected.

Does this represent the true causal effect? Probably not, as payroll isn't exactly random. But, this is a situation in which it may be okay, as it produces a payroll-adjusted number of wins.

Example 2: Evaluation-of-instructors

University instructors are typically evaluated on their teaching effectiveness based on student evaluations. But, many argue that such evaluations are highly biased by grades and class size, among other things. This means that just using an instructor's average evaluation by the students may not make for fair comparisons because of differences in these factors.

Schools can potentially adjust for these other factors. Let's take the example of grades. Unfortunately, we cannot just regress "average evaluation" on "average grade" in a class because there could be some omitted-variables bias occurring: perhaps low-quality professors give higher grades to boost their evaluations. And so, we would need a bunch of dummy variables for the instructors, making it so an instructor's evaluations and grade in a given class are being compared to his/her other classes, and not being compared to those for other instructors. This would give us a better gauge of the true causal effect of grades on the average evaluation of an instructor, which would then allow us to more accurately adjust performance based on grades.

But, this method means that *we would not be able to use the residual.* The residual would take out the instructor effect, and so all instructors would have the same average residual of zero – this will be explained in more detail in Section 8.1. And so, instructors cannot be compared to each other. Thus, we just want to adjust based on the grades, as follows:

$$Y_i = X_i\beta_1 + \beta_2 GPA_i + \varepsilon_i \tag{7.6}$$

$$Relative\ Evaluation = Y_i - \left(\hat{\beta}_2 GPA_i\right) \tag{7.7}$$

where:
- Y = average evaluation for an instructor in a given class;
- GPA = average grade (or grade point average) in the class;
- X = a set of indicator variables for each instructor, as well as a constant.

Adjusting for the constant in equation (7.7) is not important, as it would be the same for everyone. Perhaps the average "relative evaluation" can be subtracted out to make the average equal to zero, as it would be if the residual were used.

Note that there would be multiple observations per instructor, so each observation would indicate the instructor's relative performance in a given class, or his/her average evaluation for a class conditional on average grades given. These relative-performance measures could then be averaged for each instructor.

If we also wanted to factor out class size (CS), then we would have:

$$Y_i = X_i\beta_1 + \beta_2 GPA_i + \beta_3 CS_i + \varepsilon_i \tag{7.8}$$

$$\text{Relative Evaluation} = Y_i - E\left[Y_i \mid GPA_i, CS_i\right] = Y_i - \left(\hat{\beta}_2 GPA_i + \hat{\beta}_3 CS_i\right) \tag{7.9}$$

This is not a perfect method. The class-size effect (and the grade effect) could differ by instructor. So, the ideal approach would be to adjust each instructor by his/her individual β_2 and β_3. But, these would be imprecisely estimated. And so, we are forced to adjust based on an estimated average $\hat{\beta}_2$ and $\hat{\beta}_3$ across all people. Still, this gets us closer to comparing instructors' "relative performance."

What variables probably should not be conditioned on

Recruiters in the military are typically assigned to be a recruiter for 36 months. There is usually high pressure to recruit at least one person each month, and there are several awards based on how many people and how many "high-quality" people they recruit in certain periods of time, such as a 3-month period. One issue is that some unlucky recruiters are sent to Vermont or strong-economic areas (where recruiting is difficult), while others are sent to Dallas or weak-economic areas (where recruiting is easier). We cannot gauge the relative effectiveness of recruiters in these different types of areas just by comparing the number of recruits they sign. Rather, we would need to adjust the number of recruits based on the area and conditions the recruiters are given.

So, we need to determine what factors should be in the regression model and what factors should be adjusted for. Obviously, geographical indicators and economic factors would be important. Including them in the model would mean that a recruiter would be judged relative to what would be expected for their location and economic conditions.

Should we also include gender and race/ethnicity of the recruiter as explanatory variables? If we were to do so, we would be holding males and females to different standards, and we would be holding those of different races and ethnicities to different standards. For example, let's say that the dependent variable was the number of recruits signed in a year. And, let's suppose that the coefficient estimate on the variable for "female recruiter" were 3, indicating that females signed an average of 3 more recruits per year than males, holding other factors constant. If we were to factor out the gender effect, this would mean that if a male and female who were observationally equivalent (i.e., same location, time period, and characteristics other than gender) and had the same number of recruits in a year, the female's predicted success would be 3 recruits greater than the male's. This would mean that the male recruiter would be considered to have performed better because his "adjusted outcome" would be higher by 3 recruits.

To demonstrate this with an example, let's take that "female effect" of 3 and suppose that the predicted values for a female and male recruiter (Jane and John) who are observationally the same $(X = \tilde{X})$ other than their gender are the following:

- Predicted values:
  - Jane : $E(Y \mid \tilde{X}, \textit{female}) = 15$;
  - John : $E(Y \mid \tilde{X}, \textit{male}) = 12$.

And, let's say that Jane signs 14 and John signs 13 recruits in a year. Their relative performance would be:

- Relative performance:
  - Jane: $14 - 15 = -1$
  - John: $13 - 12 = +1$

Even though Jane signed more recruits than John (14 to 13), according to the model, John's relative performance would be 2 recruits better than Jane's (+1 to −1). If, however, the relative performance were not conditioned or adjusted based on gender, then Jane would have performed one recruit better than John, given that their predicted values would be the same.

The lesson from this is that you want to adjust for only the factors that you would like success to be conditioned on or adjusted for. And, gender, race/ethnicity, and other personal characteristics usually are not good factors to condition on when adjusting outcomes to gauge relative performance.

Using dummy variables to gauge relative performance

A completely different method could be used if there were multiple observations per person (or team). In that case, a model could use dummy variables for each person and compare the values of the coefficient estimates on those dummy variables. For example, with the recruiter example, the model could control for all of the factors mentioned above, making sure to exclude certain demographic characteristics and add a dummy variable for each recruiter (except one recruiter as the reference group). The recruiters with the highest coefficient estimates would be the best guess for who the most effective recruiters were.

This strategy does not work if there is only one observation for each person because then the dummy variables would perfectly predict the outcome and there would be no variation left for the location and economic factors to adjust for.

What BIG QUESTIONS are important?

If a causal effect were under-estimated or over-estimated, then it would not adjust enough or over-adjust for a given factor. Thus, in some cases, without the proper average causal effect, the comparisons become distorted. This means that, if causal effects are important, then all BIG QUESTIONS should be considered. One possible exception is mediating factors. This may not be important because, with mediating factors, the effect of the key explanatory variable is still being captured by a combination of its own coefficient estimate and the coefficient estimate on its mediating factor. Thus, the effects of the key explanatory variable would still be fully adjusted for. For example, when adjusting military recruiting success for the unemployment rate, we could also include a variable for the local wage rate, which some may say is a mediating factor for the unemployment rate. This is fine, as all that is important is that a recruiter's performance is adjusted for the unemployment rate and any effects of its mediating factors.

In other situations, having mediating factors could be problematic. For example, if we included batting average or the number of home runs in the baseball model, then we would over-adjust. Some teams may use salary effectively for big home run hitters at a cheap price. This is part of a team's relative performance. These are statistics (or characteristics) of players that higher payrolls buy more of, which should lead to more wins. But, the issue comes down to how well the teams used money or managed their players to get more production (stats and wins) for given amounts of salary. And so, these mediating factors, which could be considered outcomes, should not be controlled for.

7.4 Summary of the strategies for each regression objective

Table 7.2 offers a summary of which BIG QUESTIONS could cause a problem and what the "General Strategy" should be for each objective. A "Yes" indicates that the question does need to be asked, and

Table 7.2 Strategies and which BIG QUESTIONS need to be asked for the regression objectives

BIG QUESTION	Regression objective			
	Estimating causal effects	Forecasting the outcome	Determining predictors	Adjusting outcomes for certain factors
1. Reverse causality	Yes	Yes	Yes	Yes
2. Omitted-variables bias	Yes	No	No	Yes
3. Self-selection bias	Yes	No	No	Yes
4. Measurement error	Yes	No	Yes	Yes
5. Mediating factors as control variables	Yes	No	Yes	Depends
6. Outcomes as control variables	Yes	No, provided it precedes the dependent variable	Yes	Yes
General strategy	Avoid or address all 6 BIG QUESTIONS	Include the kitchen sink of explanatory variables	Include just one X variable, one set of categories (e.g., race), or one interacted variable per regression	Only control for factors that you want to adjust for

that problems with the BIG QUESTION need to be avoided. A "No" indicates that the BIG QUESTION is not a concern or issue for the regression objective.

The objectives of "Determining predictors" and "Forecasting the outcome" have fewer things that could go wrong (with more "No's") and are generally straightforward. "Adjusting outcomes," on the other hand, involves more thought as to what factors to condition on and what BIG QUESTIONS may be violated.

Exercises

1. Identify the regression objective of the following research questions (from the four options of estimating causal effects, forecasting/predicting an outcome, determining predictors of an outcome, and adjusting an outcome).

    a. Who was the most effective new-car salesman for Ford cars last year in the U.S., given the strength of the economy in their area?
    b. How does attending a charter school affect the test scores for inner-city minorities?
    c. How much is the amount of car sales in a local area impacted by advertising expenses?
    d. What is the best guess for how many emergency-room visits there will be from drug overdoses in each city this year?
    e. Do people who swear have higher intelligence?
    f. How much will the dollar value of U.S. imports be next year?
    g. What is the single best predictor of whether a female will give birth before age 18?
    h. How did the Clean Air Act affect the intelligence of people who grew up in large metropolitan areas?
    i. How much does consistently reading chapters ahead of class affect your grade?

2. Use the data set **births18**, which is from the NLSY starting in 1997 (Bureau of Labor Statistics, 2015). The variable descriptions are in the data description on the website. Use OLS to explore the determinants of whether a female has a child before age 18 (*birth18*), weighted by the 7th round (2003) sample weight (*wt2003*):

    - Regress *birth18* on *black, hisp, mixed, momhs, momcoll, momeducmiss, dadhs, dadcoll, dadeducmiss, notbiomom,* and *notbiodad*.
    - Regress *birth18* on *black hisp mixed*.

    (Note that the racial/ethnic variables are *black hisp mixed*, with non-Hispanic Whites as the excluded category. Also, the more appropriate model may be a probit or logit model, but that waits until Chapter 9.)

    a. Based on the four regression models, does being Hispanic (*hisp*) significantly predict *birth18*? Justify your answer.
    b. Predict the probability of having a child by age 18 based on the first model above. What characterizes those with the top 80 predicted probabilities (*b18hat* > 0.25) relative to the whole sample? (Examine the means of the explanatory variables.)

3. With the Fox News data (**foxnewsdata**), determine what the best predictor is of the change in Republican vote share (*r_vote_share_ch*), among *foxnews, male_ch, hisp_ch, black_ch, coll_ch pop_ch,* and *unemp_ch*. Use *votes1996* as the weight for the models and robust standard errors.

4. With **foxnewsdata**:

    - Regress the change in Republican vote share (*r_vote_share_ch*) on the variable *black_ch*.
    - Regress the change in Republican vote share (*r_vote_share_ch*) on the variable *male_ch*.

How could it be that the coefficient estimate on *black_ch* is about one-half of the size of that for *male_ch*, yet the R^2 for the model is higher for the model with *black_ch* (0.0102) than the R^2 for the model with *male_ch* (0.0060)?

5. With **foxnewsdata**, regress *r_vote_share_ch* on *foxnews*, *male_ch*, *hisp_ch*, *black_ch*, *coll_ch*, *pop_ch*, *unemp_ch*, *group3*, and *group4*. Restrict the sample to towns with *votes1996* ≥ 2000 and weight the model by *votes1996*.

Determine those observations with the highest-5% and lowest-5% residuals. What states do the observations from each of those groups tend to be from, relative to the sample? (Make sure to restrict the sample to those with *votes1996* ≥ 2000 for the full sample and the highest- and lowest-residual groups.)

Note

1 As will be described in Section 9.3, OLS may not be the appropriate method to use when the outcome is based on an ordered set of categories. Nevertheless, it helps to make the point here.

References

Bureau of Labor Statistics, U.S. Department of Labor. (2014). *National Longitudinal Survey of Youth 1979 cohort, 1979–2012 (rounds 1–25)*. Columbus, OH: Center for Human Resource Research, The Ohio State University.

Bureau of Labor Statistics, U.S. Department of Labor. (2015). *National Longitudinal Survey of Youth 1997 cohort, 1997–2013 (rounds 1–16)*. Columbus, OH: Center for Human Resource Research, The Ohio State University.

8 Methods to address biases

Quasi-experiments (like metaphysics) comprise a dark ocean without shores or lighthouses, strewn with many a philosophical and statistical wrecks. But, if you somehow make one work, it's wicked bitchin'.

– Immanuel Kant

You know, Hobbes, some days even my lucky rocket ship underpants don't help.

– Calvin (of Calvin & Hobbes)

Chapter 6 discussed many potential pitfalls that arise when using regression analysis to estimate causal effects. Some of these pitfalls are impossible to address. For example, if the sample is not representative of the intended population or if there is measurement error in the key explanatory variable, then there may not be a correction. Other pitfalls (mediating factors and outcomes as control variables) could often be addressed simply by changing the model. And then there are the pitfalls of non-random explanatory variables. These are sometimes addressable if you are innovative and lucky enough to find good data.

In this chapter, I discuss methods of addressing problems associated with non-randomness of the key explanatory variable – from reverse causality, omitted-variables bias, or self-selection bias. Recall from Chapter 6 that explanatory variables can have *good (exogenous) variation* and *bad (endogenous) variation*. The key to solving any problem of non-randomness is to isolate variation in the key explanatory variable that is random – i.e., the *good variation* not subject to reverse causality, omitted-variables bias, and self-selection bias. As mentioned in Chapter 6, the ideal and cleanest method would be random assignment to the treatment. But, in our observational (non-experimental) world, we often need to rely on other methods. In the rushing-vs.-passing example I gave in Box 6.2, my strategy was to attempt to strip the key X variables (passing and rushing advantages) of the endogenous component by just using first-half statistics. That is the idea of the methods of this chapter – isolate the exogenous (good) variation in the key X variables.

Some studies use what are called **Natural Experiments**. They are actually (most of the time) man-made experiments. They are "natural" in that the researcher does not need to create an experiment, but rather uses an already-created source of randomness that was probably not designed as an experiment. For example, in a study I will describe in Chapter 11, on the topic of peer effects, researchers found that the Air Force Academy randomizes cadets to roommates and squadrons, which "naturally" creates a set of exogenous peers.

It remains a rare thing that one can find a Natural Experiment to examine. And so, researchers often rely on **Quasi Experiments**. These are methods that do not have random assignment, but rather researchers design a model so that each observation is compared to other observations that are as similar as possible, except that they have different levels of exposure to the treatment. For example, with multiple observations per subject, it is possible to design a model so that a subject is compared to him-/her-/itself, pre-treatment to post-treatment, which reduces the problem of omitted-variables bias from factors determining whether a subject receives the treatment.

This chapter discusses several quasi-experimental methods. These methods are not perfect solutions, as they may have limitations for interpretation and may, at times, exacerbate other problems. Furthermore, just because one of these methods is applied does not mean that the researcher solved the problem of endogeneity. There are underlying conditions or assumptions that are needed, and so it is not always possible to validly apply these advanced methods to a particular empirical issue. But, if you were lucky and/or innovative enough to discover or create a valid quasi-experimental model, it would help towards ruling out explanations for empirical relationships that are alternative to the causal effect you are attempting to estimate.

Like in Chapter 6, in the summary for this chapter (Section 8.11), I give my judgment on the various methods using two scores: how effective the fix is and how generally feasible it is.

8.1 Fixed-effects

This is one of the longest section of the book . . . deservedly so, as it presents a simple, albeit not always perfect, solution to address various biases from omitted-variables bias and potentially reverse causality. A **fixed-effects model**, in most cases, is similar in nature to having a series of dummy variables representing the categories to be controlled for. In fact, other than a few exceptions (e.g., with heteroskedasticity corrections and non-linear models that you will see in Chapter 9), a fixed-effects model is the exact same as including a set of dummy variables.

Analyses using fixed effects can be of a few different types, based on the type of data and whether the key explanatory variable is specific to a single subject (e.g., individuals) or applies to many subjects. Here are a few types of analyses that could use fixed effects, along with some examples:

1. Examining multiple subjects over time (panel data), with a subject-specific key explanatory variable:
   - How a person's oat-bran consumption affects his/her cholesterol.
   - How having an unemployed parent affects a teenager's drug use.
   - How state tax rates affect state-level economic growth.
   - How state-level drunk-driving laws affect the number of drunk-driving arrests in the state. (Even though the law applies to everyone in the state-year, the subject in this case is the state for a given year, and so the driving law is specific to the subject.)
2. Examining how a key explanatory variable applying to many subjects affects those subjects:
   - How the state unemployment rate affects an individual teenager's drug use. (Note that the state unemployment rate applies to all teenagers in the state, as opposed to the example above in which having an unemployed parent is determined for each person.)
   - How a state-level drunk-driving law affects the probability that a person is arrested for driving drunk. (This is different from above because the subjects are individuals, not states.)

Setting up a model that could use fixed effects

Let's return to the topic from the last chapter on student evaluations of instructors and address a new issue: "Does class size affect student evaluations of instructors?" A basic approach would be to estimate the following model:

$$E_{ics} = \beta_1 CS_{ics} + \varepsilon_{ics} \tag{8.1}$$

where:
- E_{ics} is the average evaluation for instructor i in course c in course-segment (class) s;
- CS_{ics} is the class size.

We imagine that class size could have a causal effect on the average evaluation of an instructor, but could there be alternative reasons for why class size and the evaluation of the instructor would be associated with each other?

Yes! There are a few quite plausible alternative scenarios that could contribute to a relationship between class size and the evaluation. While these scenarios could be described in several ways, perhaps omitted-variables bias is the most fitting BIG QUESTION violation. Higher quality for an instructor would lead to higher evaluation scores and could lead to different class sizes: the high-quality instructors would draw more students, they may get assigned to teach larger classes (perhaps the "intro" courses) to draw in more students to a major, or they might be rewarded by his/her department with smaller classes.

Likewise, there could be omitted-variables bias from factors related to a course. An interesting course (e.g., Regression Analysis) would tend to draw more students and would generally lead to higher evaluation scores regardless of the instructor. In contrast, some courses would not be as interesting, and all instructors would tend to have lower evaluation scores when teaching the course. Or, it could be, by the nature of things or incidentally, that the larger intro courses (e.g., General Psychology) are less interesting than the smaller upper-level courses (e.g., Regression Methods in Psychology) . . . or *vice versa*. In this case, inherent, unobservable differences in the courses (how interesting it is) could affect the evaluations as well as affect the class size. Again, we would have omitted-variables bias.

Given these possible sources of omitted-variables bias, before we claim that any rela-tionship between class size and evaluations is due to a causal effect of class size, we need to rule out these alternative stories.

How can we rule out these alternative stories? Well, we probably cannot fully rule them out, but we can get closer to the true causal effect by including instructor and course **fixed effects**.

To understand how it works, let's rewrite equation (8.1) as follows:

$$E_{ics} = \beta_1 CS_{ics} + X_{ics}\beta_2 + (\alpha_i + \alpha_c + e_{ics})$$

(8.2)

where, from equation (8.1), a set of exogenous factors, X, is included and the error term, ε, is sepa-rated into three parts:

- An average effect for the instructor (α_i);
- An average effect for the course (α_c);
- The remaining error term (e_{ics}) that could capture instructor-specific effects for a given class or general variation because: (1) an instructor may have a stronger or weaker-than-normal perfor-mance in a class for some reason; (2) by natural variation or some meaningful trend, the students would be different in each class in terms of how well they receive or appreciate the material and teaching; and (3) other general sources of variation.

The problem, again, is omitted-variables bias in that factors that are part of the error term, (many of which would be captured in α_i or α_c) could be correlated with class size, presumably not by class size affecting these variables. This violates Assumption **A5** because the error term contains the effects of factors that are correlated with class size – namely, the quality of the instructor and the course. In English, this means that, by design, by the nature of things, or by an unplanned coincidence, the class size is not random with respect to the instructor evaluation because it could be determined in some way that is related to the instructor or the course, which have their own effects on the evaluations. This would be *bad variation* in the class-size variable.

One-way fixed effects

To demonstrate what including fixed effects does in correcting for omitted-variables bias (and trying to eliminate the *bad variation*), let's start by fixing the problem of differences in quality across instruc-tors. Applying instructor fixed effects to the model would simply involve:

1. Indicating in the statistical program that the model includes instructor fixed effects; or
2. Including a dummy variable for each instructor (leaving one out as the reference category).

The data do not need to be balanced in that all subjects have the same number of observations.

For pure linear methods, such as OLS, these two methods are equivalent other than the standard errors when there is a correction for heteroskedasticity or for clustering. For non-linear methods (e.g., probit and logit models, which are used for dummy-variable outcomes and will be discussed in the next chapter), it is more complicated to use fixed effects – in fact, it cannot be used in probit models. Method (2) with using a set of dummy variables to represent the factor (each instructor in this case) would be just as effective and gives a close-enough approximation to the interpretation that

I would consider it equivalent enough. But, the safer approach is to indicate fixed effects when doing heteroskedasticity or clustering corrections to the standard errors.

The one-way fixed-effect method estimates the instructor fixed effect, which is the mean value for the evaluation of each instructor, conditional on CS and the variables in X. That is, the value of α_i for each instructor in equation (8.2) is estimated (though not reported) and is usually denoted by μ_i, as follows:

$$E_{ics} = \beta_1 CS_{ics} + X_{ics}\beta_2 + \mu_i + (\alpha_c + e_{ics}) \tag{8.3}$$

Alternatively, if there is no correction for heteroskedasticity or clustering, the model can be:

$$E_{ics} = \beta_1 CS_{ics} + X_{ics}\beta_2 + \sum_{(i=2)}^{I} \gamma_i D_i + (\alpha_c + e_{ics}) \tag{8.4}$$

where D is a set of dummy variables for each instructor, excluding one as the reference instructor. The set of coefficients, γ, represents the mean values of the instructors' evaluations conditional on CS and X, relative to that for the reference instructor ($i = 1$ in this case). Note that the fixed effects (or the coefficients on the individual-instructor dummy variables) are typically not of interest and not reported in most cases. However, in this case, they could be useful, as it represents, from Section 7.3, adjusting instructor evaluations for class size. Also note that the convention is to use μ when describing a fixed effect and α when describing a component of an error term.

An important point to notice is that the error term in equations (8.3) and (8.4), the combined terms of $(\alpha_c + e_{ics})$, no longer has the inherent differences across instructors, α_i, as these differences are controlled for now. Thus, the error term should no longer be correlated with the class size (CS) with respect to the quality of the instructor. That is, as the class size varies in the model, the instructor does not change because it's held constant. It is still possible that course-specific instructor effects in the remaining error term, e_{ics}, are correlated with class size. But, this is almost certainly a smaller empirical association than that between instructor quality and class size.

What does adding fixed effects (or including the set of dummy variables) do to the model? Think back to the model from equations (4.5) and (4.6a–d) in Section 4.3 on estimating the effects of years-of-schooling on income, holding constant the effects of the AFQT quartile. The coefficient estimate on years-of-schooling in (4.5) became the average of the coefficient estimates within each AFQT quartile. That is, the estimate is based on how within-AFQT-quartile variation in years-of-schooling is related to within-AFQT-quartile variation in income.

In this case, the interpretation of β_1 in the fixed-effects model, equation (8.3), is how within-instructor differences in class size are related to within-instructor differences in the evaluations they receive, holding the factors in X constant. The estimate represents the weighted average of within-instructor coefficient estimates on the β_1's for each instructor.

Another interpretation of fixed effects models is that it transforms the data so that the instructor mean is subtracted from each variable. Thus, the estimates represent how divergences from the mean class size for an instructor affect divergences from the mean evaluation for the instructor, holding the other factors constant. That is, the model can be described as:

$$E_{ics} - \overline{E}_i = \beta_1 * \left(CS_{ics} - \overline{CS}_i\right) + \left(X_{ics} - \overline{X}_i\right)\beta_2 + \left(\tilde{\alpha}_c + e_{ics}\right) \tag{8.5}$$

where the bars above the variables indicate the average for all observations for instructor i. Note that α_i is no longer in the error term because it is a constant and becomes zero when subtracted by its average. And, $\tilde{\alpha}_c$ is now the average effect for course c, factoring out the instructor effect.

This one-way fixed effect (for instructors) would rule out any explanation to the relationship between class size and student evaluations of the instructor (β_1) that is due to inherent differences across instructors. This is a quasi-experimental method because a class for a given instructor is being compared to a very similar set of observations – other classes for the same instructor. However, it is not a perfect solution, as it does not address any inherent differences instructors may have in a certain class – they may teach a particular class well and get larger classes as a result – or a change over time in the instructor's quality.

Two-way fixed effects

Now, let's add a second set of fixed effects, for the course, to address omitted-variables bias due to "how interesting or demanding the class is" being related to class size and affecting evaluations. The model (how it could be represented in an article or report) is the following:

$$E_{ics} = \beta_1 CS_{ics} + X_{ics}\beta_2 + \mu_i + \mu_c + e_{ics} \tag{8.6}$$

where
- μ_i is the fixed effect for each instructor;
- μ_c is the fixed effect for each course.

This equation says that the evaluation of the instructor is determined by the class size, an effect particular to the instructor, an effect particular to the class, a set of other factors (X), and a random error component.

The interpretation on β_1 is now different. In equations (8.3), (8.4), and (8.5), the estimate represented how within-instructor differences in evaluations are related to within-instructors differences in class size, holding constant the variables in X. Now, with the two-way fixed effects, the interpretation is:

> **how within-instructor variation in evaluations is related to within-instructor variation in class size, holding constant the course and variables in X;**
> or
> **how within-course variation in evaluations is related to within-course variation in class size, holding constant the instructor and variables in X.**

We have now reduced the *bad variation* in class size from course characteristics that affect both class size and the evaluations. This, again, is not a perfect solution. If a course changes over time to be more or less appealing to students, in terms of how interesting or how demanding it is, there would be differences in course effects that are not controlled for with the course fixed effects. And, this could bias the estimated effect of class size on evaluations. At the very least, with the double set of fixed effects, it is likely that we would get closer to the true causal effects of class size.

Interacted fixed effects

Even with the two-way fixed effects, there could still be a correlation between the error term and class-size variable if:

- Particular instructors were stronger in particular courses than they normally are in other courses, and
- Strength in teaching a particular class well leads to more students enrolling in that class.

If these apply, then a possible variant of the model to address this problem could be an **interacted fixed effect**, as follows:

$$E_{ics} = \beta_1 CS_{ics} + X_{ics}\beta_2 + \mu_{ic} + \varepsilon_{ics} \tag{8.7}$$

In equation (8.7), the interacted fixed effects, μ_{ic} (having a double subscript and replacing the separate fixed effects, μ_i and μ_c) would effectively involve a separate fixed effect for each course that an instructor teaches. For example, if there were 20 instructors, 30 courses, and each instructor taught 4 different courses, then:

- Equation (8.6) would have 20 instructor fixed effects and 30 course fixed effects;
- Equation (8.7) would have 80 (20 times 4) instructor-course fixed effects.

The latter model would only work if instructors had multiple segments of a given course so that there would be variation in class size within the 80 instructor-course groups. The interpretation would become:

> **how variation in evaluations is related to variation in the class size in a given instructor-course combination, holding constant the factors in X.**

This would make for even more similar comparison groups. But, does this fully address the empirical problems, namely omitted-variables bias? Probably not fully. The argument for this model giving an unbiased estimate of the causal effect relies on the assumption that the class size is not correlated (in a systematic way or incidentally) with other influences on the instructor's quality/effectiveness for a given course.

Of course, it is possible that instructor quality could change over time for a given course, and students flock more to the course over time, as the instructor improves the course. As long as there are unaccounted-for differences in instructor quality over time within a course, there would potentially be omitted-variables bias. However, with the interacted fixed effects, we should get closer to the true causal effect.

The trade-off of addressing bias vs. precision

The example above with the separate instructor and course fixed effects vs. the instructor-course-interacted fixed effects demonstrates the trade-off involved with using large sets of fixed-effects. Going from 20 instructor and 30 course fixed effects in equation (8.6) to the 80 instructor-course fixed effects in equation (8.7) has the following primary advantage and disadvantage:

- Advantage: It should give a more accurate estimate, as identification of β_1 would come from how the evaluations of instructors in a specific course change when the class size changes in that course for that instructor. This reduces any potential omitted-variables bias from some instructors teaching certain classes better than others.
- Disadvantage: The greater number of fixed effects sops up a good portion of the variation, leaving less variation to get precise estimates. In other words, standard errors would likely be much larger and estimates would have less precision.

Researchers need to weigh the importance of reducing the possibility of remaining omitted-variables bias versus improving the precision in the estimates when deciding how narrow they make the fixed effects. The larger sample a researcher has, the greater latitude there would be to add more fixed effects.

Intuition on the estimated causal effect

It turns out that not all instructors would contribute equally to the estimation of the causal effect, β_1. Recall equation (4.7):

$$\hat{\beta}_1 = \sum_g \hat{\beta}_{1g} * \left[\frac{\Pr(g) \times \text{var}(X_1 \mid g, X_2)}{Z} \right] \qquad (4.7)$$

which states that the coefficient estimate represents the average of the within-group estimates, where the groups are defined by a set of dummy variables for a certain categorization (AFQT quartile, as we had it). This was demonstrated in Table 4.3 in Section 4.3.

The same equation applies for models with fixed effects. As formulated by Gibbons et al. (2014), the contribution to the estimation of β_1, the estimated effect of class size in equation (8.6), is higher for:

- (Not surprisingly) those instructors with a greater weight in the sample (i.e., more observations); and
- (Not as obvious) those instructors with greater variation in class size among his/her classes.

Think of it this way. If an instructor always had classes of 25 people, then there is no within-instructor variation in class size to explain evaluations. The estimation of β_1 would have to come from other instructors. The larger the variation in class size was for a given instructor (or instructor-course combination if using the interacted fixed effect), the more that could be explained by class size, the more precisely the effect would be estimated for that instructor, and the more the instructor's estimated effect would contribute to the overall estimate.

A similar story can be made on courses. Courses that are always around the same size would have a small contribution to the estimation of β_1, whereas courses with greater variation would contribute more to the estimate. We'll return to this concept in the next two sections.

Fixed effects do not address self-selection bias

The fixed-effects method has the potential to address omitted-variables bias and reverse causality. However, it does not address self-selection bias. A fixed-effects model essentially compares subjects before and after a treatment or at different levels of exposure to a treatment. Consider the example from Section 6.4.3 on how marijuana affects income. I suggested that the people whose income would benefit from marijuana or would be unaffected by marijuana would be more likely to use marijuana. Thus, a fixed-effects model based on a panel data set that tracks people over time would estimate the effects of marijuana more for these people (whose income benefits from or is not affected by marijuana) than for those whose income would be negatively affected be marijuana use. This is because we would not see many of the latter set of people using marijuana. Thus, we'd still have a positive bias from people selecting into whether or how much marijuana they use based on how it would affect them.

When there is self-selection bias, then a fixed-effects model does not estimate the Average Treatment Effect (ATE). Rather, it would be estimating what is called the Average Treatment Effect for the Treated (ATT). This is what we would expect to be the experiences of those who chose to receive the treatment rather than an average effect for everyone (or a random person).

Application – an actual study on class size and instructor evaluation

Some researchers examined this issue at the University of California-Santa Barbara (Bedard and Kuhn 2008). The authors have many sets of results, but Table 8.1 displays the results from their Appendix Table 1 that are the most easily summarizable. The results provide an estimated average linear effect, whereas the author's preferred specifications, rightly, had non-linear effects with quadratic and higher-order polynomial functions of class size or categories of class size. Note that a single observation represents a given class; and, for that class, the dependent variable is the average evaluation score and the key explanatory variable is the class size.

This set of results presents an interesting case. In the "quasi"-cross-sectional model in which there were no controls for the instructor or the course (the first column of results), the coefficient estimate on class size is statistically insignificant, providing no evidence for any effect of class size on instructor evaluations. But, this estimate could be affected by the various sources of omitted-variables bias. And so, the authors needed to rule out other explanations for how class size and instructor evaluations were related. So, they included instructor and course fixed effects (in the second column of results). They did not estimate models with instructor-course-interacted fixed effects, probably because there would not have been enough variation to do so precisely.

With the instructor and course fixed effects, the estimate became negative and significant (-0.0011), as might be expected. One could argue that it is not that strong of an effect, given that a 1-standard-deviation increase in the class size (of 108) would only be expected to increase evaluations by 0.12, which is less than one-fifth of the standard deviation in evaluations (0.65). Furthermore, the lower bound of the confidence interval on the estimated effect would be around -0.0003. Nevertheless, this provides some evidence for how other things besides instructor effectiveness can impact evaluations.

Application – estimating tax effects on economic growth

In Section 6.4.2 on omitted-variables bias, I discussed the problems with estimating the effects of tax rates on measures of the national economy – the unemployment rate and the real GDP growth rate.

Table 8.1 The effects of class size on average instructor evaluation from Bedard and Kuhn (2008)

	Dependent variable = average instructor-evaluation score for the class	
	Quasi-cross-section (no fixed effects) (n = 655 classes)	Fixed effects for instructor and course (n = 459 classes)
Class size	-0.0004 (0.0003)	-0.0011^{**} (0.0004)

Note: Other variables included in the model are year and quarter variables. ** indicates $p < 0.05$.

The problem was that incidental correlation with national events (the internet boom, the dot–com crash, the September 11 attacks, the Financial Crisis) causes the tax rates to get credited with or blamed for the effects of these events, likely causing bias in the estimated tax effects.

Addressing this would require controlling for these national events. However, if we use year fixed effects with the national data, then there would not be any usable variation left from the tax rate or any other X variable, as the year effects would fully describe ($R^2 = 1.000$) the annual outcomes. But, there is a potential solution. Economic and tax data at the *state* level could be used, with fixed effects for the year and the state. The year fixed effects would then pick up the average nationwide effects of the various events.

The model would be the following:

$$Y_{str} = X_{str}\beta_1 + T_{str}\beta_2 + \mu_s + \mu_{tr} + \varepsilon_{str} \tag{8.8}$$

where:

- The subscripts s, t, and r refer to the state, the time period (or year), and the region (among nine census regions);
- Y is the economic outcome (such as real Gross State Product growth rate);
- X is a set of exogenous factors particular to a state that are not constant over time and that affect the economic outcome;
- T is a set of tax rates, such as income (which combines federal and state income tax rates, including deductions for state income taxes), corporate, and property tax rates;
- μ_s is the state fixed effect;
- μ_{tr} is the interacted-region-year fixed effect.

This was the model used in Section 6.4.6 when demonstrating the effects of including outcome variables as control variables. In this model, there would be 48 observations (one per contiguous-U.S. state) for each year in the sample. Such a model may be more accurate if it were estimated as a weighted model, with the weights being based on the state's population in a given year.

The fixed effects subtract out the average effects of the state and of the year for each region. Thus, the interpretation for the tax effects, β_2, would be: *how within-state changes over time (relative to other states in a given region) in tax rates and the economic outcome are related, holding constant the average year-region effects and the other X variables*. In other words, as the tax rates change in the model, the state does not change. And, a given observation for a state is just being compared to other observations for that state, with the year effects particular to the state's region factored out.

While all states would be included in the model, some states would not "participate" in estimating the effect of a particular tax rate in T. These would be states that have the same tax rate over the period of the sample. The states with no income tax rate, for example, would not be part of the direct estimation of the effect of income tax rates. They would, however, contribute to the year-region fixed effects, which in turn could indirectly contribute to the estimated tax-rate effect.

This is not a perfect approach. There still could be certain state-related events that are incidentally correlated with changes in tax rates in that state. Nevertheless, this is the standard approach used in such studies on the effects of tax rates. Unfortunately, most of these studies violate BIG QUESTION 6 (as described in Section 6.4.6) in that they include outcomes as control variables.

Application – estimating the effects of the unemployment rate on teenage drug use

This is a case with individual-level data and a key explanatory variable that applies to many. And, it is also a case of an organization of data that I mentioned in Section 2.15.1, which I called "multiple cross-sectional periods." This type of data has a different set of subjects each year . . . or, at least they are treated as if they are different. But, subjects across periods may come from the same group, such as a state.

I discussed this research issue, on how the unemployment rate may affect teenage drug use, back in Section 6.4.5, with the following model:

$$Y_{it} = X_{it}\beta_1 + \beta_2 UR_{it} + \varepsilon_{it} \tag{6.12}$$

where Y is a measure of drug use for teenagers, X is a set of demographic characteristics, and UR is the state unemployment rate at the given time period, t. The value for UR would apply to all teenagers in the sample from that state at a given time. While I indicated that state and year controls are included in X, let's suppose that there were not any controls for year and state.

In the model, there could be omitted-variables bias in that the state unemployment rate would generally be higher or lower in certain periods that just happen to have high or low rates of drug use. For example, likely due to basketball-star Len Bias's cocaine-induced death in 1986, drug use went down among teenagers from 1986 to 1992. The very low rate in 1992 coincided with a higher-than-normal *national* unemployment rate, which means higher *state* unemployment rates. Although this particular period was not in the sample, this is an example of incidental correlation between the state unemployment rates and teenage drug use – correlation that was not necessarily due to any causal effect of the unemployment rates. Thus, the year effects could cause omitted-variables bias, if not controlled for.

Likewise, the state unemployment rate tended to be lower for the Great Plains states and higher in industrial states. To the extent that teenage drug use tends to be higher (or lower) in these states over the years, there could be incidental correlation leading to omitted-variables bias. (The omitted variable would be the state.)

The simple solution to these problems would be to add state and time-period (year) fixed effects, as follows:

$$Y_{ist} = X_{ist}\beta_1 + \mu_s + \mu_t + \beta_2 UR_{ist} + \varepsilon_{ist} \tag{8.9}$$

where the state and time-period controls are represented by the fixed effects, μ_s and μ_t, rather than being in the X vector of control variables.

The best way to interpret the coefficient on the unemployment rate, β_2, would be how within-in-state changes in the unemployment rate are related to within-state changes in teenage drug use, holding the time period and other factors in X constant. Thus, individuals are just compared to others in the same state. And, the industrial states would tend to have greater natural weight in the model than the Great Plains agricultural states because: (1) they have more observations; and (2) there is more variation in their unemployment rates.

What conditions (or assumptions) are required for this to be a valid analysis for estimating the causal effects of the state unemployment rate? The within-state variation in the unemployment rate (factoring out the country-wide year effects) must be uncorrelated with the within-state variation in other factors of teenage drug use that are not controlled for. I believe that it is unlikely that there is any factor that is not a product of the unemployment rate and would have its within-state variation be systematically correlated with the within-state variation in the unemployment rate. But, the possibility of incidental correlation remains. Still, the method should improve on a cross-sectional model in which there is a much greater likelihood of incidental correlation of the state unemployment rate and other influencers of teenage drug use.

Drawback to using fixed effects: greater bias from any measurement error

While fixed-effects models can be one of the simplest and most effective methods of addressing omitted-variables bias, it has the potential to significantly increase bias from measurement error. Going back to the analysis on class size and student evaluations, measurement error (for the explanatory variable) could occur because there could be differences between the numbers of students enrolled, showing up for class, and filling out the student evaluation. Using fixed effects eliminates some bad variation in class size (that causes omitted-variables bias), but it also eliminates good variation – i.e., variation across classes in the class size that leads to variation in evaluations. But, fixed effects do not reduce variation from measurement error. Thus, variation from measurement error will constitute a higher share of total variation in the class-size variable when fixed effects are applied. With the greater measurement-error-variation-as-a-percentage-of-total-variation-in-the-key-X-variable, there would likely be greater attenuation bias in the estimates towards zero.

Note that it is not the percentage of observations that have a mis-measured X variable that matters for the extent of measurement error bias. Rather, the extent of measurement error depends on the percentage of the (usable variation in the X variable, conditional on the other explanatory variables) that is measured with error. And, using fixed effects eliminates valid usable variation across people (or entities) – leaving just within-subject variation over time. This reduces the denominator of usable variation, meaning that the variation from measurement error is now a greater percentage of usable variation.

Let's consider the example we just used above on how the unemployment rate affects teenage drug use. A problem is that the state unemployment rate, which comes from the Department of Labor's Current Population Survey (CPS), is going to have measurement error in it. This could be based on sampling error, particularly for the smaller states. In addition, it could be from CPS respondents mis-representing their employment status. Across states, this is probably a small part of the total variation in the unemployment rate. However, for within-state changes in the unemployment rate over time, particularly if a short time period is considered, measurement error could be a much larger share of the total variation. If there were measurement error, then the estimated effect of the unemployment rate would likely be biased towards zero.

Thus, when using fixed effects, one needs to consider how much error there is in the key explanatory variable. An insignificant estimate may be attributable to attenuation bias. And, a significant estimate may be indicative of a larger effect.

The same concept will apply to first-difference methods, in Section 8.5. I will give an example that demonstrates how this problem could lead to ambiguous interpretations.

Arrellano-Bond correction when using lagged-dependent variables

A problem could arise in fixed effects when there is a panel data set (i.e., multiple observations per subject) and you have a lagged-dependent variable as an explanatory variable. The problem is that, if the lagged-dependent variable is greater than the within-subject mean, then the current dependent variable is more likely to be less than the within-subject mean. This occurs because the fixed effects make it so a person (or entity) is just being compared to him-/herself, so one observation being above the mean would necessitate that the other observations for that person would be, on average, below the mean. This would contribute a negative bias to the estimated relationship between the lagged and current dependent variables. Arellano and Bond (1991) developed an approach to address this problem, with what is called a Generalized Method of Moments model.[1]

Box 8.1 Do professional golfers behave badly (or, act irrationally) on the golf course?

Most economic theory relies on the assumption that people and firms always act in their best interest … you know the story … to maximize their utility or their profits. Well, Pope and Schweitzer (2011) uncovered some evidence that says professional golfers don't always act in their best interest. They investigated whether golfers act irrationally around the arbitrary reference point of par, which is the expected number of shots a given hole requires to complete. The idea is that golfers should almost always try to complete a hole in as few shots as possible. And so, in most situations, effort and risk should be the same, regardless of how many shots they have taken for a given hole. But, golfers may be subject to the concept of "loss aversion," which is that people tend to take costly measures to avoid a loss. In this situation, anything worse than par could be considered a "loss."

The authors aimed to compare whether golfers are more likely to make a putt for par than a putt for an eagle (two shots better than par), a birdie (one shot better than par), or a bogey (one shot worse than par. Missing the putt for par would result in a "loss." The authors used a data set of over 2.5 million putts from men's professional tournaments, with information on the location of the ball relative to the hole. They could have just compared all putts for par versus putts for the other scores, controlling for the distance to the hole. But, there could be omitted-variables bias in that better players may be more likely to have easier shots for birdie than weaker players. And so, they included in the model *player fixed effects*. This means that comparisons of birdie-vs.-par-vs.-bogey putts were just being made for each player individually and then combined into average effects. This helps rule out this potential source of omitted-variables bias. There are other potential sources of omitted-variables bias that the authors attempt to rule out with other sets of fixed effects in some models, such as fixed effects for the particular tournament-hole-round. And, all models controlled for a 7th-order-polynomial for shot distance – i.e., distance, distance-squared, …, distance-to-the-7th-power. Here are the results, based on a linear probability model, with the dependent variable being whether the player made the putt (from their Table 3, column 4, with both the player and tournament-round-hole fixed effects).

(Dependent variable = whether the player made the putt)

Variable	Coef. Est. (Std. Error)
Putt for eagle	−0.042 (0.002)***

Putt for birdie	−0.029 (0.001)***
Putt for par	(reference category)
Putt for bogey	0.003 (0.001)***
Putt for double bogey	−0.003 (0.002)

Note: *** indicates $p<0.01$.

Note that three of these estimates are highly statistically significant. So, compared to the par putt, players are an estimated 4.2-percentage-points less likely to make a putt for birdie, holding the shot distance (and player) constant. The estimates are actually similar to those without player fixed effects (column 1 in that table, which I do not report here). Nevertheless, it was worthwhile to use the fixed effects, just to make the analysis cleaner and ensure against certain sources of omitted-variables bias.

One thing these results could mean is that players try hardest when they face a potential loss (the putt for par) or greater loss (the putt for bogey). In addition, it could mean that a player's goal is shifted for the birdie (or eagle) putt from making the putt towards making sure that he keeps himself in position to make the par putt (or birdie putt) if he misses.

Subsequent research (Stone and Arkes 2016) found that players don't only bracket around the reference point of par on a single hole, but also on a rolling set of two holes and on a round (in contrast to the tournament). That is, if they are above par for the round of 18 holes (at least for Round 1 of a tournament), the evidence suggests that they try extra hard (or take greater risk) to get a birdie on the current hole to make up for being behind for the round. And, this comes at the cost of an increased chance of a bogey on the current hole as well.

8.2 A thorough example of fixed effects

Let's return to the examination of how the class size affects instructor evaluations. I created some notional data on 100 observations (classes). The setup is the following:

- A university has four instructors, each teaching a different course − A, B, C, and D.
  (Thus, there are effectively four instructor-course-interacted groups.)
- There are 25 observations (classes) per course . . . obviously this would be over several years, but we will not worry about the time factor.
- There is a range of class sizes for each course that is stipulated in Table 8.2.
- The effect of class-size on the average evaluation is also stipulated in Table 8.2, with there being no effect for two of the courses.
- I added randomness to the evaluation, so the coefficient estimates on class-size will probably not equal the effects I imposed, but should be in the general ballpark of the true effect.
- The true Average Treatment Effect that we hope to estimate is 0.0100, which is the average of the four effects for the four instructors, of −0.03, −0.01, 0, and 0 (since each instructor has the same number of classes).

Table 8.2 Course characteristics in the simulation

Course	Range of class size	Class-size effect on the average evaluation that I imposed
A	10–40	−0.03
B	100–150	−0.01
C	175–250	0
D	300–400	0

So, for the smaller two courses, there is a negative effect of class size on the average evaluation of the instructor, as would be expected. But, for the two larger courses, there is no effect, which might be expected for large enough courses.

There are two possible models:

- Cross-sectional model: $E_{ics} = \beta_1 CS_{ics} + \varepsilon_{ics}$

- Fixed-effects model : $E_{ics} = \beta_1 CS_{ics} + \mu_{ic} + \varepsilon_{ics}$

with:
- Subscript i = instructor.
- Subscript c = course. (In this simple case, either the instructor or course distinguishes the four sets of observations, A to D.)
- Subscript s = segment/class. (There are 25 classes for each course.)
- E = average evaluation of the instructor in the segment/class.
- CS = class size of segment.
- μ_{ic} = instructor-course fixed effect.

In the cross-sectional model, every class is compared to every other class, regardless of what course it is in. So, as class size changes, so does the instructor/course. But, in the fixed-effects model, classes are only compared to others in the same course, and as class size changes in the model, the instructor-course effectively does not change. This will be important, as we will see in the data.

Figures 8.1a and 8.1b show the data points and the cross-sectional model and fixed-effects model, respectively. We see from the data why it is necessary to use fixed effects for the instructor (course). Some instructors just tend to get higher ratings, and some tend to get lower ratings. Without controlling for the instructor, this would be incidental correlation that would contribute to omitted-variables bias. And, as mentioned earlier, there could be omitted-variables bias from spurious correlation in that the better instructors or more interesting courses (perhaps the instructor in course D) attract more students to their course and get better ratings.

Table 8.3 summarizes the results from the regression models, which are also seen embedded within the figures. In the cross-sectional model in Figure 8.1a, the given line is the estimated regression model, which has an unexpected positive and significant coefficient estimate on class-size of 0.0007. We know this isn't correct from how I constructed the data to have a negative effect for two of the classes and a zero effect for the other two classes. And so, it is likely due to omitted-variables bias.

The fixed-effects make it so that classes are just being compared to other classes for the same course/instructor and not to classes from other courses. In Figure 8.1b, I give the coefficient estimates

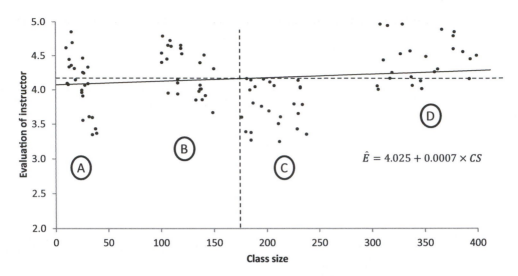

Figure 8.1a The cross-sectional representation of the class–size and instructor-evaluation issue

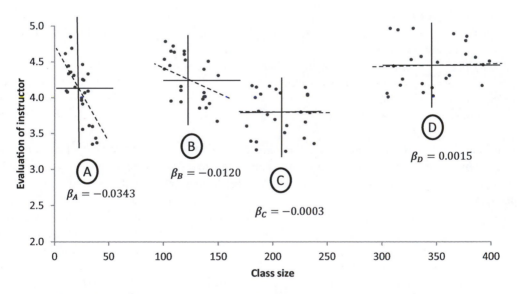

Figure 8.1b The fixed-effects representation of the class–size and instructor-evaluation issue

and show the regression line for each course. The individual models for each course produce coefficient estimates on class-size that are consistent with the class-size effect I imposed in the simulation of the data (as shown in Table 8.2). They are not the exact effects I imposed (−0.0300, −0.0100, 0, and 0) because of the randomness I injected into the determination of the evaluation. These four coefficient estimates are the inputs into the overall fixed-effect estimator, which is in the last row of Table 8.3. The coefficient estimate on class-size is now negative (−0.0027), but it is insignificant.

Table 8.3 Coefficient estimates on class-size for various models, plus variance within groups

	Dependent variable = average evaluation from the class (n = 100)	
	Coefficient estimate (standard error) on class-size	Var(class-size)
All (cross section)	**0.0007 (0.0003)****	
Course A only	−0.0343 (0.0063)***	79.32
Course B only	−0.0120 (0.0035)***	257.67
Course C only	−0.0004 (0.0031)	426.46
Course D only	0.0015 (0.0021)	911.19
All (course fixed effects)	**−0.0027 (0.0037)**	

Note: ***, **, and * indicate statistical significance at the 1, 5, and 10% levels, respectively. The heteroskedasticity-corrected standard errors are in parentheses.

Let me draw a connection to an earlier lesson on what an insignificant estimate on the key explanatory variable could mean. Recall from Section 5.5 that an insignificant estimate could be due to:

1. There actually being no effect of the explanatory variable on the outcome.
2. There being an effect in one direction, but the model is unable to detect the effect due to a modeling problem biasing the coefficient estimate in a direction opposite to the actual effect.
3. There being a small effect that cannot be detected with the available data due to inadequate power.
4. There being varying effects in the population (or sample); and the estimated effect is insignificant due to positive and negative effects canceling each other out or being drowned out by those observations with zero effects.

The overall estimated effect of an insignificant −0.0027 falls under reason 4. There actually were real effects for two of the groups (A and B), but they were drowned out by the near-zero estimates for groups C and D and no meaningful overall effect was detected. Furthermore, the estimated effect of −0.0027 is far from the true average effect of −0.100.

So, we know there is an effect, but this certainly isn't satisfying in that the full fixed-effects model is not able to detect the class-size effect we know is there for the two smaller classes, A and B. The problem is this formula again:

$$\hat{\beta}_1 = \sum_g \hat{\beta}_{1g} * \left[\frac{\Pr(g) \times \text{var}(X_1 \mid g)}{Z} \right] \qquad (4.7)$$

(Note that there are no other variables, X_2, in the basic notional example I have created.) So, the groups (courses) with the larger variances (courses C and D) are the ones that have the greater natural weights in the model. The rationale for why this weighting makes some sense is that the β_1's for courses C and D will be more precisely estimated, as can be seen with the lower standard errors for groups C and D and the highest standard error for group A, which had by far the lowest variance in CS. Note that this weighting naturally occurs, as the set of observations with the wider variance in CS would have greater deviations from the mean.

This weighting scheme makes sense if there is a constant effect (β_1) across all groups in the population. But, this is an unlikely scenario. Almost certainly, β_1 will vary in the population. In such cases, the fixed-effect estimate will be a biased estimate of the Average Treatment Effect (ATE) in the population.

Indeed, the actual ATE is -0.0100 and the average of the four estimates is -0.0113 (a not-too-far-off estimate of the true ATE), but the fixed-effects estimate is far from that at -0.0027. . . because it is overweighting the two courses that have no effect of class size. This exercise gives a larger lesson on potential problems with fixed effects: that it can shift the weights so much that it changes what sets of observations are contributing most to the effect. In the next section, I describe an adjustment to the fixed-effects estimator to obtain unbiased estimates for the ATE.

8.3 An alternative to the fixed-effects estimator

The above example demonstrated that the fixed-effects estimator could be biased when there are differing treatment effects across groups and the groups are weighted unevenly. There is a class-size effect for groups A and B, but the estimated effects (close to zero) for groups C and D are dominating the overall estimate in the fixed-effects model. The disproportionate weights for courses C and D (relative to their sample size) cause the overall fixed-effect estimate to be weighted towards their near-zero estimated effects of class size. So, varying weights due to different variances of the key X variable could cause the fixed-effects estimate to be biased.

Gibbons et al. (2014) formalize this bias when there are different (heterogeneous) treatment effects in the population. And, they find evidence for the bias from the replication of several studies from one of the top economics journals, *The American Economic Review*.

Gibbons et al. (2014) then propose a change to the fixed-effects model by re-weighting observations by the inverse of the variance of the key X variable within each fixed-effects group and conditional on the other X variables. This weight would be constant for each observation in a given fixed-effects group. They call this the **regression-weighted estimator**.

Table 8.4 first shows the original fixed-effects estimate of -0.0027 from Table 8.3. It then shows the estimate from the model Gibbons et al. suggest, with the weights for the observations being based on the within-course variance in class size. Now, it gives the exact average of the class-size effects for each course, -0.0113, which is close to the average of the effects I had imposed on the four courses (the true ATE), -0.0100. And, this is highly statistically significant.

Note that there is a trade-off here. The fixed-effects estimator naturally weights observations based on the certainty of the estimate (which depends on the variation in the key explanatory variable). This has value, but it comes at a cost of down-weighting what could be important information. This is yet another situation in which, for the sake of honesty and completeness, both sets of results should be shown to demonstrate how the results depend on the weighting of groups.

There are a few details on using this approach that need to be considered. First, if there were other variables in the model, then those would need to be factored out before calculating the weights. That is, the steps would be:

- Regress the key X variable (CS) on the other explanatory variables and fixed effects.
- Calculate the residuals for each observation from that regression.

Table 8.4 A comparison of a standard and regression-weighted fixed-effects model

	Dependent variable = average evaluation from the class (n = 100)	
	All (course fixed effects)	All (course fixed effects), weighted by inverse of variance
Coefficient estimate	−0.0027	−0.0113***
(Standard error) on class size	(0.0037)	(0.0029)

- Calculate the within-fixed-effects-group variance in the residual for each fixed-effects group.
- Apply that to equation (4.7), substituting it in for the var($X_1 | g, X_2$).

Second, sometimes the weight of one fixed-effects group comes out to be extraordinarily large due to having hardly any variation in the key X variable, particularly after adjustment for other explanatory variables. This could result in far too high a reliance or weight on an imprecise estimate. And, this could lead to higher standard errors and estimates that are far off from the true causal effect. This is where some regression diagnostics might be useful. It could be worthwhile to check the weights and perhaps delete from the sample observations that have too high a weight. It is probably better to use some standard such as requiring a certain minimum variance or standard deviation in the original key X variable or in the residual of that key X variable after factoring out the other explanatory variables and fixed effects. Unfortunately, there is no standard for what is too high a weight. This is another reason why regression is an "art."

Third, Gibbons et al. (2014) provide a method to calculate the new standard errors. This requires some complicated matrix algebra. As practitioners, the standard errors they propose should not be that different from what you would obtain naturally as you re-weight the observations. Perhaps the prudent thing to do is use a little lower p-value requirement to conclude that a hypothesis test provides evidence for an empirical relationship.

As a quick note similar to the one in Section 6.6.2, the two main statistical programs that I use (Stata and R) produce the same coefficient estimates but different standard errors for the fixed-effects models, but particularly for the heteroskedasticity-corrected standard errors. I am providing the standard errors produced by Stata, as they are larger – i.e., more conservative.

8.4 Random effects

A **random-effects model** is an alternative to fixed effects that, in some cases, can produce smaller standard errors. The requirement for a random-effects model is that the variation in effects of the subjects (such as an instructor effect or a course effect) is random with respect to the other explanatory variables. From our example, the instructor and the course effects would be uncorrelated with the class size and other explanatory variable. That is, from a generic equation with a single-dimensional fixed effect of the individual, i:

$$Y_{it} = Y_{it}\beta + (a_i + e_{it})$$

(8.10)

the following conditions must hold:

- $\text{cov}(X, \alpha_i) = 0.$

If this were to hold, then applying a random-effects model would improve the efficiency of the estimates. Furthermore, random-effects models allow one to estimate the effects of subject-specific traits that would be held constant in a fixed-effects model. For example, a model using fixed effects for instructors could not estimate the effects of instructor gender or race, but using random effects for instructors would allow one to estimate the gender and race effects.

If the random effects were not random with respect to the other explanatory variables, then it leads to inconsistent estimates, meaning that as the sample size increases, the estimates do not converge to the true population coefficients.

Basically, using random effects is a way of getting more efficient estimates (with lower standard errors), which increases the likelihood that you achieve statistical significance and narrows confidence intervals. However, it comes at the cost of not being consistent if there is any non-zero covariance (or correlation) of the effects of certain subjects (e.g., the instructor or the course) with the class size or other X variables.

One way to determine whether to use random effects is by conducting a **Hausman test**. The Hausman test has the following hypothesis test:

$$H_0: \text{cov}\left(X,\ \alpha_i\right) = 0$$

$$H_1: \text{cov}\left(X,\ \alpha_i\right) \neq 0$$

If there is a single X variable, then the Hausman test statistic is:

$$H = \frac{\left(\hat{\beta}_{FE} - \hat{\beta}_{RE}\right)^2}{\left(var\left(\hat{\beta}_{FE}\right) - var\left(\hat{\beta}_{RE}\right)\right)} \tag{8.11}$$

where $\hat{\beta}_{FE}$ and $\hat{\beta}_{RE}$ are the coefficient estimates on the single X variable for the fixed-effects and the random-effects models. This test statistic, H, can be tested under a chi-squared distribution with one degree of freedom: $H \sim \chi(1)$. In the more likely situation in which there is more than one X variable, the Hausman test statistic relies on a Linear-Algebra calculation, with vectors of coefficient estimates and covariance matrices:

$$H = \left(\hat{\beta}_{FE} - \hat{\beta}_{RE}\right)'\left[var\left(\hat{\beta}_{FE}\right) - var\left(\hat{\beta}_{RE}\right)^{-1}\right]\left(\hat{\beta}_{FE} - \hat{\beta}_{RE}\right) \tag{8.12}$$

Luckily, this is easily computed in our various computer programs.

The idea behind these test statistics is that if the differences between the coefficient estimates in the random effects and the fixed-effects models are large relative to the efficiency gains (in terms of lower standard errors), it suggests that the random-effects estimates would be inconsistent. Some argue that one should go with fixed effects if the Hausman test statistic, H, is statistically significant. But, one could argue that just because it is insignificant does not mean that the X variable and the subject-specific effects are uncorrelated. Thus, I would argue that the fixed-effects model is a more conservative approach. In addition, it has a nice interpretation of being based on within-subject effects.

As an example of an application of random effects, consider a study evaluating a new surgical procedure (the treatment) relative to a standard surgical procedure (the control).[2] The problem is that the effects of the surgical team could impact the estimated effectiveness of the new surgery relative to the standard surgery. Ideally, several surgical teams would be trained in performing both the standard and the new surgery.

If the surgical teams are then randomized for which surgery they perform, along with the patients being randomized to the surgery, then random effects can be applied as follows:

$$Y_{ij} = X_{ij}\beta_1 + \beta_2 T_{ij} + U_j + \varepsilon_{ij} \tag{8.13}$$

where:
- Y is the post-surgery outcome for patient i and surgical team j;
- X is a set of control variables;
- T is the treatment (if the patient received the new surgery);
- U_j is the random effect of the surgical team.

The idea here is that, by treating the surgical team as a random instead of a fixed factor, the results could be generalized to all potential surgical teams rather than just to the surgical teams involved in the study.

Again, using random effects relies on the assumption that the assignment of the individual factor (in our case, the surgical team) is random with respect to the other explanatory variables, including the treatment, T_{ij}. Unless you are certain that this is the case, then fixed effects is typically the more conservative approach.

8.5 First-differences

The concept of using first-difference

First-difference (FD) models are, effectively, fixed-effects models with just two observations (often over two time periods) for each subject. As with fixed effects, FD models are meant to address the problem of omitted-variables bias – from spurious or incidental correlation. The idea behind FD models is that, to eliminate an unobserved person-specific factor that may be correlated with the key explanatory variable, you examine a change over time rather than just the outcome at one point in time. So, you examine how the change in the outcome (Y) moves over a certain period with a given change in the key X variable.

The concept behind FD models is applied by most school districts, often without a regression, in how they evaluate teachers. It is generally understood that we cannot compare the end-of-year achievement of one teacher's students to the students of other teachers because there are large differences in the original preparation and background of the students that teachers have. These differences may be due to systematic patterns, as teachers in richer school districts will tend to get better-prepared students than those teaching near public housing projects. Natural variation (i.e., luck) could also cause variation in the preparedness of students a teacher gets in a given year.

To reduce the impact of differences in the preparedness of the students in the evaluation of teachers, most school districts use the average change in the students' achievement over the course of the year (or from one year to the next). This is often called the "value-added." This eliminates the influence of student-specific factors that stay constant over time. But, there still could be students who naturally learn more easily than others. So, there may still be student-specific factors, such as the ability to learn, that influence comparisons of teachers. But, these should be much less than the overall differences across students.

FD models have the potential to address omitted-variables bias and reverse causality. However, as with fixed-effects models, they do not address self-selection bias (for the same reasons). And so, as with fixed-effects models, in the presence of self-selection bias, the FD model would estimate the ATT.

First-difference example with aggregate data

Let's apply the FD approach to tackle the research issue from the prior section and build on the model on the unemployment rate and teenage drug (marijuana) use from various mentions so far. This time, we will use aggregate rates of state-level, teenage marijuana use rather than data on individuals. If we just had a cross-sectional sample (one observation per state), then we probably would experience omitted-variables bias from incidental correlation, as described in Section 8.1.

We need to rule out this omitted-variables bias and other possible explanations so that we can be more certain that the relationship between the unemployment rate and youth marijuana use is causal. To examine this, I took one observation from each state for both the 2006–07 period and 2009–10 period, averaging the youth marijuana use and the unemployment rate for the two years within each period. Two-year averages are used because that is how the youth marijuana use rates are reported to improve accuracy of the estimated use rates for smaller states.[3]

The model for the cross-sectional model is simply:

$$MJ_{st} = \beta_0 + \beta_1 UR_{st} + \varepsilon_{st} \tag{8.14}$$

where
- MJ_{st} is the youth marijuana use rate in state s in period t;
- UR_{st} is the average unemployment rate in state s in period t;
- $\varepsilon_{st} = \alpha_s + e_{st}$, where α_s is the *unobserved state effect* for marijuana use, and e_{st} is the random component of the error term.

The problem is that, even though we may not be able to create any specific story on why the unobserved state effects would be correlated with unemployment rate, there could be incidental correlation. To address this, we can estimate an FD model as follows:

$$\left(MJ_{s2} - MJ_{s1}\right) = \beta_0 + \beta_1 \times \left(UR_{s2} - UR_{s1}\right) + \left[\left(\alpha_s + e_{s1}\right) - \left(\alpha_s + e_{s2}\right)\right] \tag{8.15a}$$

or

$$\left(MJ_{s2} - MJ_{s1}\right) = \beta_0 + \beta_1 \times \left(UR_{s2} - UR_{s1}\right) + \left(e_{s2} - e_{s1}\right) \tag{8.15b}$$

where subscripts *1* and *2* on the variables, *MJ, UR*, and the error terms refer to period 1 (2006–07) and period 2 (2009–10).

Using a FD model helps to reduce any spurious correlation by eliminating from the error term the constant state effect (α_s). The interpretation will simply be:

> **How the change in state teenage marijuana use rates from one period to the next is related to the change in state unemployment rate.**

Of course, there still could be incidental correlation from the possibility that states with increases in marijuana use for non-economic reasons happened to have larger increases in the unemployment rate. But, this incidental correlation would likely be smaller than any incidental correlation with just cross-sectional data, as the perennially high (or low) unemployment rates for some states and the typically high (or low) marijuana use rates in some states would now be controlled for.

As demonstrated in Figure 8.2, this model mimics a cross-sectional model, as there is one observation per state. Every state had an increase in the unemployment rate over this time, as the latter period (2009–10) was part of the Financial Crisis. And, most states had an increase in teenage marijuana use over this period. But, these two statistics, together, do not say that the unemployment rate increases led to the increases in teenage marijuana use. Rather, a better test would be to examine whether those states with the larger increases in the unemployment rate tended to have larger increases in teenage marijuana use. Using a similar quadrant analysis from Figure 2.2 in Section 2.4, it looks like the points in the top-right and bottom-left quadrants dominate (with Arizona being a large exception). The results in Table 8.5 confirm this.

Table 8.5 shows the results of the models. Columns (1) and (2) have separate cross-sectional samples for the two periods – equation (8.14). And, column (3) shows the FD estimate from equation (8.15b). These are weighted regression models (as described in Section 3.3), for which I weight the observations by the square root of the 2010 state population.

Note that only the cross-sectional estimate on the unemployment rates for the 2006–07 analysis is positive and significant, albeit not strongly significant, as the lower bound of the 95% confidence interval is only 0.047. But, the estimate from the FD model is much lower than the other two. This suggests that there was some incidental correlation affecting the cross-sectional estimates, as the FD estimates should be much more trustworthy. That said, measurement error could become a larger problem with FD models (just as with fixed-effects models). This would likely lead to a bias towards zero in the estimates. Thus, it cannot be determined whether the reduction in the coefficient estimates

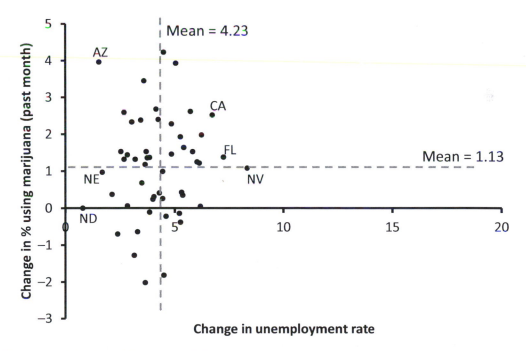

Figure 8.2 The first-difference model for the unemployment rate and teen marijuana use

Sources: NSDUH and Bureau of Labor Statistics.

Table 8.5 The effects of the unemployment rate on youth marijuana use

	(1)	(2)	(3)
	Cross section for 2006–07 averages	Cross section for 2009–10 averages	First-difference model
		Dependent variable	
	2006–07 use rates	2009–10 use rates	Change in use rate from 2006–07 to 2009–10
Unemployment rate (2006–07)	0.524** (0.237) [0.047, 1.001]		
Unemployment rate (2009–10)		0.244 (0.148) [−0.054, 0.542]	
Change in unemployment rate			0.153 (0.106) [−0.061, 0.366]
Constant	7.638*** (1.065)	8.971*** (1.406)	0.480 (0.533)
Observations	51	51	51
R-squared	0.071	0.035	0.030

Note: Standard errors in parentheses. The standard errors are corrected for heteroskedasticity. 95% confidence intervals are in brackets. The observations are weighted by the square root of the 2010 state population. *** $p < 0.01$, ** $p < 0.05$, * $p < 0.1$.

Sources: NSDUH and Bureau of Labor Statistics.

on the unemployment rate is from reducing omitted-variables bias or increasing bias from measurement error. In the end, with these data, there is no convincing evidence for an effect of the unemployment rate on state teenage-marijuana-use rates.

There is one other interesting thing to note here. The R^2 is lowest for the FD model, but it is the model we probably should place the most faith in. *This is a good example where the "goodness-of-fit" should not dictate the best model.*

Box 8.2   Are teacher qualifications important?

Who are the better teachers for our kids? How do we select the most qualified teachers? Dee and Cohodes (2008) examine how much subject-specific certifications and college majors are indicative of teacher quality (measured by student test scores). For example, a math teacher may be more effective if he/she has a math-teaching certificate or majored in math in college. The naïve approach to examine this would be to just do a comparison of student scores for teachers who have subject-specific certifications and majors to student scores for teachers without such a credential or a major. But, there could be differences in the quality of the students that a particular teacher may get. Perhaps the college math major is more likely to teach an advanced math class.

To address this issue, Dee and Cohodes estimate a first–difference model for student achievement. They use data from the National Education Longitudinal Study of 1988, which matches standardized test scores for 8th-grade students with information on their teachers from two subjects: one from math or science, and one from reading or social studies. The regression model, slightly amended from their version, is the following:

$$(Y_{1ic} - Y_{2ic}) = \lambda(Z_{1ic} - Z_{2ic}) + (\varepsilon_{1ic} - \varepsilon_{2ic})$$

where subscripts 1 and 2 are school subjects 1 and 2, i is the student, and c is the class. Y is the standardized test score (each point equals one standard deviation), and Z is the set of teacher-qualification variables. Note that the first–difference is for the student across classes. Furthermore, any student traits would fall out of the model with the first–difference, and so no student variables are included. Here are their main results, from their Table 2:

(Dependent variable = standardized test score)

Variable	OLS, with school fixed effects	First-difference
Teacher certified in subject	0.122 (0.026)***	0.042 (0.021)**
Teacher majored in subject	0.055 (0.016)***	0.009 (0.013)

Note: *** and ** indicate statistical significance at 1% and 5% levels.

Without the first–difference by student, the OLS model suggests that both subject-specific certifications and majors contribute to student learning. However, the FD model suggests the OLS model overstates those effects. There is no evidence that having a teacher majoring in the subject he/she teaches is associated with different test scores. But, there is some evidence that having a teacher certified in the subject is associated with higher test scores, with the estimate being an effect of about 4% of a standard deviation. However, note that the lower bound of the 95% confidence interval is pretty close to zero. So, the evidence may be suggestive of such an effect, but it is certainly not definitive.

Note that this is a case in which the data were not panel (multiple observations over time for a subject), but rather multiple observations per subject at the same time. The first–difference still works.

8.6 Difference-in-differences

Difference-in-difference (DD) models can be quite effective in addressing omitted-variables bias and possibly reverse causality. DD models can be used when

- A treatment and control groups can be compared over two different periods;
- The treatment occurs between periods;

- The treatment and control groups are similar enough so that, without the treatment, both would have had similar changes in the outcome between the two periods.

DD models would *not* be able to address models in which the treatment group (without the treatment) and the control group would have different changes in the outcome from period 1 to 2 or if there were self-selection bias in that the control group would have had different changes in the outcome (relative to the treatment group) if they had received the treatment as well.

Let's consider a notional example of how participating in a meditation program affects the growth in GPA from 10th to 11th grade. A naïve approach would be to regress the GPA of the students on whether the student participated in the meditation program. In this case, there would likely be omitted-variables bias. It may be the more open-minded (or hard-working and stressed) students who choose to participate in the meditation program, leading to perhaps a positive bias on the estimated effect. There is also a potential problem from self-selection bias. The ones who would participate in the meditation program would tend to be those who believe that they would benefit more from the program, which would also contribute to a positive bias. This will have implications for the interpretation below.

A DD model effectively compares the change in average student GPA, say from 10th to 11th grade (one "difference") for the treatment group and the control group (the other "difference"). Figure 8.3 shows graphically what the DD model is estimating. The DD model allows for initial differences between the treatment and control group, indicated by the different average GPA in 10th grade. But, it assumes that the hypothetical average growth rate in the GPA for the treatment group had they not had the treatment, indicated by the dashed line for the treatment group, would be the same as (parallel to) the actual average growth rate for the control group. The difference between the actual and hypothetical 11th-grade GPA for the treatment group would be the estimated treatment effect, which is positive in Figure 8.3.

As mentioned above, the validity of the model would depend on the hypothetical change in GPA for the treatment group, if they did not have the treatment, being similar to the actual change for the

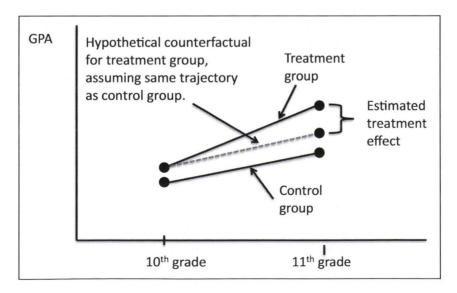

Figure 8.3 Difference-in-difference notional example

control group – i.e., that the dashed line would be parallel to the control-group line. This is something we can just theorize on, as we cannot observe the counterfactual.

Operationally, the DD model would be the following:

$$Y_{ig} = X_{ig}\beta_1 + \beta_2 \times \text{G11}_g + \beta_3 \times T_i + \beta_4 \times (T_i \times \text{G11}_g) + \varepsilon_{2i} \tag{8.16}$$

where:

- Y_{ig} = the GPA for student i in grade g;
- X = a set of other exogenous factors;
- $G11$ = an indicator for the second time period, 11th grade;
- T = an indicator for being in the treatment group; this variable gets a value of one for observations both in the pre- and post-treatment period, as it is meant to capture the average difference in achievement between the treatment and control groups.

The estimated treatment effect is $\hat{\beta}_4$, which is the coefficient estimate on the interaction of being in the treatment group (T) and being in Grade 11 ($G11$). Let us call $\overline{y}_{jg,} = Y_{j,g} - E\left[Y_{j,g} \mid X_{j,g}\right]$, where subscript j indicates the treatment (T) or control (C) group and subscript g is the grade (10 or 11). This is the average student GPA for each group after factoring out the factors in X. The estimated treatment effect is β_4, which is:

$$\beta_4 = \left(\overline{y}_{T,11} - \overline{y}_{T,10}\right) - \left(\overline{y}_{C,11} - \overline{y}_{C,10}\right) \tag{8.17}$$

or the change in average scores from 10th to 11th grade for the treatment group (T) minus that for the control group (C), after factoring out the other values in X. This is why it is called the difference-in-difference.

Does the model estimate the Average Treatment Effect?

While the DD model would address the omitted-variables bias (if the assumptions were correct), the model does not necessarily address the self-selection bias. If there were self-selection bias, then there would be a different interpretation of the estimated effect.

It is quite possible that those who choose to participate (the treatment group) would benefit more from the meditation than those who choose not to, as this could be a reason why they chose to participate. Thus, the hypothetical trajectory for the control group, if they were to participate in the meditation program, would likely be flatter than the actual trajectory for the treatment group.

This would mean that the estimated effect in the DD model would probably overstate the Average Treatment Effect (ATE) in this case, as the whole population, if given the treatment, would probably not benefit as much as the treatment group did. Rather, in the presence of self-selection bias, as with the fixed-effects and the FD models, the DD model would estimate the Average Treatment Effect for the Treated (ATT).

Application of DD models: the effects of minimum-wage increases

One of the most famous applications of DD models was Card and Krueger (1994), who examined the effect of an increase in the minimum wage in New Jersey on fast-food employment. The authors examined the change in employment resulting from the April 1992 increase in minimum wage (from $4.25 to $5.05), with observations from before (February 1992) and after (November 1992) the change. Just taking the change for New Jersey would be problematic because other things besides the minimum wage could be changing that could affect fast-food employment. They needed a control group that should have had a similar change in employment as New Jersey would have had without the treatment of the minimum-wage increase. They didn't choose Texas or Montana (or Kazakhstan) as the control group. Rather they chose New Jersey's neighbor, Pennsylvania. And so, they compared the change in employment for New Jersey to that of Pennsylvania, again relying on the assumption that the two states should have had similar changes in fast-food employment over this time period without the treatment for New Jersey.

Table 8.6 summarizes some key results, with the numbers representing average full-time equivalent (FTE) workers at fast-food establishments. The DD estimate would compare the treatment-group (New Jersey) change in employment to the control-group (Pennsylvania) change in employment. New Jersey had some increase in employment per establishment (0.59 FTE), but the estimated treatment effect, the difference-in-difference estimate (in the lower right corner of the table) is much larger at 2.76. The problem with this estimate, however, is that it is mostly driven by a drop in employment for Pennsylvania, which largely reflects much higher employment in the pre-increase period for some reason. Thus, the 2.16 decrease for Pennsylvania may have been correcting for an abnormally high initial employment rate, which is something that New Jersey did not appear to experience. This could be problematic because the assumption that they grow at the same rate between periods (see Figure 8.3) may not be valid. Thus, we may not be able to conclude that raising the minimum wage leads to a large increase in employment.

Note that this model is similar in spirit to a model that has state and time-period fixed effects. In such a fixed-effects model, the interpretation of the main coefficient estimate would be how within-state variation in employment is related to within-state variation in the minimum wage (which we see for New Jersey), factoring out the effects for other states (that for Pennsylvania).

Also note that the treatment does not have to be a dummy variable, as it could be a continuous variable. However, the common application for the DD model is using a dummy variable as the treatment.

Keep in mind that the DD method sometimes works well. But, the examples here point out that just because you use DD method does not mean that you solve the self-selection bias, omitted-variables bias, or other empirical problems. The right conditions have to hold, as outlined above.

Table 8.6 Summarizing results from Card and Krueger's (1994) Table 3 (Numbers represent average FTE workers at fast-food establishments)

	Pre-increase (Feb. 1992)	Post-increase (Nov. 1992)	Difference
New Jersey	20.44	21.03	0.59
(Treatment group)	(0.51)	(0.52)	(0.54)
Pennsylvania	23.33	21.17	−2.16
(Control group)	(1.35)	(0.94)	(1.25)
Difference	−2.89	−0.14	**2.76**
	(1.44)	(1.07)	**(1.36)**

Box 8.3   Does the Earned Income Tax Credit (EITC) affect the health of babies?

The Earned Income Tax Credit is a policy with the objective of fighting poverty while simultaneously incentivizing work. Hoynes et al. (2015) use a DD model to examine how a policy that increased credit payments in the EITC impacted the probability of having low birth weight for a baby (a sign of poor health and nutrition for the mother). Because the 1993 change to the EITC program increased payments more so for mothers with two-or-more children, babies that were first childs (parity = 1) were considered the control group, with the treatment groups being babies who were second (parity = 2) and third-or-more (parity = 3+). Thus, the difference-in-difference estimate was based on the change in the probability of having a low birth weight baby from before to after the 1993 policy change for "parity = 2" and "parity = 3+" babies compared to "parity = 1" babies.

Using "parity = 1" babies as the comparison group does not require that the probability of low birth weight is the same for those babies as higher-parity babies. Rather, the underlying assumption here is that, had there not been the increase in EITC payments, the probability of being born with a low-birth-weight would *change*, from before to after 1993, at the same rate for "parity = 2" and "parity = 3+" babies as for "parity = 1" babies. This is the assumption that needs to be assessed when evaluating a DD model. In this case, the assumption seems quite reasonable.

From a baseline rate of low-birthweight of 10.2%, the increased payments reduced the probability of a low-birthweight by an estimated 0.16 percentage points ($p < 0.05$) for "parity=2" babies and 0.53 percentage points ($p < 0.01$) for "parity = 3+" babies. This is a good indication that EITC improves the health and nutrition of mothers.

8.7 Two-stage Least Squares (instrumental-variables)

Imagine there is a rabid Los Angeles Angels (baseball) fan named Harvey who also happens to be statistically minded. Harvey notices a pattern in that Mike Trout, the Angels' star player, tends to do better when Harvey transforms his hat to a "rally cap" – turning the cap inside out. But, being both superstitious and statistical, he wonders whether there is omitted-variables bias in his informal analysis. Could it be that Harvey puts his rally cap on in situations in which Trout is more likely to get a hit? For example, it may be easier to get a hit when a pitcher is distracted by runners on base, and that is when Harvey likes to put his rally cap on. So, to test whether his rally cap is helping, hurting, or having no effect on Mike Trout's success at the plate, Harvey needs to create variation in wearing his rally cap that is random to the situation for Trout's plate appearance. One method could be to don the rally cap every other plate appearance. Another option could be to flip a coin to determine whether he puts on the rally cap. This method creates variation in "whether the rally cap is worn" that is random with respect to the game situation or who the pitcher might be. Using this "good" variation instead of the "bad" variation Harvey would naturally create would provide the necessary data to conduct an unbiased test for whether the rally cap works, provided there are enough observations.

This is the concept behind the instrumental-variables (IV) regression: isolating the random (good) variation in the key explanatory variable (wearing the rally cap) so that it does not move with other relevant yet unobservable/hard-to-quantify factors (the game situation) and is not subject to reverse causality.

The steps of the 2SLS method

The two-stage Least Squares (2SLS) method – the most common application of the IV regression – aims to eliminate non-randomness in the key explanatory variable by using only a source of random variation in the variable. The method can address bias from all three BIG QUESTIONS related to non-random explanatory variables, in addition to any bias from measurement error. The steps are the following:

1. Find a variable or set of variables, Z, that affects the non-random X variable (say, X_1) and only is related to the outcome (Y) through its effect on X_1. (This is much more difficult than meets the eye.)
2. Regress X_1 on Z and any exogenous explanatory variables (X_2).
3. Calculate the predicted value of X_1 from that equation. Thus, variation in the predicted value of X_1 only comes from variation in Z and the exogenous explanatory variables (X_2) and not from the non-random components that created the endogenous variation in X_1. Unlike X_1, the predicted value $\hat{X}_1$ should have only *good variation*.
4. Regress Y on the predicted value, $\hat{X}_1$, and the exogenous variables (X_2).
5. Standard errors need to be adjusted because using a predicted value for a regressor causes bias in standard errors. Most statistical packages will automatically fix the standard errors.

Note that:

• More than one instrumental variable can be used for a given endogenous explanatory variable.
• If there are multiple endogenous explanatory variables, then there needs to be at least one separate instrumental variable for each endogenous variable.

Figure 8.4 shows two BIG QUESTION violations, in terms of pathways:

• Omitted-variables bias in that there is an omitted (unobservable) variable X_3 (thus, the oval) that affects both X_1 and Y, causing the coefficient estimate on X_1 to pick up the effect of X_3.
• Reverse causality in that Y affects X_1.

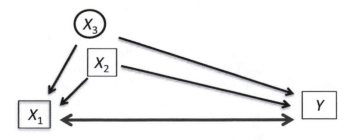

Figure 8.4 The problem with omitted variables for IV method setup

When both or one of these problems (or self-selection bias) exist, then the 2SLS method can potentially fix the problem. Figure 8.5 demonstrates the 2SLS fix for this problem. The trick, again, is finding a variable, Z, that affects X_1 but has no effect on Y other than through its effect on X_1. A predicted value for X_1 is calculated, which then is used to predict Y.

In contrast to the actual X_1 variable, the predicted variable, $\hat{X}_1$, would not be affected by the omitted variable, X_3, and should not be systematically correlated with X_3. And, addressing reverse causality, $\hat{X}_1$ would not be affected by the outcome, Y. Thus, we have isolated the *good variation* in X_1, which is not affected by the omitted variable, X_3, or the outcome, Y. As mentioned above, this method would also address any bias from measurement error in X_1.

In the case of the fan's rally cap and Mike Trout's success at the plate, the instrumental variable(s), Z, would be whether the coin flip is heads or tails. Unlike most cases, the coin flip would perfectly predict the rally-cap variable.

The problem in most applications is that there is no way to prove that Z does not have an independent effect on Y. There are "overidentification tests" for whether Z does affect Y or is independently correlated with Y, but you cannot prove the null hypothesis that there is no effect or independent correlation. If Z does affect Y, then the model is not valid because $\hat{X}_1$ would be correlated with another omitted variable (Z) that affects Y, causing omitted-variables bias. This is because Z is excluded from the equation determining Y. It is actually quite rare to come up with a valid instrumental variable.

Let's repeat steps (1) to (5) from above with the classic example on the effects of years-of-schooling on income. The problems in estimating the effects of schooling on income with conventional methods are that: (1) the years-of-schooling variable is likely affected by other factors affecting income, such as aptitude and motivation; (2) those expecting a greater return to schooling will self-select into higher levels of education; (3) there is measurement error in the education variable. The 2SLS method would be the following, now for simplicity of notation, using S rather than *educ* for years-of-schooling:

1. Find an IV or set of IVs, Z, that affects years-of-schooling (S) and only is related to income (Y) through its effect on S. (Again, very difficult.)
2. Regress years-of-schooling (S) on Z and exogenous explanatory variables (X).

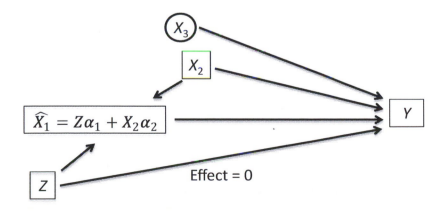

Figure 8.5 The two-stage-least-squares method

3. Calculate the predicted values of years-of-schooling (S) from that equation. Thus, variation in years-of-schooling is hopefully only *good variation*, coming from variation in Z and the exogenous X variables and not from the variation due to omitted-variables bias or reverse causality.
4. Regress income (Y) on the predicted values of years-of-schooling (S) and the exogenous variables (X).
5. Standard errors need to be adjusted because using a predicted value for years-of-schooling causes bias in the standard errors.

The formal set of equations when using the 2SLS method is the following:

$$S_i = X_i \delta_1 + Z_i \delta_2 + u_i \tag{8.18a}$$

$$Y_i = X_i \beta_1 + \beta_2 \hat{S}_i + \varepsilon_i \tag{8.18b}$$

Where $\hat{S}_i$ is the predicted value for years-of-schooling from equation (8.18a). The predicted value, $\hat{S}_i$, should not be correlated with omitted factors, and $\text{cov}(\hat{S}, \varepsilon) = 0$. Measurement error should also be less of a problem because the variable for years-of-schooling is a dependent variable (in equation 8.15a) when creating the predicted value of years-of-schooling – recall from Section 6.4.4 that measurement error in the dependent variable is minimally harmful.

Let me put all of this in English based on one of the more intriguing applications of instrumental variables (that also serves as a great example for issues we discuss below). Angrist and Krueger (1991) used a subject's quarter of birth as an instrumental variable for years-of-schooling to estimate the effects of schooling on income. The argument is that, with compulsory-schooling laws, those born earlier in the year would be able to legally leave school earlier than those born later in the year, and that the quarter of birth should have no effect on income 20–40 years later other than through the amount of schooling a person receives. While the quarter of birth would probably have little effect on years-of-schooling today, the time the subjects of their study were teenagers centered around the 1950s, which is a time period when more teenagers would quit school to work to help support their families. There was some critique of the quarter of birth as an IV (see Bound et al. 1995). But, the study certainly was innovative.

The problem with weak instrumental variables

Sometimes, there are nice, powerful (sets of) instrumental variables that explain a significant part of the variation in the endogenous key explanatory variable. Other times, the IVs are weak in that they have little explanatory power for the key X variable. Having a weak IV or set of IVs could cause large standard errors and potentially non-normal error terms. The problem is that a weak IV would lead to a relatively small amount of variation in the predicted explanatory variable. We learned back in Section 5.2 that less variation in an explanatory variable leads to larger standard errors. Furthermore, the lower amount of variation is similar to having a reduced sample size. And, this means that any problems from non-normal errors could result even though you have a sample well above 200. We discussed the consequences of non-normal error terms in Section 6.8. It basically just means that you would need to require lower p-values to conclude that there is a real relationship with any certainty.

What determines whether an IV or set of IVs is sufficiently strong? Stock and Yogo (2002) suggest that the set of IVs should have a joint significance F-test value of at least 10 in the first stage. If there were only one IV, which is the situation most of the time, then an F-statistic of 10 would be the square of the equivalent t-stat on that variable, or 3.16.

In general, the stronger is the connection between the instrumental variable and the non-random (endogenous or problematic) key explanatory variable, the more precise will be the IV estimated effect of the key explanatory variable on the outcome.

A weak connection between the instrumental variable and the endogenous explanatory variable also exacerbates any bias caused by any independent effects the instrumental variable may have on the outcome – i.e., effects not through the endogenous explanatory variable (see Bound et al. 1995).

A shortcoming of the 2SLS method

Remember in Section 2.12, I said that the OLS method produces the average effect (or, average association) across all people. Well, the 2SLS method does not quite estimate the same average effect as OLS. *Rather, for the education-income issue, it estimates the average effect of years-of-schooling on income for people whose years-of-schooling depends on the instrumental variable, Z, and for the levels of schooling that would be affected by Z* (Card 1999). This is known as the **Local Average Treatment Effect** (LATE).

Applying this concept to the Angrist and Krueger (1991) example, the estimated effect of schooling on income is based on those whose schooling depends on their quarter of birth and on the levels of schooling that are affected by the quarter of birth. Using OLS methods, there will be variation in schooling from the full distribution of schooling levels, with most variation occurring in the high school and college years. But, with the instrumental variable of quarter of birth, the variation in schooling produced by the quarter of birth should focus largely on high-school years, perhaps with some people being induced to not just stay longer in high school by the compulsory-schooling laws, but also attend college.

Thus, the 2SLS method, in this case, produces more of an effect-of-high-school-years, whereas the OLS method produces more of an effect-of-general-schooling-years, weighted more by college years – see Figure 2.6 in Section 2.6.

Also, those whose number of years-of-schooling depends on the quarter of birth are people who tended to be only marginally attached to school. They are likely different in this regard compared to the larger population of people contributing to the OLS estimate. To the extent that the returns to schooling are different for these "marginally attached students," the 2SLS/IV estimate may be different.

I will give another example of such an interpretation, in Section 8.9 below, on a 2SLS application for the effects of a parental divorce on various outcomes.

A quick note on the math behind the general IV estimator

The population parameter on an IV estimate, provided the IV variable, Z, were valid, would be:

$$\beta_{IV} = \frac{\sum_{i=1}^{n}(Z_i - \bar{Z})(Y_i - \bar{Y})}{\sum_{i=1}^{n}(Z_i - \bar{Z})(X_i - \bar{X})} = \frac{COV(Z_i, Y_i)}{COV(Z_i, X_i)} \tag{8.19}$$

This is simpler than it looks. The numerator just measures how deviations from the mean for the instrumental variable (Z) and the dependent variable (Y) move together. The denominator indicates how deviations from the mean for Z and the endogenous variable, X, move together.

The current state of the 2SLS method

The 2SLS method was popular for many years, with journals publishing papers using the method, almost regardless of how valid the instrumental variable appeared to be. But, the method has lost respect in recent years due to: (1) the unlikelihood of any instrumental variable being truly valid (i.e., having no independent correlation with the outcome, Y); and (2) the different interpretation 2SLS methods give, which is removed from what we normally want (the Average Treatment Effect, or the effects of a random change in X on the outcome, Y). The exception is for studies that combine the 2SLS methods with the regression–discontinuity approach, which we turn to in the next section.

Box 8.4   How much does school attendance affect student achievement?

Gottfried (2010) examines this issue for a sample of urban minority elementary- and middle-school students. This issue, if examined conventionally, certainly has potential BIG QUESTION violations. The author mentions the possibility of omitted-variables bias from student motivation, which could positively affect attendance and student achievement. And, there could be other factors causing omitted-variables bias, such as the importance parents place on schooling. These omitted factors would likely contribute to a positive bias on the estimated effect of attendance on student achievement. Further positive bias could come from reverse causality. If a student is not doing well in school, he/she may be less motivated to attend school when not feeling well and deciding whether to attend. Alternatively, it is possible that not doing well in school could motivate some students (and maybe the parents) to not miss any more school – this would contribute to a negative bias on the estimated effect.

Gottfried addresses these issues by: (1) using a student fixed-effects model; and (2) using a 2SLS model. I will discuss the latter. He used as an IV the distance to school. The condition needed is that distance to school should affect attendance and have no effect on achievement beyond its effect on attendance. Is this reasonable? For an urban setting, I see no great reason to believe that this is not a reasonable condition. (If this IV were used for a sample of rural students, I would not be so certain that this would be a valid IV.)

He finds, in the first stage, that each mile away from school a student lived was associated with about one-half of a day that the student misses in a school year. In the second stage, the results are surprising (to me). The estimated positive effects of attendance on student achievement (e.g., GPA and achievement test scores) are larger with the 2SLS model than the uncorrected model, with the estimates indicating that each day present at school increases one's GPA by around 0.02 to 0.03. The larger estimates for the 2SLS model may be due to the LATE-nature of 2SLS estimates – e.g., the effect of attendance could be larger for the (unidentifiable) group of students whose attendance depends on distance from school, compared to those who miss school for other reasons. Nevertheless, the results strongly suggest that attendance is important for academic success.

8.8 Regression discontinuities

The method of regression discontinuities is the current trendy approach to identifying causal effects. Many economists coming out of graduate school use this approach in their job-market paper. It involves using arbitrary threshold values that qualify someone/something for a certain treatment and uses any shift in the regression line for those beyond the threshold value to identify the impact of the treatment. Using this technique requires:

* A continuous eligibility index for a treatment (e.g., a test score);
* A defined cut-off value for eligibility.

Suppose that there is a new advanced academic program for gifted elementary students. To get into the program, a student must score at least 80 on a beginning-of-the-year test (the pre-test) designed to identify gifted students. And, suppose that the school administrators want to test whether the new program had a positive effect on the students. On the surface, we cannot just compare the results of those who are in the program vs. those not in the program, as better students will, on average, score higher and perhaps have stronger growth.

This is a perfect case for a regression–discontinuity (RD) method. The idea here is that students with a score of 80 (or a little higher) will tend to have better outcomes at the end of the year than students with a score of 79 (or a little lower) for two basic reasons:

* The students with an 80 are, on average, better students;
* The students with an 80 had the treatment of the new academic program.

The RD technique attempts to distinguish these two effects from each other and to generalize to a slightly wider range of test scores. The simple model with an RD method is the following:

$$Y_i = X_i\beta_1 + \beta_2 TS_i + \beta_3 D_i + \varepsilon_i \tag{8.20}$$

where:
* Y = the end of year achievement test score for student i;
* X = a set of demographic or other observable factors that could affect achievement;
* TS = the test score on the beginning-of-year pre-test determining acceptance into the new academic program;
* D = 1 if $TS \geq 80$ (the threshold value); $D = 0$ otherwise.

So, in this model, the TS variable has a linear effect on the outcome, Y. And, then β_3 indicates the effect of meeting the threshold value beyond the linear effect of the test score (TS). That is, β_3 indicates the effect of participating in the new advanced academic program.

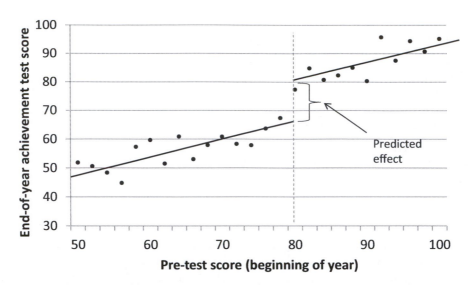

Figure 8.6 Graphical representation of a notional regression–discontinuity model

Graphically, Figure 8.6 is what this situation would look like. More advanced models could use a non-linear function to determine what the predicted scores would be without the treatment, such as:

- A spline function (see Section 3.2.3) separated at the threshold, typically modeled as two variables: (1) "score minus 80" just for values above 80; (2) "80 minus score" just for scores below 80.
- A quadratic function, from the threshold, with "distance-from-threshold" and "distance-squared" both below and above the threshold.

An example of this is in Box 8.5. See Lee and Lemieux (2010) for more details on the RD method.

Fuzzy regression discontinuities

There is a little more complexity when meeting the cut-off does not guarantee that the person obtains the treatment. This situation would call for an IV (or 2SLS) approach. This is sometimes called "Fuzzy RD," in contrast to the classic case of the threshold perfectly indicating who gets the treatment, or "Sharp RD."

A nice example comes from Ozier (2015), who estimates the causal effects of secondary schooling in Kenya on various outcomes. In a lesser-developed country such as Kenya, the self-selection bias and omitted-variables bias in this research question are likely major problems. Ozier noted that there was a cut-off score for the standardized 8th-grade examination (one close to the mean score) that gave a person an increased probability of being admitted to secondary school. Ozier uses that cut-off as the source of a regression discontinuity to examine the effect of secondary schooling on the outcomes. The model is the following:

$$\text{Stage 1:} \quad S_i = X_i\beta_1 + \beta_2 TS_i + \beta_3 D_i + \varepsilon_i \tag{8.21}$$

$$\text{Stage 2:} Y_i = \delta_{1i}\hat{S}_i + \delta_2 TS_i + \varepsilon_i \tag{8.22}$$

where

- S is a variable indicating whether the student attended and completed secondary school;
- TS is the 8th-grade test score;
- D is whether the student had at least the mean test score (TS);
- Y is one of various outcomes.

The idea here is that the variable for meeting the threshold for the 8th-grade exam score (D) has an effect on the outcome (Y), beyond the linear effect of the 8th-grade test score (TS) on Y.

In the first stage, he found that meeting the threshold was associated with a 16- and 13-percentage-points higher probability of completing secondary school for males and females, respectively, beyond the linear effect of the score on the probability of completing secondary school. Ozier noted that, for females, the IV of the regression discontinuity did not pass the Stock and Yogo (2002) F-test rule of thumb of 10. Among the statistically significant estimates, the results suggest that secondary school completion increases cognitive-test performance for men and women, increases the probability of formal employment (vs. self-employment) for men, and reduces teen pregnancy for females. There were several insignificant estimates, which may have been due to high standard errors in the 2SLS/IV models. This echoes the story that standard errors get very large if the relationship between the IV and the treatment is not very strong.

Details of the RD approach

The RD approach is considered to be pretty close to a true experiment, as it requires many fewer assumptions than other methods to address endogenous variation. This approach does have one major drawback that is similar to the drawback of the 2SLS (without accompanying RD use for creating an instrumental variable). Just as the 2SLS approach estimates the Local Average Treatment Effect (the treatment effect for those on the margin of receiving the treatment), the RD method also estimates the LATE for those close to the eligibility threshold score. If the effect were systematically different for those far from the threshold, the estimated causal effect would be biased as an estimate of the Average Treatment Effects.

One situation where the RD approach would not work is if the subjects can manipulate, to some extent, the "score" determining the assignment. For example, if some parents knew that their child was close to the cut-off score, they may encourage the child to study more or to take the test more seriously in order to meet the threshold score. This would invalidate the use of the RD approach. What to look for is whether the distribution of the qualification variable has a kink around the threshold, in the form of fewer observations than there should be before the threshold and more than there should be after the threshold (or *vice versa* if the lower value indicates qualification status).

While the RD method is a well-respected and strong approach to addressing the problems of non-random explanatory variables, it is unfortunately a rare occurrence to have such an opportunity to use the method. There needs to be a threshold based on a continuous variable that determines whether a person receives a given treatment. The research using RD largely springs from a threshold being found in policy and creating a research question from that policy rather than searching for an RD threshold for an already-established research question.

Box 8.5   Is there an advantage to a halftime deficit in basketball?

This is something I long ago noticed could be the case, but I did not have the data to examine it (nor the idea of using the RD method). Berger and Pope (2011) used data on about 12,000 NBA games and 29,000 NCAA basketball games to test whether being slightly behind at half-time affects a team's chance of winning beyond what would be expected given the score. They estimate the model:

$$(Win)_i = \beta_1 \times (losing\ at\ halftime)_i + \beta_2 \times (halftime - score - difference)_i + X_i\beta_3 + \varepsilon_i$$

They use the home team as the subject—i.e., the dependent variable was whether the home team won—but the results should be the same if the away team was used. In the set of variables in X, they include the home-team and away-team winning percentages.

For the NBA, they find that losing-at-halftime was associated with an estimated 6.2-percentage-point increase in the probability of winning ($p < 0.01$), beyond any effects of the halftime-score-difference. Using a cubic representation of halftime-score-difference, the estimated effect of losing-at-halftime goes up to 8 percentage points. For the NCAA games, the estimates were smaller and statistically significant with the linear control for the half-time-score-difference but insignificant with the cubic control for halftime-score-difference.

Why would there be a relative advantage to losing at halftime (particularly in the NBA)? It could be that players exert extra effort if they are behind, or that coaches are more likely to think that they need to make adjustments to the game plan if they are losing.

So, the idea here is that there should be a systematic relationship between the half-time-score-difference and the probability that a team wins. And, controlling for that rela-tionship, "losing" at halftime has a positive effect on the probability of winning. The authors say that it is being "slightly behind" that can have a discontinuous effect on a team's chances of winning. This speaks to the nature of the RD estimates being Local Average Treatment Effects.

8.9 Case study: research on how divorce affects children

How divorces affect children's outcomes, such as problem behavior and academic achievement, is quite a popular research topic in academia. But, as described in much detail in Section 6.10, it is ter-ribly difficult to isolate the causal effects, which apparently haven't stopped many people (including myself) from trying. The best approach for identifying the causal effect of divorces on children would be by randomizing divorces in the population. But, unfortunately I have yet to be successful at getting anyone to buy into this idea and fund me to carry out such an experiment.

So instead, researchers have been stuck with observational data. And, whereas there could be some bias from reverse causality and measurement error, the main problems would be omitted-variables bias and self-selection bias. Omitted-variables bias occurs because families that end up divorcing may be inherently different from non-divorcing families. The self-selection bias would be that parents would be more likely to divorce if they believed that the divorce would benefit or not be terribly harmful to the children.

Many different methods have been used to address these. All of them give different interpretations. None give a true causal effect – including my attempts.

There have basically been five classes of studies. All of them present different interpretations in terms of: (1) how much different respondents contribute to the estimation of the divorce effect; (2) the effect captured among the following or other possibilities:

- Inherent differences between families;
- The divorce effects itself;
- The effects of the divorce process, which could vary based on how much of the pre- and post-divorce conflict associated with the divorce would be captured in the effects.

The latter issue of what the effect is supposed to capture has largely been ignored in the literature in that researchers have not indicated what effect they aim to capture.

What follows are the five classes of studies. Note that, while I refer to "divorces" for ease of exposition, most studies, with the exception of the instrumental-variable ones, examine "disruptions" (i.e., divorces or separations).

Cross-sectional studies

Most studies, as discussed in reviews by Amato and Keith (1991) and Amato (2001), use one observation for each child (cross-sectional data), as follows:

$$Y_i = X_i\beta_1 + \beta_2 D_i + \varepsilon_i \tag{8.23}$$

where:
- Y is some outcome for a child;
- X is a set of control variables;
- D is a variable indicating that a child's parents are divorced (or the family is non-intact).

This model compares children from intact families to children from families having experienced a marital disruption or families for which there was always one parent. But, the average difference in outcomes (test scores, behavior) between children from intact vs. non-intact families, even after controlling for other factors, is probably due not just to any divorce or single parenthood, but also inherent differences that may have led to a divorce – e.g., the parents were too stressed from jobs and children, or maybe one parent was an alcoholic. Thus, the cross-sectional models estimate how children from divorced families are different from intact families, which could be the product of: (1) the divorce itself; (2) the divorce process; and (3) the inherent differences in parental behavior and interactions and family processes.

Basic longitudinal studies

There have been a few approaches using longitudinal data, which has multiple observations per person. A simple longitudinal approach has been to use a two-period model with a sample of children whose parents were still married in the first period. The model then examines the effects of a divorce between the first and second period on an outcome, including a baseline (period 1) measure of the outcome as an explanatory variable. These studies include, for example, Cherlin et al. (1991), Morrison and Cherlin (1995), and Hanson (1999).

Another longitudinal approach, applied in Arkes (2017), is to use first-difference methods, as follows:

$$\left(Y_{i2} - Y_{i1}\right) = \left(X_{i2} - X_{i1}\right)\beta_1 + \beta_2 \times \left(D_{i2} - D_{i1}\right) + \varepsilon_i \tag{8.24}$$

where the subscripts 1 and 2 on the Y, X, and D variables represent periods 1 and 2. The sample for such models often just includes those whose parents were still married in period 1 ($D_1 = 0$). Note that the quantity ($D_{i2} - D_{i1}$) equals 0 for those whose parents remain married and equals 1 for those whose parents are divorced by period 2. Thus, this type of study would compare the change in the outcome from an initial period to a second period (typically a few years later) for children experiencing a parental divorce in that interval to those not experiencing a divorce.

These models (first-difference or including the baseline measure of the outcome) address, to some extent, the differences between children from families remaining intact and families experiencing a divorce. But, there are still problems with this approach:

- Non-random factors that led to the divorce could also contribute to different changes in the outcome from the first to second period. That is, the implied assumption (that the children experiencing the divorce would have had the same change in outcome as the other children, had the divorce not occurred) is questionable.
- At the time of the first observation, children may have already been experiencing the effects of the divorce process, such as the conflict leading to the divorce and the stress of knowing that a divorce is coming. Thus, the effects of the divorce between the first and second periods may be minimal, as much of the effects of the divorce process would have been realized by the first period, even though the divorce had not occurred.
- It could be that the mechanisms of how the divorce process affects children had not fully developed by the observation of the child at the second period. This could include the long-term effects of worse economic situations and less time with parents.
- There still must have been something non-random and unobservable that caused some families that were intact in the initial period to break up before the second period.

Thus, the estimates from these studies may not capture the full effects of the divorce process if some effects had already occurred or if some effects had not developed yet. Putting this all together, the estimated divorce effects from these longitudinal studies capture: (1) any inherent differences that caused a divorce between the first and second periods; (2) the effects of the divorce process events occurring between the first and second periods; (3) an ATT rather than ATE. Again, these are potentially far off from the full causal effects of a divorce for a random child.

Fixed-effects studies

Another set of studies, also from longitudinal data, uses multiple observations for children with a fixed-effects approach (e.g., Amato and Anthony 2014), as follows:

$$Y_{it} = X_{it}\beta_1 + \beta_2 D_{it} + \mu_i + \varepsilon_{it} \tag{8.25}$$

where μ_i represents the child fixed effects.

This is equivalent to including a dummy variable for each child (with one child excluded as the reference). And, what it does is similar to what happened when we included dummy variables for each AFQT quartile when estimating the effect of years-of-schooling on income in Section 4.3. How is the estimated divorce effect determined?

- Behind the curtains, comparisons are made for each child between the averages of his/her outcome in the pre-divorce observations ($D = 0$) and the post-divorce observations ($D = 1$), factoring out other variables in the model. This produces a "divorce effect" for each child, even though that "divorce effect" for each child captures the effects of other random events. Hopefully, those random events would average out to near-zero across children.
- The divorce effects for all the children are then averaged, with the "weight" of each child in the calculation of the average based on how many observations they have and what the variance in the "divorce" variable is for each child – see equation (4.7) in Section 4.3.
- For children whose parents never divorce in the time they are observed, they have a zero variance for the divorce variable. This means that they will not contribute to the estimated divorce effect, other than by contributing to the coefficient estimates on the other variables.

These studies are subject to the same problems as the other longitudinal studies: it is not random which families end up divorcing in the study period, the pre-divorce outcomes may already reflect some of the effects of the divorce process, and the post-divorce effects may not be fully realized in the outcomes.

Divorce-timing (longitudinal) studies

A new set of articles examined how children compared to themselves in an established baseline period. The model is:

$$Y_{it} = X_{it}\beta_1 + DT_{it}\beta_2 + \mu_i + \varepsilon_{it} \tag{8.26}$$

which is similar to equation (8.25) above except that the divorce indicator (D) is replaced by DT, a set of variables for divorce-timing, or the time relative to the divorce (or separation, which was included in these studies).

Aughinbaugh et al. (2005) set the baseline period at the year of the divorce. Three studies by Arkes (2012, 2013, 2015) set the baseline period at least a few years before the divorce based on what the data allow to obtain reasonable power. For example, Arkes (2015) had as the DT variables:

- 4-or-more years *before* the divorce (the baseline period, or reference category);
- 2–4 years *before* the divorce;

- 0–2 years *before* the divorce;
- 0–2 years *after* the divorce;
- 2–6 years *after* the divorce;
- 6-or-more years *after* the divorce.

This approach allowed for a more direct examination of how children were affected in the years approaching the divorce, the years right before and after the divorce, and as time passed from the divorce. This would capture effects at different parts of the divorce process. What makes this approach unique is that children are compared to themselves at various stages of time relative to a divorce. Since children are compared to themselves (and not to other children who are not experiencing a divorce), differences in inherent family processes between intact and divorced families would not affect the estimates. In the first-difference models, the divorce may have occurred very recently in the second period for the child, so the full effects of the divorce on their achievement may not have developed. Thus, the advantage of the divorce-timing studies is that they can see how children fare as the divorce approaches, soon after the divorce, and as time passes from the divorce.

What is interesting about this approach is that not all children need to be observed in all periods relative to the divorce. Arkes (2015) calls this a "staggered-fixed-effects model." The estimated effect for a given period relative to the baseline is the sum of all one-period-change estimated effects up to that period.

But, these effects still are not the average causal effects of a random divorce in the population. The estimates produced by these studies would be an ATT. This is because only those experiencing a divorce are used to calculate the effects – those children whose families remain intact do not have a divorce year to use as a reference point.

Then again, perhaps this is the interesting statistic in this case – the Average Treatment Effect for the Treated. Divorce will not be random in the population. Perhaps the research question should be: how does divorce affect children who have experienced a parental divorce. In that sense, maybe these divorce-timing and other models estimate what is most relevant.

Instrumental-variables (IV) studies

These studies have used state laws representing the ease of divorce (e.g., no-fault divorce) as instrumental variables for whether a couple divorces (Gruber 2004; Johnson and Mazingo 2000; Corak 2001). But, applying the interpretation of IV models from Section 8.7, the estimated effects are based on the effects of divorce for those families on the margin of divorcing (i.e., those whose decision to divorce depends on the divorce law). This is not exactly a random part of the population – rather, it represents families that are vulnerable to a divorce and would be affected by these divorce laws. Furthermore, because the divorce law affects only whether the couple divorces, the estimated divorce effect does not include the effects of pre-divorce conflict. This is because the IV of the divorce law just creates variation in the probability of divorce and not the process. Thus, the IV models estimate an effect that represents something different from the other models, as it does not capture the effects of the processes leading to a divorce.

Summary

All of these models are estimating different effects, with varying levels of the divorce process being captured by the estimates and with varying success in eliminating the non-randomness of divorce. Thus, estimates from the various models are not comparable.

All studies other than the cross-sectional studies address the omitted-variables bias. The IV model is the only one that would also address any potential reverse causality and measurement-error bias, but the IV model has a narrow interpretation, as it is applicable just to families whose divorce would depend on divorce laws.

8.10 Knowing when to punt

If you ask me anything I don't know, I'm not going to answer.

–Yogi Berra

It's better to stay where you are than to go nowhere.

– Thomas Devine (California State University – Northridge)

Imagine this research question:

*   Does marijuana use cause a greater risk of a teenager engaging in unprotected sex?

This would be a difficult topic to examine because marijuana use and the propensity to engage in unprotected sex may have common factors, such as having an alcoholic parent and performing poorly in school. 'Unfortunately (again), no one funded my brilliant idea of randomizing the treatment (in this case, marijuana use) in the population so we can estimate these effects properly.' Thus, we are left with just observational data, which have the problem that, with respect to unprotected sex, it may not be random as to who uses marijuana.

Theoretically, a model using 2SLS methods (Section 8.7) could be estimated. But, this requires having an instrumental variable that affects marijuana use, but has no direct correlation with the likelihood of having unprotected sex, other than through its effect on marijuana use. This would not be easy.

Another possible type of instrumental variable would be local marijuana prices, provided that the location of the youth is known. This would rest on the dubious assumption that changes in marijuana prices were purely supply driven and not demand driven (the latter of which would make marijuana prices a product of marijuana use). Regardless, there are just not decent data available for marijuana prices in more than a select few locations over time.

Thus, this is a topic for which it is highly unlikely that a researcher would be able to identify the true causal effect. (Of course, the lack of *validity* of an instrumental variable has not stopped researchers from using such an approach.)

There are many research topics for which the pitfalls are too egregious and have no viable solution. Probably the best thing to do in such a situation (after letting it marinate for a while and not finding a solution) is to "punt," admit (to yourself) that there is hardly any way to identify the causal effect, and go on to another research topic. Alternatively, you could call it an "association" and suggest that further research attempt to somehow isolate the causal effect.

8.11 Chapter summary

In this chapter, I have introduced a few methods for addressing problems associated with non-random explanatory variables from Chapter 6 (mostly BIG QUESTIONS 1, 2, and 3). These are considered

Table 8.7 The effectiveness and applicability of the methods to address non-random explanatory variables

Modeling technique	Ability to result in an adequately valid model	Frequency with which the technique can be applied
Fixed effects	80	60
First-difference	75	65
Difference-in-difference	85	35
Two-stage Least Squares	45	10
Regression discontinuities	90	5

quasi-experimental methods, as they are designing models so that subjects are compared to themselves or to a set of subjects that are very similar.

Remember that, just because a researcher uses one of these (or other) quasi-experimental methods does not mean that the model is producing an unbiased estimate of the causal effect. All of the methods require underlying conditions or assumptions to hold be valid.

Table 8.7 shows my opinions on how effective each method is in terms of producing valid estimates and how frequently the method can be applied. These are based on a 0–100 scale. Just as with Table 6.11 to summarize the pitfalls of regression analysis, these figures are not percentages, but rather quasi-scientific, flow-of-conscious numbers (not to be cited, so I don't lose my "regression" license).

While the RD approach has the greatest potential to mimic a randomized control trial, it is rare to find the opportunity to estimate an RD model, as it requires a continuous eligibility index with a threshold indicator for eligibility of a treatment. So, the best of these approaches, from my experiences, are the fixed-effect, first-difference, and difference-in-difference techniques. While not perfect, when they can be applied, they often do a solid job to remove unobserved differences to address omitted-variables bias.

Exercises

1. Suppose that you were examining how state marijuana legalization has affected the number of car accidents in a state. Suppose that you had data over a 20-year period, during which 23 states had decriminalized marijuana. And, suppose that you have the following data (and variable names):
   - Year (Y);
   - State (S);
   - Subscripts s and y refer to the state and year
   - # accidents per capita in the state and year (A);
   - A dummy variable for whether marijuana is decriminalized in a state in a given year (MJD);
   - Population of state in the year (P) for weighting the observations.
      a. With a Simple Regression of $A_i = \beta_0 + \beta_1 \times (MJD)_i + \varepsilon_i$ why might there be omitted-variables bias?
      b. Write an equation for a regression model with fixed effects that addresses potential omitted-variables bias.
      c. Which states would be contributing to the estimated effect of decriminalization?
      d. How would you interpret the coefficient estimate on MJD, in light of the interpretations in Section 8.1?

2. From Question #5 in Chapter 7, we learned that certain states were disproportionately represented (relative to the whole sample) in the top-5% and bottom-5% of residuals. This suggests that "state" might be a confounding factor to the relationship between *foxnews* and *r_vote_share_ch*.

   a. Estimate a state-fixed-effects model (based on the variable, *statecode*) from the model in Question #5 in Chapter 7. If using Stata, use the **areg** command, as **xtreg** will not allow different weights within a fixed-effect group. What is the 95% confidence interval for the coefficient estimate on *foxnews*?

   b. Repeat (a.), but use county fixed effects (based on the variable, **countystate**). What is the 95% confidence interval for the coefficient estimate on *foxnews*?

   c. What is the difference in the interpretation of the estimated "Fox News" effect in (a.) and (b.), as to what observations are compared to what observations?

   (Note that the original Fox News study (DellaVigna and Kaplan 2007) used a wider set of control variables and a larger sample, not restricted by town size. As a result, they arrived at different estimates. To keep the models tractable, I am using a limited set of control variables.)

3. Use the **cigsales** data set. This data set comes from David Simon and is part of a preliminary analysis in an examination of how childhood exposure to cigarette smoke affects various childhood outcomes (Simon 2016).

   a. Estimate the effects of the cigarette-tax-rate-per-pack, in 2009 prices, (*tax09*), on cigarette-sales-per-capita (*cigsalepc*). Use state and year fixed effects. You may need to use fixed effects for either state or year and just a set of dummy variables for the other. Also, use robust standard errors clustered at the state level, and weight the model by the 2000 state population (*pop2000*).

   b. Estimate the same model, but add control variables for the unemployment rate (*urate*), the beer tax (*beertax*), and whether smoking is allowed in bars (*bar*) and restaurants (*restaurant*). And, add the variables for the state trends (*statetrend1–statetrend51*). Note how the estimated effect of the tax rate is affected compared to #3a.

   c. From #3b, what is the interpretation of the coefficient estimate on the tax rate, in terms of what observations are compared to what observations?

   d. What underlying condition is needed for this to be a valid model to estimate the causal effects of the cigarette tax on cigarette sales?

4. Use the **cig_1st_diff** data set. This is based on the changes from 1990 to 2000, and it is extracted from the data set used in Question #3. Estimate a first-difference model, as follows: regress *cigch* on *taxch*, *uratech*, and *beertaxch*. Weight the model by *pop2000*, and use robust standard errors. Interpret the estimate on *taxch*.

5. From Box 8.3 on the EITC, write out the regression equation for the difference-in-difference model.

6. Use **notional_eitc_data**. This notional data set (that I created) examines the effects of a general change in the Earned Income Tax Credit program that gives greater incentive for single mothers to work. This is a simplified version of Meyer and Rosenbaum (2001). (There were several changes over the years to the EITC program to increase such an incentive for single mothers, but I am simplifying it to a one-time permanent change occurring in 1990.) The sample consists of 5000 single women from before the change (1985) and 5000 single women from after the change (1995). The variables are:

- *employed* = dummy variable for being employed in past week;
- *mother* = dummy variable for whether the single woman was a mother of a child under 18 years old;
- *d1995* = dummy variable for whether the observation was in 1995 (rather than 1985).

(Note that the original data set with my notional data creation is on the website, and the formulas can be adjusted to create different-sized effects.)

    a. Estimate a difference-in-difference model to identify the causal effect of the program change on the employment of single mothers, in which the comparison group consists of single women without children. Indicate what the estimated causal effect is, its significance level, and the 95% confidence interval. (Don't forget the correction for heteroskedasticity.)

    b. What underlying condition is necessary for this technique to be valid in estimating the causal effects of the EITC change on the probability of employment for a given week?

7. Use the **notional_summer_educ** data set.[4] The idea behind this exercise is that 3rd-grade students who are at a reading level under 85 (one standard deviation below the mean of 100) are required to attend summer school. But, some students below the threshold do not attend, while some students above the threshold choose to attend voluntarily. We want to estimate how summer school improves the reading test scores for the students. Given that the threshold does not automatically dictate summer-school attendance, this is a Fuzzy RD model. The variables are:

test3 = a test at the end of 3rd grade;

test4 = a test at the end of 4th grade;

summer = a dummy variable for whether the student went to summer school between 3rd and 4th grades.

    a. Estimate a Fuzzy RD model with an instrumental-variables model to estimate the effect of summer school (*summer*) on 4th-grade test performance (*test4*). Use just a linear model to capture the discontinuity in summer-school attendance from *test3*.

    b. Estimate the same model, but use a quadratic function from both below and above the threshold of 85 for the effects of *test3* on *test4*.

    c. From (b), what is the interpretation of the estimated effect of summer school?

8. Use the data set **oecd_gas_demand**. From Question #5 in Chapter 3, add fixed effects for the country.

    a. How does the coefficient estimate on *lrpmg* change from Question #5 in Chapter 3 with the fixed effects added?

    b. How does this change which observations are compared to which observations?

Notes

1 This model uses methods we have not covered yet, including using changes in the variables rather than actual levels and using lagged values as instrumental variables.

2 This example comes from www.ma.utexas.edu/users/mks/statmistakes/fixedvsrandom.html, accessed July 10, 2018.

3 These state marijuana use rates come from the National Survey on Drug Use and Health and refer to 12–17-year-olds. The state unemployment rates come from the Bureau of Labor Statistics.

4 This notional data is based off of the concept in Jacob and Lefgren (2004). The authors used confidential data, so I created simulated data.

References

Amato, P. R. (2001). Children of divorce in the 1990s: An update of the Amato and Keith (1991) meta-analysis. *Journal of Family Psychology*, 15(3), 355–370.

Amato, P. R., & Anthony, C. J. (2014). Estimating the effects of parental divorce and death with fixed effects models. *Journal of Marriage and Family*, 76(2), 370–386.

Amato, P. R., & Keith, B. (1991). Parental divorce and the well-being of children: A meta-analysis. *Psychological Bulletin*, 110(1), 26–46.

Angrist, J. D., & Krueger, A. B. (1991). Does compulsory school attendance affect schooling and earnings? *The Quarterly Journal of Economics*, 106(4), 979–1014.

Arellano, M., & Bond, S. (1991). Some tests of specification for panel data: Monte Carlo evidence and an application to employment equations. *Review of Economic Studies*, 58(2), 277–297.

Arkes, J. (2012). Longitudinal association between marital disruption and child BMI and obesity. *Obesity*, 20(8), 1696–1702.

Arkes, J. (2013). The temporal effects of parental divorce on youth substance use. *Substance Use & Misuse*, 48(3), 290–297.

Arkes, J. (2015). The temporal effects of divorces and separations on children's academic achievement and problem behavior. *Journal of Divorce & Remarriage*, 56(1), 25–42.

Arkes, J. (2017). Separating the harmful versus beneficial effects of marital disruptions on children. *Journal of Divorce & Remarriage*, 58(7), 526–541.

Aughinbaugh, A., Pierret, C. R., & Rothstein, D. (2005). The impact of family structure transitions on youth achievement: Evidence from the children of the NLSY79. *Demography*, 42(3), 447–468.

Bedard, K., & Kuhn, P. (2008). Where class size really matters: Class size and student ratings of instructor effectiveness. *Economics of Education Review*, 27(3), 253–265.

Berger, J., & Pope, D. (2011). Can losing lead to winning? *Management Science*, 57(5), 817–827.

Bound, J., Jaeger, D. A., & Baker, R. M. (1995). Problems with instrumental variables estimation when the correlation between the instruments and the endogenous explanatory variables is weak. *Journal of the American Statistical Association*, 90(430), 443–450.

Card, D. (1999). The causal effect of education on earnings. In *Handbook of labor economics* (Vol. 3A), Orley Ashenfelter, and David Card, eds. Amsterdam: Elsevier Science and North-Holland.

Card, D., & Krueger, A. B. (1994). Minimum wages and employment: A case study of the fast-food industry in New Jersey and Pennsylvania. *American Economic Review*, 84(4), 772–793.

Cherlin, A., Furstenberg, F., Chase-Lansdale, P. L., Kiernan, K. E., Robins, P., Morrison, D. R., & Teitler, J. (1991). Longitudinal studies of effects of divorce on children in Great Britain and the United States. *Science*, 252(5011), 1386–1389.

Corak, M. (2001). Death and divorce: The long-term consequences of parental loss on adolescents. *Journal of Labor Economics*, 19(3), 682–715.

Dee, T. S., & Cohodes, S. R. (2008). Out-of-field teachers and student achievement: Evidence from matched-pairs comparisons. *Public Finance Review*, 36(1), 7–32.

DellaVigna, S., & Kaplan, E. (2007). The Fox News effect: Media bias and voting. *The Quarterly Journal of Economics*, 122(3), 1187–1234.

Gibbons, C. E., Serrato, J. C. S., & Urbancic, M. B. (2014). Broken or fixed effects? (No. w20342). National Bureau of Economic Research.

Gottfried, M. A. (2010). Evaluating the relationship between student attendance and achievement in urban elementary and middle schools: An instrumental variables approach. *American Educational Research Journal*, 47(2), 434–465.

Gruber, J. (2004). Is making divorce easier bad for children? The long-run implications of unilateral divorce. *Journal of Labor Economics*, 22(4), 799–834.

Hanson, T. (1999). Does parental conflict explain why divorce is negatively associated with child welfare? *Social Forces*, 77(4), 1283–1315.

Hoynes, H., Miller, D., & Simon, D. (2015). Income, the earned income tax credit, and infant health. *American Economic Journal: Economic Policy*, 7(1), 172–211.

Jacob, B. A., & Lefgren, L. (2004). Remedial education and student achievement: A regression-discontinuity analysis. *Review of Economics and Statistics*, 86(1), 226–244.

Johnson, J., & Mazingo, C. (2000). The economic consequences of unilateral divorce for children. University of Illinois CBA Office of Research Working Paper 00-0112.

Lee, D. S., & Lemieux, T. (2010). Regression discontinuity designs in economics. *Journal of Economic Literature*, 48(2), 281–355.

Meyer, B. D., & Rosenbaum, D. T. (2001). Welfare, the earned income tax credit, and the labor supply of single mothers. *The Quarterly Journal of Economics*, 116(3), 1063–1114.

Morrison, D. R., & Cherlin, A. (1995). The divorce process and young children's well-being: A prospective analysis. *Journal of Marriage and the Family*, 57(3), 800–812.

Ozier, O. (2015). *The impact of secondary schooling in Kenya: A regression discontinuity analysis*. The World Bank.

Pope, D. G., & Schweitzer, M. E. (2011). Is Tiger Woods loss averse? Persistent bias in the face of experience, competition, and high stakes. *The American Economic Review*, 101(1), 129–157. (Available at http://faculty.chicagobooth.edu/devin.pope/research/pdf/Website_Golf.pdf, accessed July 10, 2018).

Simon, D. (2016). Does early life exposure to cigarette smoke permanently harm childhood welfare? Evidence from cigarette tax hikes. *American Economic Journal: Applied Economics*, 8(4), 128–159.

Stock, J. H., & Yogo, M. (2002). Testing for weak instruments in linear IV regression. (Available at http://scholar.harvard.edu/files/stock/files/testing_for_weak_instruments_in_linear_iv_regression.pdf, accessed July 10, 2018).

Stone, D. F., & Arkes, J. (2016). Reference points, prospect theory, and momentum on the PGA tour. *Journal of Sports Economics*, 17(5), 453–482.

9 Other methods besides Ordinary Least Squares

The towels were so thick there I could hardly close my suitcase.

−Yogi Berra

Box 9.1   Do the shoes matter?

"Wait! Why do we have a police escort to dinner?" I asked. I glanced down at my shoes and wondered if I'd gone a bit too far with my mantra I remember from something Norm Peterson (on *Cheers*) once said: "All great thinkers [e.g., Socrates, Jesus, Larry Bird, Tim Duncan] had comfortable shoes." When told seven minutes earlier on that evening in 1999, while sitting at the hotel pool, that we were about to leave for dinner and dancing, I raced to my room, got dressed, and laced up my basketball shoes in record time. Only in response to my query about the police escort was I told that we were going to the Presidential Mansion first.

> We had earlier that day attended the inauguration of the new El Salvadoran President, Francisco Flores. And so, here I was, a relative "nobody," sitting in the living room of the President's mansion, in the company of the new President, his wife and kids, Prince Albert of Monaco, Nat King Cole's twin daughters, and four others, and I had on my basketball shoes, not quite matching my dark suit and tie. As the night later turned to dancing at a nightclub, I was clearly out-shined by everyone, particularly Prince Albert. The problem was no longer my shoes . . . but rather my dance moves (or lack thereof). In the end, wearing dress shoes would have been more appropriate for the occasion, but it wouldn't have solved the fundamental problem of the evening – my bad dancing.
>
> This is what I think of when there is a non-standard dependent variable. The appropriate-for-the-occasion method would likely be some alternative to OLS. However, in the end, using any alternative method won't make a difference if there are any meaningful biases to the coefficient estimates from non-random explanatory variables or other fundamental issues that remain unaddressed.

In some analyses, the nature of the dependent variable or the nature of the effect one is attempting to capture may dictate using a non-linear method, or something other than OLS. In this chapter, I describe different types of dependent variables and how those often warrant a different method. In particular, the estimation method used in most of the regressions discussed in this chapter is the Maximum Likelihood method. This involves finding the set of coefficient estimates that maximize the likelihood of observing the given data.[1]

9.1 Types of outcome variables

Most of the examples considered in this book have involved outcome variables that are considered continuous, in that they can basically take on any value. This, of course, is not technically true, as, for example, there are no decimal places in the income variable. But, we can innocuously assume that the variables are approximately continuous.

There are many instances in which researchers have outcomes that are not approximately continuous, but rather discrete, qualitative, or restricted in values.

- **Dichotomous (dummy) variables** take on just the values of 0 or 1. The 0-value category is typically for a "no" or for not meeting a threshold, while 1 typically indicates "yes" or meeting a threshold. Examples include: (1) whether a person uses marijuana; (2) whether a student is retained to repeat a grade; (3) whether a cancer patient survives for 10 years; and (4) whether a basketball player makes a given shot.
- **Ordinal variables** have multiple categories for which the order or value has meaning. For example, the highest degree earned would be an ordinal variable with values, say, of:
  - 0 for no high-school diploma;
  - 1 for a high-school diploma;

- 2 for an Associate's degree;
- 3 for a Bachelor's degree;
- 4 for a graduate degree.

- **Categorical variables** involve categories for which there is no obvious order. An example could be the type of car a person chooses to buy (SUV, sedan, hatchback, crossover). Other examples include the candidate a person votes for, the region of the country a person chooses to move to, and the type of college a person chooses to attend.
- **Censored variables** are (typically) approximately continuous variables for a certain set of values, but have an upper and/or lower bound for values. The censoring can occur due to limits imposed on a survey or just that values naturally do not go beyond a certain level. Income that respondents report in surveys can be censored in both directions. Surveys may have a top code for income of, say, $1 million. And, income cannot go below zero (in most cases), for those who do not work.
- **Count variables** indicate the number of occurrences of some event. It has to be an integer. If the number of possible values gets large enough and has a relatively low amount of "low numbers" (i.e., not too much bunching at the bottom end), then one can just assume that it approximates a continuous distribution. For example, with years-of-schooling as a dependent variable, the OLS method is often used, as there is little bunching at low years-of-schooling. Examples of count variables for which the OLS method may not be appropriate include: (1) the number of migraine episodes per month; (2) the number of times a person has been arrested; and (3) the number of hospital visits a person has in a year. Note that the variables listed here would likely have a relatively high proportion of observations with a value of zero.

When the dependent variable comes in one of these non-approximately continuous forms, then applying linear models (such as with the OLS method) may result in:

- Biased coefficient estimates and marginal effects;
- Biased standard errors;
- Misleading statistics related to the significance of estimates, hypothesis tests, and confidence intervals.

The correction to this problem is to use a method that is appropriate given the distribution of the dependent variable. This chapter provides basic descriptions of the various methods to use based on the type of dependent variable. While using the appropriate method is always best, the biases and other problems stemming from not using OLS (in most cases) are relatively minor compared to the problems from violations of the BIG QUESTIONS in Chapter 6.

9.2 Dichotomous outcomes

This is a common type of outcome, so I will discuss the methods used for dichotomous models with extra detail compared to the other methods. There are three basic options when the outcome is dichotomous: linear probability models, probit models, and logit models. I will introduce the three models in the next three sub-sections and then use all three models on the same data in sub-section 9.2.4.

9.2.1 Linear probability models

A linear probability model (LPM) simply uses the OLS method. Operationally, the model is:

$$Y_i = X_i\beta + \varepsilon_i \tag{9.1}$$

where Y takes the values of 0 or 1. But, effectively, the model estimates:

$$\Pr(Y_i = 1) = X_i\beta + \varepsilon_i \tag{9.2}$$

This approach has the advantage that the estimates are more directly interpretable than with the probit and logit models. In addition, certain fixes for addressing non-random explanatory variables, such as fixed effects, are often easier in the LPM than in a probit or logit model.

However, there are problems with the LPM. These include:

- Sometimes, the predicted probability will be outside of the [0, 1] range. This is less likely to be a problem when there are more X variables and when the overall probability of the outcome in the sample is not close to zero or one. But, this is one problem with LPM that should be avoided.
- Relatedly, the estimates may be biased and inconsistent. However, the magnitude of this problem may be small, depending on the situation.
- The error terms may be non-normal, which violates Assumption **A3**. This would be less of a problem with an adequate number of observations and explanatory variables. And, a high level of significance would make this assumption violation meaningless. But, it would be a concern if the level of significance was marginal, not just from reaching the typical threshold p-values, but taking into account the informal Bayes approach from Section 5.3. In such a situation, it may be worth conducting a test for the normality of the error terms.

9.2.2 Probit models

The probit model, one of the two non-linear probability models for using dichotomous outcomes, avoids the problem of predicted probabilities being outside the [0,1] range and the problem of error terms being non-normal (provided there are at least 200 observations). The model for outcome Y and a set of explanatory variables, X, is the following:

$$\Pr(Y_i = 1 \mid X_i) = \Phi(X_i\beta) \tag{9.3}$$

where Φ is the cumulative density function of the standard normal distribution. That is, Φ is a function that produces a probability between 0 and 1, with the probability being higher for higher values of $X_i\beta$. In a statistical program, you would typically just indicate a "probit" model. But behind the curtains, the estimation involves a latent variable model as follows:

$$Y_i^* = X_i\beta + \varepsilon_i \tag{9.4}$$

where $\varepsilon \sim N(0,1)$ – i.e., the error term has a standard normal distribution.

The variable Y^*, representative of (but not equal to) the propensity for Y to equal 1, is latent and is represented in the data by:

$$Y = 1 \text{ if } Y^* > 0 \text{ or } -\varepsilon < X\beta$$
$$Y = 0 \text{ otherwise}$$

(9.5)

Unfortunately, the estimates for β do not represent the marginal effects. A **marginal effect** is how the estimated probability of the outcome changes with a one-unit increase in the value of the X variable. These are not directly produced by the model, as the coefficient estimates represent how a one-unit change in a given X variable affects the latent outcome variable. Further code is often necessary to determine the marginal effects. And, the marginal effect of a given one-unit change in an explanatory variable, X_1, will vary depending on the values of the other explanatory variables (and thus, the predicted probability of the outcome). If the values of all variables put an observation at a 96% chance that the outcome will occur, there is little room for further increases in that predicted probability from a one-unit change in a variable, X_1.

Because the marginal effect for a variable depends on the values of the other variables, the common practice is to use the means of the X variables as the starting point to estimate the marginal effects of any variables. To calculate the marginal effect for an explanatory variable that is a dummy variable, you cannot start at the mean, but rather have the mean for all other variables and calculate what happens to the predicted probability going from 0 to 1 for the dummy variable.

9.2.3 Logit models

The **logit model** is another non-linear probability model that also restricts the predicted probability to be in the [0,1] range and avoids the potential problem of non-normal error terms. Again, in most statistical packages, you just specify the logit model, but behind the curtains, the model first involves the logistic function for the probability that a variable Y takes on the value of 1:

$$Pr(Y = 1) = F(X) = \frac{1}{1 + e^{-(X\beta)}}$$

(9.6)

As with the probit model, for high values of $X\beta$, this function approaches one; and for low values of $X\beta$, the denominator increases and the probability approaches zero.

Like the probit model, the logit model does not indicate the marginal effects. These marginal effects also depend on the values of the X variables. A nice feature of logit models is that they have an easy transformation to effects of the X variables on the **odds ratios**, which are the odds of an outcome occurring given the exposure to some treatment relative to the baseline odds without exposure to that treatment. (The treatment could be an extra unit of an approximately continuous variable, such as the AFQT score.) The transformation is calculated simply by exponentiating a coefficient estimate. I will show this in the next sub-section.

9.2.4 Example using all probability models

Let's do an exploratory analysis to examine what factors predicted marijuana use among a sample of youth in the year 2000. For simplicity, rather than using separate models as would be suggested as a

Table 9.1 Determinants of "whether the youth used marijuana in past 30 days," using three different probability models

	(1)	(2)	(3)	(4)	(5)
		Probit model		*Logit model*	
	LPM (OLS)	*Coefficient estimates*	*Marginal effects*	*Coefficient estimates*	*Marginal effects*
Male	0.056***	0.219***	0.057***	0.390***	0.056***
	(0.009)	(0.033)	(0.009)	(0.059)	(0.009)
Age	0.009***	0.036***	0.009***	0.064***	0.009***
	(0.003)	(0.011)	(0.003)	(0.020)	(0.003)
Race/ethnicity (non–Hispanic Whites form the reference group)					
Non-Hispanic Black	−0.082***	−0.320***	−0.077***	−0.572***	−0.076***
	(0.010)	(0.042)	(0.009)	(0.077)	(0.009)
Hispanic	−0.047***	−0.178***	−0.044***	−0.319***	−0.043***
	(0.011)	(0.044)	(0.010)	(0.078)	(0.010)
Other race/ethnicity	−0.058**	−0.222**	−0.052***	−0.394**	−0.051***
	(0.022)	(0.093)	(0.019)	(0.169)	(0.019)
Parents lived with at age 12 (excluded category is both biological parents)					
One biological parent	0.042***	0.160***	0.042***	0.287***	0.042***
	(0.010)	(0.039)	(0.011)	(0.070)	(0.011)
One bio. and one other parent	0.088***	0.316***	0.093***	0.550***	0.093***
	(0.024)	(0.077)	(0.025)	(0.132)	(0.025)
Other situation	0.020	0.078	0.021	0.134	0.020
	(0.012)	(0.049)	(0.013)	(0.088)	(0.013)
Constant	−0.005	−1.649***		−2.816***	
	(0.052)	(0.206)		(0.363)	
Observations	7995	7995	7995	7995	7995
R-squared	0.017				

Note: Standard errors in parentheses. *** $p < 0.01$, ** $p < 0.05$, * $p < 0.1$.

Source: Bureau of Labor Statistics, 2015.

strategy for determining predictors of an outcome in Section 7.2, I include several explanatory variables in the model at once.

For this analysis, I use the younger cohort of the NLSY, which started with 12–17-year-olds in 1997 (Bureau of Labor Statistics, 2015). I use data from the fourth round of interviews for this cohort, conducted in 2000–01. The dependent variable is whether the person used marijuana in the prior 30 days (coded as 1 if they had used marijuana and 0 otherwise).

Table 9.1 shows the results from using each type of probability model: LPM (using OLS) in column 1; probit model, with the coefficient estimates in column 2 and marginal effects in column 3; and logit model coefficient estimates in column 4 and marginal effects in column 5.

As discussed above, the marginal effects depend on the baseline values of the X variables. Think of it this way. Certain factors could make an outcome nearly a certainty. For example (if we had data), having an older brother use marijuana may be a very strong predictor of a person's marijuana use. For these people, the additional effects of further variables on the probability of using marijuana will probably not be as large as for other people, as there is less room for any increased probability. Typically, and in Table 9.1, the mean values of the X variables are assumed for these calculations. This is the obvious choice that would give average marginal effects for the explanatory variables.

The example in Table 9.1, not by design, turns out to be a case in which it really does not matter which model is used. The LPM results (column 1) are very similar to the marginal effects from the probit and logit models (columns 3 and 5). The largest contributor to using marijuana appears to be living with "one biological parent and one other parent" (relative to living with both biological parents), as it is associated with about an estimated 9-percentage-point higher probability of marijuana use in the past month. However, we need to be careful here in that there are alternative stories (to a causal effect) as to why those living in homes without two biological parents have higher marijuana use.

What is important here is that the differences in estimates between the models are fairly small. In fact, they are probably much smaller than any bias on the causal effects from the explanatory variables being non-random, if causal effects were our objective.

As mentioned above, logit models have a special feature. With the results from a logit model, you can calculate **odds ratios:** the change in relative odds of the outcome being "yes" ($Y = 1$), for each one-unit change of the **X** variable. The relationship between the coefficient estimate and the odds ratio is the following:

- Variable is positively associated with the outcome, *ceteris paribus*

  ➔ odds ratio > 1;

- Variable has zero association with the outcome, *ceteris paribus*

  ➔ odds ratio = 1;

- Variable is negatively associated with the outcome, *ceteris paribus*

  ➔ odds ratio < 1.

Table 9.2 shows the results from the logit model from Table 9.1, with the coefficient estimates and associated marginal effects in columns (1) and (2) copying columns (4) and (5) from Table 9.1, and the associated odds ratios in column (3). All results come from the same logit model. As an example of interpreting the model, being male is associated with an estimated 5.6-percentage-points higher probability of using marijuana in the past month, or a 47.7% higher probability of using marijuana, *ceteris paribus*. (The 1.477 odds ratio comes from exponentiating the coefficient estimate: $e^{0.390} = 1.477$.) Being non-Hispanic Black is associated with an estimated 7.6-percentage-point or 43.5% (($1 - 0.565$)×100) lower probability of using marijuana.

Table 9.2 Demonstration of odds ratios for the probability of marijuana use

	Dependent variable = whether the youth used marijuana in past 30 days		
	(1)	(2)	(3)
	Coefficient estimates	Marginal effects	Odds ratios
Male	0.390***	0.056***	1.477***
	(0.059)	(0.008)	(0.088)
Age	0.0638***	0.009***	1.066***
	(0.020)	(0.003)	(0.021)
Race/ethnicity (non-Hispanic Whites form the reference group)			
Non-Hispanic Black	−0.572***	−0.076***	0.565***
	(0.077)	(0.009)	(0.044)
Hispanic	−0.319***	−0.043***	0.727***
	(0.077)	(0.010)	(0.057)
Other race/ethnicity	−0.394**	−0.051***	0.674**
	(0.168)	(0.019)	(0.114)
Parents lived with at age 12 (excluded category is both biological parents)			
One biological parent	0.287***	0.042***	1.332***
	(0.069)	(0.010)	(0.093)
One bio. and one other parent	0.550***	0.093***	1.733***
	(0.131)	(0.025)	(0.228)
Other situation	0.134	0.020	1.143
	(0.088)	(0.013)	(0.101)
Constant	−2.816***		0.060
	(0.372)		(0.022)
Observations	7,995	7,995	7,995

Note: Standard errors in parentheses. *** $p < 0.01$, ** $p < 0.05$, * $p < 0.1$.

Source: Bureau of Labor Statistics, 2015.

9.2.5 Which probability model is best?

There are different schools of thought on which probability model to use. Horace and Oaxaca (2006) show that the linear probability model is inconsistent and biased in most cases. Others argue that the probit and logit models are likely mis-specified also, so they are no better than the LPM. (And, it is rare that the probit and logit would give meaningfully different results.)

In the grand scheme of things, it probably does not matter in most cases. (How many planets are there, again, in just our universe?) That said, the probit and logit models are more accepted, as some people are flabbergasted that someone would use an LPM. If you have a good reason to use the LPM (such as needing to use fixed effects or estimating an instrumental-variables model), it is usually accepted. If you have other reasons for using the LPM, a good strategy is to also use a logit or probit model to examine whether the answer is the same and report this in the analysis.

9.2.6 Goodness-of-fit measures for probit and logit models

Because the probit and logit estimation methods are not linear, an R^2 cannot be calculated. The R^2 can, of course, be calculated with an LPM. An alternative measure for probit and logit methods is a measure of the percent correctly predicted by the model. Most statistical packages do not compute this, so it would have to be estimated with additional code. The calculation would be comparing the actual outcome with the predicted outcome based on the predicted probability from the model – a predicted probability greater than 0.5 would indicate that the model predicts the event to occur for an observation.

The primary problem with this measure is that it only is useful for outcomes that have about a 50% overall chance of the event occurring – i.e., $Pr(Y = 1)$ is close to 0.5. If it diverges much from 50% and if there are enough explanatory variables, then a likely scenario is that all predicted probabilities will be above or below 0.5, meaning that they would all be predicted to occur or all predicted not to occur.

There are no great options for goodness-of-fit measures for probit and logit models. This may give a good reason to use the LPM when a goodness-of-fit measure is needed.

9.3 Ordinal outcomes – ordered models

This is not that common of a regression model (and not my favorite). Let's take the example of an analysis on predicting people's self-assessment of health at age 40, with data from the NLSY that we used in Table 7.1 (Bureau of Labor Statistics, 2014). In this case, we will use a sample of males and females, we'll change up the set of explanatory variables a bit, and we'll use the health outcome at age 40 instead of age 50. The choices for the outcome were (poor, fair, good, very good, excellent), coded as values 1 to 5. OLS may not be appropriate because going from, say, *poor* to *fair* (1 to 2) is not neces-sarily similar to going from *very good* to *excellent* (4 to 5) or any other transition, even though a given X variable would be estimated to have the same effect on all single-step transitions (from *poor* to *fair* and from *very good* to *excellent*). An ordered model would allow for more flexibility for varying effects.

The model would be:

$$Y_i^* = X_i \beta + \varepsilon_i \tag{9.7}$$

where Y^* is a latent variable for general health. We do not observe Y^*, but rather we observe:

$$Y = \begin{cases} 0 \text{ if } Y^* < \mu_0 \\ 1 \text{ if } \mu_0 < Y^* < \mu_1 \\ 2 \text{ if } \mu_1 < Y^* < \mu_2 \\ 3 \text{ if } \mu_2 < Y^* < \mu_3 \\ 4 \text{ if } \mu_3 < Y^* < \mu_4 \end{cases} \tag{9.8}$$

where the μ's are thresholds for the latent variable Y^* to be categorized into each level of health. The cut-off points between levels of Y^*, the μ's, are estimated by the model, and they contribute to pre-dicting the probability of a given outcome. There are different lengths of the intervals between cut-off points, which allows the X variables to have varying marginal effects on moving from one level of Y to the next level of Y. See Table 9.3.

Table 9.3 Ordered Probit results for "health at age 40" (n = 7705)

| | Dependent variable = health status at age 40 | |
	Coef. Est.	Std. Error
Years–of–schooling	0.082	(0.007)***
AFQT	0.004	(0.001)***
Black	−0.067	(0.032)**
Hispanic	−0.052	(0.035)
Male	0.145	(0.024)***
/cut1	−0.780	(0.079)
/cut2	0.093	(0.076)
/cut3	1.037	(0.077)
/cut4	2.125	(0.078)

Note: Standard errors in parentheses. *** $p < 0.01$, ** $p < 0.05$, * $p < 0.1$.

Source: Bureau of Labor Statistics, 2014.

Table 9.4 Marginal effects from Ordered Probit Model

	Poor	Fair	Good	Very good	Excellent
Years–of–schooling	−0.0039	−0.0122	−0.0155	0.0089	0.0227
AFQT	−0.0002	−0.0006	−0.0008	0.0005	0.0012
Black	0.0033	0.0102	0.0126	−0.0076	−0.0185
Hispanic	0.0025	0.0078	0.0097	−0.0059	−0.0142
Male	−0.0070	−0.0021	−0.0275	0.0157	0.0403

Source: Bureau of Labor Statistics, 2014.

The other variables are as we have used them earlier, but with the variable for years–of–schooling being from 1996 (before everyone in the sample turns 40). We see that years–of–schooling, AFQT score, being Black, and being male have significant coefficient estimates. The "cut" variables at the bottom of the table are the μ's from equation (9.8) above. These are estimated within the model. They help determine the marginal effects, which are represented in Table 9.4.

As an example of interpreting the marginal effects in Table 9.4, one extra year of schooling is associated with lower probabilities of reporting health as poor (by 0.39 percentage points), fair (by 1.22 percentage points), and good (by 1.55 percentage points); an extra year of schooling is associated with a higher probability of reporting health as very good (by 0.89 percentage points) and excellent (by 2.27 percentage points). Note that the marginal effects sum to 0 (across a row), other than some rounding errors.

In contrast to the results for schooling, being Black is associated with a higher probability of poor, fair, or good health and a lower probability of very good or excellent health. In general, note that the proportional effect of one variable relative to another stays constant across the outcomes – e.g., the marginal effects of being Hispanic are roughly three–quarters of that for the variable for Black.

As a side note, Ordered Logit Models are very similar in nature and interpretation to the Ordered Probit Model.

From my experience, the Ordered Probit/Logit Models are fairly shaky in that slight changes to the model can have disproportionate effects on the results. An alternative to ordered models is to do a series of probability models. For example, the ordered model can be broken down into probability models. For example, we could model:

- Pr(health is fair or worse);
- Pr(health is very good or worse);
- Pr(health is good or better);
- Pr(health is excellent or better).

These would be more flexible and easier to interpret. And, they would be more stable models than the ordered models.

9.4 Categorical outcomes – Multinomial Logit Model

Multinomial Logit Models can be used when:

- The outcome is categorical in that the order does not mean anything;
- The outcome is quantitative, but various factors can cause the outcome to move in opposite directions for various parts of the population as a result of a treatment; that is, the outcome may move away from or towards a central tendency.

I will present a theoretical example of using the model for categorical outcomes and an empirical example for capturing separate effects in opposite directions.

Using Multinomial Logit Models for categorical outcomes

Suppose that a political party is choosing among a field of four candidates to nominate for the presidency. The candidates and their characteristics are:

Candidate A – moderate, disagrees with the party platform on some issues;
Candidate B – tough talker, wants to pre-emptively strike Canada;
Candidate C – always agrees with the party's platform, even if it runs counter to positions he has had in the past;
Candidate D – smart person, has views mostly in-line with the party, but got caught cheating on his wife five years ago.

Let's suppose that a campaign official for candidate A wants to know what causes a potential voter to prefer one of the other candidates over candidate A.

Unlike the dependent variable in the previous section that had a clear order (level of health), there is no ordering of the candidates that has any meaning. The preferred candidate for a voter is, thus, a *categorical variable*.

If there were two categories (e.g., yes or no on some issue, such as whether the citizen voted in the election), then a probit, logit, or linear probability model could be used. But, it is more complicated in this case with multiple choices.

In the MNL model, one first chooses a baseline category, say candidate A, and then models the log odds of each choice relative to the baseline choice/outcome:

$$ln\left(\frac{Pr(y = candidate\, B)}{Pr(y = candidate\, A)}\right) = \beta_0 + \beta_1 X_1 + \beta_2 X_2 + \ldots + \beta_K X_K + \varepsilon = X\beta + \varepsilon \qquad (9.9)$$

To calculate the predicted probability of a choice, equation (9.9) would be transformed into:

$$Pr(candidate\, B) = \frac{1}{\sum_{k \neq B} e^{-X\beta}} \qquad (9.10)$$

where X includes a constant and X_1 to X_k. But, don't worry. The little green elves (the statistical program) will calculate these probabilities for you. Higher predicted values ($X\beta$) in equation (9.9) would result in a smaller denominator in equation (9.10) and a higher probability of candidate B being preferred.

Using Multinomial Logit Models for outcomes that can move in opposite directions

Let me refer back to Section 5.5, in which I argued that one reason why an estimate could be insignificant is that positive and negative effects of the treatment are canceling each other out. This could only occur when there are plausible mechanisms that could cause some subjects to be positively affected by a treatment and others to be negatively affected.

A divorce could be such a treatment, as we saw in Section 3.2.1 on interaction effects. While the conventional wisdom is that a divorce would negatively affect children, there is the possibility that a divorce could help some children, particularly if it removes them from a high-conflict household. Thus, it is possible that divorces do positively affect some children, negatively affect other children, and yet the estimated average effect that is observed in a study is insignificant because the opposing effects cancel each other out.

In a recent unpublished study of mine (Arkes 2016), I used data on children of the female respondents of the NLSY to examine how a marital disruption (a divorce or separation) affects problem behavior among children. I started with a first-difference model:

$$Y_{i2} - Y_{i1} = \beta_1 \times (A_{i2} - A_{i1}) + \beta_2 \times (D_{i2} - D_{i1}) + \varepsilon_i \qquad (9.11)$$

where:

- Y_{i2} and Y_{i1} = Behavioral Problems Index (BPI), with a higher score indicating more problems, for periods 1 and 2;
- A = age in months;
- D = an indicator variable for whether the mother was Divorced or Separated from her husband.

The samples are limited to children whose parents were still married as of period 1 and are based on the change over a two-year period. Thus, the quantity $(D_{i2} - D_{i1})$ can only take the value of 0 or 1. One sample has people aged 5 or 6 in the first period and aged 7 or 8 in the second period. The other two samples are similar two-year changes going forward to ages 9 or 10 and to ages 11 or 12. Note that it is not necessary to control for certain demographic information (e.g., gender and race/ethnicity) because they stay constant between the two periods.

Estimating equation (9.11) with OLS gives an overall, average estimated effect (using the continuous variable for actual score change) and may miss what is occurring for certain segments of the population. Using a Multinomial Logit Model may provide extra information, as it would examine effects in both directions.

For each sample, I estimated a Multinomial Logit Model based on the three outcomes that represent the change in BPI: a decrease of 5+ points, an increase of 5+ points, and a change of less than 5 points. The outcome is constructed as follows:

$$Y_i = -1 \text{ if } (Y_{i2} - Y_{i1} \leq -5)$$
$$Y_i = 0 \text{ if } \left(-5 < Y_{i2} - Y_{i1} < 5\right)$$
$$Y_i = 1 \text{ if } \left(Y_{i2} - Y_{i1} \geq 5\right)$$

A separate outcome variable was constructed similarly but based on 10-point changes.

The Multinomial Logit equations are:

$$ln\left(\frac{Pr\left(Y_i = 1\right)}{Pr\left(Y_i = 0\right)}\right) = \beta_{0a} + \beta_{1a}{\star}\left(A_{i2} - A_{i1}\right) + \beta_{2a}{\star}\left(D_{i2} - D_{i1}\right) + \varepsilon_{ia} \qquad (9.12a)$$

$$ln\left(\frac{Pr\left(Y_i = -1\right)}{Pr\left(Y_i = 0\right)}\right) = \beta_{0b} + \beta_{1b}{\star}\left(A_{i2} - A_{i1}\right) + \beta_{2b}{\star}\left(D_{i2} - D_{i1}\right) + \varepsilon_{ib} \qquad (9.12b)$$

in which the main difference is in the numerator of the dependent variable.

Table 9.5 shows the results. For the second sample (going from ages 7–8 to 9–10), the model using the OLS method (the standard approach) shows no significant coefficient estimate. However, the Multinomial Logit (MNL) models, for both Models 2 and 3, show that there are significant coefficient estimates in both directions. Using the marginal effects (M.E.), experiencing a parental divorce/separation in those two years is associated with an estimated 5.5-percentage-point increase in the probability of a decrease in the BPI by 5+ points (improved behavior) and an estimated 8.3-percentage-point increase in the probability of having an increase in BPI by 5+ points (worsening behavior). *The Multinomial Logit Model was able to uncover real effects on children that were masked by the models using the OLS method.*

For the younger sample, there were no significant coefficient estimates. And, for the older cohort, the standard estimated divorce effect (with OLS) is weakly significant, but it is more strongly significant when separately examining just increases in behavioral problems (for both 5-point and 10-point increases).

9.5 Censored outcomes – Tobit models

In some cases, an outcome is censored at the bottom or top level of the distribution. For example, SAT scores are bottom- and top-coded at 200 and 800. So, the scores are not able to distinguish between the abilities or aptitudes of those who score 800. As mentioned in the chapter introduction, another example is income, which is censored at 0 for those who do not work. This means that there is a relatively large percentage of observations with a value of 0, particularly for women, who have lower labor force participation rates.[2] Furthermore, the income data we have used from the NLSY is top-coded for 3.9% of the sample.

Table 9.5 Coefficient estimates of a marital disruption on problem behavior

	Dependent variable = Behavioral Problems Index		
	Sample		
	From 5–6 to 7–8 years old (n = 3144)	From 7–8 to 9–10 years old (n = 3332)	From 9–10 to 11–12 years old (n = 2781)
Dependent variable			
Model 1 (OLS)			
Change in scores	−0.584	1.262	2.722*
	(1.228)	(1.213)	(1.578)
Model 2 (MNL)			
Decrease of 5+ points	0.077	0.597***	0.389
	(0.203)	(0.228)	(0.250)
	M.E. = 0.040	M.E. = 0.055	M.E. = 0.011
Increase of 5+ points	−0.223	0.675***	0.629***
	(0.214)	(0.217)	(0.237)
	M.E. = −0.059	M.E. = 0.083	M.E. = 0.100
Model 3 (MNL)			
Decrease of 10+ points	0.065	0.407*	0.273
	(0.228)	(0.239)	(0.272)
	M.E. = 0.011	M.E. = 0.032	M.E. = 0.017
Increase of 10+ points	−0.080	0.661***	0.584**
	(0.240)	(0.213)	(0.246)
	M.E. = −0.015	M.E. = 0.098	M.E. = 0.089

Note: Standard errors in parentheses. *** $p < 0.01$, ** $p < 0.05$, * $p < 0.1$.

Source: Bureau of Labor Statistics, 2014.

One can imagine that women (like men) who have very low levels of education are less likely to work because the income would be too low. So, they choose not to work or are unable to get a job. An extra year of schooling, which should make them more productive, can then have two effects:

1. increase the likelihood that the woman works and earns income;
2. increase income for those already working.

When there are these two separate effects, OLS is problematic because it results in inconsistent estimates. James Tobin developed a model to address this, which became known as the **Tobit model**. The model is:

$$Y_i^* = X_i\beta + \varepsilon_i \tag{9.13}$$

Where $Y_i^\star$ is a latent variable that is observed for values of Y greater than zero (provided that 0 is the censor point):

$$Y = \begin{cases} Y^\star & if\ Y^\star > 0 \\ 0 & if\ Y^\star \leq 0 \end{cases} \tag{9.14}$$

This model, also estimated by maximum likelihood, uses the assumption that the error terms are normally distributed. A problem with the Tobit model is the ambiguity for what expected value to use and, thus, what marginal effects to calculate. The coefficient estimates themselves are on the latent variable, $Y^\star$, and so they are not interpretable themselves. The potential expected values could be:

- The expected value of the latent variable: $E[Y_i^\star] = X_i\beta$, which comes straight from the reported output, but $Y_i^\star$ typically has no useful meaning;
- The expected value of the outcome, conditional on X and being positive: $E[Y_i \mid Y_i > 0, X]$;
- The expected value of Y conditional on just $X, E[Y_i \mid X]$.

The latter two are more complicated to calculate, as they incorporate how the X variable affects the probability that the person has positive income.

Given the ambiguity of the Tobit model, a common approach is to estimate two models that are more concrete:

- How the X variables affect the probability that the person has a positive value for the dependent variable;
- How the X variables affect the dependent variable, conditional on the dependent variable being positive.

This would be more tractable, and it would have more straightforward interpretations. Remember that, often, simpler is better.

9.6 Count variables – Negative Binomial and Poisson models

As mentioned in the chapter introduction, most variables are not truly continuous (i.e., being able to take on any value), but can be approximated as continuous based on having an adequate amount of variation. Other variables, however, are clearly discrete, such as a "count" variable. Let's take the example of the number of children a teenage female desires to have. This variable would be censored at zero, highly concentrated at low values, and highly skewed to the right.

Using OLS causes problems because: (1) the error terms are not normally distributed, violating Assumption **A3** for OLS; and (2) the model may give predictions that are less than zero, which cannot actually occur.

There are two models that are commonly used with count data: the Negative Binomial regression model and the Poisson regression model. Both have the general format of:

$$\log[E(Y \mid X)] = X\beta$$

or

$$E(Y \mid X) = e^{X\beta} \tag{9.15}$$

This means that the coefficient estimate indicates the percentage increase in the count outcome associated with a one-unit increase in X. This is not exactly a marginal effect, but rather a quasi-elasticity.

(Behind the curtains, there are some extra details and differences between the Poisson and Negative Binomial models, but they are very math intensive and presenting them would be contrary to the spirit of this book.)

The Negative Binomial model is the more flexible of the models and should be used most of the time. Poisson is better when there is "under dispersion," meaning there is less variation in the model than expected – I know, a very abstract concept. You're safer sticking with the Negative Binomial model.

Example: How educational expectations affects fertility in one's youth

To demonstrate count models, I examine the issue of how much females' educational expectations affect their fertility outcomes. I take a sample of the 1331 16–17-year-old females from the initial NLSY round in 1979 who had not had any kids as of their initial 1979 interview and were still in the sample 5 years later. I then examine how various factors affect the number of kids they had by their interview about 5 years later, in 1984 (Bureau of Labor Statistics, 2014).

Figure 9.1 shows the histogram of the outcome. It obviously is not a continuous outcome, having only five different values. Plus, there is the bunching at zero. Thus, it is unlikely that the error terms would be normally distributed if OLS were used.

Table 9.6 shows a comparison of results from a Negative Binomial, Poisson, and linear model using the OLS method, along with marginal effects of the Negative Binomial and Poisson models. The primary explanatory variable of interest is expected years of education. For 16–17-year-old females, each expected year of schooling is associated with about 14% fewer births over the next 5 years (from the primary Negative Binomial and Poisson models – columns 1 and 3), holding the other factors constant. These translate into a marginal effect of 0.051 fewer births – columns 2 and 4. The OLS estimate,

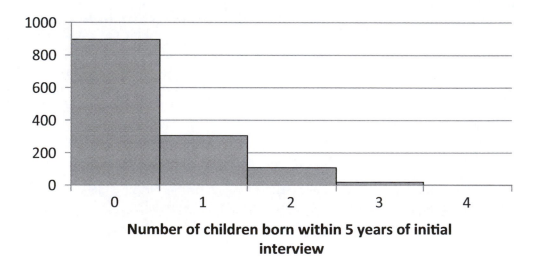

Figure 9.1 Frequency of number of children born in first 5 years of NLSY survey

Table 9.6 Results from Negative Binomial, Poisson, and OLS

	Dependent variable = number of births				
	Negative Binomial model		Poisson model		Linear model using OLS
	(1)	(2)	(3)	(4)	(5)
	Estimates	Marginal effects	Estimates	Marginal effects	Estimates / Marginal effects
Expected years of schooling	−0.138***	−0.051***	−0.137***	−0.051***	−0.062***
	(0.024)	(0.009)	(0.024)	(0.009)	(0.010)
AFQT	−0.012***	−0.005***	−0.012***	−0.005***	−0.004***
	(0.003)	(0.001)	(0.003)	(0.001)	(0.001)
Race/ethnicity (non–Hispanic and non–Black is the reference group)					
Black	0.402***	0.165***	0.397***	0.163***	0.197***
	(0.108)	(0.050)	(0.108)	(0.050)	(0.053)
Hispanic	0.212*	0.0849	0.209*	0.083*	0.094*
	(0.121)	(0.052)	(0.120)	(0.051)	(0.055)
Constant	1.255***		1.245***		1.385***
	(0.275)		(0.276)		(0.131)
Observations	1331	1331	1331	1331	1331
R-squared					0.113

Note: Standard errors are in parentheses and are corrected for heteroskedasticity.

*** $p < 0.01$, ** $p < 0.05$, * $p < 0.10$.

Source: Bureau of Labor Statistics, 2014.

also in terms of the change in the number of births, is 0.062 fewer births. Being Black is associated with about 40% (or 0.16) more births.

While OLS may sometimes give very similar results, in this case, the results are a bit different. I would trust the Negative Binomial and Poisson results more than OLS, given that the OLS estimates will be inconsistent. One last note is that a Poisson model gives almost the exact same results as the Negative Binomial model, in this case. In most cases, it likely will not matter which model you use, but the more conservative approach, again, is using the Negative Binomial model.

9.7 Duration models

Duration models are used to examine the factors contributing to the event of ending time in a given state of existence. For example, one may want to investigate what factors contribute to:

* Businesses failing,
* Cancer patients in remission having a recurrence,

- People leaving a spell of unemployment,
- A couple divorcing,
- How long a machine lasts before malfunctioning.

Duration models are also called:

- Survival models (e.g., the machine surviving in the "working" state);
- Hazard models (the hazard of a machine malfunctioning).

The survival time is the amount of time that a subject remains in a certain state. That is, how long will a cancer patient remain in the state of "remission"? How long will the unemployed person remain in the state of "being unemployed"? The survival time may be censored in that not everyone will change states by the end of the study period. Also, it could be the case that not everyone is observed when first going into the initial state (e.g., remission). That is not ideal, but duration models can account for this.

The survival function, $S(t)$, represents the probability that a subject survives in a given state for t periods, and is represented as:

$$S(t) = \Pr(T > t) \tag{9.16}$$

where T is the actual survival time.

The hazard function, $h(t)$, would then be the probability that the subject changes to the other state in a given period t:

$$h(t) = \frac{f(t)}{S(t)} \tag{9.17}$$

where $f(t)$ is the value for a given t in the probability density function of the distribution of the survival time of T.

Choosing the correct probability density function $f(t)$ and hazard function $h(t)$ unfortunately presents a researcher with several options. The two choices that are most often used, based on flexibility of the model, are:

- Using the Weibull distribution. This has flexibility over what the distribution of the survival time (T) is, but it requires the researcher to make assumptions on what that distribution looks like. It allows varying underlying hazard rates (probability of failure) as the survival time increases.
- Using the Cox proportional–hazards model. This does not require any prior knowledge of the hazard distribution. The downside is that it requires the underlying hazard rate (before the effects of other explanatory variables are accounted for) to be constant for each value of t, meaning, for example, that the underlying divorce rate would be constant at each year of marriage in the model if there were no influences from other factors. The basis of using the Cox proportional-hazards model is that the hazard (and survival) distribution is not known, so assigning an incorrect distribution causes more bias than assuming no distribution.

The safest approach typically is using the Cox proportional-hazards model. The model is:

$$h(t \mid X_i) = \Pr(\text{subject } i \text{ changes states in period } t) = h_0(t) \times e^{X_i \beta} \qquad (9.18)$$

where $h_0(t)$ is the baseline hazard for a given period and X is the set of explanatory variables.

This means that the estimated effect of a one-unit change in an X variable on the probability of the person changing states (i.e., not surviving in the current state) is the exponential of the coefficient estimate on that X variable. Sounds strange, but it works well. Trust me!

As mentioned above, the model can incorporate censored data – cases in which a person is first observed after the initial state has begun (e.g., unemployment) or before the initial state ended (finding a job). The censored points just need to be indicated in the statistical program.

Application: The effects of the unemployment rate on the probability of a divorce

A colleague and I examined how the strength of the economy, proxied by the state unemployment rate, affects the probability of a divorce (Arkes and Shen 2014). We examined the effect of the lagged unemployment rate (during the $(t-1)$th year of marriage) on the probability that the couple's marriage survives through year t. For example, how does the average unemployment rate in the 3rd year of marriage determine whether the couple survives through the 4th year of marriage. We used the lagged unemployment rate because of the likelihood that divorces take time to be carried out.

Table 9.7 shows a summary of the two primary models, displaying the estimated hazard ratios and standard errors (as reported in the article), not the coefficient estimates. Each estimate represents the estimated change in the odds of a divorce, relative to the baseline odds, from a 1-percentage-point increase in the unemployment rate. Model (1) estimates the effects for all married couples, while model (2) estimates separate effects by length of marriage.

Table 9.7 Cox proportional-hazards model for the effects of state unemployment rates on the probability of a couple divorcing (n = 95,472)

	Using state unemployment rates	
	(1)	(2)
unemployment rate	1.034*	
	(0.021)	
(unemployment rate) × (in years 1–5 of marriage)		1.014
		(0.030)
(unemployment rate) × (in years 6–10 of marriage)		1.079***
		(0.029)
(unemployment rate) × (in years 11+ of marriage)		1.004
		(0.036)

Note: The models also control for demographic factors, religion, age of marriage for both spouses, 3-year-group indicators, and state indicators. *** $p < 0.01$, ** $p < 0.05$, * $p < 0.10$.

Source: Bureau of Labor Statistics, 2014.

There is a weakly significant positive estimated effect of the unemployment rate on the probability of divorce. However, when estimating separate effects by length of marriage, the evidence is stronger that a higher state unemployment rate increases the probability of a divorce for those in their 6th to 10th years of marriage. The point estimate (the best guess for the estimated effect of the unemployment rate) for this group says that a 1-percentage-point higher unemployment rate would lead to a 7.9% higher risk of divorce, relative to the baseline odds. There is no evidence that the unemployment rate affects the probability of divorce in those in other stages of marriage.

One factor to keep in mind is the point from earlier about the measurement error in the state unemployment rates. And, these models had state and year controls, which is almost equivalent to fixed effects. This means that one reason why there were insignificant estimates on the unemployment rate might be that there was a large bias towards zero from measurement error.

Earlier, I argued against the use of national variables. For example, using national unemployment rates for estimating the effects of the economy on drug use or using national tax rates to estimate the effects of tax rates on economic growth (Section 6.4.2) introduces a great potential for omitted-variables bias. With divorces, however, one could argue that national unemployment rates could be used because divorce rates do not change much at a national level within short periods of time other than due to the strength of the economy. (If we were wrong on this assumption, then our results when using the national unemployment rate should not be trusted.) Exceptions may include the September 11 attacks (which some argue brought families together more) and a well-publicized domestic violence incident (which could encourage more women to leave marriages).

By including 3-year-group controls (i.e., fixed effects), the effect of the national unemployment rate is identified by how within-3-year-period variation in the national unemployment rate is related to such variation in the probability of divorcing. With the national unemployment rates, the results (not shown here) were much stronger: a higher national unemployment rate was estimated to lead to a higher probability of divorcing for those couples in their 6th to 10th year of marriage by 23.4%. Note that this does not mean that a 1-percentage-point increase in the unemployment rate leads to an increase in the probability of a couple divorcing from 3.1% to 26.5%. Rather, it would be 23.4% on top of 3.1% (or 3.1% times 1.234), which would mean 3.8%.

9.8 Chapter summary

This chapter presented alternative methods to use in certain situations, mostly in cases in which the dependent variable is not continuous or approximately continuous. As stated earlier, using OLS when the error terms are not normally distributed could cause:

- Inefficient estimates;
- Biased estimates;
- Misleading statistics related to the significance of estimates, hypothesis tests, and confidence intervals.

That said, sometimes using these models presents new problems or makes it impossible to apply a correction for non-random explanatory variables, creating even worse biases to the estimates. In general, the biases or inconsistency resulting from the improper model being used is much smaller than the biases associated with the pitfalls from Chapter 6. The best approach is to use the appropriate model, as outlined in this chapter, unless it prevents the use of proper methods to address certain biases.

Exercises

1. From Chapter 7, Question #2, using **births18**, use a probit model to regress *birth18* on *black*, *hisp*, *mixed*, *momhs*, *momcoll*, *momeducmiss*, *dadhs*, *dadcoll*, *dadeducmiss*, *notbiomom*, and *notbiodad*. What is the marginal effect of the variable *black* on the probability of a teenager having a birth before age 18?
2. Repeat Question #1, but use a logit model instead of a probit model.
3. Are there any major differences between the estimated marginal effects in the probit or logit model in Questions #1 and #2, compared to the estimates from OLS in Question #2 in Chapter 7?
4. What is the odds ratio of having a birth before age 18, based on one's mother having a high-school diploma (*momhs* = 1), relative to the baseline odds? Interpret this odds ratio.

Notes

1 More specifically, the Maximum Likelihood method involves finding the set of coefficient estimates that give the highest likelihood of the data occurring as it did. That is, the likelihood function maximizes $\ln[\Pr(Y_1, Y_2, Y_3, \ldots Y_n \mid X_1, X_2, X_3, \ldots X_n)]$ for the n observations, with the X's representing all explanatory variables.
2 The same issues occur if the dependent variable is "truncated," meaning that only observations meeting a certain threshold for the dependent variable are included in the sample. Examples of this include restricting samples to: honor students with a GPA of 3.5 or better; low-income individuals who earn no more than the poverty level; people with a minimum of $10,000 of income.

References

Arkes, J. (2016). On the misinterpretation of insignificant coefficient estimates. SSRN Working Paper. (Available at http://papers.ssrn.com/sol3/papers.cfm?abstract_id=2821164, accessed July 10, 2018).

Arkes, J., & Shen, Y. C. (2014). For better or for worse, but how about a recession? *Contemporary Economic Policy*, 32(2), 275–287.

Bureau of Labor Statistics, U.S. Department of Labor. (2014). *National Longitudinal Survey of Youth 1979 cohort, 1979–2012 (rounds 1–25)*. Columbus, OH: Center for Human Resource Research, The Ohio State University.

Bureau of Labor Statistics, U.S. Department of Labor. (2015). *National Longitudinal Survey of Youth 1997 cohort, 1997–2013 (rounds 1–16)*. Columbus, OH: Center for Human Resource Research, The Ohio State University.

Horace, W., & Oaxaca, R. (2006). Results on the bias and inconsistency of ordinary least squares for the linear probability model. *Economics Letters*, 90(3), 321–327.

10   Time-series models

The future ain't what it used to be.

—Yogi Berra

The future ain't what it was, but "what it used to be" *might* help predict the future. **Time-series models** involve one entity or subject (e.g., a country, a business) that is followed over many periods. This contrasts with a cross-sectional model, which has many subjects in just one period. And, time-series models are different from panel models, which have multiple subjects over multiple periods.

Time-series models can be categorized in two ways:

- **Contemporaneous (static) models** that examine the contemporaneous (current) effects of an X variable on an outcome;
- **Dynamic models** that examine how lagged values of an X variable and/or lagged values of an outcome determine the current value of the outcome.

These models are often for the purpose of forecasting the outcome and estimating causal effects of various factors on the outcome. Either way, time-series models are useful when a dependent variable has inertia or some factor could have drawn-out effects over time. For example, an oil-price increase could cause airline ticket prices to increase, but the effect may not be immediate, as there could be contracts for jet fuel purchases in the short term.

Time-series models have so many subtleties that whole textbooks are written on the various types of time-series models for different situations. So, this chapter represents just an introduction to time-series models. I emphasize some of the most common problems to be conscious of when conducting time-series analysis.

10.1 The components of a time-series variable

A time-series variable can be decomposed into four basic components:

- A trend component – the value may tend to move over time;
- A seasonal component – the value may tend to be different in certain periods, such as parts of the year;
- A cyclical (often called "irregular") component – the value may go through cycles, such as macroeconomic business cycles or drug epidemics;
- A random-disturbance component – this is just due to the random things that happen in life.

Not all time-series variables will have all of these components. For example, whereas a quarterly unemployment rate would have a seasonal component (the rate is typically higher in the winter quarter), an annual unemployment rate would not have any seasonal component. And, many time-series variables will not have any trend.

Figure 10.1 demonstrates the different components of the time-series variable, the average U.S. gas price, based on the first Monday of each quarter. The lines are:

- Price = actual price for the given date;
- Trend = linear trend from the model: $\widehat{(Price)}_t = 1.023 + 0.013 \times t$;
- Seasonal = quarterly effects:

$$\widehat{(Price)}_t = 1.204 + 0.092 \times (spring)_t + 0.118 \times (summer)_t + 0.119 \times (fall)_t ;$$

- Irregular: $\widehat{(Price)}_t = 0.202 + 0.854 \times (Price)_{t-1}$;
- Random disturbance (residual) = the residual from including all other components in a joint model:

$$\hat{\varepsilon}_t = (Price)_t - [0.213 + 0.004 \times t + 0.134 \times (spring)_t + 0.091 \times (summer)_t + 0.069 \times (fall)_t + 0.725 \times (Price)_{t-1}] .$$

Some of these components will be integral for subsequent lessons. For example, the irregular component will be the basis for autoregressive models in Section 10.3.

10.2 Autocorrelation

Consider three time-series variables:

- The winning percentage for your favorite sports team (I'll use mine, the San Antonio Spurs);
- The number of minutes a doctor spends with a patient;
- The daily percentage change in the stock price of Google.

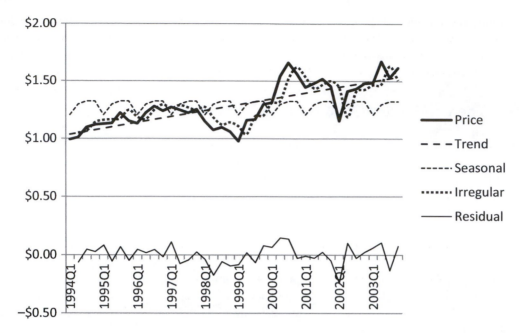

Figure 10.1 Decomposition of a time-series variable (quarterly gas prices)

And, consider how these variables might move over time. Specifically, think about how a given observation might be correlated with prior observations.

I would expect:

- The winning percentage for the Spurs to be positively related to recent, prior years, as most key players stay the same from one year to the next;
- The number of minutes a doctor spends with a patient to be negatively related to prior patients because more time spent with prior patients means the doctor will feel more rushed;
- The daily percentage change in Google's stock price would not depend in any systematic way on prior daily changes.

These are indicators of the extent of **autocorrelation** (also called **serial correlation**) in a variable. Autocorrelation is a situation in which a variable is correlated with its lagged values. Technically, autocorrelation would come from the correlation of the errors. First-order autocorrelation would be the case in which, from a time-series regression with an error term of ε_t:

$$\varepsilon_t = \rho\varepsilon_{t-1} + \eta_t \tag{10.1}$$

where η_t is the part of the error term that is truly random and independent of any other error term and assumed to be normally distributed. In the examples above, the estimate for ρ would likely be positive for the Spurs' winning percentage, negative for the number of minutes a doctor spends with a patient, and close to zero for the daily change in Google's stock price.

Any autocorrelation could be due to correlated period effects (such as having a star player for certain years) or due to some factor or event having lasting or drawn-out effects. For example, in an analysis of opioid overdoses, epidemics could cause higher-than-normal overdose rates for a few years, leading to a positive correlation of the error terms. And, with drawn-out effects, oil-price increases could have lagged effects on airline prices, as contracts might have contracted jet fuel prices. And so, the airline prices might have effects that last long after the oil prices have returned to their normal price range.

The concept of autocorrelation is similar to that of **spatial correlation**, which is the case in which locations close to each other would have correlated values of a variable. In spatial correlation, the correlation is by geographical proximity, whereas autocorrelation is the correlation of observations that are in proximity by time.

To demonstrate what positive vs. negative correlation looks like, let's consider two different time-series variables for the Spurs:

- Their winning percentage each season;
- The change in their winning percentage from the prior season.

Figure 10.2 shows the time series for these two variables for every year that the Spurs have been part of the National Basketball Association. As expected and discussed above, it appears that there is a positive correlation between successive values for the winning percentage. However, for the change in winning percentage, it appears that there is a negative correlation between values. That is, when one value is high (positive), the next value appears to decrease or be negative. And, when one value is low, the next value tends to be higher. This actually makes sense, as an increase in winning percentage in one year may partly be due to random luck, and reversion to the mean would then cause a tendency for the change to the next year to be negative. These, again, are cases of autocorrelation, positive in the first case and negative in the second case.

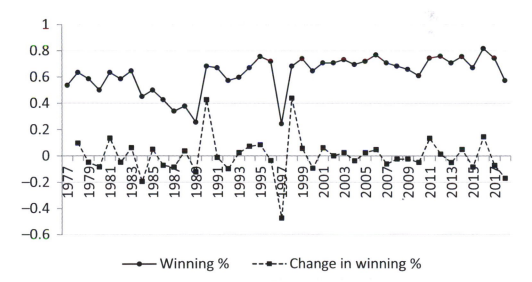

Figure 10.2 San Antonio Spurs winning percentage and change in winning percentage, by year

Autocorrelation creates problems if one is using time-series variables to analyze the relationship between different variables, particularly when there is a lagged-dependent variable. This partly occurs because the effective sample size decreases, as there are fewer independent observations when there is autocorrelation. And, there is also the possibility of biased coefficient estimates. I will discuss these problems in Section 10.5. But first, I will introduce the autoregressive and distributed-lag models in the next few sections, with the autoregression in the next section being a way to model autocorrelation.

10.3 Autoregressive models

Just as regressions represent a method to model correlations, autoregressive models represent a method of modeling, or approximating, autocorrelation. They involve regressing a time-series variable on one or more lags of the variable.

The typical autoregressive model involves some national economic outcome, such as the annual inflation rate or Gross Domestic Product growth rate. Instead, I will initially focus on something that provides much more meaning to many people and has become, to some, the center of Western-civilization culture: Trump's Twitter tweets. Let's test how the number of tweets in a given week can be predicted by the number of tweets in prior weeks.

If Trump's number of tweets in a given week can be predicted by the number of his tweets from recent weeks, then it could mean a few things:

- Perhaps he gets in tweeting modes or anti-tweeting modes (or modes of resistance to anti-tweeting-advice from senior advisors);
- Perhaps his number of tweets depends on big events that last for a few or several weeks.

Let's start with a visual examination of his weekly number of tweets, as shown in Figure 10.3. While there are occasional single-week dips and peaks, there does seem to be occasional clumping

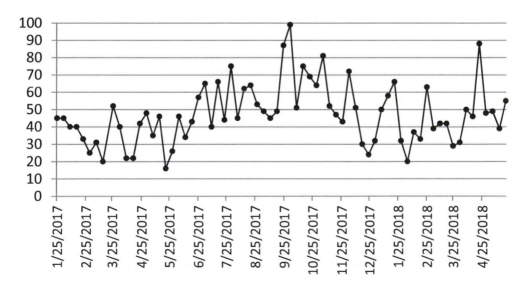

Figure 10.3 President Trump's weekly tweets while president (through April 2018)

of the amount of tweets – perhaps not incidentally, "clumping" is what some would have called a Clinton-Trump presidential ticket, if it ever would have happened (or would happen in the future, with Chelsea and Don Jr.).

To formally test whether the number of weekly tweets can be forecasted by that for recent weeks, we would estimate an **autoregression**, which is a regression of a time-series variable on some of its lagged values.

A first-order autoregressive model, AR(1), would be:

$$Y_t = \beta_0 + \beta_1 Y_{t-1} + \varepsilon_t \tag{10.2}$$

A jth-order autoregressive model, AR(j), would be:

$$Y_t = \beta_0 + \beta_1 Y_{t-1} + \beta_2 Y_{t-2} + \ldots \beta_j Y_{t-j} + \varepsilon_t \tag{10.3}$$

There is a trade-off in that higher-orders to the autoregressive model (i.e., adding more lags) may provide important information that can help forecast current values, but it also brings greater imprecision to the estimates of the coefficients on the existing lags. This occurs because there may be high correlation between explanatory variables, which are all lags of each other.

How do you choose the optimal order (i.e., number of lags) to use for an autoregression? You may need to use BIC, AIC, and AICc (corrected AIC), which were briefly mentioned in Section 6.5. The idea behind them is to evaluate models based on how much additional variables contribute to the explanation of the data, while punishing the model, to some extent, for having to add more variables. The following is a brief description of each, with $\hat{L}$ being the maximum value of the model's likelihood function (see the endnote in the Introduction of Chapter 9), k being the number of parameters to estimate, and n being the sample size:

- BIC $= \ln(n) \times k - 2 \times \ln(\hat{L})$
- AIC $= 2k - 2 \times \ln(\hat{L})$
- AICc $= $ AIC $+ \dfrac{2k^2 + 2k}{n - k - 1}$

The AICc was created because BIC is considered by some to penalize added variables too much, and AIC does not penalize extra variables enough, particularly for small samples. And so, AIC is more likely to say that models with more variables are "better." The AICc statistic adds a little extra penalty for adding X variables – recall that a lower value means a better model.

In Table 10.1, I present the AR(1) to AR(4) models for Trump weekly tweets and the BIC, AIC, and AICc values. I restrict the data to weeks starting February 26, 2017, so that the first week can have four lags available (in the Presidential term) and the number of observations is the same for each model.

The first lag, Y_{t-1}, has a statistically significant coefficient estimate and is fairly high, suggesting a strong connection between the number of tweets last week and this week. (Note that the estimate on a lag would rarely be above 1.0.) The coefficient estimate on the first lag remains fairly steady as more lags are added. This is some evidence that the President gets into tweeting (and/or anti-tweeting modes). When the second and further lags are added, none of their coefficient estimates turn out to be statistically significant. This means that we have no evidence that Trump's tweeting modes/anti-modes, on average, last more than two weeks.

Table 10.1 Autoregressive models for President Trump weekly tweets

	AR(1)	AR(2)	AR(3)	AR(4)
Dependent variable = number of tweets in the week				
Y_{t-1} (# tweets in prior week)	0.410***	0.350**	0.351**	0.353**
	(0.117)	(0.138)	(0.141)	(0.138)
Y_{t-2}		0.146	0.149	0.127
		(0.116)	(0.123)	(0.129)
Y_{t-3}			−0.009	−0.0645
			(0.116)	(0.118)
Y_{t-4}				0.153
				(0.102)
Constant	28.11***	24.09***	24.31***	20.68***
	(5.482)	(6.043)	(6.738)	(7.127)
Observations	65	65	65	65
R-squared	0.168	0.186	0.186	0.205
BIC	553.9	556.6	560.8	563.5
AIC	549.5	550.1	552.1	552.6
AICc	549.7	550.5	552.8	553.6

Note: Heteroskedasticity-corrected standard errors are in parentheses.

*** $p < 0.01$, ** $p < 0.05$, * $p < 0.10$.

So, which of these is the optimal model? The R^2 is highest for the AR(4) model, indicating that we can better explain Trump's weekly tweets. But, note that the standard error on the first lag is lower in the AR(1) model than in the AR(4) model. And, note that the BIC, AIC, and AICc all have the lowest values for the AR(1) model. This points to the AR(1) model being the optimal autoregressive model for modeling Trump's weekly tweets.

Lagged scatterplots

Sometimes, a basic autoregressive model may not represent well the actual extent of autocorrelation. A good check might come from using a **lagged scatterplot**, which is a scatterplot of a time-series variable with its lagged value. The lagged value could come from the prior period or from several periods ago.

What a lagged scatterplot could indicate is:

- Whether, despite insignificance in an AR model, there is a non-linear relationship between the lagged values and current values;
- Whether there are any outliers that could be driving the autocorrelation.

Figures 10.4a and 10.4b show the lagged scatterplots for the Spurs' winning percentage and the change in winning percentage (corresponding to the lines in Figure 10.2). Figure 10.4a appears to show a clear positive correlation between the variables, and this is confirmed in Model (1) in Table 10.2. But, Figure 10.4b shows a less certain relationship and, in particular, a single outlier (the 1998 observation) that could be driving the negative autocorrelation. Indeed, as shown in Table 10.2, with an AR(1) model based on the change in winning percentage, the coefficient estimate on the lagged-winning-percentage is reduced by a large amount when the 1998 observation is excluded

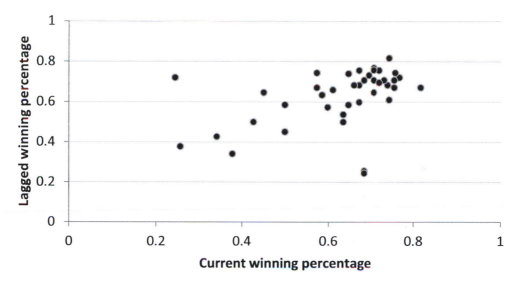

Figure 10.4a Scatterplot of current versus lagged winning percentage for the Spurs

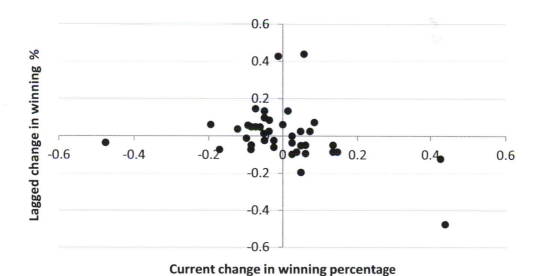

Figure 10.4b Scatterplot of current versus lagged change in winning percentage for the Spurs

Table 10.2 AR(1) model for the Spurs winning percentage and change in winning percentage

	Dep. Var = winning percentage (Y_t)		Dep. Var = change in winning percentage (ΔY_t)
	AR(1)	AR(1) (all obs.)	AR(1) (excludes 1998)
Y_{t-1} (winning % in prior season)	0.442**		
	(0.205)		
ΔY_{t-1}		−0.367	−0.145
		(0.225)	(0.165)
Constant	0.350**	0.000	0.010
	(0.137)	(0.022)	(0.022)
Observations	41	40	39
R-squared	0.197	0.132	0.019

Note: Heteroskedasticity-corrected standard errors are in parentheses.

*** $p < 0.01$, ** $p < 0.05$, * $p < 0.10$.

(Model (3)), although the coefficient estimate on the lagged-change-in-winning-percentage is insignificant both with and without the 1978 observation.

Autocorrelation functions (ACF) and partial autocorrelation functions (PACF)

The **autocorrelation function** (ACF) indicates how correlated different observations are based on how many periods away the observations are from each other. Typically, the further away two data points are, the closer would be their correlation to zero, but this is not always the case.

The **partial autocorrelation function** (PACF) is the same, but it factors out other variables. In particular, it typically just factors out the correlations of the other lags.

Figure 10.5a shows the ACF for the number of weekly Trump tweets. The shaded area represents 95% confidence intervals. Anything beyond the shaded area would represent a statistically significant correlation (at the 5% level).

Even though no lagged-dependent variable beyond the first lag has a statistically significant coefficient estimate (from Table 10.1), observations are still statistically significant for five and six periods away. This could be because the cumulative set of autocorrelations from successive periods away make the 5th and 6th lagged observations correlated to a current observation.

The correlations do approach zero as the lags increase, but they strangely start becoming negative and somewhat large in magnitude at the 17-period lag. I cannot think of any logical explanation for this other than pre-orchestrated chaos meant to throw off researchers who are trying to explain patterns in the number of weekly Trump tweets. That said, the estimated correlations are statistically insignificant. More evidence for my conspiracy theory on pre-orchestrated chaos in the number of Trump tweets comes from the PACF. The PACF, in Figure 10.5b, shows that observations are significantly *negatively* correlated for lags of several lengths, between 15 and 31 weeks away.

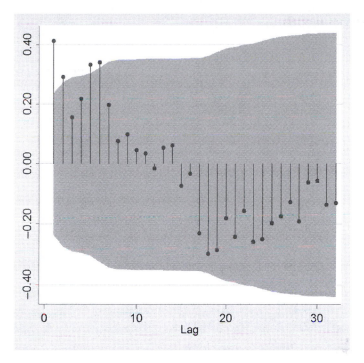

Figure 10.5a Autocorrelation function (ACF) of the number of weekly Trump tweets

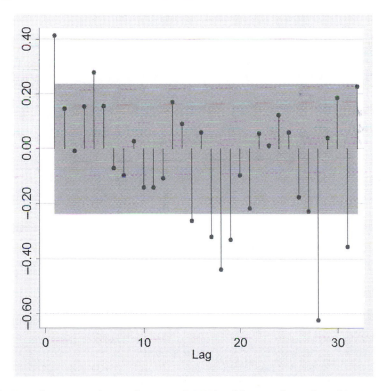

Figure 10.5b Partial autocorrelation function (PACF) of the number of weekly Trump tweets

For the record, I do not really believe that there is a conspiracy of pre-orchestrated chaos in the number of tweets to confuse the throngs of us doing time-series analyses of Trump tweets.

Perhaps more intuitive ACF and PACF's come from that for the pattern of wine consumption per capita in the U.S. Figures 10.6a and 10.6b show these graphs.[1] The ACF demonstrates a much smoother function, with correlations that tend towards zero the further away the observations in time are.

The two-period lag (the second data point in these figures) provides a good demonstration of the difference between the ACF and the PACF. Observations from two years apart are positively correlated by a significant amount (as indicated by the point in the ACF being outside the shaded region representing the 95% confidence interval). But, observations from two years apart are not significantly correlated with each other after factoring out the other correlations, particularly the one-year-apart correlations. This may suggest just an AR(1) process for wine consumption per capita.

10.4 Distributed-lag models

Sometimes, you may expect some factor to have an effect on an outcome that lasts for several periods. The classic example, from economics, is that a country's income growth could affect growth in consumption for several quarters or perhaps a few years. In such a situation, the optimal model may be a distributed-lag model.

The distributed-lag model is of the form:

$$Y_t = \beta_0 + \delta_0 X_t + \delta_1 X_{t-1} + \delta_2 X_{t-2} + \ \ldots \ + \delta_p X_{t-p} + \varepsilon_t \tag{10.4}$$

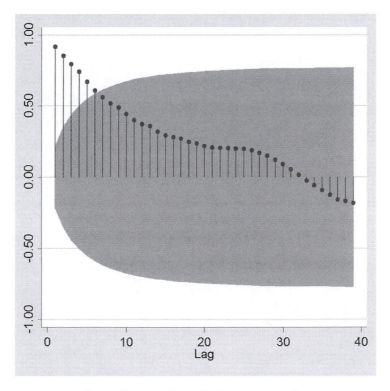

Figure 10.6a The autocorrelation function for U.S. wine consumption

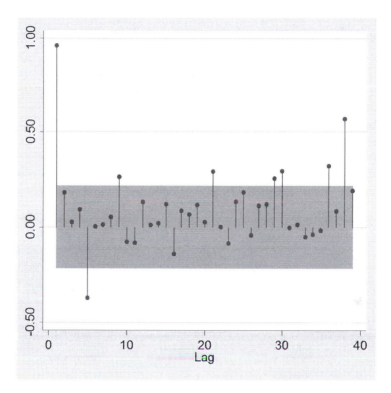

Figure 10.6b The partial autocorrelation function for U.S. wine consumption

Unfortunately, it is rare that any theory would dictate a certain number of lags, so the lags should often be determined empirically. Perhaps the information criterion (BIC, AIC, and AICc) would be useful measures rather than relying on the statistical significance of each lagged-X variable.

The distributed-lag model can be problematic because the lagged values of the X variable are often highly correlated with each other. This could cause:

- Large standard errors and greater imprecision of the estimates;
- Challenges in interpreting the estimated contribution of a given lagged-X variable, while holding constant other lagged-X variables; and
- Coefficient estimates on successive lags that have sign-reversing or non-monotonic decreases in coefficient estimates as lags increase, which probably makes little theoretical sense – this occurs because the highly correlated lags often battle each other for explanatory power.

The easiest approach to address these problems is to estimate a model with the current X variable and a lagged Y variable:

$$Y_t = \alpha + \beta Y_{t-1} + \delta_0 X_t + \varepsilon_t \tag{10.5}$$

If you iteratively plug in the equivalent equation for Y_{t-1}, you get:

$$Y_t = \alpha + \beta \times \left(\beta Y_{t-2} + \delta_0 X_{t-1} + \varepsilon_{t-1} \right) + \delta_0 X_t + \varepsilon_t \tag{10.6}$$

And so, the effect of X_{t-1} on Y_t is $\beta \times \delta_0$. In fact, the effects of lagged X variables are constrained to be smooth in this model, and the jth lag of X will have an effect on Y_t of $\beta^j \times \delta_0$.

Table 10.3 demonstrates the model with an analysis of the relationship between Trump tweets and Trump approval ratings (from Gallup's weekly tracking poll of Trump's approval). Models (1) to (4) are distributed-lag models, with up to four lags. Model (1) may not be ideal, as there could be further lagged effects of the approval rating. Sure enough, according to the BIC, AIC, and AICc, the subsequent lagged models are better fits, and the optimal model appears to be Model (4), despite the lack of statistical significance of any single lagged variable. But, we see the problem of having multiple lags, as the standard errors tend to be larger with more lags because the lagged approval variables are likely highly correlated with each other. In addition, as can be seen in Models (3) and (4), the coefficient estimates on the consecutive-lagged-approval variables jump around in terms of sign and magnitudes, which is again the result of the lagged variables being highly correlated with each other.

The correction for these problems, as stated above, would be to use equation (10.5), which includes the lagged value for tweets and the current value of approval, as depicted in Model (5). The coefficient

Table 10.3 The relationship between approval ratings and tweets for President Trump

	Dependent variable = number of tweets in the week				
	(1)	*(2)*	*(3)*	*(4)*	*(5)*
Tweets					
1-week–lagged					0.32**
					(0.12)
Approval–rating variables					
Current level					−1.73**
					(0.84)
1-week–lagged	−2.05**	−2.17	−2.07	−1.49	
	(0.89)	(1.36)	(1.38)	(1.53)	
2-week–lagged		−0.18	1.42	1.20	
		(1.35)	(1.81)	(1.85)	
3-week–lagged			−2.40**	−1.05	
			(1.19)	(1.51)	
4-week–lagged				−2.14	
				(1.44)	
Constant	126.47***	137.97***	164.97***	181.77***	99.06***
	(34.79)	(41.68)	(48.45)	(51.71)	(35.75)
BIC	584.5	580.7	574.3	568.6	
AIC	580.1	574.1	565.5	557.7	
AICc	580.3	574.5	566.2	558.8	
Observations	68	67	66	65	68
R–squared	0.063	0.070	0.110	0.139	0.204

Robust standard errors in parentheses

*** $p < 0.01$, ** $p < 0.05$, * $p < 0.1$.

estimate on the current approval rating is statistically significant, although the lower value of the 95% confidence interval for that estimate (0.08) is not that large. Whereas Model (5) addresses the problems of the distributed-lag model, it has its own problems stemming from autocorrelation, as will be described in the next section.

Granger Causality tests

The Granger Causality test examines whether the lags of the X variables have significant coefficient estimates. But, this would not necessarily be a true test of *causality*, as the name implies. Yes, any lagged values of approval would certainly precede the values for the number of tweets in week t and thus avoid a violation of BIG QUESTION 1, reverse causality. But, it could be subject to a few other BIG QUESTION violations. The most likely, perhaps, would be omitted-variables bias in that there could be common factors determining approval in week $t-1$ and weekly tweets in week t. Furthermore, there could be measurement error in the approval rating, as there is a margin of error associated with the approval rating, as in any poll. This measurement error would likely be random with respect to the number of tweets, and therefore likely lead to a bias towards zero. So, this would not be a true test for causality.

Nevertheless, the model for Granger Causality is based on an **autoregressive–distributed-lag model**, which would include both lagged values of the dependent variable and the explanatory variables, as follows:

$$Y_t = \beta_0 + \beta_1 Y_{t-1} + \delta_1 A_{t-1} + \varepsilon_t \tag{10.7}$$

This tests whether Trump's number of weekly tweets moves with his approval rating. Table 10.4 presents the results in column (1). There is no evidence that the weekly number of tweets tends to move

Table 10.4 Granger Causality model for Trump's weekly tweets and approval rating

	(1)	(2)
	Granger Causality	*Granger Causality with Newey-West standard errors*
	Dep. Var. = # tweets in a week	
Y_{t-1} (# tweets in prior week)	0.37***	0.37***
	(0.13)	(0.11)
A_{t-1} (lagged approval rating)	−0.98	−0.98
	(0.88)	(0.95)
	[−2.73, 0.77]	[−2.88, 0.92]
Constant	67.80*	67.80*
	(37.10)	(40.16)
Observations	68	68
R-squared	0.183	--

Note: Heteroskedasticity-corrected standard errors are in parentheses. The 95% confidence interval is in brackets for lagged approval rating.

*** $p < 0.01$, ** $p < 0.05$, * $p < 0.10$.

with Trump's lagged approval rating. I only use one lag, but such models could use multiple lags. (The second column for Table 10.4 will be referred to below.)

10.5 Consequences of and tests for autocorrelation

Consequences for models without lagged-dependent variables

Autocorrelation is a violation of Assumption **A2** from Section 2.10 – that the error terms are independent and identically distributed. This would mean that the OLS-estimated standard error would be biased, which implies that the hypothesis tests would be unreliable. This means that the OLS estimator would no longer produce the minimum-variance estimator of the coefficient estimate. The logic for why these problems occur, as with clustered standard errors (Section 6.6.3), is that having correlated observations means that there are fewer independent observations that create variation for more precise estimates. Thus, the effective sample size is lower, and the estimates should be less precise.

Consequences for models with lagged-dependent variables

When a model contains a lagged-dependent variable as an explanatory variable, then autocorrelation could also (in addition to biasing standard errors) cause *biased coefficient estimates*.

Combining the equations for the autocorrelation (10.1) and the model to address problems with distributed-lags (10.5),

$$\varepsilon_t = \rho\varepsilon_{t-1} + \eta_t \tag{10.1}$$

$$Y_t = \alpha + \beta Y_{t-1} + \delta_0 X_t + \varepsilon_t \tag{10.5}$$

we would have:

$$Y_t = \alpha + \beta Y_{t-1} + \delta_0 X_t + \rho\varepsilon_{t-1} + \eta_t \tag{10.8}$$

Because the lagged error and lagged-dependent variable (ε_{t-1} and Y_{t-1}) are positively correlated with each other, the current error and lagged-dependent variable (ε_t and Y_{t-1}) are correlated with each other in equation (10.5). This causes a violation of Assumption **A5**, and it comes in the form of omitted-variables bias. The likely outcome of this would be that the coefficient estimate $\hat{\beta}$, would be overstated (positively biased if $\rho > 0$ and $\beta > 0$). This would then bias the coefficient estimate on X_t, $\hat{\delta}_0$.

Let's consider what's occurring operationally. If we were to estimate how opioid prices affect opioid overdoses, there could be positively correlated errors (e.g., due to epidemics) that would lead to an overstated estimated effect of the prior periods' opioid overdoses on that for the current period. This leaves less variation in the number of opioid overdoses (Y_t) for the current price (X_t) to explain, leading to a downward-in-magnitude bias in $\hat{\delta}_0$. This bias occurs only if a lagged-dependent variable is used as an explanatory variable and there is autocorrelation.

Tests for autocorrelation

In models without a lagged-dependent variable, the test for autocorrelation has historically been the **Durbin–Watson test**. This can be used if the following conditions hold:

- The regression model includes an intercept term;
- The error terms have a first-order structure ($\varepsilon_t = \rho\varepsilon_{t-1} + \eta_t$);
- (As stated above) there are no lagged-dependent variables;
- The explanatory variables are purely exogenous.

The test statistic is:

$$d = \frac{\sum_{t=2}^{T}\left(\hat{\varepsilon}_t - \hat{\varepsilon}_{t-1}\right)^2}{\sum_{t=1}^{T}\hat{\varepsilon}_t^{\,2}} \tag{10.9}$$

This test would produce:

- A value of 0 if there were perfectly positive autocorrelation, as the numerator would equal 0;
- A value of 2 if there were no autocorrelation (this can be seen if the quantity in the numerator were expanded);
- A value of 4 if there were perfectly negative autocorrelation, as the numerator would equal $\sum\left(2\hat{\varepsilon}_t\right)^2$.
- The critical values for the test statistic are a lower value (d_L, less than 2) and an upper value (d_H, greater than 2). One would conclude that there were autocorrelation if the test statistic, d, were less than d_L (indicating positive autocorrelation) or greater than d_H (indicating negative autocorrelation). The critical values are available at various websites.[2] But, statistical packages will conduct the test and determine its significance for you.

The Durbin–Watson test is likely biased by the inclusion of lagged-dependent variables. In particular, there is a bias towards a test statistic of 2, which would indicate no autocorrelation. In addition, the Durbin–Watson test cannot test for autocorrelation beyond a one-period lag. In such cases (with lagged-dependent variables or autocorrelation beyond a one-period lag), the best test is the **Breusch–Godfrey test** (also known as the Lagrange Multiplier Serial Correlation test).

Step 1 of this test is, from equation (10.5), to estimate the residuals as:

$$\hat{\varepsilon}_t = Y_t - \left(\hat{\alpha} + \hat{\beta}Y_{t-1} + \hat{\delta}_0 X_t\right) \tag{10.10}$$

Step 2 is to regress the residuals on the same set of explanatory variables plus the lagged residual:

$$\hat{\varepsilon}_t = b_0 + b_1 Y_{t-1} + b_2 X_t + b_3 \hat{\varepsilon}_{t-1} + \eta_t \tag{10.11}$$

Step 3 is to calculate the test statistic of multiplying the sample size (n) by the R^2 for equation (10.11), which effectively tests whether $b_3 = 0$:

$$nR^2 \sim \chi^2(1).$$

The null hypothesis is that $\hat{\rho} = 0$ (from equation (10.8) above), meaning the error terms are not serially correlated. This chi-squared test has one degree of freedom because only one lagged residual is being tested. But, if one were to test for correlation with p lagged error terms, then there would be p degrees of freedom for the chi-squared test. Furthermore, the test can be conducted with other forms (e.g., with multiple lags of Y or X).

From Model (5) in Table 10.3, the Breusch-Godfrey test produces a $\chi^2(1)$ statistic of 0.730, which gives a p-value of 0.393. And, a Breusch-Godfrey test for two lags of autocorrelation produces a test statistic of 1.159 (p = 0.560). Likewise, the Granger Causality model in Table 10.4 produces a $\chi^2(1)$ statistic of 0.859 (p = 0.354). Both show no evidence for autocorrelation.

Some would argue that the Breusch-Godfrey test should always be used rather than the Durbin-Watson test, given the restrictions and assumptions on the Durbin-Watson test. I would agree with this.

Can you correct for autocorrelation in models without lagged-dependent variables?

With the problem being biased standard errors in models without lagged-dependent variables, there are two potential methods to address the bias in the standard errors. First, there is what is called a Generalized Least Squares method, which typically requires a complicated two-step, iterative model, with the Cochrane-Orcutt and Prais-Winsten methods being perhaps the most commonly used approach (Cochrane and Orcutt 1949; Prais and Winsten 1954) – the latter is just an extension to save the very first observation, but that most likely does not matter in relatively large samples. In my view, for purposes other than forecasting, this is not worth the effort, in part because it produces a different set of estimates from what OLS produces. And so, I will leave this for Section 10.8 below, on forecasting, for which the method would likely generate more accurate forecasts.

A simpler (albeit imperfect) solution, when forecasting is not the goal, is to use **Newey-West standard errors** (Newey and West 1987) Again, it's a complicated calculation (behind the scenes), but the concept for calculating the Newey-West standard errors is similar in nature to the correction for heteroskedastic standard errors. The Newey-West standard errors are still biased, but they are typically more accurate than OLS standard errors in the presence of autocorrelation. The typical correction is that they would be larger than OLS standard errors, resulting in a lower likelihood of achieving statistical significance. Further caution should be used for formal hypothesis tests, given the remaining bias in these standard errors.

Model (2) from Table 10.4 above applies the Newey-West standard errors to the Granger Causality model. The standard error on the coefficient estimate on the lagged approval rating is now higher, producing a wider confidence interval.

Can you correct for bias in coefficient estimates from autocorrelation in models with lagged-dependent variables?

Are bears Catholic?

In most cases, there is no correction for the bias in coefficient estimates from autocorrelation in models with lagged-dependent variables. There is an approach using Generalized Least Squares, as just described a few paragraphs up. But, this approach requires large samples and adjustments to the standard errors; furthermore, there are problems under various circumstances (Betancourt and Kelejian 1981). Another approach is to use the instrumental-variables method (Section 8.7). Every so often, someone comes up with an innovative instrumental variable that affects the lagged-dependent variable, Y_t, but is uncorrelated with ε_t. But, this happens not much more frequently than bears being Catholic.

10.6 Stationarity

Perhaps one of the most important characteristics for a time-series variable to have is **stationarity**. A stationary time-series variable, X_t, has:

- A constant mean over time;
- A constant variance over time;
- A correlation coefficient between X_t and one of its lagged values, X_{t-j}, that depends solely on the length of the lag (and no other variable).

If any of these do not hold, then the time-series variable would be nonstationary. Nonstationarity can cause problems for time-series models, typically leading to biased estimates of the relationship between variables. This is often called a **spurious regression** because the key explanatory variable and the outcome are related at least in part because they both are changing over time.

Examples based on autoregressive models

Let's consider an autoregressive model (without an intercept term):

$$Y_t = \beta Y_{t-1} + \varepsilon_t \tag{10.12}$$

with $\varepsilon_t \sim N(0, \sigma^2)$. And, let's consider three cases of values of the actual values of β:

- $|\beta| < 1$: This means that $E(Y_t)$ will approach zero in the long run. Thus, while the mean value could be larger in magnitude as it takes the time to approach zero, the eventual mean should be stable around zero, with a constant variance. So, such a time-series variable would be stationary.
- $|\beta| > 1$: The value of Y_t, in this case, would grow in magnitude over time. It is possible that a value of $\beta < -1$ could cause a mean to be steady around zero, but the variance would increase over time. Thus, this time-series variable would not be stationary.
- $|\beta| = 1$: This is a case called **unit root** or **random walk** ($Y_t = Y_{t-1} + \varepsilon_t$). This is also a case in which the time-series variable would not be stationary. One reason for this is that a random drift away from a temporary mean could persist.

What these examples demonstrate is that a time-series variable that is unit root or a value of $|\beta|$ that is greater than one will be nonstationary. Thus, time-series regressions using time-series variables with a unit root (or worse) would be subject to spurious regression. And so, a test is often needed to ensure that a time-series variable is indeed stationary.

Spurious regression is not the only problem that results from unit roots. In an AR(1) model for a unit-root variable, in which the coefficient (β) should be one, there is a bias on $\hat{\beta}$, as $E(\beta) = 1 - 5.3 / T$, where T is the number of observations in the time series. This would affect forecasting if there was indeed a unit-root autoregression. Furthermore, the distribution for the t-statistics for the coefficient estimates would be non-normal, meaning that the t-tests and p-values would be incorrect.

Test for nonstationarity

An initial check for nonstationarity could come from a visual inspection of the variable over time. If it looks like the mean is changing or not converging, or if the variance of the variable appears to change over time, then there is likely nonstationarity.

The most common formal approach to testing for nonstationarity is the **Dickey–Fuller test** (Dickey and Fuller 1979). This is a test to determine whether there is sufficient evidence to determine that $|\beta| < 1$ in equation (10.12), which would indicate that the time-series variable is stationary. From equation (10.12), Y_{t-1} is subtracted from both sides of the equation, which would give:

$$Y_t - Y_{t-1} = (\beta - 1)Y_{t-1} + \varepsilon_t \tag{10.13}$$

or

$$\Delta Y_t = \gamma Y_{t-1} + \varepsilon_t \tag{10.14}$$

where $\gamma = \beta - 1$.

Thus, the hypothesis test becomes:

$H_0: \gamma = 0$ (nonstationarity);
$H_1: \gamma < 0$ (stationarity).

Note that the default (null hypothesis) is nonstationarity, so the test is whether we can conclude that there is stationarity. This Dickey-Fuller test is based on the assumption that equation (10.12) is the correct model for Y_t. However, the model could also include a constant term or a trend.

With a constant, the model would be:

$$\Delta Y_t = \alpha + \gamma Y_{t-1} + \varepsilon_t \tag{10.15}$$

And, with a constant and a trend, the model would be:

$$\Delta Y_t = \alpha + \gamma Y_{t-1} + \delta \times t + \varepsilon_t \tag{10.16}$$

where the variable t is a trend, taking on the values, sequentially, of 1, 2, 3, . . . T. Including a trend would capture natural "trends" over time in a variable. For example, we know that stock prices generally go up over time, and the coefficient estimate on the trend would capture that.

In addition, an **augmented Dickey–Fuller test** can be estimated for higher-order autoregressive models (i.e., with more than one lag). The model testing for stationarity based on an AR(p) model would be:

$$\Delta Y_t = \alpha + \gamma Y_{t-1} + \lambda_1 \Delta Y_{t-1} + \lambda_2 \Delta Y_{t-2} + \ldots \lambda_p \Delta Y_{t-p} + \varepsilon_t \tag{10.17}$$

Regardless of the model, the hypothesis test would be the same, as it would test whether the coefficient estimate on the lagged variable is less than zero – that is, $\gamma < 0$. The critical values do not follow from the standard Student t-distribution table. However, most statistical packages will conduct the test and determine the level of significance and the p-value.

Tests for stationarity tend not to be very reliable, as they depend on the assumption of constant variance. Nevertheless, this may be the best test available. And so, not being able to conclude stationarity of a time-series variable suggests that measures should be taken to address the nonstationarity.

Cointegration

As described above, one of the most harmful products of nonstationarity is spurious regression, in which two nonstationary time-series variables may have their estimated association with each other biased. The most likely cause of this is that both variables have changing means over time.

However, just because two time-series variables (a dependent variable and X variable) are nonstationary does not necessarily mean that it causes a spurious regression. If the two variables have "matching" degrees of nonstationarity in that the residual from the regression is stationary, then the two variables are said to be **cointegrated**. And, this would mean that the model is not a spurious regression.

Any type of time-series model with two variables that we have seen so far could be tested for cointegration. From a model with a trend of:

$$Y_t = \beta_0 + \beta_1 X_t + \beta_2 t + \varepsilon_t \tag{10.18}$$

the test would involve first calculating the residual:

$$\hat{\varepsilon}_t = Y_t - \beta_0 - \beta_1 X_t - \beta_2 t \tag{10.19}$$

Next, a Dickey-Fuller test would be conducted on the residuals. In this case, while the standard Students-t distribution does not exactly apply, the adjusted critical values are not that different from the actual Students-t distribution.

If the residuals were found to be stationary, then that is evidence supporting the notion that X_t and Y_t are cointegrated. And, this means that the original model, (10.18), could be used. On the other hand, if there were no evidence for stationarity, then we have to assume there is nonstationarity and another approach is needed.

How to address nonstationarity

In the case in which nonstationarity between two variables cannot be concluded from a Dickey-Fuller test on each variable or from a Dickey-Fuller test on cointegration, then a simple correction for this problem may be to just take the first-difference of the model. Thus, the model, from (10.18), would be:

$$Y_t - Y_{t-1} = \left(\beta_0 + \beta_1 X_t + \beta_2 t_t + \varepsilon_t\right) - \left(\beta_0 + \beta_1 X_{t-1} + \beta_2 t_{t-1} + \varepsilon_{t-1}\right) \tag{10.20a}$$

or

$$\Delta Y_t = \beta_1 \Delta X_t + \beta_2 + \varepsilon_t - \varepsilon_{t-1} \tag{10.20b}$$

This does not always fix the problem. If there is seasonality, then equation (10.20b) would be problematic because it confounds the relationship between lagged and current values of a time-series variable, and so a seasonal term would be needed in conjunction with any differencing. Also, it is possible that important information on the levels of X_t or Y_t would be lost with this approach. However, this is certainly not always the case, and it may be the only approach to address a spurious regression in the presence of nonstationarity.

Example with the price of oil and the stock market

Let's explore the relationship between the price of oil and the stock market. We will use as data:

- Price of oil: based on crude oil, West Texas Intermediate;[3]
- Stock market: S&P 500 index.

And, we will examine this relationship for two different 5-year periods: 1990–94 and 2010–14. Let's first do a visual examination of the data. Figures 10.7a and 10.7b show the trends in these two variables for the two time periods, respectively.

From the figures, it looks like there could be trends in the data, some that are subtle. And, these trends could make it seem like the two variables were related, even if they were not. Table 10.5 shows the results of the Dickey-Fuller tests. Only in one of the four cases (oil price in the first period) is there evidence of nonstationarity for the variable. This suggests that a regression using these two variables could result in biased estimates that largely would reflect how the trends of the variables move with each other, particularly for the later period.

In Table 10.6, for both time periods, I estimate the model as both a regular dynamic model and a model transformed to use changes in the variables to address the nonstationarity. There are a few

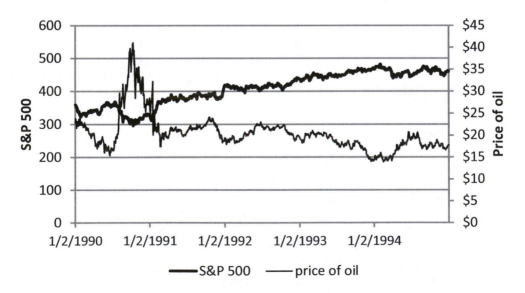

Figure 10.7a Daily prices for the S&P 500 and oil, 1990–94

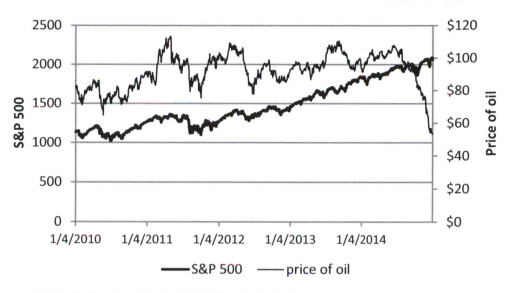

Figure 10.7b Daily prices for the S&P 500 and oil, 2010–14

Table 10.5 Dickey–Fuller tests for nonstationarity

	1990–94 (n = 1265)	2010–14 (n = 1257)
S&P 500	−1.020 (p = 0.746)	−0.005 (p = 0.958)
Price of oil	−4.439 (p = 0.003)	−1.327 (p = 0.617)

Table 10.6 The relationship between oil prices and the S&P 500 index

	1990–94		2010–14	
	(1)	(2)	(3)	(4)
	S&P 500	Δ(S&P 500)	S&P 500	Δ(S&P 500)
1-day-lagged S&P 500	0.994***		0.999***	
	(0.002)		(0.002)	
Current oil price	−0.076**		0.063	
	(0.033)		(0.042)	
Δ(oil price)		−0.477***		3.732***
		(0.178)		(0.354)
Constant	4.212***	0.078	−3.932	0.820**
	(1.535)	(0.081)	(3.766)	(0.347)
Observations	1,265	1,265	1,257	1,257
R–squared	0.997	0.030	0.998	0.175

Note: Robust standard errors in parentheses. Changes are one-day changes.

*** $p < 0.01$, ** $p < 0.05$, * $p < 0.1$.

interesting results here. First, the estimated effects of oil in the differenced models – Models (2) and (4) – are significantly different from their non-differenced corresponding estimates in Models (1) and (3). This is likely a result of the spurious (biased) regression resulting from the nonstationarity. The trends in the variables are dominating the actual effects of the variables. Second, practically speaking, oil-price increases appear to negatively affect the stock market in 1990–94, but positively affect the stock market in 2010–14. This could be due to the combination of reduced reliance on oil in the U.S. economy (partly from the shift away from manufacturing) and the increased production of oil products in the U.S. economy.

10.7 Vector Autoregression

The **Vector Autoregression (VAR) model** involves multiple time-series regressions that include the lagged values of each variable in the model. The individual equations within a VAR are estimated by OLS, although with an extra feature. The models allow the error terms to be correlated between each other. (This is similar to a Seemingly Unrelated Regression [SUR] model.) A model with two variables, X_t and Y_t, and p lags would be characterized as a VAR(p) model with the following two equations:

$$Y_t = \alpha_0 + \alpha_1 Y_{t-1} + \alpha_2 Y_{t-2} + \ \ldots \ + \alpha_p Y_{t-p} + \beta_1 X_{t-1} + \beta_2 X_{t-2} + \ \ldots \ + \beta_p X_{t-p} + u_t \qquad (10.21)$$

$$X_t = \delta_0 + \delta_1 X_{t-1} + \delta_2 X_{t-2} + \ \ldots \ + \delta_p X_{t-p} + \lambda_1 Y_{t-1} + \lambda_2 Y_{t-2} + \ \ldots \ + \lambda_p Y_{t-p} + v_t \qquad (10.22)$$

The VAR model can have more than two variables. Having five variables would mean five equations with p lags for each variable in each model. The optimal number of lags could be determined by BIC, AIC, or AICc, as described above in Section 10.3.

Alternatively, one could conduct an F-test for the joint significance of the lagged variables in the individual equations within a VAR. For example, we may want to test whether the last lag is jointly significant. And so, the null hypothesis would be:

$$H_0 : \alpha_p = 0, \beta_p = 0, \delta_p = 0, \lambda_p = 0.$$

VARs can be used for forecasting, as well as attempting to estimate causal relationships. In fact, the VAR is just an extended form of a Granger Causality model (from Section 10.4). Still, one must be cautious of all of the BIG QUESTIONS from Chapter 6, as well as any problems with nonstationarity, before concluding that relationships are causal.

I perform a VAR model, with President Trump's weekly approval ratings and tweets. Preliminary Dickey-Fuller tests for stationarity yielded tests that indicated stationarity, with p-values of 0.0000 (for **tweets**) and 0.0037 (for **approval**). This suggests that there is no need to correct for stationarity.

Model (1) is the same as the Granger Causality test in Model (2) of Table 10.4 in determining the number of tweets, for which the coefficient estimate on the 1-week-lagged approval rating was insignificant. But, it looks like I was interested in the wrong thing in Table 10.4. I should have explored whether and how tweets might affect the approval rating. And, sure enough, it looks like there is a significant negative relationship between the lagged number of tweets and President Trump's approval rating, with a 95% confidence interval of [−0.045, −0.005]. Perhaps there is a common factor

Table 10.7 Vector Autoregression (VAR) for Trump tweets and approval

	(1)	(2)
VARIABLES	*Number of tweets*	*Approval rating*
1-week-lagged tweets	0.370***	−0.025**
	(0.117)	(0.010)
		[−0.045, −0.005]
1-week-lagged approval rating	−0.981	0.619***
	(0.954)	(0.084)
	[−2.852, 0.889]	
Constant	67.80*	15.91***
	(39.27)	(3.44)
Observations	68	68
R–squared	0.183	0.583

Note: Robust standard errors are in parentheses. 95% confidence intervals are in brackets.

*** $p < 0.01$, ** $p < 0.05$, * $p < 0.1$.

determining the prior week's tweets and the current week's approval rating. But, this might be indicative of a negative effect of the tweets on President Trump's approval rating. See Table 10.7.

10.8 Forecasting with time series

Much of the prior examples in this chapter dealt at least implicitly with the objectives of estimating causal effects or determining predictors. As described in the introduction of this chapter, a common use of time-series models is to forecast an outcome. I discussed forecasting in Section 7.1, and how the optimal strategy was pretty much to throw in all variables you could, other than those that may result in reverse causality. The goal in Section 7.1 was more to predict values for a subject based on a set of known X values. For example, an insurance company may want to predict the likelihood that a potential customer would get in a car accident based on data on other people. Forecasting with time-series models involves trying to forecast/predict future values for a time-series variable based on the subject's prior values. This section discusses some of the issues involved with forecasting time-series variables.

All of the models used in this chapter could be used for forecasting. But, the presence of non-stationarity or autocorrelation could cause problems. Stationarity might be fixable with a differenced model. With autocorrelation, the Generalized Least Squares method (the Cochrane-Orcutt or Prais–Winsten method) would likely improve the forecast.

Generalized Least Squares correction for autocorrelation

Recall that the problem with autocorrelation is that part of the error term would include a component of the error terms from prior observations. This would mean that the T observations in a time-series model are not independent, and the effective sample size is lower, as there are not T independent observations. While the correction can be done with practically any time-series model, let's take equation (10.18) and say we want to forecast the value of Y_{T+1}. We can combine equation (10.18) with the autocorrelation equation (10.1):

$$Y_t = \beta_0 + \beta_1 X_t + \beta_2 t_t + \varepsilon_t \tag{10.18}$$

$$\varepsilon_t = \rho\varepsilon_{t-1} + \eta_t \tag{10.1}$$

to get:

$$Y_t = \beta_0 + \beta_1 X_t + \beta_2 t_t + \rho\varepsilon_{t-1} + \eta_t \tag{10.23}$$

Addressing autocorrelation would involve removing ε_{t-1} from equation (10.23), by first lagging equation (10.18) and multiplying by ρ:

$$\rho Y_{t-1} = \rho\beta_0 + \rho\beta_1 X_{t-1} + \rho\beta_2 t_{t-1} + \rho\varepsilon_{t-1} \tag{10.24}$$

and subtracting that from equation (10.23):

$$Y_t - \rho Y_{t-1} = \beta_0(1 - \rho) + \beta_1(X_t - \rho X_{t-1}) + \beta_2 t_t - \rho\beta_2 t_{t-1} + \eta_t \tag{10.25}$$

Now, the model is free of any autocorrelation. Operationally, this is estimated by Generalized Least Squares. The method involves iteratively solving for $\hat{\rho}$ and the $\hat{\beta}$'s, all through OLS, until the estimate $\hat{\rho}$ converges to a steady value. From this, transformations can be made using equation (10.25) to generate forecasts of Y_{T+1}.

This method is easily done for you in Stata and in R – see the documents with code for the Prais–Winsten method on the book's website. As mentioned above, this method should produce more accurate forecasts.

The ARIMA model for forecasting

Perhaps the "it" thing now in forecasting is the **autoregressive-integrated-moving-average (ARIMA)** model or the **autoregressive-moving-average (ARMA)** model, which excludes any independent (X) variables. From a basic model with just an intercept and error term:

$$Y_t = \alpha_0 + \varepsilon_t \tag{10.26}$$

the ARMA model is:

$$Y_t = \alpha_0 + \underbrace{\lambda_1 Y_{t-1} + \lambda_2 Y_{t-2} + \ldots + \lambda_p Y_{t-p}}_{\text{autoregressive part}} + \underbrace{\delta_1\varepsilon_{t-1} + \delta_2\varepsilon_{t-2} + \ldots + \delta_p\varepsilon_{t-p}}_{\text{moving-average part}} + \varepsilon_t \tag{10.27}$$

The autoregressive part is that Y_t depends on its prior values. The moving-average part is that Y_t depends on past random errors.

If Y_t is nonstationary, then we need the ARIMA model, which uses ΔY_t. Basically, the differencing is the "integrated" part of ARIMA.

With the 2010–14 data on the S&P 500 stock-market index, I used an ARIMA model, with one lag, two lags and three lags. I present these in Table 10.8. The arguments for an ARIMA(a,b,c) model are that *a* is the number of lags for the autoregressive part of the model, *b* is the number of times the variable was differenced to address stationarity (typically just one), and *c* is the number of lags for the moving-average part of the model. These models will be used next for determining how accurate the forecast is.

Determining the accuracy of the forecast

Testing how accurate a forecast is requires some out-of-sample observations, which was mentioned in Section 7.1. Such observations could come from:

- Observations that have yet to be realized (that you are forecasting), or
- Observations at the end that you leave out of the sample.

Table 10.8 ARIMA models for daily S&P 500, 2010–14

	Dependent variable = daily S&P 500 index		
	ARIMA(1,1,1)	ARIMA(2,1,2)	ARIMA(3,1,3)
S&P 500 variables (Y_t)			
1-day-lagged	−0.847***	0.101	0.403
	(0.097)	(0.136)	(0.751)
2-day-lagged		0.820***	0.731***
		(0.106)	(0.203)
3-day-lagged			−0.229
			(0.572)
Residuals ($\hat{\varepsilon}$)			
1-day-lagged	0.797***	−0.167	−0.450
	(0.107)	(0.132)	(0.757)
2-day-lagged		−0.792***	−0.678***
		(0.104)	(0.253)
3-day-lagged			0.186
			(0.548)
Constant	0.737**	0.746***	0.744***
	(0.370)	(0.205)	(0.231)
Standard error of the residual	13.47***	13.44***	13.43***
	(0.393)	(0.400)	(0.398)
Observations	1,257	1,257	1,257

Note: Standard errors in parentheses.

*** $p < 0.01$, ** $p < 0.05$, * $p < 0.1$.

For the latter, there is a trade-off: the more observations you leave out for testing the forecast accuracy, the stronger will be the test but the weaker will be the model (as it would have fewer observations).

With the above ARIMA(1, 1, 1) model, I used the first five trading days in 2015 as the out-of-sample prediction. Sometimes, the explanatory variables (in this case, the lagged dependent variables and residuals) would need to be forecasted as well. But in other cases, as I do here, the explanatory variables are available. From the forecasts, I calculate two common measures of forecast accuracy/error:

- Mean absolute percent error (MAPE);
- Root Mean Square Error (RMSE), which is the square root of the mean square error, from equation (2.16).

The first one, MAPE, is exactly what it sounds like. Table 10.9 shows the *absolute forecast error* for each of the first five observations of 2015, based on the ARIMA(1,1,1) model. From these five observations, the MAPE is the average of the absolute forecast error, which is 1.2%. The RMSE is then the square root of the average squared forecast error, which comes to 27.2.

Forecast intervals

At home games for the New York Mets, at Citi Field, there is a sushi bar near the right-field corner. The Mets probably want a good forecast of how much sushi to stock for a given game. But, the point forecast may not be enough information. If they order the point forecast for every game, they would not have enough sushi about 50% of all games, causing them to miss out on selling something that probably has a nice profit margin. And, they would have ordered too much on about 50% of the games, which means they would likely have to give the sushi away to staff, as sushi probably will not stay fresh for the next game.

In this situation, the Mets would probably want a confidence interval for the forecast, or a **forecast interval**. The forecast interval for the next value from a forecast model (with T observations) of an outcome, Y_{T+1}, is:

$$Y_{T+1} \pm s_F \times t_c \qquad (10.28)$$

where s_F is the standard error of the forecast and t_c is the critical t value for the given confidence interval.

Table 10.9 Forecasts and statistics for first 5 trading days of 2015 for the ARIMA(1,1,1) model

	S&P 500	Predicted value	Residual	Absolute forecast error
1/2/2015	2058.2	2060.6	−2.4	0.1%
1/5/2015	2020.6	2058.2	−37.6	1.9%
1/6/2015	2002.6	2023.8	−21.2	1.1%
1/7/2015	2025.9	2002.3	23.6	1.2%
1/8/2015	2062.1	2026.3	35.8	1.7%

The formula for s_F, in the case of there being one explanatory variable, X_t, is:

$$s_F = \sqrt{1 + \frac{1}{T} + \frac{\left(\hat{X}_{T+1} - \bar{X}\right)}{\sum_{t=1}^{T}\left(X_t - \bar{X}\right)^2}} \qquad (10.29)$$

This is somewhat complicated, and you probably will not need to calculate this, as your statistical program will do so. But, what's important is that the standard error of the forecast will be lower if:

- There are more observations in the forecast model (T);
- The value of X_{T+1} is closer to the mean value of X.

Let's suppose that:

- Y_t = the number of orders for sushi (assuming they count the people who ask for sushi after they run out);
- X_t = the internet average price of a bleacher (standardized) seat.

The average price of a bleacher seat may be a good composite indicator of the expected attendance and the willingness among the audience to pay for the expensive sushi. The forecast interval would be narrower with more observations in the model and the closer is the value of X_t to its mean (or the internet average price for the game to the sample average price for a bleacher seat).

The formula for the standard error of the forecast would obviously be more complicated with more variables added. But, the same concepts would apply in that the forecast would be more accurate (with a narrower forecast interval) with a larger model and with X values (or lagged-dependent variables) closer to their mean values.

10.9 Chapter summary

This chapter introduced time-series models and noted some of the more common problems, most notably autocorrelation and nonstationarity. Keep in mind that, if the objective of the regression is causality (whether it be a contemporaneous model, a Granger Causality model, or a Vector Autoregression), all of the BIG QUESTIONS from Chapter 6 need to be checked before concluding causality. Corrections for nonstationarity (with using changes in the variables rather than actual values) may be one method of avoiding any biases associated with omitted-variables bias.

Exercises

1. Use the data set **ford_amazon_2017**, which has the 2017 daily change in stock prices (adjusted for splits and dividends) for Ford and Amazon.
   a. Estimate an AR(2) model for both Ford and Amazon stock-price changes, using robust standard errors. Conduct individual and joint tests of significance of the lagged stock-price changes at the 5% significance level.
   b. Estimate an autoregressive-distributed-lag model by regressing the change in Ford's stock price on the lagged change in Ford's and Amazon's stock price, using robust standard errors. What can you conclude?

For Questions #2 through 6, use the data set **wine_beer**, which indicates the per-capita wine and beer consumption in the U.S. from 1934 to 2016.

2. Estimate AR(1) to AR(4) models for beer consumption per capita, using robust standard errors. Use BIC, AIC, and AICc to decide which is the best model.
3. Test beer and wine consumption for stationarity using the Dickey-Fuller test, based on one lag. What can you conclude?
4. Estimate a Granger Causality model for how wine consumption affects beer consumption. Adjust the model as you see fit based on the results of the stationarity tests from Question #3. What does the model tell you?
5. From the model in Question #4, test for autocorrelation using the Breusch-Godfrey test. What does the test tell you?
6. Estimate a VAR model, with two lags, for wine and beer consumption. Adjust the model as you see fit based on the results of the stationarity tests from Question #3. What does the model tell you?

Notes

1 The source for these data is: https://pubs.niaaa.nih.gov/publications/surveillance110/tab1_16.htm
2 One website with a table of the critical values is: https://www3.nd.edu/~wevans1/econ30331/Durbin_Watson_tables.pdf, accessed July 10, 2018.
3 This oil-price data comes from https://fred.stlouisfed.org/series/DCOILWTICO

References

Betancourt, R., & Kelejian, H. (1981). Lagged endogenous variables and the Cochrane-Orcutt procedure. *Econometrica*, 49(4), 1073–1078.

Cochrane, D., & Orcutt, G. H. (1949). Application of least squares regression to relationships containing auto-correlated error terms. *Journal of the American Statistical Association*, 44(245), 32–61.

Dickey, D. A., & Fuller, W. A. (1979). Distribution of the estimators for autoregressive time series with a unit root. *Journal of the American Statistical Association*, 74(366a), 427–431.

Newey, W. K., & West, K. D. (1987). A simple, positive semi-definite, heteroskedasticity and autocorrelation consistent covariance matrix. *Econometrica*, 55(3), 703–708.

Prais, S. J., & Winsten, C. B. (1954). *Trend estimators and serial correlation* (Vol. 383, pp. 1–26). Chicago: Cowles Commission discussion paper.

11 Some really interesting research

11.1 Can discrimination be a self-fulfilling prophecy?
11.2 Does Medicaid participation improve health outcomes?
11.3 Estimating peer effects for academic outcomes
11.4 How much does a GED improve labor-market outcomes?

In this chapter, I review a few relatively recent articles that I found to be interesting and soundly conducted and that had multiple lessons using the concepts from this book. I must relate my experience in writing this chapter. I browsed through some of the top journals in economics, business, and the social sciences in order to find articles to discuss for this chapter, and there were few articles that had insignificant estimates on the key explanatory variables. This is something to note for the next chapter.

11.1 Can discrimination be a self-fulfilling prophecy?

The first article we will discuss is: "Discrimination as a Self-Fulfilling Prophecy: Evidence from French Grocery Stores," by Glover et al. (2017). The article examines whether minority cashiers at a grocery-store chain in France are less productive and more likely to be absent when they have a work shift under a manager with greater bias against minorities. I chose this article because it applies several important concepts from this book: interacted variables, fixed effects, difference-in-difference models, linear probability models, several potential BIG QUESTION violations, and a convincing method to address the primary BIG QUESTION violations. I had briefly described this study back in Box 3.1. Here, I give a much fuller description, now that we have more skills to analyze the study.

Study questions

If you want to test your knowledge, you can read the article and consider these study questions before reading the description of the study I give below:

1. Why might there be reverse causality in this study?
2. What is the explanation the authors give for why there may not be reverse causality?

3. Why could there be omitted-variables bias in a basic model on this topic (i.e., not with the methods this article uses)?
4. How do the authors address the main source of omitted-variables bias?
5. Why is there likely bias from measurement error for the key interacted explanatory variable? What is the likely implication for the results from any bias from measurement error?
6. With the combination of fixed effects for the worker, what variation is identifying the effect of minorities working for more-biased managers?

Background

The entry-level cashiers at this grocery-store chain are new workers hired under a government-subsidized six-month contract. The authors chose these workers because, unlike the established workers, the new ones do not have any choice on their schedule. A computer program determines their schedule. The workers know their shift times and which manager will be on duty during their shifts several weeks in advance. These are large stores (30 to 80 registers in each store), as they typically have 100 to 250 cashiers for a given store, with around 5 different managers for the cashiers.

Sample

Whereas data was obtained on 218 workers, only 204 are part of the sample because some had to be excluded due to there not being data on the bias of the manager for their shifts. For those 204 workers, there are a total of 4371 shifts as the primary sample. Of the 204 workers, 28% are classified as minorities. For a reason that you will see soon, the sample includes non-minorities as a control group for the difference-in-difference approach.

Outcomes

The government program is meant to give a trial work period to these young (often inexperienced) workers. The stores end up offering employment contracts to 30–40% of them. To be able to make informed decisions, the chain keeps excellent records and has invested in creating some performance metrics. The productivity outcomes for the analysis are:

- Whether the worker was absent on a given day;
- Minutes worked in excess of schedule;
- Articles scanned per minute;
- Time between customers.

Key explanatory variables

The key explanatory variable is an interaction of two variables, both of which are likely measured with error:

- *Minority worker.* The race/ethnicity of workers is not allowed to be collected in France, but names are. The authors had experts in France give their best guess to the minority status of each worker based on their name. Obviously, the experts may have made mistakes.

- *Manager bias (towards minorities):* This is based on an Implicit Association Test (IAT) (Greenwald et al. 1998; Lane et al. 2007). The test is standardized so one unit is a standard deviation and a positive (negative) value indicates bias against (for) minorities. The average score among the managers was 1.35, meaning that the managers were, on average, 1.35 standard deviations away from neutrality or unbiasedness with regards to race. As with any test, there could be error in this variable. The IAT was taken, on average, 17 months after the data on worker shifts were collected.

Potential sources of bias (violations of the BIG QUESTIONS)

Let's consider what potential biases could occur in a naïve model for worker performance:

$$Y_i = \beta_0 + \beta_1 \left(minority_i \times bias_i \right) + \varepsilon_i \tag{11.1}$$

where Y is the worker-productivity measure. So, β_1 indicates the interacted effect of a minority worker and a manager's level of bias. The following are the potential sources of bias or other problems.

- *Reverse causality.* This could occur if poor performance of the worker affected the manager's bias. The authors note that this is unlikely for a few reasons. First, 85% of the managers had worked there for more than 10 years, so any bias would likely not be appreciably affected by a few some-what recent, less productive, minority cashiers. Second, the managers oversee 100 to 250 cashiers at a given time (not per shift), and so one less productive minority cashier should not affect them. Third, the Implicit Association Test (see the study for the description) uses male names, but over 90% of the cashiers are female.
- *Omitted-variables bias.* There are two main sources of omitted-variables bias. First, any manager bias could be correlated with other aspects of the manager that would make any cashier less productive. Second, the workers with the worse (or better) outcomes might be more likely to be assigned to the more-biased managers, just due to randomness. I will explain how these were addressed when discussing the model below.
- *Self-selection bias.* The workers cannot select their schedule, so they cannot choose to work with a manager with low bias. Thus, this is not an issue.
- *Measurement error.* As mentioned above, this could occur due to mis-measurement of the minority status of the worker (which again is done by experts analyzing the name of the cashier) and error in the Implicit Association Test in measuring the extent of any manager bias against minorities. The bias on the coefficient estimate for the interaction of "minority" and "manager-bias" should be in the direction towards zero. If so, then the estimates may understate the relationship between manager bias and worker productivity.
- *Error terms may be correlated (not a big question violation).* A given store may be very busy, and so there would be greater pressure for cashiers to work fast. Thus, the error terms for workers for a given store may be correlated for some of the performance metrics.

Overall, the major concern should be for omitted-variables bias. Now, I'll demonstrate how these problems are corrected for.

The model

Their model is the following:

$$Y_{ist} = \beta_0 + \beta_1 \left(minority_i \times bias_{ist}\right) + \beta_2 \left(bias_{ist}\right) + \delta_i + X_{ist}\beta_3 + \varepsilon_i \qquad (11.2)$$

where:
- Subscripts are for the worker (i), the store (s), and the day (t);
- Y = one of four dependent variables listed above (for worker i on shift s in time period t);
- $minority$ = whether the cashier is believed to be a minority;
- $bias$ = bias measure (based on an "implicit association test") measure for the shift manager for worker i's shift s in time period t;
- $(minority \times bias)$ = interaction of the two variables;
- X = a set of other shift characteristics (which are not terribly important);
- δ_i = worker fixed effects.

This is both a fixed-effects and difference-in-difference model. The primary fixed effects are on the worker, δ_i. Let's think about what this means for the source of variation. Now, minority workers are being compared to their individual selves. That is, for each minority worker, there is an estimate for how the worker's performance changes with having a shift manager with a one-unit (i.e., 1-standard-deviation) increase in bias against minorities. The estimate for β_1 would be the weighted average of each of these individual-worker estimates. This avoids the possibility of omitted-variables bias from better- (or worse-) performing workers just happening to be assigned in the same shift as higher-bias managers.

The inclusion of the *bias* variable alone addresses the other potential source of omitted-variables bias that managers with greater bias (i.e., against minorities) might systematically (across all racial/ethnic groups of cashiers) encourage different worker productivity than managers with less bias.

This effectively makes the problem a difference-in-difference with the following controls:

- Each worker is controlled for with fixed effects (this effectively controls for *minority*).
- The variable *bias* is controlled for.
- The interaction of *minority×bias* is then the key explanatory variable.

The coefficient estimate, $\hat{\beta}_1$, indicates how minority workers respond to higher manager bias against minorities relative to how non-minority workers respond to the same higher bias (also against minorities).

To address the potential for correlated error terms, the authors cluster at the store level. That is, they allow correlation of error terms for all observations from a given store. There is no reason to include store fixed effects because that is probably captured by the worker fixed effects, assuming almost all cashiers only work at one store while in the sample.

Key results

Table 11.1 summarizes the estimated effects of the interaction of *minority* (cashier) and *bias* (from the manager) on four dependent variables, measuring some form of productivity. The first outcome

Table 11.1 Key results from Glover et al. (2017), Tables III and IV

Dependent variable measuring some form of productivity (positively or negatively)	Coefficient estimate on the interaction of minority × bias
Indicator for being absent for the shift	0.0177***
(n = 4371)	(0.0042)
Minutes worked in excess of schedule	−3.327*
(n = 4163)	(1.687)
Articles scanned per minute	−0.233**
(n = 3601)	(0.108)
Inter-customer time (measured in seconds)	1.417**
(n = 3287)	(1.649)

Note: Standard errors are in parentheses. *** $p < 0.01$, ** $p < 0.05$, * $p < 0.10$.

indicates that workers are significantly more likely to be absent from their shift when getting scheduled with a manager with more bias ($p < 0.01$). In addition, minority cashiers scan fewer items and allow slightly more time between customers when working under more-biased managers ($p < 0.05$). Of lower significance is that the minority cashiers work fewer minutes beyond their schedule with more-biased managers ($p < 0.10$). Despite the statistical significance of these estimates, note that the 95% confidence intervals for the interacted effects of *minority* and *bias* are fairly wide and include values that are near zero for three of the outcomes.

What are the mechanisms at play?

The authors conducted a survey of the cashiers, in which they asked about particular managers, which the authors then merged with the productivity data. Their more important findings were that:

- Interestingly, minority cashiers tended to rate the more-biased managers more positively, more enjoyable to work with, and that the cashiers had more confidence working with them, although all of these differences were statistically insignificant. This is evidence against any animus by the more-biased managers leading to lower work performance.
- More-biased managers are less likely to ask minority cashiers to do the unpleasant task of closing their register and doing cleaning duties (at the end of the shift). This is consistent with the theory that more-biased managers interact less with minority cashiers.
- Workers had greater productivity working under managers whom they had more interactions with.

What this suggests, in the end, is that manager–worker interaction is the key ingredient that appears to lead to greater productivity of the workers. This is a lesson many of us could use.

General things I liked about this article

The authors were forthright about potential problems. They gave their honest take of whether it could be a problem in the end. Furthermore, they used a quite straightforward approach with easy interpretations. They did not get unnecessarily complicated. If I would consider how interesting the results were for how much I like the article, then I would add that as another reason to like the article. But, I won't do that, as we should focus on methods and soundness, both of which the authors do extremely well with.

11.2 Does Medicaid participation improve health outcomes?

Medicaid, a joint federal and state program, provides a low-cost form of health insurance to several disadvantaged groups, including those with low income, the disabled, and the elderly. In the last several years, some states have opted to expand Medicaid in an effort to improve health outcomes. But, it was uncertain how much this would actually improve health.

How Medicaid participation affects health outcomes would normally be a difficult topic to examine because it is far from random who applies for Medicaid. The potential problems are the following:

- *Reverse causality*. This could work two opposite ways. It could be the ones who are in need of health care who are more likely to apply for Medicaid. This could contribute to a negative bias on the causal effect of Medicaid participation on health. On the other hand, it may be the more health-conscious people who are interested in getting health insurance are the ones more likely to apply, which would contribute to a negative bias.
- *Omitted-variables bias*. There could be common factors for health and whether someone applies for Medicaid. Perhaps difficulty finding a job makes a person have health problems from stress and also makes the person apply for Medicaid, being in need of health insurance.
- *Self-selection bias*. It would likely be those who think they could benefit most from Medicaid (in terms of health-outcome improvement) who are more likely to apply for Medicaid.

Oregon, thankfully, made it simpler for the researchers by instituting a lottery to determine eligibility in an expansion of its Medicaid program. The state randomly selected roughly 30,000 of 90,000 on the Medicaid waiting list. Those 30,000 were then offered Medicaid if they met the eligibility requirements.

Baicker et al. (2013) designed a study to examine the effects of this Medicaid expansion in Oregon. Their model involved a 2SLS approach, with the lottery as the IV determining Medicaid participation and the predicted Medicaid participation then included in a series of models to determine its effects on various health outcomes. Not everyone who won the Medicaid lottery ended up enrolling in Medicaid, as some became ineligible (e.g., due to income increasing) or may have chosen not to take it. The identification was based on the assumption that the lottery determining eligibility for Medicaid would not affect health other than affecting Medicaid participation. (One of the great features of this study is that the authors outlined their whole methods in a publication before they collected and compiled the final data for their analysis.)

While this study design is likely the best that could be done with available data, it is not perfect. There could be attenuation bias (towards zero) because those not on Medicaid could be:

- People with low income who still receive treatment (perhaps paid for by the state) when needed;
- People who ended up getting health insurance through a job.

The results were:

- No statistically significant effects of Medicaid participation on clinical outcomes (e.g., blood pressure and cholesterol), with the exception of increasing the likelihood of a diabetes diagnosis and using medication for diabetes.
- Significantly reduced risk of screening positive for depression, although the 95% confidence interval was quite wide and bordered near zero: (-16.7 to -1.6 percentage points).
- Significantly greater health-related quality-of-life, although also with a 95% confidence interval close to zero.
- Significantly reduced out-of-pocket expenses, and reduced risk of having medical debt or needing to borrow money to pay medical expenses.

The finding that there was no evidence for most clinical outcomes being affected by Medicaid coverage is quite interesting. However, we need to keep in mind that some of the insignificant estimates may be due to attenuation bias.

Why I liked this article

One nice feature of this article is that, instead of the standard errors, they gave the 95% confidence intervals and p-values. In some sense, these are more valuable than the standard error. Also, given that I had such a difficult time finding studies that had insignificant estimates on key explanatory variables, I liked that many of the key estimates in this article were insignificant (for the clinical outcomes). It is also good that the authors published their methods before conducting the analysis. This held all parties to an implicit contract that the authors had to follow these methods and the journal (*New England Journal of Medicine*) couldn't decide not to publish it afterwards. This is a good practice to follow, to publish your methods online in a working paper before conducting the primary analyses.

11.3 Estimating peer effects for academic outcomes

Teenagers and young adults are an influential lot. They generally want to fit in. And so, teenagers can be highly influenced by their peers in many regards. This could include academic success, as teens can learn study habits from their friends; or, teens could get distracted from studying by friends (who may be less interested in academics) introducing them to other time-consuming or non-enriching ventures.

Examining peer effects for academic outcomes would typically involve a model as follows:

$$Y_i = \beta_0 + X_i\beta_1 + \beta_2\left(Y^P\right)_i + \varepsilon_i \tag{11.3}$$

where:
- Y is some measure of academic success for person i;
- Y^P is the measure of academic success or qualifications for person i's peers or friends;
- X is a set of demographic and contextual factors for person i.

Potential sources of bias

Figuring out the BIG QUESTION violations on this topic is like shooting fish in a barrel, as there are plenty of problems with the standard approach to estimating peer effects.

- *Reverse causality.* There are two types of reverse causality here. The direct type is that the youth's friends may be positively (or negatively) influenced in their academic outcomes as a result of the subject youth's academic success (or lack thereof). So, cases in which the youth's level of academic success affects that of his/her friends would contribute to an upward bias for β_2. In some sense, any reverse causality would be evidence itself for peer effects, but it would upwardly bias any estimated effects of peers. The second type of reverse causality is that a teenager intent on doing well academically may seek out friends who are academically successful. Likewise, someone who has little interest in doing well would not choose friends based on their academic success. Thus, something closely tied with the dependent variable would determine the value of the key explanatory variable. Some call this the "selection effect" in that you select your friends based partly on whether their own outcome is desirable. And, this could be *self-selection bias* in that those who expect greater academic benefits from smart friends are more likely to choose smart friends.
- *Omitted-variables bias.* Just as with reverse causality, there are a few types of omitted-variables bias on this empirical issue. First, a youth and his/her friends may have common factors of academic success. This could include positive factors, such as the prevalence of a good role model among an older sibling for one of the friends or successful parents. And, it could include negative factors, such as being from a neighborhood with a lot of violence and not having much peace to study well. In addition, the friendship may have been initially formed non-randomly. Perhaps the youth had formed these friendships long ago over factors that could contribute to better academic outcomes (e.g., playing computer games) or worse academic outcomes (e.g., interest in substance use). Thus, the level of academic success use for the subject and his/her friends would be positively correlated due to the reasons leading them to become friends in the first place. Again, this would contribute towards a positive bias in the estimated peer effects.
- *Measurement error.* There could be measurement error from the youth misrepresenting how academically successful his/her friends are. Also, it could result from the youth not listing his most academically influential peers. Perhaps the youth would have a few sets of friends – some that he identifies with academically and others he identifies with to activate his fun side. The youth may indicate the latter if he/she is responding to questions about friends, even though the academic friends are entirely different. These cases would not be random measurement error, so we cannot determine the direction of the bias on the estimate of β_2 from measurement error.

Let me note that the story on all of these biases would be more interesting if we were discussing peer effects for marijuana use.

Addressing the BIG QUESTION violations

Random assignment of peers or friends would be the optimal solution to be able to correctly estimate peer effects. Unfortunately, I don't think we can convince any youth, for the larger good of knowledge and some researcher getting a decent publication, to accept a situation in which he/she is randomly assigned friends. But, a few researchers realized that some youth (college freshmen) are randomly assigned roommates. Few schools use random assignments, but when they do, this presents the opportunity for a Natural Experiment. And so, these researchers examined how the pre-college traits of a college freshman's roommate and other randomly assigned peers affect the freshman's outcomes.

Perhaps the most notable such study regarding peer effects for academic outcomes is by Carrell et al. (2009), who use roommate and squadron random assignments at the Air Force Academy (AFA) to examine the effects of peer SAT scores and other pre-college characteristics on the freshmen's first-semester course grades. Cadets at the AFA are randomly assigned to their roommate and to one of 36 squadrons, each of which has 120 students (from Freshmen to Seniors), with about 33 per freshmen class. And, freshmen are not allowed to enter the premises of other squadrons for the first seven months, meaning that they have limited contact with those from other squadrons, other than in their classes. This suggests that the roommate and squadron may indeed be the relevant peers. Furthermore, the first-semester courses are standard for all freshmen, and they cannot choose their professors or sections. Thus, the courses and sections, usually around 20 students, are exogenous as well.

Carrell et al. (2009) estimate the following equation (changed somewhat from their version for the purpose of simplification):

$$GPA_{ics} = \beta_0 + X_{ics}\beta_1 + \left(X^P_{ics}\right)\beta_2 + \mu_{cs} + \varepsilon_{ics} \qquad (11.4)$$

where:
- i = the individual cadet;
- c = the course;
- s = the section;
- GPA = the GPA of the cadet's grade in the given course;
- X = the pre-AFA characteristics of the cadet;
- X^P = the pre-AFA characteristics of the cadet's peers (the roommate(s), and the other squadron freshmen);
- μ_{cs} is the fixed effect for the course–section (a class).

One aspect that is essential to their study, in order to avoid reverse causality, is that the measures of the quality of the peers (the variables in X^P) occur before the freshmen are exposed to each other. These measures of quality include verbal and math SAT scores, as well as academic and leadership scores (based on high-school experiences) and a fitness score (which also presumably occurs before exposure to each other in the squadrons).

The course-section (class) fixed effects mean that the relationship between the peer pre-AFA characteristics and the cadet's GPA in a given course (holding the other factors constant) is estimated for each of the roughly 1000 sections (classes). The overall effect, β_2, is the weighted average of the 1000-or-so β_2's for each section.

Table 11.2 summarizes the primary results, which come from the first two columns of Table 3 in the study. Interestingly, only one of the roommate pre-Air-Force characteristics had a statistically significant coefficient estimate – that for leadership, although the lower bound of the 95% confidence interval is quite close to zero. The stronger results come from the characteristics of the other freshmen in the squadron, where two of the characteristics have significant estimates. The one for SAT verbal seems reasonable, as having squadron members who are better at verbal skills may help a given student do better in his/her classes. Also, freshmen with squadron members who had greater pre-Air-Force

Table 11.2 Summary of the main results from Carrell et al. (2009), Table 3

	Dependent variable = grade (GPA) in a given class	
	Model (1)	Model (2)
	Roommate	Other freshmen in squadron
SAT verbal	0.003	0.338***
	(0.019)	(0.107)
SAT math	0.005	0.119
	(0.021)	(0.097)
Academic composite	0.0004	0.018
	(0.005)	(0.032)
Fitness score	0.022	0.153**
	(0.013)	(0.064)
Leadership composite	0.012**	0.024
	(0.006)	(0.041)

Note: Models also include the own characteristics for each subject, course-section fixed effects, and year fixed effects.

fitness scores also do better in their classes. While this empirical relationship is plausible, it is also possible that this may be a Type I error, as I am not aware of an obvious mechanism underlying this effect. Further evidence (not shown here) suggests that there is some evidence suggesting that this verbal-SAT effect is stronger for students whose own pre-AFA characteristics are weaker.

There have been a few studies using random college roommate assignments regarding substance use – e.g., Duncan et al. (2005) on marijuana use. The more interesting Kremer and Levy (2008), combining the concepts of substance use and academic outcomes, found that, for males, having a freshman roommate who drank in the year before college had a quarter-point lower grade point average (GPA).

What I like about this study

The study takes advantage of randomness that someone else instituted. Overall, there is not overwhelming evidence for peer effects. That is okay. This is a well-executed and pretty clean study in terms of the lack of alternative stories that could explain the results.

11.4 How much does a GED improve labor-market outcomes?

Many Americans who choose not to (or are not allowed to) complete high-school attempt to earn a General Equivalency Diploma (GED). The GED is supposed to be an "equivalent" to a high-school diploma. And so, it serves somewhat as a signal to employers that the GED holder may be a few steps ahead of other non-high-school-grads. And, a GED is typically required for those wanting to further their education with college or other professional courses.

There have been many attempts to estimate how earning a GED affects one's labor-market outcomes. But, such a topic could have the same empirical problems as one would have estimating the effects of years-of-schooling on income. Just like it isn't random how many years-of-schooling a person would obtain, it wouldn't be random who (among those without a high-school diploma) would earn a GED.

Two of the most notable problems may be omitted-variables bias and self-selection bias. There could be omitted-variables bias because, among non-high-school-grads, those with higher motivation and intelligence would likely have a higher probability of taking and passing the GED and would, on average, do better in the labor market. Self-selection bias may occur because those who earn a GED may tend to be the ones who believe they can highly benefit from having one. Thus, they may be more motivated to earn one.

Jepsen et al. (2016) devise a regression-discontinuities model to estimate the effects of the GED on a few labor-market outcomes. The authors focus on roughly 44,000 males and 42,000 females who first took the GED test in Missouri between 1995 and 2005. Restricting the sample to those who took the GED reduces one source of omitted-variables bias – the motivation to take the GED – but, perhaps not the motivation to do well on the GED. The GED is a national test, although there have historically been small differences across states in what is required to pass. The requirements for passing in Missouri were scoring at least 400 on all five sub-tests and 2250 total (out of 4000). People were allowed to retake the test, and their sub-scores and total score (and pass status) would be based on the highest of each of the five sub-test scores over the prior two years. The authors find high retake rates for those who score just under the 2250. And, (in their Figure 1) they find a discontinuity for final score (after retakes), with a big jump right at the passing score of 2250. This demonstrates that few people stick with a score right below 2250 without retaking the test.

Given that 2250 does not necessarily dictate passing the GED (due to sub-scores potentially being too low), the situation calls for a *Fuzzy RD* model. But, there is a problem with using the final total score. Recall back in Section 8.8, I said that an RD model will have problems if the subjects can manipulate the scores. And, that would be the situation if the authors used the final score, as subjects could conceivably keep taking the test until they passed and it wouldn't be random which subjects did so. Their solution is to use the first-test total score as the continuous variable underlying whether the person passes the GED. They demonstrate (in their Figure 3) that there does not appear to be a discontinuity at the score for first-scores, in contrast to final score after retakes.

Their model involves:

- *Stage 1*. Regression of GED certification on a dummy variable for meeting the 2250 threshold on the first test and quadratic variables below and above the threshold.
- *Stage 2*: Regression of the labor-market outcome on the predicted-GED probability from Stage 1 and the same quadratic variables below and above the threshold. The excluded variable is the dummy variable for meeting the 2250 threshold on the first test.

Let's recall that RD models produce LATE's, so what these authors estimate is the effect of a GED for those right by the threshold on the first test.

With the outcome of quarterly earnings, examined for each of the 30 quarters after the first test, the authors find mostly no significant effects for males and females, with a few exceptions for males. For males, for quarters 6 to 9 after the first test, the estimated effect of the GED was significant at the 5% level, with estimated effects ranging from about $430 to $600 in quarterly earnings. Being only significant at the 5% level, the 95% confidence intervals included values not far off from zero.

For the outcome of whether the person was employed in a quarter (i.e., had positive income), there was only one of 60 estimated effects (30 quarters times 2 genders) that had a significant estimate. Thus, there is no evidence that having a GED affected a person's probability of employment.

There was one alternative story that could not be ruled out by the RD model. Earning a GED could increase one's probability of attending further schooling, which would then reduce earnings while in school. The authors do find evidence that the GED does indeed increase the probability that someone is enrolled in a post-secondary school. But, they describe and show in an Appendix not included in the main article that restricting the sample to those not enrolled in school results in a similar set of results as described above.

What I like about this study

This is a sound study, for which I could not come up with any alternative stories that the authors had not considered. Again, I like the general finding of insignificant effects, although in this case, the insignificant estimates make for quite an interesting result: there is little evidence that a GED improves labor-market outcomes, on average.

References

Baicker, K., Taubman, S. L., Allen, H. L., Bernstein, M., Gruber, J. H., Newhouse, J. P., . . . Finkelstein, A. N. (2013). The Oregon experiment – effects of Medicaid on clinical outcomes. *New England Journal of Medicine*, 368(18), 1713–1722.

Carrell, S. E., Fullerton, R. L., & West, J. E. (2009). Does your cohort matter? Measuring peer effects in college achievement. *Journal of Labor Economics*, 27(3), 439–464.

Duncan, G. J., Boisjoly, J., Kremer, M., Levy, D. M., & Eccles, J. (2005). Peer effects in drug use and sex among college students. *Journal of Abnormal Child Psychology*, 33(3), 375–385.

Glover, D., Pallais, A., & Pariente, W. (2017). Discrimination as a self-fulfilling prophecy: Evidence from French grocery stores. *The Quarterly Journal of Economics*, 132(3), 1219–1260.

Greenwald, A. G., McGhee, D. E., & Schwartz, J. L. K. (1998). Measuring individual differences in implicit cognition: The implicit association test. *Journal of Personality and Social Psychology*, 74(6), 1464–1480.

Jepsen, C., Mueser, P., & Troske, K. (2016). Labor market returns to the GED using regression discontinuity analysis. *Journal of Political Economy*, 124(3), 621–649.

Kremer, M., & Levy, D. (2008). Peer effects and alcohol use among college students. *The Journal of Economic Perspectives*, 22(3), 189–206.

Lane, K. A., Banaji, M. R., Nosek, B. A., & Greenwald, A. G. (2007). Understanding and using the implicit association test: IV. What we know (So Far) about the method. In *Measures of attitudes* (pp. 59–102), Bernd Wittenbrink, and Norbert Schwarz, eds. New York: Guilford Press.

<table>
<tr><td>

12
</td><td>

How to conduct a research project
</td></tr>
</table>

Box 12.1   Is it art?

"Boy, that went well," Calvin gloated, as he emerged from the Pentagon, having presented his Army reenlistment model to Defense officials who, in turn, would soon report his results to Congress.

"They believed you on everything," Hobbes replied, "even the part about being able to perfectly predict which Soldiers would reenlist."

"Yeah. . . .You didn't notice me sweating, did you?"

Hobbes paused a moment. "Yogi Berra once said, 'If you ask me anything I don't know, I'm not going to answer.'"

Calvin stopped in his tracks and turned to Hobbes. "Listen, you furry, omnivorous, baboon-posing-as-a-feline stuffed animal. My research is *art*! People always make the mistake of thinking art is created for them. But really, art is a private language for sophisticates to congratulate themselves on their superiority to the rest of the world. As my 'artist's statement' explains, my work is utterly incomprehensible and is therefore full of deep significance."

Bewildered, Hobbes replied, "I thought you were doing regression analysis."[1]

Kanye West had a great song lyric that I wanted to use to open this chapter (or even Chapter 1), but my people couldn't find his people to get his permission to use it. So, let me paraphrase. He said that he's had many "wrongs" in life that he'd like to correct for. But, at the same time, he doesn't regret his wrongs because they aided him in writing the song that this lyric is in.

This is how I feel. I have committed wrongs in my research life. I never manipulated numbers or knowingly neglected to mention certain limitations to a study, but I searched for significance – i.e., trusted a model more and reported it if it gave significant estimates. And, I have sometimes been in the "convincing" mode rather than the mode of "these-possible-alternative-explanations-to-my-results-are-distinct-possibilities-and-should-not-be-discounted-as-being-remote-possibilities" (in cases in which the alternative explanations were indeed distinct possibilities). I recognized my wrongs when I saw it in other articles, and it hit me that this ain't right. This doesn't contribute to public knowledge. I had to right my wrongs, and so I wrote this song on regression analysis.

In this chapter, I describe how to conduct a research project. This includes strategies on choosing a topic, conducting the analysis, and writing up the report.

12.1 Choosing a topic

There are four general approaches to choosing a topic that I will describe:

- Searching data sets to come up with a topic;
- Choosing a topic and searching for data to address it;
- Finding better ways to approach an existing issue that others have examined;
- Being on the lookout for randomness and other things.

Searching data sets to come up with a topic

There are plenty of data sets available with rich data. Some data sets have individual-level information on academic achievement and social, behavioral, and economic outcomes. These include the NLSY, National Educational Longitudinal Survey (NELS), Early Childhood Longitudinal Survey (ECLS), National Survey on Drug Use and Health (NSDUH), Behavioral Risk Factors Surveillance Survey (BRFSS), and many more. There are many sources for economic data at the national and state/local level. There are data sets on business financial data. And, more and more big data is becoming available on things such as sports and internet searches. Browsing through these data sets could be quite fruitful for finding interesting empirical relationships to explore and test, around which there might be an interesting theory you could develop.

Choosing a topic and searching for data to address it

Alternatively, you could choose a topic that interests you and try to find data for it. The topic could come from discussions with friends on human behavior. You might read about some topic in the news, and that could spark a thought on a tangential topic.

It is easier to write about a topic that you know something about. This could make it easier for understanding the mechanisms or theory underlying any empirical relationships you are testing for. Furthermore, having some knowledge about the topic could give some perspective on interpreting results – particularly, surprising results. We have seen the problems of Nobel Prize winners, who have probably never played basketball, incorrectly interpreting results on the hot hand in basketball. That said, you would need to be careful about bringing pre-conceived notions to the project.

With your topic, you can search for data. If feasible, you could even create your own data by conducting a survey. This is easier said than done, as there is a science behind conducting surveys to obtain a high level of honesty in the responses and an adequate response rate. And, there are strict rules on human-subject protections, with a review typically required by your institution's Institutional Review Board.

Finding better ways to approach an existing topic

Another method is to read through existing studies (browsing titles to start with) to find a topic that you believe could be examined in a better way. You may come across a research finding that you find preposterous – e.g., the finding that "the hot hand in basketball is a myth." Think of ways you can develop a model that produces a more accurate test for the topic. Or, consider whether there are potential empirical problems in a study, such as BIG QUESTION violations. And, evaluate how well the study addressed them and whether you had a better approach. Or, perhaps you could merely test for evidence of the bias you hypothesize, without necessarily claiming to identify the true causal effect.

Be on the lookout for randomness and other things

Think of the discrimination study we discussed in Section 11.1. I do not know how the authors came up with the idea. Perhaps one of the authors became aware of the great performance metrics that the grocery chain had been collecting and noted the possibility of issues regarding young, inexperienced, minority cashiers and managers who may have bias against minorities. Or, the authors may have found out that the cashiers are randomly assigned to their shifts.

And, think of the study by Carrell et al. (2009) on peer effects at the Air Force Academy (Section 11.3). They knew that the Air Force Academy assigned freshmen to roommates and squadrons pretty much randomly, making sure demographic groups were fairly evenly split. They were then able to create a study around that random (good) variation.

The bottom line is that you could be on the lookout for:

- Unique data;
- Some random source of variation determining an endogenous treatment variable (such as a lottery for Medicaid);
- Thresholds dictating eligibility for a treatment (for regression-discontinuity models);
- Panel data that track people over multiple time periods.

All of these could be the ingredients for a great research paper.

12.2 Conducting the empirical part of the study

Gathering data

The empirical part of the study begins with collecting data. This may involve collecting multiple data sets and merging data. Perhaps there is geographical information (such as state unemployment rates) that can be merged with data that have the corresponding geographical information for the merge/match. And, it may involve collecting your own data by a survey.

Creating the proper sample

With the data, one must choose the proper sample. The sample should be representative of the population on which you wish to make inferences. If the analysis is on people, then consider what age groups to use. Are there certain characteristics that make some observations less relevant? Studies that examine how state tax rates affect state economic growth often exclude Alaska and Hawaii, as capital and businesses are not easily moved to or from these states, as they would be for the 48 contiguous states. Thus, it is theorized that tax rates have less of an effect on these states. Is that a good reason to exclude them? I'll let you consider that. Also of consideration is how to keep observations with missing data, which I describe below.

Dependent variable

There may be one obvious dependent variable that you have in mind. But, having multiple dependent variables can be helpful in painting a sharper picture on what outcomes the treatment may have an impact on and on whether the treatment has a consistent impact on various outcomes. For example, the Oregon Health Study (Baicker et al. 2013), as described in Section 11.2, examined how Medicaid coverage affects a wide set of health-outcome measures.

Key explanatory variable

The key explanatory factor may be obvious, as it would likely be part of the initial choosing of a topic. However, it is worthwhile to consider how to characterize the factor. If it is a yes/no treatment, then it is simple. But, for continuous variables, one could consider non-linear effects (Section 3.2). Furthermore, there could be interacted effects if the effect could vary across observations based on some factor. Do you want to estimate an overall effect or how the effect varies by group?

Control variables

The choice of control variables should be based on the guide presented in Section 6.5, if the objective is estimating causal effects. For other objectives of regression analysis, Table 7.2 in Section 7.4 should be considered. Although often it is a good idea to control for variables that would otherwise present an omitted-variables-bias problem, it is also good to be judicious about not throwing too many control variables into the model.

Check the data

Check the frequency of the values for each variable used in the regression. Sometimes, in survey data, missing values are coded as negative numbers, with codes for various reasons why the value is missing for the observation. If left as is, this could have a large impact on the regression results. It is also good to check for incomprehensible values of a variable.

Correcting for missing data

It is rare that data for regressions are perfect. There is often missing information. This may be due to coding errors, a respondent choosing not to answer a question, or the data just not being available. How missing data can be treated depends on what information is missing, and it may not be necessary to throw out an observation with missing data.

Missing data on the dependent variable

In this situation, there is nothing that can be done. The observation would need to be excluded from the regression. You may want to think about whether there is a pattern based on which types of observations have a missing dependent variable. Any pattern should be noted, as it speaks to one of the "things that could go wrong" in regression analysis, *non-representative samples* (Section 6.7).

Missing data on the key explanatory variable

If the key explanatory variable is missing, then this is another situation in which the observation should be dropped. To impute a number would introduce measurement error (BIG QUESTION 4). Again, the data should be investigated for patterns in having the key independent variable missing.

Missing data on other explanatory variables (the control variables)

This is the one case in which it may be best to keep the observation. Control variables, again, are ones that are included just to obtain more accurate estimates on the key explanatory variables. The strategy for including the observation is to:

* Assign the same value to the missing variable for all observations missing that variable – the mean value is a good choice;
* Create a new dummy variable equaling one if the original value was missing on that variable and zero otherwise.

For example, with the NLSY data, the AFQT percentile score is missing for about 6% of the sample (Bureau of Labor Statistics, 2014; 2015). In the models above, I just excluded these 6% from the sample. But instead, I could have assigned 50 (the national median) to the AFQT score for these people (or the sample average of 43.8) and created a variable, *afqtmiss*, which equals one if the *AFQT* was originally missing and zero otherwise.

The idea here is that the observations have value in describing the relationship between the key explanatory variable (and other control variables) and the outcome. Excluding observation because they have missing data on non-key-explanatory variables would cause us to lose any information the observations provide. So, we assign them a value near the middle of the distribution (so it has a minimal effect on the estimate on the AFQT score) and then have an extra variable in there to see if those with a missing AFQT score have systematically higher or lower outcomes than others, holding other factors constant. Generally, more observations produce more precise estimates, and so saving observations from the chopping block can be a good thing, if done correctly.

Assessment of the study and corrections

As part of the assessment, one should consider the BIG QUESTIONS and the potential problems with standard errors. If there were a problem with mediating factors or outcomes included as control variables (BIG QUESTIONS 5 and 6), then the solution would be to simply remove them, provided there were no ambiguity in whether the variables would cause harm either omitted or included (see Section 6.4.5). If there were measurement error, there would most likely be nothing that could be done. But, there may be a solution if the problem stems from a non-random key explanatory variable, provided a method from Chapter 8 (or another innovative method) could be applied. Also, any issue with the standard errors (i.e., multicollinearity, heteroskedasticity, or correlated error terms) could be corrected with the methods indicated in Section 6.6.

Extra analyses

There are various reasons to estimate variants of the primary model. Make sure you do not overdo it, but the following are some reasons that could justify estimating multiple models:

- Conduct a sensitivity analysis. This is meant to test whether the results are "sensitive" to alternative specifications or characterizations of the treatment. For example, the key explanatory variable might be characterized as a spline or quadratic function.
- Split by demographic group to see if there is a stronger/weaker empirical relationship for particular groups.
- Demonstrate the effects of a correction for a BIG QUESTION violation. For example, you may want to show the results from what happened without and with fixed effects (to address omitted-variables bias). This could be indicative of how much of an omitted-variables-bias problem there was initially. But, be aware of other interpretations with the fixed effects, such as the potential for greater bias from measurement error and a re-weighting of groups of observations.
- When there is an ambiguous modeling decision (e.g., whether to include a variable or whether to use OLS or probit), you could estimate the model both ways to determine whether the results are relatively stable or if they meaningfully change with different modeling decisions.

12.3 Writing the report

The main things I keep in mind as I write a paper or report is to: (1) keep the report as readable as possible; and (2) make it so someone could skim through the article and get the general gist within a few minutes. To this end, I attempt to avoid complicated language. And, I try to make tables as clear as possible so that a reader does not have to check elsewhere in the paper to understand the table.

General components

The following is the general order of the components of a paper or article:

- Abstract,
- Introduction,

- Theoretical/Conceptual Framework,
- Data,
- Methods,
- Results,
- Conclusions/Discussion,
- References.

Having these distinct sections improves the readability of the paper, as it makes it easier for a reader to find a particular point they are searching for and it just breaks up the paper. While some journals require a fixed format (that may not follow this exact ordering), often there is flexibility in some of the ordering and which components are necessary. Sometimes sections are too short to stand on their own, and so it is better to incorporate them into other sections. For example, the conceptual framework (which discusses the mechanisms for why there should be the empirical relationship you are hypothesizing) could be quite simple and straightforward. Thus, it could be part of the Introduction or the Methods section. And, the Data section may be small enough to be included in the Methods section. Sometimes more sections are needed. If there are multiple research questions or just a long set of results, it may be worthwhile to split the Results section into two or more sections. Finally, note that other names are often used to title a section. The same general concepts apply.

Abstract (or executive summary)

The Abstract should summarize most of the research project: the research question, data, methods, results, and conclusions (and maybe the contribution relative to prior studies, if space allows). How much detail you go into depends on how much space you have. For academic articles, you may be limited to 100 words, or sometimes you may be allowed as much as 250 words. And sometimes, the abstract is allowed to be free-flowing, and sometimes it needs to be structured into specific sections.

For non-academic reports (e.g., to sponsors), there is often an Executive Summary instead of or in addition to an abstract. The "Executive" reading the "Summary" should be able to understand what was done in the report within a few pages. They can then refer to the body of the report for more detail.

Introduction

There is typically not any standard form for an Introduction. The Introduction should provide a concise description of the whole study. Some say that you should introduce your topic in the first paragraph. But, if the title of the paper is self-explanatory and you describe your topic in the abstract, then you should have a little "artistic license" for how to start your paper. Although few do so, starting the Introduction with some captivating story could draw in readers. Let me suggest that we start a trend of beginning a paper/report with a short story that leads into the introduction of your topic. This could be a quick, funny story from your life that has some meaning for the research topic. It could be a story you make up, such as the foul-shooting contest I had with LeBron James in my head. Alternatively (or, in addition to), you could include a relevant quote from one of our great philosophers: e.g., Socrates, Yogi Berra, Bob Dylan, Gregg Popovich, Andy Dufresne, or Calvin. If you're not sure it works, take a chance. I'm sure I misfired on some of my stories in this book or quotes that I thought were funny. But, I hope that a few worked. Remember, this is supposed to be fun ... in addition to being informative.

One important component of the Introduction is your empirical objective. Your topic should not just be exploring the relationship between two variables, but indicate whether your objective is to estimate a causal effect, determine the best predictors of some outcome, forecast the outcome, gauge relative performance, or some other purpose that guides your research.

Another important component of the Introduction is some discussion on why the topic is important. Why might the world (or some segment of the world) benefit from this research?

The last part of the Introduction is often a brief map of the structure of the paper. This may not be necessary, as structures of reports are fairly standard, and a reader could easily skim through the paper to see this.

In some academic fields, a new trend is to have a Positionality Statement included in the Introduction. (I was recently asked to do this for a journal article.) This is a statement that indicates how your world views or your experiences may have bearing on the research. And, it may include some statement on how you became interested in the research topic in the first place.

Literature review

This is the section in which you highlight how your research fits into the general literature on the research topic. This will indicate what your contribution will be. Sometimes, if brief, the Literature Review is folded into the Introduction.

The topics to cover in this section include:

- What, if anything has been done on your specific topic?
- What has been done on related topics (if nothing has been studied specific to your topic)? Generally, it is not necessary to discuss the methods of each article you describe. But, it would be useful to do so for a few key articles that are closely aligned with your study.
- Is there a hole in the literature for this topic?
- Why have prior studies been inadequate in addressing the research question, or why is it worthwhile to do another study on the issue? This could be that prior studies used poor methods, had inadequate or old data, or had mixed evidence with no definitive or convincing answer. Or, it could just be that there are few studies on an issue, and it merits another examination to provide further evidence.
- What will your contribution be? This could be a new question never examined before (to your knowledge). Or, for topics that have been addressed, your contribution may be a new approach or method, better data, updated data, or merely another study to add to the existing studies.

Theoretical/conceptual framework

In this section, you indicate why there should be the relationship that you are hypothesizing. There are two general approaches:

1. You would take an existing theory, extend an existing theory, or develop a new theory. You would then make predictions or hypotheses about what behaviors, actions, or relationships should be observed based on that theory. You would then empirically test those predictions.

2.   You start with a hypothesized empirical relationship, and you then use theory to explain why there could be such a relationship. Of course, the hypothesized empirical relationship might be based on some basic theory to start with (e.g., that basketball players can get into a higher level of play and have the hot hand), but the emphasis would be on the empirical relationship.

Some academic journals like to see a full theoretical model with utility or production functions (along with a little Calculus). Sometimes, such models may have some value. But often, just describing the mechanisms that could be at play should be adequate.

Sometimes, in the second approach above, the mechanisms are obvious enough that they could be described very briefly. In this situation, the options are:

- Just incorporate the theory into the Introduction.
- Combine the theory with the Literature Review, and call it a "Background" section.
- Put the theory in the Methods section.

The Theory or Conceptual Framework may require an extra review of the literature. That is, some mechanisms may have some literature supporting it as a mechanism, and that may give your theory more credibility.

This section could be placed before the Literature Review. Which ordering is better is situation-specific and depends on how you weave the story.

Data

This section could be combined with the Methods section (which comes next); it largely depends on whether one or both of these are long and complicated on their own, or if at least one of them could be described fairly briefly.

The descriptions for the data collection and creation of the sample should be detailed enough so that someone could easily replicate what you did in terms of compiling and preparing the data. The main components for describing the data include the following:

- Data source(s) and how the data were accessed;
- Sample criteria, along with reasons for using non-obvious criteria;
- Perhaps how various sample criteria affected the sample size;
- The final sample size, or the range of sample sizes if the sample varies based on the dependent variable or the model used.

The variables used should be indicated. This could go under the Data or the Methods part of the description. They include indications of:

- The dependent variable(s) – i.e., outcome(s);
- The key explanatory variables;
- The control variables.

After describing these variables, it is conventional to present a table with some descriptive statistics, such as the mean and standard deviation of the variables. One practice that could help with clarity is to have separate panels in this table for the dependent variable(s), the key explanatory variable(s), and the control variables.

Methods

The components of the Methods description should include:

- What challenges are involved with estimating the model (e.g., there is omitted-variables bias, and so you need to design the model to address that).
- What method is used (e.g., OLS, fixed effects, logit model, etc.).
- Why you chose that method if it is not obvious (e.g., how does it solve your research issue).
- What the different specifications you estimate are and why. For example, you may want to estimate a model with and without certain fixed effects to demonstrate what the "fix" you apply does to the estimated effects.
- Some want to see the formal hypotheses, but the mere topic (even from the title sometimes) should have enough information so that explicitly laying out the hypotheses would be unnecessary.
- The limitations of your analysis. Are there any BIG QUESTION violations that remain? Often, it is uncertain but a possibility that there are remaining BIG QUESTION violations. You want to say that. Oh, and only people who have read this book know what is meant by "BIG QUESTION violations," so you may not want to use that terminology, but indicate the actual problem – e.g., measurement error. Remember that our objective is the truth, and your job is to present evidence and not convince.

If the situation calls for Model Diagnostics, then it is typically a good idea to discuss in the Methods section if any change in method is required. For example, you could describe a heteroskedasticity test you conducted, and due to the results, you correct for heteroskedasticity – although, you really should almost always do this, as it is a costless fix. Another example is that, if the situation presents the possibility of non-normal errors and there is borderline significance (to be discussed in the Results section next), it may dictate the use of a certain method (e.g., logit method instead of OLS for a dummy-variable dependent variable).

Recently, in my research articles, I have started to include a table at the end of the Methods section that summarizes the main points from the data and methods descriptions. This includes points such as: the data source, the sample size, the dependent variable, the key explanatory variable(s), the control variables, the method (e.g., OLS), any fixed effects used, and the relevant potential limitations. This is a general list; yours may not have all of these points and may include others. For most people who look through articles, they want to get the idea quickly (as they may have many articles they're sifting through). This is an easy reference for the readers to use to get the main gist of what you did. See Table 1 in Arkes (2017) for an example. (This is another trend I'd like to start.)

Results

This section is for presenting and interpreting the results of the quantitative analysis. (In Section 13.4 below, I summarize some of the main points from this book, including important points on interpretations.) You will present and describe table(s) of results, which often should be placed at the end of the paper. This description should include the interpretation in terms of what the magnitude of the estimates indicate and how statistically significant they are, taking into account the critiques of the p-value from Section 5.3. If the coefficient estimate on the key explanatory variable is insignificant, consider the four reasons for insignificance. Is it possible that there are counteracting positive and negative effects? Is the confidence interval for the estimate narrow enough to conclude that there is no meaningful effect?

If you have a large set of explanatory variables, focus on the interpretations for the key explanatory variables and perhaps a few notable control variables – maybe those control variables with surprising results or those that appear to have the highest levels of significance. Describing the estimates and significance on each variable would not be fun for the reader. They can see the results in the tables.

There may be extra models you want to estimate to test for the robustness or sensitivity of your results. These are, in one sense, beneficial for representing how "robust" or "shaky" any key result is. However, researchers have generally gone too far with these tests, which have increased the length of research articles in the last few decades, which I mention below in Section 13.3. Some semi-consequential sets of results can be described very briefly, but have the results in an Appendix, in an online version of the paper for anything published in an academic journal, or just made "available upon request."

Each table should be able to stand on its own and not require someone to read the text to understand it. Some people just look at the tables, and so you want them to see the table and understand the results. Here are a few presentation tips for tables to make it easier for the reader:

- Give the sample size and what each model does (e.g., what fixed effects are included).
- Clearly identify the dependent variable in either the table title, above all models (if it is the same for each model), or at the top of each column (if it varies by model).
- Indicate what each explanatory variable is (use short variable descriptions if possible and not hard-to-decipher variable names).
- Present estimates on the key explanatory variables first.
- Group categories together and indicate the reference group (see Table 9.1 as an example).
- While some present the t-stats under or next to the coefficient estimate (in parentheses), most people prefer to see the standard errors so they can construct their own quick confidence intervals. Also useful would be the 95% confidence interval and indicators for meeting key p-value thresholds – or, the p-values themselves, as Baicker et al. (2013) present (see Section 11.2). But, do not overstate the importance of the p-value, given our discussion on the drawbacks of the p-value from Section 5.3.
- Don't overdo the decimal places. Having 3 significant values is usually enough (which may mean zero decimal places), with 3 or 4 decimal places being the maximum it should ever be. Sometimes, more decimal places are needed, depending on the scaling, to give the reader a better gauge of the t-stat.

Conclusions/discussion

This is where you draw everything together. You can briefly remind the reader what the objective of the analysis was and what the holes in the literature were. You then briefly discuss the important findings, regardless of whether they were statistically significant. Next, provide a discussion of what this means for the research question, in relation to the prior literature (if there is any). Beware of your pre-conceived notions and cognitive biases (see Section 13.1).

Be honest again about the study's limitations. Frankly, this impresses me more in a researcher than significant estimates do. The limitations should include alternative stories that could explain your results – i.e., stories that are alternative to your hypothesized theory. Again, a researcher's job is to present evidence and give an objective interpretation. One can give their interpretation and opinion on the final result. But, that should be backed up with evidence. If you need to make some leaps of faith, then you're convincing.

The Conclusions section should include a discussion on what the implications of the findings are for policy or anything else – e.g., business strategy, health behaviors. In addition, if there were subsequent research topics that you could recommend, that would be a good point to end on . . . unless you have another great quote to sum up the paper.

References/bibliography

Provide a list of references at the end of the report or perhaps before any Tables and Appendices. The format will depend on your discipline or the requirements of the academic journal.

Note

1 From this story, only part of Calvin's last quote came from one of Bill Watterson's actual comic strips: "People always make . . . full of deep significance." The rest of the story was my *artistic* interpretation of the context. CALVIN AND HOBBES © Watterson. Reprinted with permission of ANDREWS MCMEEL SYNDICATION. All rights reserved.

References

Arkes, J. (2017). Separating the harmful versus beneficial effects of marital disruptions on children. *Journal of Divorce & Remarriage*, 58(7), 526–541.

Baicker, K., Taubman, S. L., Allen, H. L., Bernstein, M., Gruber, J. H., Newhouse, J. P., . . . Finkelstein, A. N. (2013). The Oregon experiment – effects of Medicaid on clinical outcomes. *New England Journal of Medicine*, 368(18), 1713–1722.

Bureau of Labor Statistics, U.S. Department of Labor. (2014). *National Longitudinal Survey of Youth 1979 cohort, 1979–2012 (rounds 1–25)*. Columbus, OH: Center for Human Resource Research, The Ohio State University.

Bureau of Labor Statistics, U.S. Department of Labor. (2015). *National Longitudinal Survey of Youth 1997 cohort, 1997–2013 (rounds 1–16)*. Columbus, OH: Center for Human Resource Research, The Ohio State University.

Carrell, S. E., Fullerton, R. L., & West, J. E. (2009). Does your cohort matter? Measuring peer effects in college achievement. *Journal of Labor Economics*, 27(3), 439–464.

13 Summarizing thoughts

You had me at "holding other factors constant."

– Anonymous

13.1 Be aware of your cognitive biases

I've got plenty of common sense . . . I just choose to ignore it.

– Calvin (from Calvin and Hobbes)

All researchers and their readers are subject to cognitive biases, just like other members of the animal kingdom. Sometimes, a cognitive bias is the result of hubris, but often it is an innocent subconscious thought process. Regardless, it could cause misguided research strategies, improper interpretations of research, and unjustified acceptance/rejection of others' research. Being conscious of your cognitive biases could help your research.

One important cognitive bias is **confirmation bias**, which is a situation in which people have prior beliefs on some issue, and they reject any new information that is contrary to their beliefs or what they want to hear, and they accept/absorb any new information that is consistent with their beliefs. One of the most tragic examples of confirmation bias is the case of Reggie Lewis. Lewis was the Boston Celtics' leading scorer for two seasons (1991–92 and 1992–93). He fainted in a play-off game in 1993. The Celtics assembled a "dream team" of 12 cardiologists, who concluded that Lewis should not play basketball again.[1] He went for a second opinion, and a single doctor gave a diagnosis of a fainting condition and gave Lewis clearance to return to basketball. Lewis collapsed two months later while shooting baskets and died at the hospital. Lewis listened to the single opinion he wanted to hear rather than the collective opinion of the 12 experts.

Evidence on how prevalent confirmation bias is in society comes from the correlation of viewpoints on some political issues. I imagine that there is a strong correlation of viewpoints between: (1) whether humans are contributing to global warming; (2) whether gay marriage should be allowed and recognized; (3) whether tax rates should be lower; (4) whether there should be more stringent guns laws; (5) whether the U.S. should have invaded Iraq; and (6) whether marijuana should be legalized. Yet, these are independent issues that, I believe, should have no common factor other than how consistent a given viewpoint is with a political party's platform. Thus, followers of one political party will want to listen to what their party leaders have to say, form their initial opinions, and then discount any opposing evidence or arguments.

Here is how confirmation bias could affect research. A researcher may estimate a model and obtain some result that is contrary to what he believes to be the case. He may then change the model (for the worse) until he obtains a statistical relationship that is more in line with what he believes or what he wants to be the case.

A peer reviewer subject to confirmation could recommend that a paper does not get published if the paper has findings that are contrary to what his prior belief was on the topic. Likewise, a peer reviewer may be too quick to accept research with questionable methods if it produces a result consistent with their prior views. Avoiding confirmation bias is important when reading and properly assessing research.

Learning the proper methods, pitfalls, and interpretations of regression analysis should reduce the leeway researchers have to be subject to confirmation bias and to "regression fish" for good results. And, it should reduce the leeway that consumers of research have in letting their cognitive bias get in their way of gaining knowledge.

How else would you avoid confirmation bias? A simple lesson may come from the famous British philosopher and intellectual, Bertrand Russell. A *New York Post* writer, Leonard Lyons, discussed Russell in a 1964 story.[2] Lyons recounted how he had once asked Russell whether he would die for his beliefs. Russell replied, "Of course not. After all, I may be wrong." The lesson is that the key to avoiding confirmation bias is to know that, almost always, you *may* be wrong.

So, the most important thing to do when conducting or reading research is having an open mind. You can have strong pre-conceived notions of the answer to the research question. But, you will give a more thorough and objective assessment of the research if you at least entertain the notion that the issue is not settled and your pre-conceived notion, even if it is based on prior research, may be wrong. This strategy will help to offset any confirmation bias you may have on the topic.

Besides confirmation bias, there are a few other cognitive biases that you should be aware of to avoid succumbing to them. Here are a few.

- **Anchor-point bias**. This is closely tied with confirmation bias. It occurs when someone observes an initial estimate on a statistical relationship (e.g., increasing the minimum wage 10% reduces employment by 2%) and discounts any study that finds anything far off from 2%. The 2% estimate was their "anchor."
- **Exception fallacy**. This is a case in which a person discounts a research finding because he knows an exception to the finding. For example, there may be a study that demonstrates a positive association between marijuana use and depression. Someone may respond that he has a friend who smokes pounds of marijuana and is the happiest person he knows, and so the finding can't be true. Other than in the hard sciences, there are few deterministic relationships in the world. Just

because marijuana use and depression may be positively related does not mean that everyone who uses marijuana is depressed and everyone who doesn't use marijuana is not depressed. Remember, regressions indicate how two variables move together, on average. They typically do not indicate a singular effect/association that fits everyone.

- **Ecological fallacy.** This is almost a reverse of "exception fallacy." It occurs when someone takes a general research finding and makes conclusions about an individual. Using the example above, based on the positive association between marijuana use and depression, assuming someone who is depressed is using marijuana (or *vice versa*) would be committing the ecological fallacy.

13.2 What betrays trust in published studies

Most published studies are based on objective, well-intentioned analyses. However, strong incentives researchers face could affect the quality of some of the studies that become disseminated. Furthermore, the peer-review process is not as strong as one might think.

I discuss these issues to make you aware of further incentives (for researchers and reviewers) that could affect the quality of research. And, this highlights that a research article should not be trusted just because it is published in a respectable journal.

Funded research and incentives for researchers

This issue makes me think of a movie I once saw on a criminal trial (but I can't think of the name of the movie). I probably have some details wrong, but I believe someone was on trial for murder, and the prosecution brought in a psychologist as an expert witness. Here is my recollection of the defense lawyer questioning the psychologist:

Psychologist: "The defendant is mentally fit, and was not insane when he committed this crime."
Defense lawyer: *"How many trials have you been an expert witness for?"*
Psychologist: "About 160."
Defense lawyer: "How many of those 160 cases have you found the defendant to not be mentally fit?"
Psychologist: (sheepishly) "None."

The problem, as you have probably figured out, is that the psychologist is being paid by the prosecutor to give certain testimony. The psychologist had been a reliable witness for the prosecutor, always giving the answer consistent with their story. And so, the psychologist kept getting hired for his expert testimony. The same holds for any type of expert witness in a criminal or civil trial.

There is a similar problem with funded research. If researchers are being paid by oil companies to investigate whether humans' use of fossil fuels is contributing to global warming, it is unlikely that the researcher will produce and disseminate any research finding that human activity is actually contributing to global warming. Three reasons for this are:

- The sponsors would likely search for researchers who have shown sympathy to their argument that humans are not causing global warming;
- The sponsors would not release a study contrary to their viewpoint;
- The researcher would have the incentive to find that humans are not contributing to global warming if they hope to get funded by these sponsors again.

Anyone reading research should be aware of incentives researchers (and their sponsors) have. Academic journals typically require authors to disclose who funded the research, and that is typically reported with the article. But, when research is cited or is discussed on the news, there is rarely a mention of who the funder of the research was. Yet, this is critical information.

Trust research more if it isn't funded by organizations with vested interests, such as the oil industry and pharmaceutical companies – not to say that ALL research funded by these types of organizations is biased.

Publication bias

In a 2010 article in *The Atlantic*, David Freedman (2010) wrote:

> Imagine . . . that five different research teams test an interesting [medical] theory that's making the rounds, and four of the groups correctly find no evidence for the theory, while the one less cautious group incorrectly "proves" the theory true through some combination of error, fluke, and clever selection of data. Guess whose findings your doctor ends up reading about in the journal, and you end up hearing about on the evening news?

It is natural that people tend to find statistically significant estimates more interesting than insignificant estimates. So, as journals compete for readers, they tend to be hesitant to publish a finding of "no effect" as readers would be less interested in it and would be less likely to build further research off of a no-effect finding. That would mean fewer citations and a lower ranking for the journal. Some academic journals are realizing the problems this cause and are reported to be more receptive of "no effect" findings. For example, the well-regarded *American Journal of Public Health* has a stated policy that "Studies with negative results, or those challenging previously published work or widely held beliefs, receive equal consideration." There are even new journals in a few fields that focus on publishing "negative results," called *All Results Journals*.

What I have described here is called **publication bias**, which is the tendency for journals to publish results that have significant results. The bias would be in the direction of larger and significant effects, as the smaller, insignificant results are less likely to be published. In Freedman's example above, if just the first study was published and no journal would accept the other four studies, then 100% of the studies (1 of 1 study) on this topic find the theory to be true. But, the reality is that only 20% (1 of 5 studies) found evidence supporting the theory to be true.

But, the bias doesn't stop at the journal. It has secondary effects on some researchers, who strategize their behavior given the biases by journals. I can think of two reactions, one of which is understandable and the other one not being okay. Both contribute to publication bias. The first reaction – the understandable one – is that, if they do research and find a non-interesting result, researchers may choose to shift their focus away from that research and towards some topic that has better prospects (for journal quality and the probability of getting published). So, these presumably valid results would never be known to the research community.

The less understandable reaction is when researchers change the model until the results are more interesting. This leads to misinformation for the public. This is called **p-hacking** because the researcher is trying to "hack" the p-value. It is possible that p-hacking is due to the authors having a certain belief about what an effect could be, and so they change the model until they get the effect they think it should be. But, it could also be that the authors are just trying to get results that could be published. The result of p-hacking would be a disproportionately large share of p-values just below key significance values (particularly, 0.05) and a smaller-than-expected share of p-values just over the key significance values. Some evidence for p-hacking can be seen in Head et al. (2015), which demonstrates the distribution of p-values has a disproportionate concentration of values just below the key significance level of 0.05. That said, the study also finds no evidence that p-hacking is a widespread-enough phenomenon that it would meaningfully affect any general consensus on research findings.

Along the same lines as publication bias, among the dozens of job-market candidates (coming out of graduate school) I have seen over the years at my organizations, I cannot remember one who had insignificant primary results. The problem is that dissertations are tomes that typically involve developing a theory and testing it empirically. If there were an insignificant result, some people assessing the candidate may take it as a signal that the candidate developed a theory that is not supported by data. Thus, there is the incentive for the job-market candidates to produce a dissertation with significant estimates. As with publication bias, this could collectively be the product of some candidates finagling the model until something significant comes up, or it may be due to candidates switching topics if they do not find anything significant.

Personally, I would really appreciate a candidate who had insignificant results because it would be a good signal that they didn't keep playing with the model to find something significant. One of the candidates I was impressed by had a nice significant result, but said that she tried everything she could to "kill the effect" (i.e., make it insignificant) and was unable to do so.

Hopefully, readers will be mindful of publication bias (and these incentives) and use the BIG QUESTIONS in Chapter 6 to guide them to develop the best possible model, regardless of the result.

The not-so-great scientific-review process

The scientific/peer-review process is what determines what studies receive funding, what studies get published, and in what journals they get published. Researchers choose a journal to submit a paper to. An editor of the journal then decides whether the journal would be interested in the research, and if so, sends the paper to a few referees for a peer review. These referees are typically not known to the researcher, and often, the author is not known to the referees. The referees critique the study and make recommendations to the editor for whether to reject the paper, offer the authors the opportunity to revise and resubmit the paper, or accept the article for publication. Regardless, the authors typically receive a set of comments by the referees.

Most researchers would agree that the peer-review process is highly random, and many consider it extremely flawed. From my personal experience, I will share a few stories. There is one journal to which I have sent four different articles for publication. The only one they accepted was the least informative and least innovative of the four. In another case, a colleague of mine tells a story of how she and co-authors submitted an article to a high-quality journal, got rejected, subsequently submitted the paper to six other lower-quality journals, and continued getting rejected. They then submitted again to the original high-quality journal (forgetting they had already done so), and it got accepted for publication!

These are two of numerous anecdotes that researchers can tell. But, more formal tests of the peer-review process, as discussed in Section 1.3, demonstrate the random nature of the process. And, there are also conflicts of interest for referees, who are often people who have researched the issue before. Thus, if the results are contrary to what the referees had found, they may be (perhaps subconsciously) more critical of the paper.

I likely experienced this first hand with my basketball-hot-hand research. In Arkes (2010), my evidence for a hot hand in basketball was contrary to the existing literature that claimed that the hot hand in basketball does not exist. At the first journal to which I sent my article, the referee recommended rejecting the paper because my results had to be wrong because it had been "proven" that the hot hand does not exist. This may have been one of the prior authors, or at least someone who had bought into the hot-hand-is-a-myth story. Regardless, it was "confirmation bias" in that the referee discounted my research, not based on the methods, but based on the fact that the findings were different from past research.

Referees of papers in which they are cited may have the incentive to get the paper published, as it would provide a citation for their own research, which boosts their count on "Google Scholar Citations Index" or other such citation counts. And, of course, referees are not always well-conversed in the pitfalls of regression analysis.

The bottom line is that the media and other consumers of research should not rely on the peer-review process and where the article is published to determine the quality of a research study. Nor should you rely on the peer-review process as you assess others' research. Judge articles on your own.

13.3 How to do a referee report responsibly

The average article in the top economic journals is three times lengthier than it was in the 1970s (Card and DellaVigna 2013). Are these articles anywhere close to three times as informative? Heck no! And, they are about 5.2 times more painful to read . . . on average.

The likely cause of the increase in article length is greater demands for revisions by referees. Yes, the refereeing process has run amok! Referees demand many checks on the results to make sure they stand up to different specifications. While such checks can be useful at times, they need to be applied more judiciously.

In a recent article in *Journal of Economic Perspectives*, Berk, Harvey, and Hirshleifer (2017) give several much-needed recommendations on how to conduct a responsible referee report, which should help towards improving the scientific-review process. These recommendations include the following:

- Weigh the importance/relevance/contribution of the research along with how sound it is. That is, be prudently more forgiving of flaws for more important research, as no research is perfect. (Of course, make sure that the authors acknowledge those flaws.)
- Be clear on what comments are necessary for the author to address and what comments are just suggestions for improving the paper.
- The comments that you deem to be necessary to address need to be scientifically justified.
- Be properly skeptical of evidence for an effect that has low prior probabilities, particularly if the p-value is not sufficiently small. Consider the informal Bayesian approach (Section 5.3).
- Be courteous and impartial.
- Decline performing the review if you have conflicts of interest.
- Generally, use the criterion of whether you would have been proud to have written the paper.

13.4 Summary of the most important points and interpretations

The effects of all of the problems mentioned so far in this chapter (cognitive biases, incentives for researchers, publication bias, and the poor refereeing process) could be largely mitigated if the research community and consumers of research had a better understanding of regression analysis and the right questions to ask when assessing research. The better scrutiny would, hopefully, force researchers to put forth more solid research. This section summarizes the main questions to ask to assess research, whether it's your own or someone else's. In addition, it provides key interpretations that are often misunderstood.

The various objectives of regression analysis

Regression analysis is mostly used to estimate the causal effects of some factor on an outcome. But, there are other uses of regressions. Regressions can forecast or make a prediction for an outcome. They can determine the strongest predictors of some outcome. And, regressions can be used to adjust outcomes to eliminate the influences of factors unrelated to the performance so that the outcomes can be compared across subjects – e.g., how strong an instructor's evaluations are, adjusting for the difficulty of the class taught and the class size. Keep in mind that the strategies for properly estimating regression analyses differ based on the objective.

What does "holding other factors constant" mean?

One of the most beautiful aspects about regressions is that one can design a model so as to isolate the relationship between one factor and the outcome while other related factors are not moving. That is, we effectively see what happens to the outcome from variation in one explanatory variable without other explanatory variables changing with it. This concept should then guide the choice of the optimal set of control variables, as some factors should vary as the key explanatory variable changes (e.g., mediating factors) while other factors should not vary (e.g., common factors of the key explanatory variable and the outcome).

Be careful of the proper reference group

When estimating the effect of some variable on an outcome, it is important to understand what the reference group (or "implicit reference group") is. If we were estimating the impact of the amount of cell phone usage on brain functioning, we would essentially be comparing extensive users vs. light users (or non-users). But, who would be in the light/non-user group? It could include people who are using their tablet or computer to do all the things that people do with their cell phones. And so, we may not detect any difference in brain functioning, as a good share of the light users would have their brain functioning affected by substitutes to cell phones. Thus, we would want to factor out the heavy tablet and computer users from the "light users" of cell phones. The lesson is to always consider who is being compared and what the reference group would be, even for continuous key explanatory variables.

Assessing research for biased estimates

Research can be, in some ways, open to interpretation and at times ambiguous. Researchers may find a given empirical result that is "consistent with a given theory." So, they may conclude that the theory is true. But, there may be stories that can give alternative explanations to the empirical result. These sprout from the limitations of a model in controlling for certain factors.

Remember that a regression just indicates how two variables move together, holding other factors constant. Any conclusion of causality (if that is the objective) must rely on how well the researchers were able to rule out any alternative explanations to the variables moving (or not moving) together. And, this typically comes down to whether the BIG QUESTIONS are addressed (so you can answer "no" to them). These BIG QUESTIONS, applying to the objective of estimating causal effects, are:

1. Is there reverse causality?
2. Is there omitted-variables bias?
3. Is there self-selection bias?
4. Is there significant measurement error?
5. Are there mediating factors (mechanism variables) used as control variables?
6. Are there outcome variables used as control variables?

These are the questions that need to be asked regardless of whether the results indicate a real empirical relationship between two variables or no evidence for such a relationship. If there are alternative stories and the researchers did not take measures to correct for the pitfalls, then any conclusion on the existence or magnitude of the causal effect has to be questioned. At the same time, the severity of the empirical problem needs to be considered. There may be misdemeanors in research (or mild violations of the BIG QUESTIONS) that would probably not create any meaningful bias on the estimated effects.

Coefficient estimates represent estimated average effects (or associations)

A coefficient estimate (or its associated marginal effect for certain models) represents how two variables move together, on average, in the sample. If the model is free from biases, then the estimate represents an *average effect*. There may be some subjects that are affected more by the treatment than others; and there may be some that are not affected at all. Also, what appears to be a small effect may be a rather large effect for some combined with a zero effect for others. For example, a parental divorce may harm 3% of children experiencing one, while the rest of children may be unaffected by a parental divorce. Combining them, the average effect may be negligible. In this case, the conclusion that a divorce does not affect children would be incorrect.

What does an insignificant estimate mean?

An "insignificant coefficient estimate" could be the result of:

1. There actually being no effect of the explanatory variable on the outcome;
2. A modeling problem causing a bias;

3. Inadequate power to detect an effect; and
4. Varying and counteracting effects in the population.

Thus, whereas an insignificant estimate is often referred to as evidence of "no effect" or "no relation-ship" between the variables, the proper interpretation of an insignificant estimate is that "there is no evidence of a significant relationship." If, on the other hand, the confidence interval (95% or greater) is narrow and near zero on both ends, then you could conclude that there is not any meaningful rela-tionship between the variables. Remember, there is no evidence that there is other intelligent life in the universe . . . nor is there evidence that we are alone!

Statistical significance is not our goal

Our goal is advancing knowledge. Our goal is *not* to find a statistically significant coefficient estimate. Our goal is *not* to come up with some amazing result that will wow people. Well, that would be nice, but it should come within the parameters of honest and objective research.

13.5 Final words of wisdom

I never said most of the things I said.

−Yogi Berra

For those who have read this far (rather than waiting for the motion picture to come out), let me end with a few thoughts and one more Yogi quote.

One of my greatest revelations in life came to me in 2015: that officials in the Department of Defense (DoD), for which I have done much of my career work, tend to put more faith in research and models that are more complicated and that they understand the least. These DoD officials are not the only ones who do so. But, based on my experience, the simpler and more direct models tend to be the more robust and reliable models. From Chapter 8, the better methods to address non-random explanatory variables are the simpler ones: first-differences, and fixed effects. More complex methods, such as instrumental variables, are typically less stable, highly dependent on questionable assumptions, and representative of an effect for a smaller segment of the population.

Summing up the past 312 pages, remember when you conduct and read/assess research:

- Have an open mind.
- Entertain the notion that your pre-conceived notions on the topic may be wrong.
- Understand that a more complex model does not mean it's producing a result that is any closer to the truth.
- Assess whether other possible explanations can be ruled out.
- Be honest about the limitations of your models.

Understanding this will keep the researchers (or yourself) honest and make them do strong, sound research. If we do this, we will have the potential to make better decisions for ourselves and for society. And, maybe someday some visitor from another planet will find, on this planet, "intelligent" life, along with "intelligent" policies and practices based on high-quality research.

Notes

1 This comes from a *Time Magazine* article, "Did Reggie Lewis Have to Die?" by Christine Gorman, http://tinyurl.com/oc7l7hh, accessed July 10, 2018.
2 1964 June 23, *New York Post*, Section: Post Daily Magazine, The Lyons Den by Leonard Lyons, Quote Page 27 (Magazine Page 3), Column 3, New York.

References

Arkes, J. (2010). Revisiting the hot hand theory with free throw data in a multivariate framework. *Journal of Quantitative Analysis in Sports*, 6(1).

Berk, J., Harvey, C. R., & Hirshleifer, D. A. (2017). How to write an effective referee report and improve the scientific review process. *Journal of Economic Perspectives*, 31(1), 231–244.

Card, D., & DellaVigna, S. (2013). Nine facts about top journals in economics. *Journal of Economic Literature*, 51(1), 144–161.

Freedman, D. H. (2010). Lies, damned lies, and medical science. *The Atlantic*. November 2010 issue. (Available at www.theatlantic.com/magazine/archive/2010/11/lies-damned-lies-and-medical-science/308269/, accessed July 10, 2018).

Head, M. L., Holman, L., Lanfear, R., Kahn, A. T., & Jennions, M. D. (2015). The extent and consequences of p-hacking in science. *PLoS Biology*, 13(3), e1002106.

Appendix of background statistical tools

This chapter reviews some statistical tools that will serve as building blocks to the concepts covered in this book. There will not be any Calculus (other than in two endnotes); it just isn't necessary for understanding regression analysis (despite what others say).

Before beginning, we need to understand these two terms:

- A **parameter** is a number that describes a population, such as a mean.
- A **statistic** is a number describing a sample from the population.

We calculate statistics from samples to estimate what the population parameters are.

A.1 Random variables and probability distributions

Random variables are variables that quantify the product of a random process. This could be something from a known probability distribution, such as rolling a die. Or, it could be something that has a prior unknown probability distribution, such as the number of Donald Trump tweets in a given week.

Random variables typically are represented by a capital letter, with Y being a common variable name for an outcome and X being a common variable name for a factor that predicts the outcome.

Just because we call them random variables does not mean that the variables are completely random. Obviously, certain events can cause Trump to tweet more on a given day. But, there is also a random component determining the values of these variables.

There are two types of random variables:

- **Discrete random variables** have a set number of possible values, such as rolling a die, which has only 6 possible values.

- **Continuous random variables** have an infinite number of possible values. This would include any variable measuring time, weight, height, volume, etc. Also, some variables that are discrete but have many possible outcomes are often approximated as continuous.

Continuous random variables will be more relevant to regression analysis, but understanding discrete random variables helps towards understanding the theory behind continuous random variables.

Discrete random variables have probability distributions, as depicted in Figure A.1 on rolling a 6-sided die. The value of the random variable, we'll call X, takes on the value of the die roll. Each possible value has a probability of 1/6, or 0.167.

Note that the sum of the probabilities equals one. With the probability distribution, we can calculate the probability of various events occurring. For example, $Pr(X \geq 5) = Pr(X = 5) + Pr(X = 6) = 1/6 + 1/6 = 1/3$.

As you can imagine, the probability distribution is more complicated for a continuous random variable, as there is an infinite number of possible values. Thus, what is used is a **probability density function** (PDF). Let's consider the easiest PDF possible in Figure A.2: a uniform distribution between 0 and 5, with a height of 0.2. Note that, analogous to the probability distribution for the die roll above, the area under the density function equals one (5×0.2).

The probability of a range of values for the random variable will now be the area under the probability density function between the two values. For example, $Pr(1 < X < 3) = 2 \times 0.2 = 0.4$. This is the base times the height of the area between 1 and 3. What this also means is that the probability of any one value is equal to 0. This is true for all continuous distributions.

Another important function is the **cumulative distribution function** (CDF), which indicates the probability that the random variable will have a value less than or equal to a given value. For example, the CDF corresponding to the uniform distribution in Figure A.2 would be that shown in Figure A.3. It increases by 0.2 for each unit and reaches 1 at a value of 5, which is the right end of the uniform distribution.

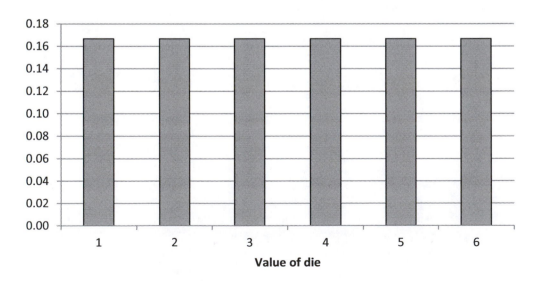

Figure A.1 Probability distribution for the value of a roll of a die

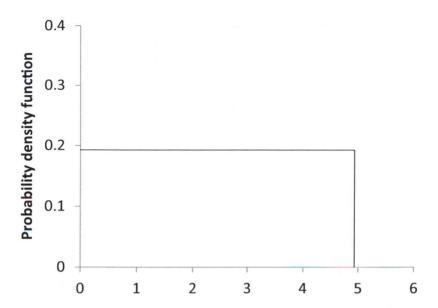

Figure A.2 Probability density function of a (continuous) uniform distribution

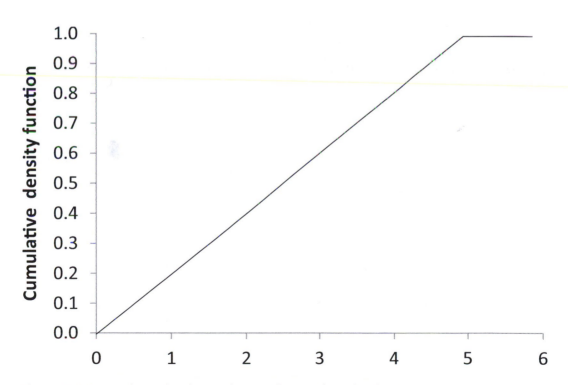

Figure A.3 A cumulative distribution function for a uniform distribution

The continuous distribution that is most commonly used is the normal distribution, which is the bell–shaped, symmetrical curve that many of us are familiar with. We will discuss that in the next section. Note that not all continuous distributions are smooth and symmetrical as that for the uniform or normal distribution. Imagine the distribution for how long it takes people to get ready in the morning to meet the world. My notional example is in Figure A.4. This distribution has two spikes, for those who set their alarm exactly 30 minutes and 60 minutes before they need to leave their home. Also, the distribution would be considered skewed to the right in that there are many people in the right tail of the distribution. In other words, from the mean value (maybe somewhere around 0.8 hours), the values range much farther above than below the mean.

Expected values and means

There are various measures of the central tendency of a variable. There is the median (the middle value), the mode (the most common value), and the mean (the average). With regression analysis, we are mostly concerned with the mean, or **expected value**, of a variable or distribution.

The expected value of a discrete random variable will be the probability-weighted average of the values. With the random variable of the value of a die roll, the expected value, $E(X)$, would be:

$$E(X) = \mu_x = \left(\frac{1}{6} \times 1\right) + \left(\frac{1}{6} \times 2\right) + \left(\frac{1}{6} \times 3\right) + \left(\frac{1}{6} \times 4\right) + \left(\frac{1}{6} \times 5\right) + \left(\frac{1}{6} \times 6\right) = 3.5 \qquad (A.1)$$

This would be the mean value, μ_x, of an infinite number of rolls of the die.

For the expected value of a continuous random variable, it is based on the same concept in that it is the average of the range of values, weighted by the probability of each small range of values. To keep my promise of avoiding Calculus, I will relegate the formal definition to this endnote.[1] For a symmetrical PDF, the expected value will be the median value. For our continuous uniform PDF, there is no singular mode, but the expected value is the median, or 2.5.

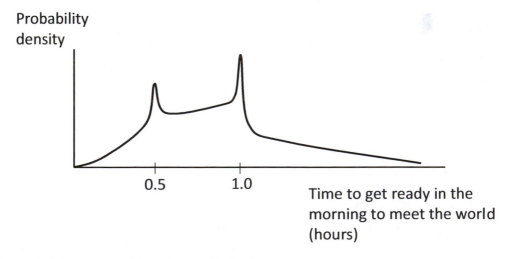

Figure A.4 A non–standard continuous distribution

Perhaps a useful application of expected value is for a bet on a roulette wheel. A roulette wheel has 38 slots:

- 18 numbers between 1 and 36 that are *red*;
- 18 numbers between 1 and 36 that are *black*;
- 2 numbers that are *green* (usually 0 and 00).

A typical bet would be on the color red or black. If you get it correct, you win the amount you bet. If you get it wrong, you lose the money you bet. Let's call the random variable, X, the amount that you win. So, the expected value of a \$1 bet on, say red, would be:

$$E(X) = \Pr(red) \times (gain\ or\ loss\ if\ red) + \Pr(not\ red) \times (gain\ or\ loss\ if\ not\ red)$$
$$E(X) = \frac{18}{38} \times (\$1) + \frac{20}{38} \times (-\$1) = -\$0.053 \tag{A.2}$$

Thus, for every dollar bet on a color for the roulette wheel, you should expect to lose 5.3 cents, provided that you do not have any secrets to the universe.

Variances and standard deviations

Whereas the expected value indicates the central tendency of a random variable, the variance and standard deviation indicate how spread out the values of the random variable are. This is known as a "measure of dispersion." Recall from basic statistics that the variance of a set of observations is:

$$s^2 = \frac{\sum_{i=1}^{n}(x_i - \bar{X})^2}{n-1} \tag{A.3}$$

That is, the variance is the sum of the squared differences of the value for each observation from the mean, divided by the sample size minus one. The standard deviation of the set of values would then be the square root of the variance.

The same concept applies for random variables with a fixed probability distribution, but it is weighted by the probability of each value (or small range of values) so that there is no need to divide by the sample size. The calculations for variance and standard deviation of the random variable of the value of the die roll are:

$$V(X) = \sigma_X^2 = \left(\frac{1}{6} \times (1-3.5)^2\right) + \left(\frac{1}{6} \times (2-3.5)^2\right) + \left(\frac{1}{6} \times (3-3.5)^2\right) + \left(\frac{1}{6} \times (4-3.5)^2\right)$$
$$+ \left(\frac{1}{6} \times (5-3.5)^2\right) + \left(\frac{1}{6} \times (6-3.5)^2\right) = 2.917 \tag{A.4}$$

And, the standard deviation of $X = \sigma_X = \sqrt{\sigma_X^2} = 1.708$.

Again, the formula for a continuous distribution is relegated to a footnote.[2]

Joint distributions of two random variables

Table A.1 shows a **joint probability distribution** of two variables: age group (random variable X) and whether the teenager uses Facebook (random variable Y). This distribution indicates the probability

Table A.1 Example of a joint probability distribution

	Does not use Facebook	Uses Facebook
	$Y = 0$	$Y = 1$
Age 15–17 ($X = 0$)	0.5	0.1
Age 18–19 ($X = 1$)	0.1	0.3

that certain values of the two variables occur jointly. The sum of the probabilities equals one, just as with a probability distribution or probability density function for a single random variable. From the joint probability distribution, we can calculate several important probabilities and statistics.

Unconditional (marginal probability)

This is just the probability of the value of one particular variable. For example, $\Pr(X = 0) = 0.6$ (which is the sum of all the probabilities in the "$X = 0$" row, 0.5 and 0.1).

Conditional probability

This is the probability of the value of one random variable, given a certain value for the other random variable. The formula is:

$$\Pr(Y = 1 | X = 0) = \frac{\Pr(Y = 1, X = 0)}{\Pr(X = 0)} = \frac{0.1}{0.6} = 0.1667 \tag{A.5}$$

A good way to think of conditional probability is with poker. From the cards you observe in your hand and on the table, you may be able to figure out the probability that a player has a certain card or set of cards that can beat you. But, conditional on the other player betting large, the conditional probability that they have that winning card would be higher (depending on how often that player bluffs).

Conditional expectation

This is the expected value of one variable, given a certain value of another variable. This normally would involve variables with a larger range of values than just the two values Y has, but the idea is the same. The formula, for a case with j different values of the Y variable:

$$E(Y | X = x) = \sum_{i=1}^{j} y_i \times \Pr(Y = y_i | X = x_i)$$

$$E(Y | X = 1) = (0 \times 0.25) + (1 \times 0.75) = 0.75 \tag{A.6}$$

The conditional expectation will be seen in Chapter 2, with the predicted value of the outcome (Y), given value(s) of the predicting variables (X's). For example, from a regression, we can estimate the predicted income for someone with 11 years-of-schooling (and perhaps other predicting variables).

One other important statistic is the *conditional variance*, $V(Y \mid X = x)$. You would probably never or rarely need to calculate this, but the idea will be important for an essential concept mentioned in Chapter 2 and discussed in greater detail in Chapter 6, called *heteroskedasticity*.

Covariance

This measures how two random variables tend to move with each other. The calculation for the covariance is:

$$cov(X,Y) = \sigma_{XY} = E\left[(X - \mu_X)(Y - \mu_Y)\right] = \sum_{i=1}^{a}\sum_{j=1}^{b}(x_i - \mu_X)(y_i - \mu_Y)Pr(X = x_i, Y = y_j) \quad \text{(A.7)}$$

where a and b are the number of values for variables X and Y.

If a covariance is positive, it means that when one variable is above its mean, the other variable tends to be above its mean. In contrast, a negative covariance indicates the opposite in that when one variable is above the mean, the other variable tends to be below the mean.

Other than the sign (positive vs. negative), the covariance has no meaning by itself, as it needs to be considered in light of how much variation there is in one of the variables. For example, if the X variable measured the weight of something, the covariance would have quite different values based on whether the weight is measured in grams, pounds, kilograms, or manatees.

When the covariance is combined with the variation in the explanatory variable, we will find out how much one variable (an outcome) tends to move with a one-unit change in the other variable (the explanatory factor). And, this is what we want to find out in regression analysis.

Correlation

Unlike the covariance, the correlation has a bounded range of −1 to 1 by dividing the covariance by the variance of the two variables and, thereby, making it independent of any unit. The formula is:

$$corr(X,Y) = \frac{cov(X,Y)}{\sqrt{V(X)V(Y)}} = \frac{\sigma_{XY}}{\sigma_X \sigma_Y} \quad \text{(A.8)}$$

A positive correlation means that X and Y tend to move in the same direction, while a negative correlation indicates that X and Y tend to move in opposite directions. The sample correlation between X and Y is indicated as: $r_{X,Y}$

Independence

Two variables are said to be independent if the value of one variable has no bearing on the value of another variable. This would mean that:

- $COV(X,Y) = 0$
- $corr(X,Y) = 0$
- $E(Y \mid X) = E(Y) = \mu_Y$

Linear functions of random variables

To later understand the distribution of combinations of variables, it is important to learn how the expected value and variance of transformations of random variables are calculated. Consider the case of the two random variables, X and Y:

$$Y = a + bX$$

Or, with our die example, let's say that Y depends on the die roll as follows:

$$Y = 3 + 2X$$

The mean, variance, and standard deviation of random variable, Y, would be:

- $E(Y) = E(a + bX) = a + b \times E(X)$
- $V(Y) = V(a + bX) = b^2 V(X)$
- Standard-deviation$(Y) = b\sqrt{V(X)}$

With the die example:

- $E(Y) = \mu_Y = E(3 + 2X) = 3 + 2 \times E(X) = 3 + 2 \times 3.5 = 10$
- $V(Y) = \sigma_Y^2 = V(3 + 2X) = 2^2 V(X) = 4 \times 2.917 = 11.667$
- Standard-deviation$(Y) = \sigma_Y^2 = \sqrt{11.667} = 3.416$

Note that the constant, a, has no bearing on the variance. It merely shifts the distribution and does not affect how spread out the data are.

Other calculations that will come in handy deal with combinations of multiple random variables. The formulas are:

$$E(X + Y) = E(X) + E(Y) \tag{A.9}$$

$$V(X + Y) = V(X) + V(Y) + 2COV(X, Y) \tag{A.10}$$

A.2 The normal distribution and other important distributions

The normal and standard normal distributions

Perhaps the most important distribution in statistics is the normal distribution. This is the bell-shaped distribution that can describe many things in life – e.g., intelligence, motivation, height, weight, grumpiness-in-the-morning, and more.

The normal distribution is denoted as $N(\mu, \sigma^2)$, with μ being the mean and σ^2 the variance. This distribution has several nice properties:

- It is symmetrical, so the median, mode, and mean are all in the middle of the distribution.
- 68.3% of all observations are within one standard deviation of the mean.

- 95.4% of all observations are within two standard deviations of the mean.
- 95% of all observations are within 1.96 standard deviations of the mean.

Given these features, to the extent that we can use normal distributions, our interpretations will be much easier.

Any normal distribution can easily be transformed into a **standard normal distribution**, which has a mean of zero and a standard deviation of one: N(0,1). The transformation for a value from the distribution simply involves subtracting the mean (μ) from a normal variable and dividing by the standard deviation (σ) as follows:

$$Z = \frac{X - \mu}{\sigma} \tag{A.11}$$

The resulting value of the standard normal variable, commonly denoted as Z, has the nice property that it represents the number of standard deviations below or above the mean.

Furthermore, the standard normal distribution has a known PDF and CDF that allow one to easily calculate the probability of various values. The cumulative probability for a given value can be calculated in Excel (NORM.S.DIST function, with the Z value as the first argument and "true" as the second argument).

Let's take the simple case of IQ, which has a population mean of 100 and a standard deviation of 15. You are probably thinking that IQ is usually reported as discrete variable, but it is often approximated as a continuous variable, given the fairly large number of possible values. The probability calculations require a transformation of the random variable to the standard normal (Z) distribution by subtracting the mean and dividing by the standard deviation.

The probability that a random person has an IQ above 115 is:

$$\Pr(IQ > 115) = \Pr\left(\frac{IQ - \mu}{\sigma} > \frac{115 - 100}{15}\right) = \Pr(Z > 1) = 1 - \Pr(Z < 1) = 1 - 0.8413 \tag{A.12}$$
$$= 0.1587$$

Note that on both sides of the inequality, I subtracted the mean and divided by the standard deviation – the symbols (μ and σ) on the left side to transform the random variable to Z, and the actual population parameters (100 and 15) on the right side to determine the Z value we are using in the calculation. Furthermore, the probability usually given is from the CDF for the Z distribution. That is why I transformed [$\Pr(Z > 1)$] to [$1 - \Pr(Z < 1)$].

The probability that the IQ of a random person is less than 105 is:

$$\Pr(IQ < 105) = \Pr\left(\frac{IQ - \mu}{\sigma} < \frac{105 - 100}{15}\right) = \Pr(Z < 0.3333) = 0.6305 \tag{A.13}$$

The probability that the IQ of a random person is between 97 and 106 is:

$$\Pr(97 < IQ < 106) = \Pr(-0.2 < Z < 0.4) = \Pr(Z < 0.4) - \Pr(Z < -0.2) \tag{A.14}$$
$$= 0.6554 - 0.4207 = 0.2347$$

While most calculations for hypothesis testing and similar statistical applications will rely on the Student's t-distribution (briefly described next), the same concepts as those in the standard normal distribution will apply.

The Student's t-Distribution

The **Student's *t*-distribution** is a normal distribution that is used for hypothesis tests and confidence intervals of coefficient estimates in regression analysis. In regression analysis (and other types of hypothesis tests using distribution statistics based on samples), the standard deviation of the population parameter is unknown, which creates another source of uncertainty. Thus, the distribution will be wider than the standard normal distribution, which is associated with a known population variance and standard deviation. With a wider distribution than a standard normal distribution, hypothesis tests and confidence intervals (which you'll learn about in Chapter 5) will be more conservative. The Student's *t*-distribution approaches the standard normal distribution as the sample size increases, and with a sample of around 100 or more, the Student's *t*-distribution is pretty close to the standard normal distribution.

The chi-squared distribution

The chi-squared distribution with k degrees of freedom, $\chi(k)$, represents the distribution for the sum of k standard normal variables that are independent from each other. This distribution will be used for tests for heteroskedasticity (Section 6.6.2).

The F-distribution

The *F*-distribution is based on the ratio of two chi-squared distributions. This means that two separate degrees-of-freedom are needed. The most common uses of the *F*-distribution are to test whether all or some of the coefficient estimates in a regression are jointly statistically significant in a hypothesis test, which comes from Chapter 5.

A.3 Sampling distributions

When there is polling for, say, an upcoming presidential election, one random sample from the population would likely be different from another random sample from the population. If a sample is drawn randomly from the population, then the values of variables from those observations in the sample would be a random variable. It follows that the sample statistics resulting from the random draw from the population, particularly the sample mean, are themselves random variables. And, these random variables often have features that, again, make life easier for us.

From our samples, we are using statistics to make inferences on parameters for the population. When doing so, we want to know how confident we can be about the value of the population parameter or the likely range of values that the population parameter falls in. The larger is our sample, the closer the statistics will be to the population parameters.

The key sampling distribution is that for the sample mean. If we were to roll 3 dice (or roll the single die 3 times), giving you values (x_1, x_2, x_3), we would get a certain sample average, $\overline{X}$. The next sample of 3 dice will likely give you a different $\overline{X}$. Those $\overline{X}$'s, if calculated an infinite number of times, would have a certain probability distribution. As long as each observation is independent and identically distributed (meaning they come from the same possible distribution), then the sample-mean random variable will have the following properties:

- $E(\bar{X}) = \mu_{\bar{x}} = \frac{1}{n}\sum_{i=1}^{n} E(X_i) = \frac{1}{n}\big(E(X_1) + E(X_2) + E(X_3)\big) = \frac{1}{3}(3.5 + 3.5 + 3.5) = 3.5.$

- $V(\bar{X}) = \sigma_{\bar{x}}^2 = \frac{1}{n^2}\sum_{i=1}^{n} V(X_i) + \frac{1}{n}\sum_{i=1}^{n}\sum_{j=1, j\neq1,}^{n} cov(X_i, X_j) = \frac{\sigma_X^2}{n} = \frac{2.917}{3} = 0.972.$

  (The covariance between any two observations equals zero if all observations are independent of each other.)

- *Standard deviation* $(\bar{X}) = \frac{\sigma_X}{\sqrt{n}}.$

So, the expected value of a sample mean is equal to the population mean. And, the variance of the sample mean is equal to the population variance of the random variable divided by the sample size.

Note that when we know the population variance, we use the term *standard deviation of the sample mean*. However, if we do not know the population variance, the estimator for the standard deviation of a population mean is called the *standard error of the population mean*. In regression analysis, we will use the term *standard error* for the standard deviation of the estimated relationships between variables (coefficient estimates) because we will not know the underlying population variance for those relationships.

Are the dice-roll observations independently and identically distributed? Yes, because the value of a die roll does not depend on the value of another die roll, and the distribution of possible values is the same. Sometimes, in regressions, this condition is violated. There could be siblings in a sample with correlated outcomes (due to correlated factors). Or, in an analysis of stock-market returns, companies from the same industry may have correlated observations. In these situations in a regression, there is a simple correction for this, which is described in Chapter 6.

Recall the nice properties that normal distributions have. If we can somehow get a normal distribution to work with, we can finish our work earlier and go have some other form of fun. With the sampling distribution of the mean, if the underlying population were normal, such as for IQ, then the sampling distribution of the mean would be automatically normal, regardless of the size of the samples taken. However, for other types of distributions that are not normal, the sampling distribution of the mean is *not necessarily* normal, but it will be with a large enough sample. This leads us to the Central Limit Theorem.

The Central Limit Theorem

The **Central Limit Theorem** says that the sampling distribution for a sample mean, if the sample size is sufficiently large, will be approximately normal. The term that is often used is that the distribution is **asymptotically normal**. So, what is a sufficient sample size to get the sample mean being approximately normal? It depends on how approximately normal you want to be and how skewed the underlying distribution of the random variable is. For an even distribution such as dice rolls, getting to around a sample size of 30 would normally be adequate. For a more skewed distribution, it may take a bit more.

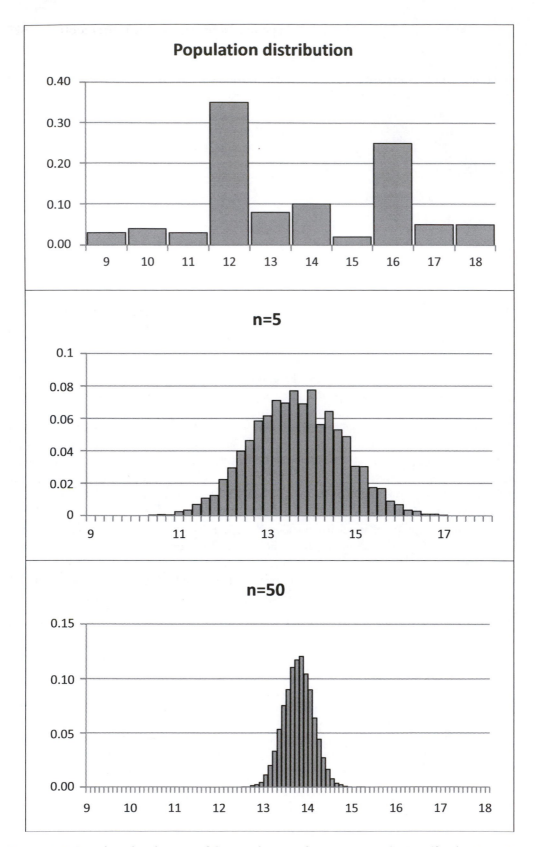

Figure A.5 Sampling distributions of the sample mean for various sample sizes (for the Central Limit Theorem)

Figure A.5 demonstrates the Central Limit Theorem with some notional data on the distribution of years-of-schooling in the population. The first panel is the underlying distribution in the population I made up, obviously simplified to be between 9 (9th grade) and 18 (a college degree plus two years of graduate school). Note that I created spikes in the distribution at 12 and 16 years-of-schooling – a high-school diploma and a 4-year college degree. The other three panels are sampling distributions from the underlying population. I approximate an infinite number of samples with 10,000 samples drawn for each sample size: n = 5, and n = 50.

Even with the samples with just 5 observations, the distribution of the sample mean is starting to look normal, albeit with a few kinks. This would be good enough for me to consider normal (given all the other things that could go wrong and the conservative interpretations I espouse in this book), but others may disagree. By a sample size of 50, it's starting to look even more normal.

Note also that the distribution gets tighter as the sample size increases. This is what should happen given that the sample size is in the denominator of the formulas for the variance and standard deviation, as seen above.

If we have an approximately normal distribution, we can then use the normal distribution to calculate probabilities. And, for a sample mean, there is a similar transformation to the Z variable as was the case with a single value:

$$Z = \frac{\bar{X} - \mu}{\sigma/\sqrt{n}} \tag{A.15}$$

For example, if I wanted to know the likelihood that the sample mean of 25 dice rolls would be at least 4, the calculations would be:

$$\Pr(\bar{X} > 4) = \Pr\left(\frac{\bar{X} - \mu}{\sigma/\sqrt{n}} > \frac{4 - 3.5}{1.708/\sqrt{25}}\right) = \Pr(Z > 1.464) = 1 - \Pr(Z < 1.464) = 0.072 \tag{A.16}$$

For a random sample of 100 people, the probability that their average IQ is less than 95 is:

$$\Pr(\overline{IQ} < 95) = \Pr\left(\frac{\overline{IQ} - \mu}{\sigma/\sqrt{n}} < \frac{95 - 100}{15/\sqrt{100}}\right) = \Pr(Z < -3.3333) = 0.0004 \tag{A.17}$$

This says that a sample as small as 100 is unlikely to get a sample mean as far as 5 points away from the mean.

Finally, for a problem that is analogous to the hypothesis tests we will do in Chapter 5, the probability that the average IQ from the sample of 100 is more than 2 standard deviations away from the mean is the following equation (note that the standard deviation of the mean, from equation (A.17), is 1.5, so the values 97 and 103 would be 2 standard deviations [of the sampling-distribution-of-the-mean] above and below the mean):

$$\Pr\left((\overline{IQ} < 97) or (\overline{IQ} > 103)\right) = \Pr(Z < -2) + \Pr(Z > 2) = 0.02275 + 0.02275 \tag{A.18}$$
$$= 0.0455$$

Thus, it is slightly less than a 5% chance that we get a sample statistic more than 2 standard deviations away from the population mean.

A.4 Desired properties of estimators

When drawing samples of observations that are independent and identically distributed, then we can say that the estimators (namely, the sample mean, variance, and standard deviation) are *unbiased* and *consistent*. Here is what they mean:

- An estimator is **unbiased** if its expected value is the true value of the coefficient being estimated.
- An estimator is **consistent** if the estimator converges to the true estimate as the sample size increases.

This is what we will eventually desire in our regression models – unbiased and consistent estimators of the population parameters for how variables are related to each other. But, this does not always occur. For the purpose of understanding these concepts better, I give two examples where one of these properties holds and the other does not.

Example of an estimator being unbiased (which is good) but inconsistent (bad)

From a sample of n independent observations of some variable X, $\{x_1, x_2, x_3, \ldots x_n\}$, say the true (and unknown) mean is μ. Consider the following estimator for the mean:

$$F(X) = x_1 \tag{A.19}$$

That is, the estimator of the mean is just the first observation.

This is *unbiased* because $E(x_1) = \mu_x$.

However, it is *inconsistent* because as the sample increases (say, going from a sample of 5 to a sample of 1000), just taking the first observation will not get you any closer to the true mean of μ_x. In contrast, using the sample mean of 1000 observations versus 5 observations would get you closer to the true mean.

Example of an estimator being consistent (good) but biased (bad)

From a given sample, suppose that your estimate for the mean was:

$$F(X) = \frac{1}{n} \sum_{i=1}^{n} x_i + \frac{1}{n} \tag{A.20}$$

The first component is the sample mean, which is an *unbiased* estimator for the true mean. Thus, adding the second component, $1/n$, causes the estimator to be biased. However, it is a *consistent estimator* because as n increases, then the second component will go to zero, and the estimator will converge to the true sample mean.

Applications to regression analysis

When evaluating whether a regression model is producing the correct estimates, researchers often use these terms – biased-vs.-unbiased and consistent-vs.-inconsistent. The more important property, for your sake, is "unbiasedness," as the most common pitfalls to regression analysis will center on whether the estimate is biased due to mis-specification. In fact, almost anything that is biased will be inconsistent too. But, "consistency" will also pop up a few times.

Notes

1 The expected value for a continuous random variable is: $E(X) = \int_{-\infty}^{\infty} xf(x)\,dx$, where f(x) is the height of the probability density function for a given value, x, of the random variable X.

2 The variance for a continuous random variable with a known probability distribution is: $V(X) = \int_{-\infty}^{\infty} (x - \mu_X)^2 f(x)\,dx$, with the standard deviation being the square root of that.

Glossary

Adjusted R-squared: A version of R^2 (see below) that is adjusted for the number of explanatory variables in the model.

Akaike Information Criterion (AIC) and corrected (AICc): Estimators of the relative quality of a regression model, in terms of being able to explain data.

Anchor-point bias: A situation in which someone observes an initial number or statistic and relies too heavily on that number/statistic when making decisions or drawing inferences on a population.

Attrition bias: A situation in which those who stay in a longitudinal sample are different from those who leave or stop responding to a survey.

Autocorrelation (serial correlation): A situation in which a variable is correlated with its lagged values.

Autocorrelation function (ACF): A function indicating how correlated different observations are based on how many periods away the observations are from each other.

Autoregression: A regression of a time-series variable on some of its lagged values.

Autoregressive-integrated-moving-average (ARIMA) model: A model that regresses a time-series variable on the lagged values of that variable and lagged values of the random error from its mean value, with "integrated" referring to having the variable differenced to avoid problems from potential nonstationarity.

Average forecast error: The average of the absolute values of the difference between the actual outcome and the forecasted/predicted outcome.

Average Treatment Effect (ATE): The average effect of the treatment in the population; or, if the treatment were assigned to everyone, how would a given outcome change, on average.

Average Treatment effect for the Treated (ATT): The average effect of the treatment on an outcome, for those who receive the treatment (as opposed to the whole population).

Bayesian Information Criterion (BIC): One of a few estimators of the relative quality of a regression model, in terms of being able to explain data.

Biased: The expected value of the coefficient estimate does not equal the true (unknown) population coefficient.

Breusch–Godfrey test (also known as the Lagrange Multiplier Serial Correlation test): A test for autocorrelation, which is often used in the presence of second-or-higher-order autocorrelation or in models with lagged-dependent variables.

Breusch–Pagan test: A test for heteroskedasticity.

Categorical variable: The values of the variable are based on some qualitative feature, and the order of the values have no meaning.

Causal effect: The effect that one variable has on another variable.

Causation: A situation in which one variable has an effect on another variable.

Censored variable: A variable whose value is only partially known, often due to there being an upper and/or lower bound for values.

Central Limit Theorem: The sampling distribution for a sample mean will be approximately normal if the sample size is sufficiently large.

Ceteris paribus: Holding other factors constant; Latin, meaning "all other things equal"; and French, meaning "Don't put all of those damn things in my coffee at once so that I know what ingredients make it perfect."

Clustering: A situation in which certain observations are correlated with each other in a model.

Coefficient estimate: An estimate for how much higher or lower a dependent variable (Y) is, on average, with one extra unit of an explanatory variable (X), holding other factors constant.

Cointegration: A situation in which two time-series variables that are nonstationary become stationary when considering a linear combination of the two variables.

Conditional probability: The probability of an event occurring, given that another event has occurred.

Confidence interval: A specified interval in which there is a certain probability that the true population coefficient lies within it.

Confirmation bias: The tendency to take evidence in favor of one's prior views as being confirmatory of these views and to discount any evidence contrary to one's prior views.

Consistent: A property of an estimator that involves the estimator converging towards the true population parameter as the sample size increases.

Constant term (intercept): In a regression, the expected value of the dependent variable (Y) when all of the explanatory variables equal zero.

Control variable: The set of variables included in the model to help identify the causal effects of the key X variable(s).

Correlation: The extent to which one variable moves with another variable, standardized on a -1 to 1 scale.

Count variable: A variable that can only take on only non-negative integer values representing the count of some event occurring.

Covariance: A measure of how two random variables tend to move with each other; the value depends on the scales of the variables. More technically, the mean value of the product of diversions from the mean for two variables divided by.

Cross-sectional data: A set of data with one observation per entity (e.g., person), typically at a particular point of time.

Cumulative distribution function (CDF): A function whose value is the probability that a variable will take on values less than or equal to a given argument of the function.

Degrees of freedom: The number of values that are free to estimate the parameters, which is the sample size minus the constraints (parameters to be estimated).

Dependent variable: (Also called the *outcome*, *response variable*, *regressand*, or *Y variable*), the variable that is being explained in a regression model.

Dichotomous variable: See dummy variable.

Dickey–Fuller test: A test for unit root, which indicates nonstationarity.

Difference-in-difference (DD) model: A model in which a treatment and control group are compared from a period after the treatment to a period before the treatment.

Differential measurement error: A case in which the measurement error in a given X variable is related to the value of that X variable or another X variable.

Dummy (dichotomous/binary) variable: A variable that just takes on a value of 0 or 1 (typically to indicate whether a certain condition is true or not).

Duration model: A model that examines the factors explaining the event of ending time in a given state of existence or how long it takes until an event occurs.

Durbin–Watson test: A test for autocorrelation that requires, among other things, the error terms to have a first-order lag structure, the model not having lagged dependent variables as control variables, and the X variables being purely exogenous.

Dynamic model: In a time-series model, an examination of how lagged values of X and/or Y determine the current Y variable.

Ecological fallacy: A situation in which someone takes a general research finding and makes conclusions about a person or subject based on that finding (under the presumption that the general finding applies to all subjects).

Endogenous variable: A variable that is determined within the model, with the variation in the variable being related to the dependent variable, not just by affecting the dependent variable.

Error term: The difference between the actual value of the dependent variable and the expected value from the true regression model. (The actual observed error term is the residual.)

Exception fallacy: A case in which a person discounts a research finding because he or she knows an exception to the finding.

Exogenous variable: A variable that derives its variation from outside the model and not anything related to the dependent variable.

Expected value: In general statistics, a predicted value of a variable, based on the possible values and the probability of them occurring. In regression analysis, the predicted value of the dependent variable based on certain values of the explanatory variables.

Explained Sum of Squares (*ExSS*): Total variation in the dependent variable explained by the regression model.

Explanatory variable (or, X variable): A variable that is used to explain the dependent variable.

False negative: A test result that says the null hypothesis (e.g., the coefficient is zero) is not rejected even though the alternative hypothesis is true (and the null hypothesis is false).

False positive: A test results that says the null hypothesis (e.g., the coefficient is zero) is rejected even though the null hypothesis is true.

First-difference (FD) model: A model, with one observation per subject, in which observations are based on the change from the one period to the next (typically, with the same two periods for each subject).

Fixed-effects (FE) model: A model that separates subjects by certain groupings, making it so subjects are only compared to other subjects in the same group.

Forecast interval: A confidence interval for the forecasted value of a particular observation.

Fuzzy regression discontinuities: A regression-discontinuities model in which the threshold value does not perfectly predict the likelihood that the subject receives the treatment.

Goodness-of-fit: The extent to which the observed data can be explained by the regression model.

Hausman test: A test to determine whether to use a random- or fixed-effects model.

Hazard function: From a duration model, the probability that the subject changes to another state in a given period t.

Hazard model: See Duration model.

Hazard ratio: In a survival model, the ratio of the risk of leaving a given state for two different values of an explanatory variable (e.g., when a treatment is applied vs. when a treatment is not applied).

Heteroskedasticity: A violation of the condition for homoskedasticity, which leads to biased standard errors.

Homoskedasticity: The variance of the error term, ε, is uncorrelated with the values of the explanatory variables, or $var(\varepsilon | X) = var(\varepsilon)$.

Hot hand: A situation in which a player has a period (often within a single game) with a systematically higher probability of making shots (holding the difficulty of the shot constant) than the player normally would have.

Incidental correlation: A situation in which two variables are correlated with each other by coincidence and not by any deterministic or systematic relationship.

Inconsistent: The estimator does not converge to the true coefficient as the sample size increases.

Independence: The characterization of two variables if the value of one variable has no bearing on the value of another variable.

Independent variable: A (bad) term to use for the explanatory (X) variable.

Interaction effect: The coefficient estimate on a variable that represents the product of two or more separate factors.

Instrumental variable: A variable used in a two-stage Least Squares Model that is assumed to affect the endogenous explanatory variable but have no effect on the dependent variable other than by affecting the endogenous explanatory variable.

Intercept: See constant term.

Joint probability distribution: A set of probabilities for all possible joint values of two or more variables.

Key explanatory (X) variable(s): (For regressions with the objective of estimating causal effects), the variable or set of variables for which you are trying to identify the causal effect; (for regressions with other objectives), the more important variables used for determining predictors, forecasting the outcome, or adjusting outcomes.

Lagged scatterplot: A scatterplot of a time-series variable with its lagged value.

Lagged variable: A time-series variable that is a set number of periods before the current value for a given observation.

Linear-log model: A model with a dependent variable in original form and an explanatory (X) variable that is measured as a natural logarithm.

Linear probability model: A model that uses Ordinary Least Squares for a dichotomous dependent variable.

Logit model: A non-linear model used to explain a dependent variable that is a dummy variable.

Log-linear model: A model with a dependent variable measured as a natural logarithm and an explanatory (X) variable that is measured in its original form.

Log-log model: A model with both the dependent and explanatory variables measured as natural logarithms.

Longitudinal data: A data set in which subjects are tracked over several periods.

Marginal effect: How the outcome (or the estimated probability of the outcome for probability models) changes with a one-unit increase in the value of the X variable.

Mean Square Error: The average of the squares of the residuals from a regression.

Measurement error: A situation in which a variable (typically an explanatory variable) is measured with error or does not represent well the concept the variable is meant to capture.

Mechanism: A full reason why a change in an X variable would cause a change in the Y variable, with the pathways and maybe a mediating factor.

Mediating factor: A factor through which the key explanatory variable affects the dependent variable.

Model selection: The process of choosing the optimal set of control variables.

Moderating factor: A variable for which different values of it are associated with different values of a coefficient estimate on another variable.

Multicollinearity: A situation in which having explanatory variables that are highly correlated with each other causes the coefficient estimates to have inflated standard errors.

Multiple Regression Model: A regression model with more than one explanatory variable.

Natural Experiment: A model in which the variation in the key X variable is random due to natural processes or a policy or system that was designed to be random for other purposes.

Negative results: Results that are not statistically significant.

Newey–West standard errors: Standard errors that are imperfectly corrected for autocorrelation. (They are considered an efficient way to address autocorrelation, despite being imperfect.)

Non-differential measurement error: A situation in which any measurement error in a given X variable is independent of the values of that X variable and other X variables.

Non-random explanatory variable: A variable that is endogenous to the dependent variable.

Nonstationarity: A property of a time-series variable that has a mean or variance that changes over time.

Normal distribution: A continuous, bell-shaped probability distribution that has the same mean, median, and mode and has a standard percentage of observations falling within a given number of standard deviations from the mean.

Odds ratio: The odds of an outcome occurring given the exposure to some treatment (which could be one extra unit of an explanatory variable) relative to the baseline odds without exposure to that treatment.

Omitted-variables bias: A situation in which the coefficient on one X variable is capturing the effects of another factor that is not included as a control variable.

Ordinal variable: A categorical variable with the values having no meaning other than the order.

Ordinary Least Square: A method to estimate a regression model that determines the coefficient estimates that minimize the sum of the squared residuals.

Out-of-sample prediction: A predicted value for an observation that is left out of the sample, based on the coefficient estimates of a regression model with a given sample.

Panel data: A set of data that follows multiple entities over time.

Parameter: A number that describes a population, such as a mean.

Partial autocorrelation function (PACF): The same as autocorrelation function, but it factors out other factors.

Partial effect: (In this book), an estimated effect that is missing part of the full effect of a key explanatory variable on a dependent variable due to having mediating factors or other outcomes controlled for in a model.

Perfect multicollinearity: A situation in which one X variable is an exact linear transformation of another X variable or set of X variables.

p-hacking: A situation in which researchers change the model to generate a more interesting result, which usually involves a lower p-value, typically in attempts to get below key threshold values of 0.10, 0.05, and 0.01.

Power: (Generally) the ability of a model to detect a significant relationship if one exists; (technically) the probability that a model would reject a null hypothesis if it were false, with a statistic of a certain size.

Practical significance: The coefficient estimate has a value that would suggest a meaningful relationship between the X and Y variable.

Predicted value: What we would expect the value of the dependent variable would be, given the coefficient estimates from the regression and a given set of values of the explanatory variables.

Prior probability: (In regression analysis), a subjective probability that there is a relationship between two variables, before any formal test for a relationship.

Probability density function (PDF): A function of a random variable that indicates the relative likelihood of the variable taking on certain values.

Probit model: A non-linear model used to explain a dependent variable that is a dummy variable.

Publication bias: A bias in the distribution of primary results from published studies stemming from the results of the analyses affecting the likelihood that a given study gets published.

p-value: The likelihood that, if the null hypothesis were true, random processes (i.e., randomness from sampling or from determining the outcomes) would generate a statistic as far from the null-hypothesis value as it is.

Quadratic model: A regression model that has both an X variable and its square as explanatory variables.

Quasi-experiment: A model that does not have random assignment in the key X variable, but rather has a research design that makes each observation be compared to other observations that are as similar as possible.

Quasi-omitted-variables bias: A situation in which a control variable that is included to avoid or reduce omitted-variables bias has a biased coefficient estimate itself, which means that some omitted-variables bias remains even though the variable is not "omitted."

Random-effects model: An alternative to fixed-effects models that requires that the variation in effects of the subjects (such as an instructor effect) is random with respect to the other explanatory variables.

Random explanatory variable: A variable that is exogenous to the dependent variable.

Random variable: A variable that quantifies the product of a random or uncertain process.

Random walk: The property of a time-series variable in which the value of the variable equals the prior value plus a random error term and perhaps a drift or trend.

Reference group: In characterizing a categorization, this is the group that does not have a dummy variable in the model so that any coefficient estimates are considered in reference to this group.

Regression-discontinuity model: A regression method that uses a threshold value of some variable (Z) that determines whether someone receives a treatment and, essentially, compares the outcomes for people right above and below the threshold to estimate the causal effect of the treatment.

Regression model: An equation that represents how a set of factors explains an outcome and how the outcome moves with each factor (not necessarily causally).

Regression-weighted estimator: A new estimator for fixed effects that weights observations within a group by the inverse of the conditional variance of the key X variable.

Rejection region: The part(s) of the sampling distribution for an estimator that indicates that a null hypothesis should be rejected.

Residual: The difference between the actual dependent variable (Y) value and the predicted Y value based on the regression equation; this is the predicted error term.

Residual Sum of Squares (RSS): The total variation in the dependent variable remaining unexplained by the regression model.

Reverse causality: A situation in which the dependent variable (Y) affects an explanatory variable (X).

Robust standard errors: Standard errors that are corrected for any bias from heteroskedasticity.

Root Mean Square Error (RMSE): The square root of the Mean Square Error; also equal to the Standard Error of the Regression.

R-squared (R^2): The proportion of the variation in the dependent variable that is explained by the X variable(s).

Sample–selection bias: A situation in which the sample is non-random due to subjects (observations) being selected for the sample based on some factor related to the outcome.

Sampling distribution: A probability distribution for a statistic based on an ample number of samples drawn from a population.

Sampling error: A deviation of a sample statistic from a true population parameter due to the sample being non–representative of the population; this can occur from random sampling from a population due to natural variation.

Self-selection bias: (Based on my definition), a situation in which the subject chooses the value of an explanatory (X) variable based on the perceived effects of the X variable on the outcome.

Serial correlation: See Autocorrelation.

Significance level: For a hypothesis test, the error allowed for a Type I error (incorrectly rejecting a null hypothesis).

Simple Regression Model: A regression model with just one explanatory variable; also called a Bivariate Regression Model.

Spline function: A regression that allows for different coefficient (slope) estimates at different values of the explanatory variable.

Spurious correlation: A situation in which two variables were correlated with each other by the nature of things, or due to having a common factor.

Standard error (of a coefficient estimate): The standard deviation of a sampling distribution for the coefficient estimate.

Standard error of the forecast: The standard deviation of the forecasted value of an observation.

Standard normal distribution: A normal distribution with a mean of zero and standard deviation of one. Each unit of the distribution represents one standard deviation.

Standardized effect: Based on the coefficient estimate on an X variable, how many standard deviations higher or lower the Y variable tends to be with a one-standard-deviation increase in the X variable.

Stationarity: The property of a time–series variable that the variable has a constant mean, variance, and covariance with its lagged value over time.

Statistic: A number describing a sample from the population.

Statistical significance: A status for a coefficient estimate attained when it is far enough from the null–hypothesis value that makes it unlikely (i.e., below a given significance level) to have occurred by chance.

Subject: A person or entity that is being examined in a statistical analysis.

Survival function: A function representing the probability that a subject survives in a given state for t periods.

Survival model: See duration model.

t-**statistic:** In regression analysis, the coefficient estimate divided by the standard error.

Time–series data: A set of data that follows one entity (e.g., a country) over time.

Total Sum of Squares: The total variation in the dependent variable, measured as the sum (across the observations) of the squared deviations from the mean.

Treatment: The procedure or exposure for which the effects on the dependent variable are being estimated. This is typically the key explanatory variable. It can be a dichotomous variable for yes/no on having received the treatment, or it can be a variable measuring different levels of the treatment.

Trend: A component of a time-series variable that shows a general movement over time.

Two-stage Least Squares: A regression method that involves a first stage of predicting an explanatory variable that is likely endogenous and a second stage of regressing the dependent variable on the predicted value of the endogenous explanatory variable. This method requires an instrumental variable for the first stage.

Type I error (false positive): The null hypothesis is true, but it is rejected by the hypothesis test.

Type II error (false negative): The null hypothesis is false, but the hypothesis test fails to reject the null hypothesis.

Unit of observation: What an observation represents in a regression model.

Unit root: (See Random walk.) The property of a time-series variable in which the value of the variable equals the prior value plus a random error term and perhaps a drift or trend.

Unobserved heterogeneity: See Omitted-variables bias.

Vector Autoregression model (VAR): Multiple time-series regressions that include the lagged values of each variable in the model and allow the error terms of each regression to be correlated with each other.

Weighted Least Squares: A regression model in which different observations have different weights (i.e., importance/contribution) in the model.

Index